Goethe's "Wilhelm Meister's Apprenticeship": A Reader's Commentary

Goethe's *Wilhelm Meisters Apprenticeship* is commonly acknowledged to have played a pivotal role in founding the genre known as the Bildungsroman. Although a wealth of critical material has accumulated since its publication in 1795–96, a detailed commentary in English on this novel of "apprenticeship" has been lacking from the corpus. Jane V. Curran's full-length commentary fills this gap. In her analysis, Curran presents the standard material familiar from traditional commentaries, but includes passages hitherto neglected, presenting new insights in a new form. Curran stresses the importance of narrative techniques, traces the development of the characters, and draws the reader's attention to the intertextual echoes, the use of symbols, and the many instances of irony. She also points out parallels between Wilhelm Meister's experiences and Goethe's life, and illuminates contemporary issues that are touched on in the novel, particularly the development of the German theater. The book provides notes with pertinent information for the interpretation of Goethe's work, along with factual details of general interest, scholarly sources, and background information. This is a vade mecum not only for students of Goethe and of German literature, but also for all who are interested in the development of the Bildungsroman.

Jane V. Curran is Chair of the German Department at Dalhousie University, Halifax, Nova Scotia.

Studies in German Literature, Linguistics, and Culture

Edited by James Hardin
(*South Carolina*)

Goethe's
Wilhelm Meister's Apprenticeship

A Reader's Commentary

JANE V. CURRAN

CAMDEN HOUSE

First published 2002
by Camden House

Camden House is an imprint of Boydell & Brewer Inc.
PO Box 41026, Rochester, NY 14604–4126 USA
and of Boydell & Brewer Limited
PO Box 9, Woodbridge, Suffolk IP12 3DF, UK

ISBN: 1–57113–118–3

Library of Congress Cataloging-in-Publication Data

Curran, Jane Veronica.
  Goethe's Wilhelm Meister's apprenticeship: a reader's commentary / Jane V.
Curran.
    p. cm. – (Studies in German literature, linguistics, and culture)
  Includes bibliographical references and index.
  ISBN 1–57113–118–3 (alk. paper)
    1. Goethe, Johann Wolfgang von, 1749–1832. Wilhelm Meisters
Lehrjahre.   I. Title. II. Studies in German literature, linguistics, and culture
(Unnumbered)

PT1982 .C87 2002
833'.6—dc21

                                                          2001043901

A catalogue record for this title is available from the British Library.

This publication is printed on acid-free paper.
Printed in the United States of America

For Tom

Contents

Acknowledgments

I AM INDEBTED to Steve Dowden and to James Hardin of Camden House for their suggestions and encouragement from the very start.

The Dalhousie University Faculty of Arts and Social Sciences kindly granted me the Burgess Award for one semester, which enabled me to spend a greater proportion of my time on the preparation of the manuscript.

I am very grateful to my colleagues and friends, students and family for their interest, patience, and loyal support.

J. V. C.
September 2001

Abbreviations

DVjs	*Deutsche Vierteljahrsschrift für Literaturwissenschaft und Geistesgeschichte*
FA	Johann Wolfgang Goethe, *Wilhelm Meisters Lehrjahre* (Frankfurt: Deutscher Klassiker Verlag, 1992)
GJ	*Goethe-Jahrbuch*
GLL	*German Life and Letters*
GQ	*German Quarterly*
HA	*Goethes Werke*, Vol. 7, ed. Erich Trunz (Munich: Beck, 1982)
JbDShG	*Jahrbuch der Deutschen Shakespeare-Gesellschaft*
JbDSG	*Jahrbuch der Deutschen Schillergesellschaft*
JbFDH	*Jahrbuch des Freien Deutschen Hochstifts*
JWGV	*Jahrbuch des Wiener Goethe-Vereins*
MA	Johann Wolfgang Goethe, *Sämtliche Werke nach Epochen seines Schaffens*, Münchener Ausgabe, Vol. 5, ed. Hans-Jürgen Schings (Munich: Hanser, 1988)
PEGS	*Publications of the English Goethe Society*

Introduction

"I**T IS MORE** of a business to interpret the interpretations than to interpret the texts, and there are more books on books than on any other subject: all we do is gloss each other."[1] Montaigne's disheartening assessment of the scholarly enterprise surely becomes increasingly accurate with each successive generation. In addition, the fashion for commemorating anniversaries of the birth or death of a great author, such as the 250th anniversary of Goethe's birthday in 1999, gave rise to a sudden additional influx of publications on the market. How, then, can another commentary, and one on so celebrated a writer as Goethe, be justified? It could still be useful if, in accordance with the hermeneutical principle, existing commentaries no longer speak to the contemporary age, or if, because of cultural differences, a group of readers is not being well served by existing works. If, like Thomas Carlyle's translations (which, incidentally, received the seal of approval from Goethe himself), these employ an idiom no longer in current usage, a more modern translation is called for. A commentary, too, must address its readers in the right idiom and it must answer the right questions. And while any new commentator must take into account those who have gone before, it is important not to lose sight of the text itself.

Previous commentators on *Wilhelm Meisters Lehrjahre* form an illustrious succession; first and foremost among contemporary documents is the exchange of letters that took place between Goethe and Schiller during the actual period of composition of *Wilhelm Meisters Lehrjahre*. This has always been recognized as a valuable tool for the interpretation of the work, since Goethe often takes up a suggestion of Schiller's, sharpening or polishing when his friend felt there was a need.[2] Schiller was not alone among Goethe's contemporaries to draft an assessment of the novel. Others include Friedrich Schlegel, who

---

[1] Michel de Montaigne, *Essays* (On Experience), trans. M. A. Screech (London: Penguin Classics, 1991), 369.

[2] These letters, together with Goethe's post-1796 remarks about *Wilhelm Meisters Lehrjahre,* are usefully presented in the Reclam *Erläuterungen und Dokumente* prepared by Ehrhard Bahr (1982) as well as in various editions.

wrote one of the earliest essays on the subject, *Über Goethes Meister* (1798), first published in the journal *Athenäum* of which he and his brother August Wilhelm Schlegel were joint editors, and who also wrote a review of Goethe's works in 1806; Novalis, whose less systematic comments are scattered throughout various volumes of his fragments; Schelling, who in his *Philosophie der Kunst* (1802–3) focuses on the struggle between real and ideal in the novel; and Madame de Staël, who in *De l'Allemagne* (1810) contrasts Voltaire's type of doctrinaire philosophical novel with Goethe's sweeping, less narrowly committed work.[3] Prominent writers and thinkers of the nineteenth and twentieth centuries carried on the tradition, and so we have an assortment of comments from such prominent writers and critics as Eichendorff, Fontane, Hesse, Hofmannsthal, Thomas Mann, Lukács, Habermas, and Martin Walser.[4]

Karl Morgenstern first coined the term "Bildungsroman" in a lecture given in 1819, and pointed to *Wilhelm Meisters Lehrjahre* as the prototype of this genre. Hegel refers to "Lehrjahre" in his *Lectures on Aesthetics* (1823) as attempts by the individual to change the world, or at least to create a personal paradise within it. Dilthey takes up the term Bildungsroman, to imprint it on all subsequent discussions, in his *Leben Schleiermachers* (1870). More recent studies of the novel bring a wide variety of methodologies to bear. As a consequence, the axis has shifted from a preoccupation with the meaning of the term Bildungsroman with Lukács, and moved ahead to encompass sociological, psychoanalytical and structuralist analyses (Kittler, Eissler, Hörisch).[5]

This is the first English commentary to deal at length, in a connected text, with the whole of *Wilhelm Meisters Lehrjahre*. It follows the linear arrangement of the novel itself, and begins each chapter with a purely chronological description of the action and the figures. Where appropriate, these are connected to the events of the previous chapter, but only rarely to future twists and turns. The summary leads directly into the analytical commentary, which draws attention to narrative technique, intertextual echoes, leitmotifs, irony of all kinds, dramatic touches, and nuances. It identifies parallels with Goethe's life and with the theatrical, religious and social issues of the day, as well as offering

---

[3] A list of these sources is provided in the 1992 Deutscher Klassiker edition, commonly referred to as the Frankfurter Ausgabe (*FA*).

[4] Bahr briefly introduces and edits each of these contributions.

[5] A survey of the more recent studies can be found in Uwe Steiner, "Wilhelm Meisters Lehrjahre," *Goethe-Handbuch*, Vol.3: Prosaschriften (Stuttgart/Weimar: Metzler, 1997), 140–43.

new insights at various points. With few exceptions, each chapter concludes with footnotes containing pertinent information for the interpretation of the text. Everyday phenomena, obsolete customs, literary and social debates, religious controversies, parallels in other works by Goethe, and biblical references may all be found there. In preparing the material, I looked to other commentators for support, but saw no necessity to present exhaustive lists of further reading at every stage. Similarly, I resisted the temptation to refer to other commentators merely in order to take issue with their conclusions.

The text is taken as given; I rarely felt the need to quote from it, and have consciously avoided doing so in order to circumvent difficulties that might have arisen for readers restricted to the use of an English translation. Where I refer to an English version of the text, I am always thinking of Blackall and Lange's (Suhrkamp, later Princeton UP, 1989). I have kept the reader at the forefront of my mind, and by that I mean the novice reader who does not know how it will all turn out. This policy has definite consequences for the perspective of this commentary; themes are traced backward, in retrospect, not projected forward, so that, in a sense, the reader progresses in tandem with the protagonist. Rather than offer an all-embracing interpretation, I have tried to observe and shed light on the details and structure of the work, the echoes and the themes. The pace is established by the work's own intrinsic momentum. So the book aims to embrace the seasoned Goethe scholar, the graduate student, the comparativist, the cultural or aesthetic historian, and the celebrated general reader as well.

There is no complete handwritten manuscript of *Wilhelm Meisters Lehrjahre;* only book seven has survived in handwritten form. In preparing my commentary, I have used the various critical editions of Goethe's works. The *Weimarer* or *Sophienausgabe* of 1898, reprinted in 1987 in a handy paperback version, is now also available in an expensive CD ROM edition. The *Sophienausgabe* provides variant readings, but no notes. The twenty-two volume *Berliner Ausgabe* published by the Aufbau Verlag between 1960 and 1978 offers more in the way of commentary than does the Cotta edition, which began appearing in 1949 and comprises precisely the same number of volumes. Although Erich Trunz's commentary in the fourteen volume *Hamburger Ausgabe* (original edition 1950–1968; revised edition 1981) is still extremely useful, two more recent critical editions, the *Münchener* (1988) and the *Frankfurter* (1992) have now broadened the field.

Whereas the *Hamburger Ausgabe* reproduces the text of the *Sophienausgabe* of 1898, both these newer editions revert to the original 1795–96 text, and the editors of the *Frankfurter Ausgabe* explicitly state their conservative policy in this regard. Hans-Jürgen Schings provides copious explanatory notes in the *Münchener Ausgabe;* his interpretations display socio-historical leanings and a particular interest in the influence of Spinoza. The lack of bibliography in this edition is regrettable, especially since the editors of the *Frankfurter Ausgabe* do provide a welcome selection of secondary literature, including recent and foreign language works. Both editions reinstate the settings for the songs by Johann Friedrich Reichardt, which, although undoubtedly approved by Goethe, had been omitted by successive editors since the 1795–96 edition in which they appear in a fold-out format.[6] The Frankfurter edition follows the lead provided by the Reclam commentary volume of 1982 by reproducing two versions of the painting of the ailing prince, one by Januarius Zinck and the other by Antonio Belucci. A brief summary at the beginning of each book, as provided by the *Frankfurter Ausgabe,* is a good substitute for the chapter-by-chapter one-line summary at the back of the *Hamburger Ausgabe.* To my constant surprise, I found that all these commentators conspired to pass in silence over passages, and sometimes whole chapters, which seemed to me to be of crucial importance to the internal development of the novel. This confirmed my determination to interpret the text and not the interpreters.

Much has been written about the status of *Wilhelm Meisters Lehrjahre* in the debate about the precise definition of the term Bildungsroman.[7] There is considerable dissenting opinion on the usefulness of such a term at all, although the sheer volume of writings about this phenomenon surely constitutes its own sort of validation. Without wishing to enter the debate, I would simply like to emphasize the basic features of the work that, in some combination, are generally considered to be symptomatic for novels following *Wilhelm Meisters Lehrjahre* that are usually identified as belonging to the same genre, such as Gottfried Keller's *Der grüne Heinrich* (1854–55; 1879–80) or Adalbert Stifter's *Der Nachsommer* (1857).[8]

---

[6] Only two of the songs are actually attributed to Reichardt — possibly Goethe was signalling his disapproval in a response to Reichardt's support for the French Revolution.

[7] A useful sampling of views is collected in *Reflection and Action: Essays on the Bildungsroman,* ed. James Hardin (Columbia: U of South Carolina P, 1991).

[8] A detailed discussion of the question can be found in Jürgen Jacobs, *Wilhelm Meister und seine Brüder. Untersuchungen zum deutschen Bildungsroman* (Munich: Wilhelm Fink, 1972).

The central figure of the genre typically develops towards a goal that he is not in a position to see clearly. Indeed, especially during his time with the theater, Wilhelm often seems to be working against the prescribed course, with his repeated errors of judgment, wrong turnings, and misguided ambitions. But Wilhelm's course has been prescribed for him all along by his natural endowment with particular abilities and by members of the Tower. Irony is very much at work throughout the narrative and there are very few who escape from it. Through irony, the Tower's hocus pocus and utopian ideal are undermined and Wilhelm is constantly being made to look foolish by a remark from the narrator. A sign that the protagonist has achieved the desired stage in his development by the end of the novel is that he recognizes and accepts his position in life and ceases to strive for the wrong things. In a sense, the conclusion of the novel is a type of irony turned in on itself: harmony appears to have been established between the will of the Tower and Wilhelm's subjective wishes, and yet much is left incomplete, and much remains implicit or unresolved. The inconclusive ending is a typical feature of the Bildungsroman; an ideal harmony is not the usual end stage.

In its initial form, however, this novel was less about the individual's confrontation with the world than it was about the state of the contemporary German theater. *Wilhelm Meisters Theatralische Sendung* (variously translated as "Theatrical Calling" or "Theatrical Mission") is first mentioned by Goethe in 1777.[9] In 1786 his journey to Italy interrupted work after six books were all but completed. The novel remained a fragment and was not included in the eight volumes of Goethe's works that appeared between 1787 and 1790. *Wilhelm Meisters Theatralische Sendung* was considered lost until its miraculous rediscovery in 1910.

On returning to the work in 1794, Goethe's first step was to rewrite the existing material, compressing the six books of the *Theatralische Sendung* into four. In 1795, he worked out a scheme for connecting books five and six to the four compiled earlier, and the entirely new books, seven and eight, occupied Goethe in the first half of 1796. As each book was completed, Goethe eagerly sought Schiller's critical comments, and so the first commentary was generated in record short order.

Because the novel is inconclusive, there are grounds for arguing that Goethe uses the techniques of realism in the final pages. Realism plus irony, however, still does not give the total sum. To stop there would

---

[9] Available in English as *Wilhelm Meister's Theatrical Calling,* ed. and trans., John R. Russell (Columbia: Camden House, 1995).

be to ignore the presence of the unexplained and the mysterious. For even with Jarno's eventual explanation of the ghost and other mysterious visitations, there are still some perplexing elements in the story. As Nicholas Boyle points out, there is an air of magic realism about *Wilhelm Meisters Lehrjahre*, of which the likes of Umberto Eco and Gabriel García Márquez are the indirect inheritors.[10] In keeping with Goethe's own method, I propose now to look backward, as so often occurs in *Wilhelm Meisters Lehrjahre*, that is to say, to turn away from comparable works of the twentieth century and rejoin Thomas Carlyle, who already felt it necessary to assert, "Goethe's world is every way so different from ours; it costs us such effort, we have so much to remember, and so much to forget, before we can transfer ourselves in any measure into his peculiar point of vision. . . ." Carlyle then adds that "helps may be given, explanations will remove many a difficulty; beauties that lay hidden may be made apparent; and directions . . . will at length guide [the reader] into the proper track for such an inquiry."[11] In the spirit of Carlyle, this commentary aims to offer just such guidance to the contemporary reader.

---

[10] Nicholas Boyle, *Goethe: The Poet and his Age. Vol. 2, Revolution and Renunciation, 1790–1803* (Oxford: Oxford UP, 2000), 424.

[11] Thomas Carlyle, *Critical and Miscellaneous Essays in Five Volumes* (London: Chapman and Hall, 1899) I: 209.

Book One

Chapter One

THE FIRST CHAPTER opens on a scene full of anticipation. Mariane, a young actress, is expected home at any moment from the theater. Barbara, her serving woman, looks forward to showing her a parcel that has just arrived. She is hoping Mariane will show gratitude towards the benefactor who sent the items. Mariane barely glances at the objects and refuses to think about Norberg, who sent them and will return soon. She is preoccupied with thoughts of the one she truly loves. Barbara wants her to change out of her costume, an officer's uniform, and adopt a more feminine attitude. Wilhelm enters and he and Mariane embrace.

The chapter introduces three characters: the lovers — Wilhelm and Mariane — and old Barbara, serving woman to Mariane. There is also a more oblique mention of one other character, also a suitor of Mariane's, the same Norberg who sent the parcel. The characters enter in ascending order of importance. Although he is a vital topic of discussion, Wilhelm, the eponymous central character, actually enters in person only briefly, at the very end. Mariane, Wilhelm's beloved and his principal inspiration, will preoccupy Wilhelm's thoughts and indirectly determine his path for some time to come. Barbara, with her down-to-earth ways, acts as a foil to the starry-eyed idealism of the lovers, and as a catalyst for the narrative, but does not herself play a large part.

Mariane is an actress and has been appearing on stage in an epilogue. That is to say, she is not among the performers taking part in the main feature of the program, rather, she is acting in some sort of skit at the end of the evening.[1] Her secondary role on the stage foreshadows the brevity of her physical presence in Wilhelm's life. Wilhelm's entrance is heralded by the pragmatic Barbara's negative views of him.

---

[1] The epilogue, in German "das Nachspiel," was a short piece performed at the end of an evening's theatrical entertainment. It was often a sort of comic relief and completely unrelated to the full-length play which preceded it. Several examples can be found in the full-length study of this genre by David G. John.

She sees in Wilhelm a merchant's son of small means (and thus unsuitable for Mariane) and is exasperated by his lovesickness. Although the reader does not feel encouraged to side with Barbara against Wilhelm, Barbara does have a useful function to perform here. She tells the reader in a few words the salient points about Wilhelm's background and identifies the main factors which will trigger his actions and determine his future course.

Mariane introduces the motif of textiles and costumes which weaves its way through the novel, sometimes effecting a link between characters and events, sometimes forming part of a mystifying trail of clues and adding to the build-up of suspense. In this chapter, Mariane receives a gift of muslin and ribbons from the still-absent Norberg. The muslin is to be made into a nightgown, a garment which will increase her feminine allure. The mention of the nightgown is offset by references to the very masculine officer's uniform which Mariane wears on the stage; she causes Barbara distress by not changing out of it immediately on returning home. Barbara links the male attire with a headstrong and foolhardy attitude on Mariane's part, but she is also conscious that the girl's altered appearance expresses her hidden divided loyalties. The military uniform supports Mariane in her stalwart sense of purpose with regard to her relationship with Wilhelm. It undermines the feminine side of her nature and renders her impervious to Barbara's championing of the absent Norberg to whom they owe their livelihoods (Larrett 40).

When Wilhelm rushes into the room, he embraces not Mariane but the "red uniform and the white satin vest." Synecdoche reduces the person to a costume. The description of this action sends out two signals. First, Wilhelm is attached to Mariane's stage persona rather than to her real self, and thus is inclined to prefer the world of illusion to the world of reality. Second, he is attracted to the female form in a masculine aspect, which Mariane presents here and which other characters will display at later points in the novel. Thus, the military costume contributes to the textile motif but also makes Mariane the first in a series of female characters who appear, to a greater or lesser extent, visibly masculine. All these women are significant for Wilhelm, but whereas he meets some in the flesh, there are others he has only read about.

The striking and fertile first sentence of this chapter throws the reader into the midst of events. Unlike the situation in the opening of *Wilhelm Meister's Theatrical Calling,* there is very little indication here of the time or place in which these events are occurring. But this first sentence, which appears to describe an event of secondary importance (we never do find out which play it was) actually conveys some very important information. It emphasizes a central theme, the theater, which will dominate the first five books. However, the significance of the theater extends beyond Wilhelm's literal experiences, his enthusiasm and idealism: it has implications for the style and interpretation of the novel as a whole. The word *Schauspiel* also conveys the additional, less neutral connotation of a spectacle or unnecessarily elaborate theatrical display; the choice of this word carries with it a suggestion of Barbara's impatience. Combined with the mention of length, it predicts, in the opening sentence, the many and varied vicissitudes of Wilhelm's development (Reiss 1951, 115–17).

By the end of the chapter, a pattern of influence stemming from theatrical practices has clearly imprinted itself on the narrative technique in the novel. The narrative voice begins in omniscient mode, informing the reader about the characters' thoughts, reactions, and circumstances. The initial emphasis lies with Barbara's perspective, but in the last paragraph, with the rhetorical question, "Who would dare to describe . . .?," there is a sudden temporary break in the narrative omniscience. The narrator has given up the objective stance and finally addresses the reader directly. This device has the effect of suggesting that the narrator, who at the beginning knew what motivated Barbara's actions, now knows only as much as the reader does. But by the very act of drawing the reader *aside,* away from the happy lovers, the narrator is, paradoxically, drawing the reader *into* the events. It is as though the reader were present in the scene but, following the narrator's example, chose to turn away. The teasing narrative pattern is already established. It tantalizes the reader by alternating between disguising the facts and disclosing them, between a display of knowledge and the illusion of ignorance (Schlaffer *Mythos,* 209).

Already in this opening chapter there are several indications that life and the theater stand in an interesting relation to one another. Alongside its other connotations, the first noun, "das Schauspiel" (the play), conjures up the conflict between illusion and reality (Reiss 1951, 115). When Barbara tries to run down Wilhelm's reputation, Mariane retaliates. As a measure of her sincerity, she declares that the love she feels is the real thing and that she knows how to distinguish it from the passion she has so often feigned on the stage. Theatrical illusion stands in fundamental contrast to everyday reality. But on another level, the idealized view Wilhelm has of life in the theater has little to do with the hardships of this profession. As a sign of the centrality of this theme, the mutual overlapping of reality and illusion, Goethe employs a number of features which serve to undermine the traditional divisions between reality and representation and between the novel and drama genres.

The narrator, in effect, draws the curtain on the scene with the happy lovers at the end of this chapter and the reader is made to feel like a spectator in the theater (von der Thüsen 624). Elsewhere, the narrator affects to know nothing, or sometimes declines to reveal anything, beyond what the actions of the characters communicate. At these moments, the narrator appears to take on the role of a director, while the characters in the novel become the actors. Performances of songs are interspersed throughout the narrative and this too has the effect of undermining the epic form, the norm for the novel, and of suggesting a dramatic performance. But the theatrical feature which is most striking and pervasive has to do with credibility. More or less mysterious characters appear and then fade from sight, only to reemerge in an important connection much later on; concealments and misconceptions abound. Difficulties are repeatedly solved by the most artificial of means. These are the techniques of the stage, designed to guarantee maximum involvement on the part of the spectator. The plan involves a cast of thousands and the scheme is too unwieldy for a classical structure; if the reader and Wilhelm are expected to learn about life through this experience, it has to be a "theatrum mundi," in which the theater is an allegory for life (Storz 1953, 64).

The final sentence of this chapter shows old Barbara going offstage, as it were, and it is easy to visualize the curtains closing. In between Chapters One and Two, the props will have to be rearranged, because the next scene takes place in Wilhelm's house. The seven chapters to follow are largely made up of Wilhelm's childhood reminiscences by way of explaining the origins of his interest in the theater. But there are also regular interruptions caused by returns to the present moment and to Wilhelm's listeners. Mariane and Barbara are somewhat distracted, as they listen to Wilhelm's account, by thoughts of the future, in particular of the imminent arrival of Norberg, as announced in this first chapter. The structure, then — and it is one which characterizes the novel as a whole — incorporates not only a linear development in time but also a kind of circularity produced by the constant and necessary movement backwards and forwards.

Chapter Two

Chapter Two is composed of a conversation between Wilhelm and his mother. Wilhelm's mother does not have a sustained role in the work and here too she is restricted to speaking on her husband's behalf. Wilhelm, she says, is wasting too much time at the theater. In turn, Wilhelm criticizes his father's style of life. His mother feels responsible because she made Wilhelm a gift of some puppets years earlier and so began his passion for the theater. Wilhelm recalls the excitement of that Christmas and the David and Goliath performance and rushes off to retrieve the puppets.

Wilhelm's mother, in reporting her husband's views and in attempting to dissuade her son from visiting the theater with such regularity, argues on two fronts. From her own point of view, and based on her experiences, the danger lies in allowing free rein to the emotions and thus disturbing the equilibrium required for normal, day-to-day life. She associates the theater with stimulus and the passions, and in Wilhelm's case, she is right. As a self-appointed troubleshooter and mediator, she also reports Wilhelm's father's question: what use is the theater? Wilhelm's spirited response gives a hint of the fundamental tension in his home life: his father would like Wilhelm to follow in his own footsteps and make a profitable living in trade and commerce. Although Wilhelm's whole nature rebels against such an expectation, the problem cannot be resolved at this stage and will keep returning to preoccupy him.

In this chapter, the dispute is couched in terms that describe the competing claims of aesthetic and monetary values. Wilhelm's argument is designed to pinpoint a contradiction in his father's position: since not everything in their house has a practical purpose and some things are purely decorative, the father has no right to judge the theater by the yardstick of utility or assess his son's visits to the theater in terms of financial benefit. Unfortunately, the English style of furniture, more practical and less ornate than the French, was not a good example for Wilhelm to choose; it does not provide a clear illustration of his contention that some of his father's valued possessions are without practical use. The tension between father and son here is very significant because it will ultimately become a tension within Wilhelm himself. But for now, Wilhelm makes the transition back to the topic of the theater by likening the ornamentation on the wallpapers in his house to the curtain in the theater.

This chapter, like the last one, displays some features borrowed from the stage. The father's reported disapproval forms a kind of backdrop to Wilhelm's reminiscences in praise of the puppet theater of his childhood. The conversation with his mother acts as a prologue: she makes the causal connection between his present passion for the stage and the puppet theater which she gave him for Christmas twelve years earlier. And when Wilhelm animatedly adduces his father's taste in wallpaper and furniture to prove his point, it is easy to picture him indulging in a grand and sweeping gesture, indicating that the whole room is an ample demonstration of useless ornamentation. The reader is now able to begin building up a composite picture of Wilhelm but, employing yet another dramatic technique, Goethe has made secondary figures the mouthpieces for these first impressions. Having heard Barbara's objections to Wilhelm as a suitor, the reader now learns of Wilhelm's father's disapproval of his habits, although not directly; they are transmitted by a third party, Wilhelm's mother.

Wilhelm, remembering the puppet show, launches into the lengthy recollections of his childhood which, with the occasional change of scene, continue to form the main subject matter up to Chapter Eight. The puppets themselves, which Wilhelm retrieves at the end of the chapter, are a tangible device which permits him to reenter his childhood. In his reverie, he remembers thinking he could make them real by speaking for them and manipulating them; now, in handling the puppets again, he brings that period of his childhood vividly back to mind. Goethe, too, is reliving his own youth; in *Dichtung und Wahrheit* I, 2 he tells of the puppet theater with the figures of David and Goliath, which he and his sister received, and which had come from their grandmother. In the same work, Goethe mentions the providential puppet show that he saw as a child in Frankfurt; it told the story of Dr. Faust. Even the father's somewhat censorious attitude reflects Goethe's representation of his own father's disposition.

As a literary theme, then, the puppet theater has biographical foundations in Goethe's life as well as historical ones in the history of German theater. Traveling puppeteers and troupes of players brought dramatic productions to the public in the German states before permanent, fixed stages were eventually established. In a parallel chronology, Wilhelm's passion for the puppet theater as a child is the embryonic form of his fascination with the theater as an adult. The puppet theater is the real stage *in nuce,* just as the boy displays the characteristics which appear more fully developed in the man. And Wilhelm now hopes that his dreams of a life on the stage can also be coaxed into becoming a reality.

The arguments Wilhelm makes in favor of the theater culminate in the example of the curtain which, although ornate, has a function, which differentiates it from the ornamentation in his father's house. And so the textile theme appears again. Whereas the house and its furnishings symbolize the materialism and philistine attitudes he so resents in his father, the curtain in the theater promises a performance "to entertain, enlighten and elevate."[1] Now, in the description of the first

---

[1] The phrase "to entertain, enlighten and elevate" is reminiscent of the Horatian poetic precept which had become a commonplace at least since Gottsched's version of the *Ars Poetica* in 1737:

puppet show, the curtain is described as "mystic" and "half transparent." This refers to a biblical prototype: the curtain behind which the Arc of the Covenant is kept, the veil which keeps the Holy of Holies concealed (Exodus 26:31–33). There is of course both bathos and irony in drawing this parallel with a stage designed for puppets and intended for the entertainment of children (Bahr 14), but the comparison is nevertheless compatible with the content of the first puppet show performance now being relived by Wilhelm. The play is derived from the biblical story of David and Goliath (1 Samuel 17) and probably seemed to Wilhelm's highly principled father a suitable and improving theme to choose for children.[2]

David, the victor in the story, gains the hand of the king's daughter and Wilhelm bestows on him the epithet "lucky prince" (Glücksprinz; Seitz 125). His regret at the dwarflike stature of the puppet representing David suggests that Wilhelm identified with the hero for his brave deeds but would wish, in his own case, for a physical appearance capable of reflecting the greatness displayed by his actions. This is the first instance of Wilhelm's habitual practice of identifying with a hero he has read about or seen depicted in some art form (Wuthenow 74–86).

The theater begins, in this chapter, to show something of the rich and significant symbolic function it acquires in the novel. As entertainment, it counteracts the sterility and materialism Wilhelm finds at home; it allows the passions free play and nurtures the imagination. Already in the form of a puppet show, the stage, as well as the figures represented on it, promises delights to compensate for the less than pleasing aspects of Wilhelm's home life. In the year of his youth when the puppet theater became his chief consolation, Wilhelm's discontent stemmed from having to try and settle into a new and unfamiliar house. In his present situation, visits to the theater help Wilhelm escape from the standards and expectations his father seeks to impose.

The conversation in this chapter reverts, for the reader's benefit, to the beginnings of what Wilhelm's parents think of as a wild addiction to the theater. It also shows his mother to be more understanding of his behavior, which she hopes will help her to establish a peaceful and harmonious household. No doubt partly in order to gain sympathy

---

> Aut prodesse volunt, aut delectare, poetae;
> aut simul et iucunda et idonea dicere vitae (*Ars Poetica* 1.333–34)

Here Horace emphasizes the dual task of poets: to combine entertainment and instruction in their works.

[2] In the account of the action, the "son of Jesse" is a reference to David, while "the Philistine" is Goliath.

from Wilhelm, she blames herself and her gift of the puppet theater for the present trouble. Wilhelm insists that she should not feel any remorse for a generous act by which she has caused so much pleasure. In addition to her regret, she also has a sense for the quirks of destiny; she sees that gift of the puppets so long ago as the cause of the present domestic unrest surrounding Wilhelm's frequent visits to the theater. This relationship of cause and effect belongs to a series of unexpected connections, a pattern of unpredictable outcomes and a web of unsuspected relationships which make up the structure of the entire novel.

Chapter Three

Wilhelm entertains Mariane by showing her the collection of puppets.[1] He has curtailed his visits to the theater but after everyone else has gone to bed he slinks away to join Mariane. On this occasion, aside from the puppets, Wilhelm has provided the money for some oysters and champagne, which Barbara shares with them.[2] Then he returns to the account of the puppet theater and his boyhood. Some time has elapsed, since Barbara refers to a ballet performance Wilhelm had mentioned.[3] Wilhelm's story has continued offstage, as it were.

A commonplace about the delights of first love opens the chapter.[4] This device has a twofold function. The first concerns the role of the

---

[1] When Wilhelm unwraps the puppets, their wires are tangled. This indicates that they are marionettes, not hand puppets.

[2] Mariane's favorite puppet — and she is adamant about this — is Jonathan. He was the son of Saul, whose close and loyal friendship with David is legendary. Jonathan is mentioned in passing in the previous chapter as well; here, he seems to have instilled in Mariane the devotion for which he is known. It remains to be seen whether her capacity for devotion, like her embraces, will be transferred from the puppet to Wilhelm.

[3] Wilhelm's description of the "Moors, the shepherds and the dwarves" identifies the ballet as a Rococo pastoral type. The German text speaks of each of these types in pairs — both masculine and feminine forms are given. This is an important factor which provides for the conventional happy ending (Anger 70).

[4] The practice of beginning a chapter with a commonplace is typical for the German novel of the Enlightenment period. This is especially characteristic of the novels of C. M. Wieland, such as *Geschichte des Agathon* (1766–1767), which is often seen as the forerunner to *Wilhelm Meister's Apprenticeship* in the history of the *Bildungsroman,* and in which the narrator's didactic or ironic interventions constantly interrupt the narrative time frame.

narrator, who is permitted to step forward here and comment on Wilhelm's situation from an uninvolved perspective. Narrator and reader join forces for a while; theirs is the universal point of view, whereas Wilhelm, as the individual living through the events, is set apart. The narrator calls the reader on side, by placing the inclusive pronoun forms "we" and "us" over against the phrase "our hero," to denote Wilhelm. The subsequent function of the commonplace is to introduce a note of doubt. The reader is led to suspect that the term "our hero" is gently ironic, and this suspicion is upheld by the hypothetical and detached means of introducing the commonplace. The word "if," as the first word in the chapter, brings about a very effective separation of the narrative voice from the point of view it is about to state, even before this point of view is expressed. By way of contrast, the narrator then goes on to describe the normal course of events, the way things happen for the rest of us. The common lot, it seems, includes a bumpy ride and a few limited pleasures but, at the end, nothing more than resignation. But because Wilhelm's presumably preferable and favored status is dependent upon the truth of the initial proposition, an element of doubt takes hold and the reader is gently encouraged to wonder whether Wilhelm will, after all, take the path most of us take, as described by the narrator.

Love continues to be one of the main topics in this chapter and the reader hears both from the narrator and from Wilhelm on the subject. The narrator makes an explicit connection between Wilhelm's love for the theater and his love for the actress, Mariane. Again, an implied note of warning creeps in; the theater by definition belongs to the realm of representation, of appearance rather than reality. An image links Wilhelm's desire with the "wings of imagination" and this again suggests something which exists purely in the mind and does not translate into real terms. Wilhelm and Mariane's love may turn out not to have the substantial and enduring qualities Wilhelm expects of it. An impression engendered by the narrator is having an unsettling effect on the reader. It would appear that Wilhelm believes in the power of his own sentiments above all else, in determining future events (Blackall 1976, 110). In addition, there is Mariane's "ambiguous situation," her relationship with Norberg, which means that in everyday life as well as when she performs on the stage, Mariane leads a double existence. Even the perceptible traces of this tension within Mariane give misleading indications of their true source. Unable and unwilling to detect any duplicity in his beloved, Wilhelm does not read these as signs of anxiety and dilemma but as alluring modesty.

From Wilhelm's perspective, the relationship with Mariane has brought definite benefits which extend beyond the immediate pleasure of her company. It has helped him to come to a clearer delineation of his capabilities, priorities, and future plans. Love's beneficial influence has given him the ingenuity to devise a plan which would keep his father happy, pacify his mother, and enable him still to see Mariane regularly. The reader, however, becomes painfully aware that this arrangement, too, is based on duplicity. When Wilhelm describes his disappointment at discovering that the puppet theater has been dismantled after the performance, he compares the sense of loss to a lover's despair at losing his beloved. For the reader, this comparison constitutes one more ominous sign of how fragile love is, particularly that between Wilhelm and Mariane. Ironically, this message comes across at the precise moment when Wilhelm is brimming with confidence, convinced that he has no fear of losing Mariane.

At the end of the chapter, the narrator allows the reader, Mariane, and Barbara a deeper insight into the state of affairs than Wilhelm has attained. Wilhelm is out of touch with reality, as the details about his relationship to Mariane make clear. Mariane is not the only one playing a role here; Wilhelm, too, because of his tendency to identify with a literary figure, is acting out a part. When recounting the method of Wilhelm's nocturnal escapes, the translation describes Wilhelm's emotional state with this phrase, "his heart beating fast like that of a young lover in a play." This is a useful paraphrase and explanation but does not reproduce the effect of the original phrase *"alle Lindors und Leanders im Busen."*[5] With the mention of these two names, the narrator shows that Wilhelm fancies himself as playing the part of a heroic and dashing lover in a play and this reference contributes to the impression that Wilhelm likes to identify with a role model. As examples of this tendency multiply, it becomes clear that it is not only the remnant of a childish game but an inner necessity, the condition most essential to the development of Wilhelm's character (Schlaffer *Mythos,* 82). In this case, the standard is not provided by one specific character, but rather by a type. The names Lindor and Leander were popularly used on the French comic stage to designate the young lover. There is also a faint but detectable note of ridicule; a hint of youthful naiveté is discernible in this description of Wilhelm's aspirations.

Barbara's desire for Wilhelm to continue his reminiscences has little to do with any actual interest in the subject matter. She is keen to pro-

---

[5] Beaumarchais, in *Le Barbier de Séville* (1775), has Count Almaviva refer to himself by the name of Lindor when he makes an amorous approach. Lessing adopts the name Leander for the lover in the comic plays *Damon oder die wahre Freundschaft* (1747), *Der Misogyn* (1748), and *Der Schatz* (1750).

tect her mistress from having to reveal her origins, to comply with the
suggestion, made by Wilhelm, that to talk of one's past, including past
mistakes, is a pleasurable pastime. This increases the dramatic sense of
foreboding: Wilhelm, however, acts in complete ignorance of the ominous atmosphere in the room.

The curtain of the puppet theater is once again described as "mystic." For Wilhelm, it transforms the doorway between two rooms into
something completely different. As a boy, he was seemingly transported
into a different dimension, an illusion which did not immediately leave
him, even after the structure had been dismantled. His story stresses the
difference between his own reaction and that of his siblings who were
completely unconcerned by the disappearance of the stage. In his mind,
there is reason enough to interpret these feelings as a definite sign that
he has always had a special affinity for the theater. The metaphor which
compares the disappearance of the theater with the loss of a lover seems
apt to Wilhelm, especially on that intimate evening at Mariane's house.
But for the reader, as for Mariane and Barbara, there is an uncomfortable irony in his words and it is made all the more painful by his confident and loving glance in Mariane's direction.

Chapter Four

This short chapter comprises further reminiscences from Wilhelm. He
continues with another demonstration of his father's moral rigidity. A
young lieutenant had built the theater and provided voices for the puppets. Wilhelm's father agreed to another performance at this man's request. The lieutenant was keen to inaugurate a new "Hanswurst" or
clown figure.[1] Wilhelm becomes increasingly curious about the mechanics
of the show and peeks behind the curtain.

Wilhelm is no longer simply telling of his childhood and the beginnings
of his enthusiasm for theater in all forms. By the time he describes the second performance, he is already embarked on an account of the transition
from childish innocence to a knowledgeable state. He is torn, in this tran-
sitional stage, between wanting to submit himself entirely to the all-

---

[1] The origins of Hanswurst go back as far as Sebastian Brant's *Narrenschiff*
(1519) and Martin Luther's *Wider Hanns Worst* (1541). He is related to the
Pickelherring of the English comedians and Harlequin of Commedia
dell'arte. Hanswurst is typically a person of insatiable appetites, good humor,
word games, and off-the-cuff flashes of wit. German traveling groups in the
latter half of the seventeenth century adopted the practice of appending a
Hanswurst piece as a epilogue to the main part of the program.

encompassing, wondrous illusion, and the desire to know how the illusion is produced. He wants both to be enchanted and to be the enchanter. In fact, what he wants is something much larger, and this is borne out by the concluding sentence of this chapter. He wants an insight into the reality behind the world of appearances and a grasp of his own relation to it.

His quick glance behind the curtain allows Wilhelm to discover the answers to some of the questions about the techniques of puppet-show production. He discovers, for example, that the lieutenant is working behind the scenes. To his dismay, Wilhelm also finds out that the puppets, despite their ability to convince the audience of their individual personalities, emotions, and antagonisms during the performance, are handled with a decided lack of respect when it is all over. He catches sight of them all being packed away into the same drawer (the German text makes this clearer) with complete disregard for the allegiances or conflicts between the characters they represent. Knowing that the animation of the puppets is an illusion, Wilhelm nevertheless clings to his conviction that they have personalities and are subject to human emotions. The sight of the lieutenant in the "sanctuary," preparing for the epilogue, detracts somewhat from Wilhelm's enjoyment of the rest of the performance, but it is clear from the use of the word "sanctuary" that he still thinks the theater is a mystical experience.

The epilogue is less satisfying for Wilhelm than what preceded it. As a consequence, the recollection that when Mariane first appears (in Chapter One) she too has been performing in an epilogue is vaguely disturbing for the reader. It is apparent that many of the details from Wilhelm's account reflect on his present situation in subtle ways. (The importance of even the smallest detail even at this early stage in the novel is something Friedrich Schlegel admired in his essay "Über Wilhelm Meister" [1798; *FA* 1287].) The parallels between Wilhelm's personal development and the history of German theater also continue. When Wilhelm expresses his distaste for the "Hanswurst" figure, there is a reference to Gottsched's plans to reform the repertoire of the German stage, including placing a ban on the use of this clown figure.[2]

The chapter describes a deeply divided state of affairs and there is no attempt to effect a resolution at this point. Wilhelm's unstoppable

---

[2] Johann Christoph Gottsched (1700–1766), a dramatist and critic. His *Versuch einer critischen Dichtkunst* (1730) urged German playwrights to imitate French models, to write in accordance with the dictates of reason, and above all to follow the rules. He sought to banish the Hanswurst figure from the German stage on the grounds that it was vulgar, and enlisted the support of Friederike Neuber and her troupe in staging a ceremony in 1727 to mark its demise. But by 1740 Hanswurst had returned to the stage and Gottsched's influence was on the wane.

compulsion to destroy the illusion he cherishes so much by analyzing its means of operation leaves him vacillating between calm and unrest. The whole structure of the novel is characterized by the juxtaposition of such contrasting elements and oppositions (Blackall 1976, 122–23). A small gain in knowledge only reveals the extent of his ignorance, and Wilhelm thus becomes conscious of the need to pursue knowledge. Even at the time of the puppet show he knew that what he lacked was a sense of the "enterprise as a whole" and he still sees this as his most important goal. The final statement shows that Wilhelm is interpreting his growing but still incomplete understanding of the workings of the puppet show. He sees this process as analogous to a growing consciousness of oneself in relation to the world. What he expresses at the end of this chapter becomes the central endeavor in the whole of his subsequent development (*FA* 1387, n. 370).

Chapter Five

This chapter is also entirely devoted to Wilhelm's narrative. It opens by comparing children with mice. Wilhelm's unaccompanied sortie into the pantry satisfies his taste for the food stored there and for the puppet theater he discovers. The chapter tells how Wilhelm learned the text of the David and Goliath puppet show and used lumps of wax to represent the characters.[1] It also mentions Wilhelm's initiation into the secrets of the puppet theater.

The chapter opens, like Chapter Three, with a commonplace. But this time it is formulated by Wilhelm himself and not by the narrator. This has the effect of drawing the reader in, to listen to Wilhelm. The commonplace with which Chapter Three opened contained an irony designed to draw the reader away from the scene and thus provide an opportunity for assessment. But in this chapter the narrator has no place; Wilhelm has subsumed this role by speaking both to his audience in the room and directly to the readers of the novel. His commonplace simply constitutes his observation and analysis of an endearing childish attitude.

For the reader, the ending of the chapter contains a rather unexpected development: Wilhelm is to be allowed to learn to manipulate the puppets and put on a show. This comes about, not surprisingly, first at the instigation of Wilhelm's mother and then through a request from the lieutenant. The reader has come to expect that no such offer

---

[1] Wax was the obvious material to choose for forming the figures as it can easily be softened and made malleable. It was also readily available, as candles would have provided the main source of lighting.

would be forthcoming directly from Wilhelm's father and there is the implied suggestion that an approach by his son would have been unequivocally rejected. Even though this was an important step forward for Wilhelm, much less space is devoted to it here than to the description of the mouselike tactics which led to Wilhelm's procuring of the text. Goethe delights in the detailed description of the pantry — its enticing smells, its various types of intriguing containers, and the sheer luxuries that these "chests, sacks, boxes, cases and jars" contain.[2] All Wilhelm's senses are on the alert. Against the background of the church bells ringing, he must listen for any movement which might indicate a disturbance; he smells the spices and can almost taste them too. His eyes light up on seeing the puppets' wires, which he then unfortunately touches and manages to tangle.

Goethe also dwells on the stealth involved in Wilhelm's method of entering the pantry. The boy takes advantage of a moment's inattention on his mother's part and his movements are quiet and hurried, spurred on by the imminent danger of interruption. But his selections are haphazard: the unexpected chance to fulfill a desire leaves him no time to plan. Unexpected too is his discovery of the boxes with the telltale evidence that they contain the puppets. The situation is dictated by Wilhelm's need to be quick and so he is unable to take full advantage of his serendipitous discovery. He pilfers a handful of dried fruits and, more importantly, manages to snatch up the text of the David and Goliath puppet show.[3]

When Wilhelm thinks about the puppets, both here and at the end of Chapter Two, he speaks of them as potentially coming to life. They do so, at least in a figurative way, insofar as the whole experience with the puppets does seem to reflect on later events. The episodes from his childhood that Wilhelm rehearses continue to parallel events that contribute to his subsequent development. He stumbles across the puppets, and his actions before and after are characterized by subterfuge — a resemblance to the means he adopts in order to spend time at the theater and with his beloved Mariane. Both actions involve a strategy for evading his parents. When he enters the pantry, his mother has gone out and the rest of the household is asleep; to visit Mariane, he must wait until his parents are asleep and then creep away. And then,

---

[2] Before the days of refrigeration, the pantry, where dried foodstuffs were stored, was an important room in every house, and rats and mice were real threats.

[3] The "pomegranate skin" should in fact be "bitter orange." Pomegranate skin is brittle and without flavor and would not constitute a delicacy, whereas the citrus peel imparts a definite piquancy to any dish.

both the dried fruit and the puppets have a heightened appeal for Wilhelm because they are kept hidden away and he eagerly anticipates access to them. This is also an aspect of his relationship with Mariane: his days are spent in anticipation of their evenings together. Thus, the precipitate actions of entering the pantry, snatching up the booty, and dashing out will develop in time into a definite pattern of behavior. A tendency of Wilhelm's to throw himself headlong into a given situation is already visible.

The stealth needed for the acquisition of the book must continue while Wilhelm commits to memory the speeches contained in it. His devotion to this task brings about the illusion in him that he has actually become David and Goliath. In his account, Wilhelm draws attention to his youthful ambitious nature: although he managed to learn all the parts, he really only saw himself in the main roles and paid much less attention to the minor parts. But it is also remarkable that he did not select only one hero, *either* David *or* Goliath, with whom to identify. At this early stage, Wilhelm already sees himself in a number of different roles; he thinks he has real ability as an actor. For the reader, however, this seems a less than ideal situation. Again Wilhelm is patterning himself on a literary figure (*FA* 1387) but in this case it is immaterial to him which of the two sworn enemies he imagines himself to be. As acting and the theater are images for life and the world, Wilhelm's indifference here would seem to indicate a moral indifference born of self-centeredness. Even on the more literal level it is evident that the supposed talent for the theater is largely the product of the boy's imagination.

Once again, Wilhelm describes his mother and father as being very different in their respective attitudes towards children and their upbringing. His father believes in delivering praise and blame evenhandedly, as a matter of principle, even if the blame is undeserved. The praise is frequently not even expressed, as Wilhelm indicates when he says his father "secretly praised" his son's good memory. The German text describes the father, when he attends the puppet show with Wilhelm as co-puppeteer, as apparently peeking through between his fingers (er selbst schien nur durch die Finger zu sehen; Steiner *Sprache,* 94). The image conveys an atmosphere of childish play which at one and the same time fits in with the scene of childhood delights and condemns the father's attitude as unworthy of an adult. His mother, on the other hand, can be relied upon to show clemency in the face of Wilhelm's confession and to continue her role as mediator between her son and her husband.

Chapter Six

Wilhelm shows a disarming sense for the follies, confusions, and exaggerated reactions of childhood. He describes his first performance of a puppet show in front of children. An unfortunate slip gave his father the chance to dwell on his son's mistake. Wilhelm then grew up reading other plays and opera libretti. He began to construct props and strayed away from producing shows. His interest was only in the melodramatic fifth act and the special effects needed.

Mariane has not been paying attention. Wilhelm wants to hear something of her childhood, but Barbara intervenes. The chapter closes with the suggestion that such a harmonious scene is unlikely to occur as often as Wilhelm hopes.

Wilhelm begins his account by filling in the details of his initiation into the art of puppeteering, an event to which he had alluded only briefly in the previous chapter. His anticipation finally ends in the sheer joy of being invited into the room where the theater is set up and seeing the puppets arranged in order. From the elevation of a step provided for the puppeteer, Wilhelm looks down on to what he describes in German as "the little world" (über der kleinen Welt) and this expression is repeated soon after, when Wilhelm refers to the fact that he was even happy to be in charge of the "little world" of puppets when he had no audience. The puppets offer Wilhelm a sphere separate from his daily life and one in which he can give his imagination free rein. When he sees them as constituting a world, he also sees himself controlling this world. It is an expression of his desire, doubtless still a subconscious one, to take control of his life and determine his own destiny, a desire that gains support from the unfair treatment he feels he receives from his father.

The second time Wilhelm pictures himself in charge of the "little world" of the puppet theater, he mentions his imagination, and this is the key to the dissolution of the delightful world of illusion. Wilhelm imagines the love he shares with Mariane to be secure. And yet the relationship itself was described in Chapter Three as soaring on the "wings of imagination." The suggestion is that the contents of Wilhelm's imagination do not usually accord with reality. Wilhelm imagines that Mariane will be entertained by his narrative but it soon emerges that this is not the case. Also, his fascination for the theater, with Mariane as its representative, is in fact far removed from a true picture of life on the stage. All in all, imagination plays far too great a part in this relationship; even Mariane says in Chapter One that love is something she has only acted out on the stage until now (Gilli 202–3).

There seems to be a general confusion between what is imagined, what is acted, and what is real.

Wilhelm's account does not shy away from including the embarrassing mistake he made in dropping the Jonathan puppet during the performance, but he also says that, after spending a miserable evening, he found he had recovered from this humiliation the next morning. In his own estimation — and his mother concurred — he had really done very well indeed, especially in producing the voices for David and Jonathan. Set against this is the father's critical attitude, rapidly becoming a theme in these first chapters.

Wilhelm discovers and reads with great interest a collection of plays published under the title *Die Deutsche Schaubühne* (The German Stage).[1] The publication of this collection between 1740 and 1745 was part of a campaign to base the repertoire seen on German stages on the French classical model. And so, in a sense, Wilhelm's story runs parallel to the development of the German theater, as biblical topics give way to the French classical stage. The five-act structure was standard for the plays included in *Die Deutsche Schaubühne* and so it was easy for Wilhelm to know that a stabbing or other violent action could be found there. Indeed, it seems unlikely to have been the classic structure of the plays which attracted Wilhelm, since he mentions a predilection for opera, where much greater freedom would have been at his disposal (Bahr 18). In keeping with his drastic editing of these plays, Wilhelm only mentions three isolated characters from different plays by name (though one is replaced by the paraphrase "some tyrant" in the English version): Chaumigrem, Darius, and Cato.[2]

Wilhelm's childhood discovery of new plays allowed him to indulge his taste for the sensational and to try his hand at making new props, an

---

[1] Johann Christoph Gottsched published a collection of plays under the title *Die Deutsche Schaubühne* (1740–45). The plays, carefully edited to reflect the practices of the ancient dramatists, were intended to provide a repertoire for the German stage similar to that of the French classical stage. Some were translations from the French, others were original German works, including some from the pen of Gottsched and his wife.

[2] Chaumigrem is a tyrant in the 1689 novel by Heinrich Anselm von Zigler und Kliphausen, *Die asiatische Banise oder Das blutige doch mutige Peru*. He terrorizes and plunders neighboring territories in India and takes captive the beautiful princess Banise. *Die Deutsche Schaubühne* contains a tragedy, "Banise," by Melchior Grimm, based on that novel. Cato is the hero of Gottsched's tragedy "Der Sterbende Cato" (1732), also contained in *Die Deutsche Schaubühne*. Darius is the eponymous hero of Friedrich Lebegott Pitschel's "Darius," another of the plays included in the same collection.

activity at which he proved quite adept. So that the puppet troupe could take on new roles, individual puppets also had to be provided with changes of costume. As a result, textiles again become the subject of discussion for a while. Ribbons and taffeta accumulate into an extensive wardrobe, but unfortunately the continuous need for new costumes and props began to absorb Wilhelm more than the need to produce new plays to a high standard. The highly superficial aspects of the theater — the special effects and the costumes — appealed to him most and overrode his interest in the plays themselves. This of course is a comment on the superficiality of his acquaintance with the realities of theater life as well as on the state of the German stage at the time (Seitz 125). Wilhelm now freely admits that it was a mistake to let his childish preoccupation go so far. The mistake, as he says, was to allow himself to live entirely in his imagination and not to see that in doing so he had "destroyed the very foundations of this small world." The use of the term "world" once again alerts the reader to the possibility of applying this lesson to identify the dangers inherent in Wilhelm's present "world."

In case this parallel is not clear enough, the narrator now steps in to start a new paragraph by describing Mariane's reaction to Wilhelm's story. Despite the solemn judgment with which her lover concludes this part of his life story, and despite the exciting moments and high points of his childhood to which she has been treated, Mariane is bored and sleepy (Seitz 125). Here again is an indication that Wilhelm is not in tune with Mariane's sentiments and has mistakenly imagined that she would be entertained by this sort of narrative. Worse still, despite the gestures she uses to cover up her wandering thoughts, gestures which could be used to wonderfully ironic effect on stage, he fails to notice her inattention and is easily persuaded to continue. Neither does he notice the melancholy glance Mariane casts in Barbara's direction at the close of the chapter.

Wilhelm's analysis of his mistake contributes to one of the main themes which influence the structure of the novel (Viëtor 39–40; Mahoney 57). At the beginning of Wilhelm's reminiscences in Chapter Three, he refers to the pleasure of recollecting past but harmless mistakes. Dropping the Jonathan puppet was a mere mishap, but the mistaken perspective Wilhelm has just described may entail serious consequences in due course and will become part of a pattern of mistakes which make up the vagaries of his development.

The roots of one more important theme are detected in this chapter by some critics. The theme revolves around the importance of first impressions (Graham 187–90; Schings 717; Riemann 198 ff). Wilhelm asks Mariane to tell of her early impressions of childhood because he wants to know more about the woman he loves. The implication is that Wilhelm believes an individual's character to be formed by impressions, and his subsequent references to impressions substantiate this. Mariane and Barbara both appear to think that such an account of childhood and first impressions from Mariane's lips would reveal elements of her formation that would be unwelcome to Wilhelm's ears. Wilhelm insists and entreats Mariane to comply with his wishes; he speaks of sharing her past in his imagination and of imagining that they could regain lost time. The repeated reference to what is imaginary is another signal that Wilhelm fails to recognize the distinction between reality and appearance. In fact, with unconscious irony, Wilhelm is demonstrating that his love for Mariane is based on an idealized version of her. He has elevated her to the level of muse (Riemann 211) and has yet to discover the baser truths to which the reader is already privy.

Chapter Seven

Wilhelm moves on to the amusement he and his friends derived from acting. Wilhelm made the swords, decorated the sleds, transformed huntsmen and knights into an ancient army. Wilhelm was more interested in changing themes and costumes than in activity.

Tasso's *Jerusalem Delivered,* in a German translation, caught Wilhelm's fancy.[1] He was especially taken with the character of Chlorinda and her fatal armed encounter with Tancred.[2] The next step was to perform the episode. Wilhelm enlisted adult help in finding a space for the performance and materials for the scenery. But the production was a disaster because Wilhelm had relied on his enthusiasm instead of a script. David and Goliath and an improvised clown stepped

[1] Torquato Tasso (1544–1595) completed his epic poem *La Gerusalemme liberata* in 1575, although the first printed edition did not appear before 1581. The First Crusade forms the basis for the story, but romantic and fabulous elements have been added. The translation to which Wilhelm refers is by Johann Friedrich Kopps and is dated 1744. In *Dichtung und Wahrheit,* Goethe describes his own youthful enthusiasm for this work and says that he memorized parts of it. Goethe's father's library contained a 1705 edition of the poem in the original language as well as Kopps's translation.

[2] Chlorinda is a beautiful but warlike Ethiopian princess in *La Gerusalemme liberata.* Tancred, the Norman, falls in love with her but, without realizing it, kills her in combat. Armida is a Syrian enchantress who lures the Christian army, under their leader, Godrey, to her "bower of bliss." They are rescued by Rinaldo, with whom Armida falls in love.

in. Wilhelm vowed never to push ahead with a play before all the preparations are complete.

Wilhelm makes a transition at the opening of this chapter from self-sufficiency to a wider society. Children's make-believe games, in which a spirit of cooperation necessarily emerges, laid the foundation for acting in earnest. Wilhelm both knew how to make costumes and props and had a knack for persuading others to lend a hand in their manufacture. The restlessness that prevented him from staying with one play from beginning to end while he was manipulating the puppets later meant that he was constantly changing the themes of the games he played with his friends. But he now appears to see this willingness to move from one role to another as a welcome characteristic in someone who has ambitions as a professional actor.

Wilhelm's stories from his childhood have nothing haphazard about them. Always, an event is mentioned as exemplifying an attitude, not simply as an entertaining aside. As narrator, he exercises a definite control and discipline in his choice of material; there is a continuous theme, and each event illustrates a stage in a kind of psychological history. Nevertheless, he relates the events with an endearing irony and sense of the follies of childhood. When describing the unfortunate Tancred and Chlorinda performance, Wilhelm speaks of how his speech moved from first to third person in midstream. The change was an indication of Wilhelm's increasing self-consciousness, a sign that he had become better able, through this event, to take the important step of assessing himself. He was learning how to distance himself from the situation and, if necessary, to shoulder the blame himself when things went wrong. Wilhelm has become aware of the necessary connection between error and the acquisition of knowledge, a connection which constitutes, from one perspective, the main force responsible for propelling the hero on his way and the novel forward.

The transformation of the group of playmates from a Roman army into crusading knights came about through Wilhelm's sudden intense preoccupation with the story of Tancred and Chlorinda. Wilhelm's enthusiasm for what he had read of this text resulted in delusions of grandeur: whereas his friends held back and doubted their competence, Wilhelm urged them on and convinced them that they could play these roles from Tasso before an audience.[3] But again, he had placed the de-

---

[3] The theater in the second half of the eighteenth century saw an increase in the tendency to dramatize narrated events, as opposed to creating new drama. The German theater was slow in developing, in comparison with the same

tails before the substance; he had neglected to rehearse his little troupe and had given them no practical instructions for the performance. The stop-gap solution to this crisis was twofold and both facets recall stages in the development of German drama. First, the recycling of a biblical story and its conversion from puppet-theater material to the stage proper reflect a real transition in the history of the theater. In addition, the improvised clown act is an exact parallel to the custom of bringing on the popular *Hanswurst* figure to fill in time during a break. Goethe even takes the further step of having Wilhelm voice his disapproval of this clown figure, on the grounds that he undermined the seriousness of the play. This is clearly a reference to Gottsched's campaign to ban *Hanswurst* from the German stage. And so the account of Wilhelm's "inner history," with Wilhelm himself taking over as narrator, continues to run parallel to the emergence of a national theater in Germany.

The episode is significant because some important themes, destined to recur at crucial points in the novel, come to the fore here. In Chlorinda, whose attraction for Wilhelm lay in the quality of "masculine femininity," there is an extension of the characteristics first suggested by the person of Mariane. The importance attached to the officer's uniform Mariane wears for her stage performances served to alert readers to the fact that Wilhelm is drawn to women who demonstrate masculine as well as feminine traits. There is a link between Wilhelm's fascination with women who display masculine traits and his drive to develop harmony and balance in his own person (*FA* 1388). This question of wholeness and how an individual may attain it was a common preoccupation among Goethe's contemporaries. The view was that human nature is perfectible if a harmony can be achieved through balancing the constituent parts. According to Wilhelm von Humboldt (in a view that originates with Plato) male and female designations are to be seen as one-sided and restrictive.[4] The perfected human form would rise above such restrictions by combining the characteristics of each (Larrett 54).

---

process in France and England. In Germany, the theater really acquired stability, largely through patronage, only in the last quarter of the century.

[4] Wilhelm von Humboldt (1767–1835) was a political theorist, philologist and prominent subscriber to the humanistic view that held the study of ancient languages and classical ideals to be essential to the education of a well-rounded individual. He worked with Goethe and Schiller on the journal *Die Horen* and later, as founder of the University of Berlin and as a Prussian Minister of the Interior, was able to exert his influence by having his ideas introduced into the education system.

Wilhelm's tendency to identify with heroes of the printed page is again evident in his enthusiasm for the story of Tancred and Chlorinda's love and its tragic end. But it now develops one step further. As Chlorinda is a heathen, Tancred must keep his love a secret, and this relationship has several features in common with that of Wilhelm and Mariane. In his despair at having killed his beloved, Tancred gives vent to his emotion by striking a tree. Immediately, a voice addresses him with the warning that he is destined to "harm everything he ever loved." The reader is bound to suspect that this is yet another signal pointing to the fate of Wilhelm and Mariane's love. And in general, the impression persists that Wilhelm, both in the attitudes he adopted as a child, and in those apparent in him as he tells his tale, is unable to maintain a clear enough distinction between appearance and reality. This failing is to blame for the breakdown of the Tancred and Chlorinda performance because he imagined that, having been inspired by the poem, he would simply be able to reenact the events on stage without further ado. This inability to draw a line between the content of his thoughts or wishes and the actual state of affairs also prohibits Wilhelm from recognizing a profound reluctance in Mariane to reveal any details about her own past.

Chapter Eight

Chapter Eight is the last to be exclusively devoted to Wilhelm's narration. It has a slim narrative frame: the narrator describes the attitudes of Wilhelm's listeners and concludes with another brief intervention. Wilhelm describes how he turned almost anything he read into a scene to be performed. He began with the tragic ending and thought he could act almost any part. The efforts of Wilhelm and his friends were disorganized and unprofessional in the extreme, yet they were blissfully unaware of this. They took it for granted that their audiences would understand what was being conveyed. The young actors used whatever was available for props, and the boys also played the female roles. Eventually the sisters of some of the boys were admitted and they all received some instruction from the lieutenant. The introduction of female members led to romantic attachments and other minor dramas. Tragedy was considered easiest to perform. Wilhelm sees all this as valuable training, decisive for his future plans.

Wilhelm was expected to follow his father into the world of commerce. He now describes an allegorical poem he wrote at the time, as a means of giving vent to his resentment. The poem contrasts a godlike female figure representing tragedy and an old woman representing commerce. The hero rejects the material richness proffered by the goddess of commerce and turns to the muse. Wilhelm turns the muse into a compliment for Mariane.

At the outset of the chapter, as Wilhelm prepares to continue his story, the narrator informs the readers, with a delightfully ironic touch, that Mariane is asleep. The irony is compounded by the fact that in Chapter Six Wilhelm had made it clear that he set great store by an exchange of childhood reminiscences as a way of adding a further dimension to their relationship. Although it was mostly Barbara who encouraged him to go on with his story, Wilhelm's pleasure in these occasions derives from Mariane's presence. And so, now, he places his arm around her and continues to speak, oblivious of the fact that she is leaning on him not out of affection, but for support while she sleeps. This entertaining vignette places *Wilhelm Meisters Lehrjahre* in line beside C. M. Wieland's *Geschichte des Agathon* in the series of German novels commonly referred to by the term Bildungsroman.[1] In Wieland's novel, the fourth chapter of Book Seven contains a comparable situation and the narrator offers the amusing principle that a female listener's tendency to fall asleep is proportionally heightened if her beloved's story is exciting and true, the images vivid and the expressions lively. In contrast to the slumbering Mariane, Barbara knows how to profit from a situation and pours the remainder of the wine for herself. Wilhelm is too preoccupied with telling his story to be interested in drinking wine. This small detail of Barbara's behavior accords with what the reader already knows about her pragmatic, calculating outlook on life. Unlike Wilhelm, she does not suffer from any confusion between illusion and reality.

Wilhelm's autobiographical account continues to emphasize his mental or spiritual state. For example, he begins with a reference to the embarrassment of the Tancred and Chlorinda episode. He then goes on to use nouns such as "passion," "determination," "imagination," "delight," "preference," and verb forms such as "thinking," "believed," "felt." Always, his intentions or reactions are the important element; events are chosen more for the light they can shed on the account of

---

[1] *Geschichte des Agathon* (1767) is generally considered to be the first Bildungsroman (Swales, Beddow). Wieland's novel shares with *Wilhelm Meisters Lehrjahre* the characteristic of being to a certain extent a portrayal of its author's life and development. A feature of the Bildungsroman which Agathon and Wilhelm both display is the importance of error in determining the path the hero takes. What unites them here is the use of devices which undermine the traditional fictional construct to be found in novels.

his spiritual development and less for any entertainment value they might incidentally have. As narrator, however, he is able to comment on the ideas, feelings, and reactions of his younger self. He consistently draws attention to the fond misconceptions, the ill-advised decisions, the consequences of poor preparation, the over-ambitious plans — in short, all the errors of the enterprise, of which the children themselves were blissfully ignorant at the time. In the light of the accumulation of evidence to the contrary, the children's belief that they know more than the lieutenant could teach them about the business of acting and staging appears all the more ludicrous.

The tendency for reality and appearance to overlap is apparent at several points in this chapter. An exceptionally active imagination in Wilhelm as a child leads him to think of himself as able to portray all of the parts in any given play. Then the children think that the power of their own imaginations, which, when necessary, can transform a piece of wood into a dagger, will make this transformation apparent for the audience as well. And despite the makeshift character of the whole, it does not occur to them that the audience could be somewhat confused about which character each individual actor or actress is supposed to represent. The romances which subsequently develop between the actors and actresses are considerably enhanced by their costumes: a young man dressed to appear as a dashing hero or a young lady adorned with bows and ribbons can the more readily be idealized by the other party.

In Wilhelm's estimation, it is quite an improvement when the girls are allowed to join the troupe. The first step was achieved by having boys dressed in costumes which allowed them to portray female characters. This practice ties in with the theme which emphasizes textiles and costumes for their symbolic value. In addition, it mirrors the situation which drew attention to Mariane dressed as a male officer. Both versions of the phenomenon conjure up von Humboldt's view of human nature achieving perfection through a unity of male and female. A hint of this perfection is attained, even at this stage, when the couples pair off and form their romantic unions.

Having already confessed a weakness for melodramatic and tragic endings, Wilhelm mentions that the group felt best able to perform tragedy well. The real reason is that they found more opportunity to rant and stamp their feet in a tragedy, but they were also able to justify their choice more objectively. They had heard that, as a general rule, tragedy was easier to write and perform than comedy. This refers to a topos from Horace's *Epistles* 2.1, where Horace claims that, although comedy is thought to be easier to write because it draws on everyday life for its subject-matter, yet it is actually harder to succeed with a comedy, because audiences will judge it more harshly.[2]

Here as before, Goethe closely follows the details of his own childhood as recollected much later in *Dichtung und Wahrheit* (Flemming 7–9). Parallels occur in the importance of the puppet theater, in the son's obsessive interest in the stage, and in the father's disapproving attitude. Also, of course, Wilhelm in adulthood looks back on his youth and relates it in narrative form, just as Goethe does *in Dichtung und Wahrheit.*

The allegorical poem Wilhelm recalls writing at this juncture was an outpouring of his unhappiness at the prospect of being obliged to adopt a way of life so completely opposed to the profession which he was so passionately determined to pursue. He calls the idea behind it "trivial," which is a translation of the German word "gemein." The German word also has the meaning of "common," in the sense of "unoriginal" and this seems closer to the intention of this passage. The theme of the poem is that of "Hercules at the Crossroads," a fable in which the young hero must choose between pleasure and virtue. Its origins lie in antiquity with Prodicus of Ceos and Xenophon (Bahr 26) and there is a 1773 poem by Wieland with the same theme.[3] But it is also possible that Wilhelm is making a more general point: what he views as "unoriginal" is the widespread literary practice of personifying ideas (*MA* 720; Bahr 21; *HA* 629).

Judging by Wilhelm's description of it, the poem (which may have resembled a one-act play) seems to display many features which one also finds in stage performances. The lively dispute between the two figures is a dramatic scene of the kind for which Wilhelm had a particular penchant. The costumes are described in detail and both the women bear symbolic objects which would make them identifiable at a glance. The muse of commerce carries a distaff and keys and wears spectacles; the other figure is overburdened with "crowns and daggers, chains and masks."[4] Their manners of speaking are also quite distinct, each designed

---

[2] The line is taken from one of Horace's two great literary epistles, the other being 2.3, commonly known as *Ars Poetica*. Horace's view is reiterated in a more concise form in Jean Paul's *Vorschule der Ästhetik* (1804), paragraph 39.

[3] The motif was used by Wieland for his Singspiel *Die Wahl des Herkules.*

[4] A distaff is a stick used to hold the bunch of flax, or wool, for spinning. Schings (*MA*) sees the significance of this object as reaching beyond its function within the poem. He refers to a passage in *La Gerusalemme liberata* (II, 39) in which Chlorinda is described as disdaining flax, distaff, needle and thread. Womanly occupations are not sufficiently demanding for her. Thus, the figure representing commerce is also diametrically opposed to the much-admired Chlorinda.

to complement her persona. It has been observed that these two female figures sum up Mariane and Barbara (Schlaffer *Mythos,* 136).

At the close of the chapter, the narrator returns to describe Mariane's awakening. She has not heard any of Wilhelm's final installment and has presumably also missed the extravagant compliment addressed to her, which Wilhelm had tacked on to the end of his story. It is an amusing situation: Wilhelm's gesture and dramatically raised voice wake Mariane, but the content of his rhetoric is completely lost. Presented on stage, it could have been part of a comic skit. Again, Goethe introduces into his novel scenes and gestures which seem designed for the stage.

The conclusion is interesting for its narrative technique. The narrator refers to Wilhelm as "our hero." This signals a shift in perspective away from Wilhelm, who has virtually taken over as narrator in recent chapters. Whereas Wilhelm's remarks were directed towards Mariane and Barbara, the narrator now addresses the reader directly. By using the inclusive form "our," the narrator is counting on a like-minded reader and is standing in the way of any tendency to identify with the protagonist. Whereas Wilhelm maintained an ironic distance from his younger self, the narrator takes the reader's agreement as given and uses the equally ironic but also gently mocking term "our hero." In expressing the hope that Wilhelm will have more attentive listeners in the future, the narrator drops a number of hints. Mariane does not seem very interested in Wilhelm's story, but Wilhelm — rather unheroically — is so enjoying the opportunity to reminisce that he continues, in a state of self-absorption, quite unaware of Mariane's inattention. Mariane's indifference is hardly surprising. After all, for Mariane, the stage is part of her everyday existence, her bread and butter. Performing on stage is a nightly routine and the acting profession holds no glamor for her now, if it ever did. Wilhelm's fascination for the theater in all its aspects is an idealized dream, far removed from the life with which Mariane is so familiar. The meeting of minds which should have taken place between Mariane and Wilhelm on this occasion has failed. And their failure to communicate is symptomatic of a deeper rift, also evident in the fact that they do not belong to the same class of society. A final note of doom strikes when Wilhelm sets up a contrast between the fictional muse in his poem and the reality of life with Mariane. As the reader well knows, Wilhelm's enthusiasm is misplaced: what he takes for reality in his present situation is largely a construct of his imagination (Gilli 199).

Chapter Nine

The reader gains some insight into Mariane's state of mind in this chapter, but in the third person. The narrator describes Mariane's thoughts without reference to events prior to her involvement with Wilhelm and the beginning and end deal with Wilhelm's current aspirations. Mariane's thoughts are revealed only to the reader, while Wilhelm remains in the dark. This increases the sense of an ever-widening rift between the lovers. Wilhelm, on the other hand, has difficulty in preventing himself from expressing his thoughts out loud, even when alone.

The opening paragraph makes it clear that Wilhelm is confident of Mariane's love and that she agrees with his plans and hopes for the future. He has made the transition from the nervous anticipation in the early stages of a love affair, to the contentment of a relationship on a secure footing. Not that he takes Mariane for granted; on the contrary, he holds her in high esteem. He idealizes her and is profoundly grateful for her reciprocation. She fills his thoughts at every moment. Mariane has been swept along by Wilhelm's passion, although she is periodically subject to guilt and is painfully aware of her difficult choice. Mariane's life seems lackluster; her love for Wilhelm has increased accordingly. Each sees the other as a means of escape.

After giving an analysis of Mariane's unsettled thoughts, the narrator returns to Wilhelm in his blissful state. Totally unaware of Mariane's distress, he bubbles over with feelings of love and gratitude towards her and indulges in exclamatory self-address, incredulous as he is at his good fortune. Wilhelm believes that his relationship with Mariane is a sign that his destiny lies with the theater. Mariane appears to be offering him a means of escape from the bourgeois existence he finds so distasteful. He feels renewed by her presence and able to pursue his intention to leave his family without regret.

This short chapter has an important function. First, it emphasizes the lack of understanding between the lovers and Wilhelm's obliviousness. But then near the end, the narrator gives some more precise contours to Wilhelm's dreams. He has a lofty goal that seems less remote when viewed from the stable perspective he feels he has attained through his bond with Mariane. Goethe introduces a topical theme: Wilhelm hopes to be able to found a national theater.[1] Contemporary writers strongly desired to establish a truly national German theater with financial support. Such an institution would replace, in part, the traveling groups which were almost the sole providers of theater at the time.

The final sentence describes how Wilhelm attempted to gather together his thoughts and form a mental tableau out of them. The image is that of a painting suffused with the colors of love. The background is hazy and the figures difficult to distinguish, but it is precisely this which Wilhelm, in his euphoric optimism, finds appealing. The murkiness serves to underline the lack of clarity both in Wilhelm's grasp of his present situation and in the idealism of his plans for the future. In forging a connection between painting and the imagination, Goethe gives an inkling of the important role which certain paintings will play in Wilhelm's development.

---

[1] The term "national theater" held tremendous significance in the contemporary cultural community. The desire to establish a theater which concentrated on home-grown material for its repertoire was shared by all the leading lights. Not only would German writers thus be encouraged to compose new works, but the German public's discerning palate would be schooled as well. The people were in need of education through exposure to the right types of art. This would promote the formation of a more refined aesthetic taste, and provide a moral or ethical dimension as well. Whereas during the Baroque period education centered around the Church, and whereas the Enlightenment insisted on the importance of reason and knowledge, the classical concept of education through art was now taking hold.

Gottsched had laid the basis for the idea of a national theater, using the French classical stage rather than ancient precedents as his model. Under his influence, Johann Elias Schlegel produced the first German national play, *Herrmann*. He then moved to Denmark and founded a national theater there. Several writers developed the theme of a national theater in essays, lectures, and theoretical works. Johann Georg Sulzer, in his *Allgemeine Theorie der schönen Künste* (1771–1774), isolates three types of drama and the third type stresses the need for emphasis on relevance for the nation. Schiller discusses the moral impact of the stage in two essays dated 1783 and 1784. The first experiment in establishing such a theater in Germany took place in Hamburg in 1767, under the direction of Gotthold Ephraim Lessing. Although this first attempt to found a national theater was short-lived, it gave rise to Lessing's work *Hamburgische Dramaturgie* in which he envisages a German theater with a repertoire that would attain a complete unity between art and nature and at the same time would truly belong to the nation. After other similar enterprises had taken root in Mannheim and Berlin, the theater in Weimar — which was to be completely molded by its director, Goethe himself — was established in 1791.

Chapter Ten

Wilhelm's friend Werner delivers a speech outlining the benefits of an association with the world of trade. His down-to-earth business sense forms a counterbalance to Wilhelm's dreamy hopes for a successful and pioneering role in the theater. Werner appears as Wilhelm is packing his books and criticizes Wilhelm's unfinished projects. The friends engage in a discussion that will be significant for Wilhelm's development. They discuss whether seeing a project through to the end is a good thing in itself. Werner, too, was involved in the puppet theater, supplying the required materials. Werner refers dismissively to Wilhelm's allegorical poem with its uncharitable portrait of the female figure representing commerce. The impassioned encomium which follows amply redresses the balance.

The chapter begins with the pronoun "he" and in doing so seems to suggest an uninterrupted flow out of the previous chapter and into this one. In fact, the narrator has passed over several intervening stages which would explain how Wilhelm's dreams of breaking away are now significantly closer to being realized. The details of the arrangements are deferred until the next chapter, so that the reader can first hear a spirited defense of precisely the lifestyle and preoccupations Wilhelm despises most.

The first sentence describes the scene, with Wilhelm at home, sorting through his books and papers; the reader is placed in the position of an onlooker. Already in the second sentence an account of Wilhelm's thoughts, recollections, and intentions takes over from the description of his current physical activity. Wilhelm is establishing principles which will help him decide what to take and what to leave behind. Before Werner interrupts, two such principles have taken shape: nothing must be taken along which will remind him of the past and only works of good taste are to be included. The principles Wilhelm formulates here bear a close resemblance to those upheld by Gottsched and the members of the movement to establish a German national theater. A movement away from using ancient Greek or seventeenth-century French classical drama as models was deemed an essential prerequisite for founding a national theater which could stand on its own merits. Wilhelm's thoughts also touch on the issue of good taste, and this too is reminiscent of one of the reformers' principles: that the German theater was intended to refine the tastes of the theater-going public.

Wilhelm mentions both poets and critics in the category of works of good taste. The combined qualities of composing poetry and judging it according to certain precepts are characteristic of the central concept of taste in eighteenth-century aesthetic theory (*MA* 722–23). But Wilhelm has not so far been able to dedicate himself with equal enthusiasm to the works of poets and those of critics. The poetry volumes were well thumbed and he had tried his hand at imitating the style of those works he admired, but the critical works had been largely neglected; their pages were still uncut.[1] Wilhelm pictures himself developing into a writer, and the method he adopts in order to refine his talents in this direction is imitation. The practice of imitating the acknowledged masters as a way of schooling oneself in the art of poetry or rhetoric is part of a long tradition. And yet here the reader's feeling, derived from certain hints, is that whatever the merit of his model texts, Wilhelm's literary efforts are probably misguided and inferior.

Werner is critical of Wilhelm's seeming inability to complete any of the projects he takes up with such enthusiasm. Wilhelm maintains that it is a good thing to try one's hand at a variety of activities if one hopes to learn. Furthermore, when one of these pursuits turns out to be unsuitable, there is no particular virtue in completing the project simply for the sake of having it finished. This dispute expresses *in nuce* the central issue about the structure of *Wilhelm Meisters Lehrjahre* as a Bildungsroman. The development this protagonist undergoes does not culminate in the sort of conclusion that satisfies all the separate strains of Wilhelm's ambition. Wilhelm does undergo changes, but he does so without reaching any very clear and decisive goal or one that relates to his earlier plans. The ending does not simply bring unity to his inner divisions and many plans are left unrealized, including the plan to spend his life on the stage, which was an all-consuming ambition at the beginning of the novel. The dispute continues and Wilhelm, in turn, accuses Werner of exploiting the situation; it emerges that he persuaded Wilhelm to accumulate a large collection of puppet costumes so that he himself could supply the materials and make a profit.

These childhood recollections support an impression that the characters of the two young men were already established in their childhood. The behavioral tendencies each displayed then are still typical for them now that they are about to become independent young adults. Werner sums up their differing attitudes with good-natured irony when

[1] Book sizes are determined by the number of times a large sheet of paper is folded in order to form the pages. Books of the size known as "quarto" are put together from large sheets of paper folded into four leaves. Readers would have had to slit along the folded edges and thus separate the pages in order to read the book. Some of the smaller French publishing houses continue to produce volumes with uncut pages even today.

he describes himself accumulating a good profit while Wilhelm was preparing to deliver Jerusalem.[2] Werner juxtaposes the realm of the imagination, where Wilhelm thrives but which Werner himself sees as folly, with the practical and very real sphere in which he himself feels at home.

It is very likely true that Wilhelm's allegorical poem lacked artistic merit, but Werner mainly objects to its unflattering portrayal of the figure representing the world of business. Werner argues on behalf of his "Goddess" that her emblems of the olive branch and a golden crown designate the benefits she brings to her adherents.[3] According to Werner, involvement in the world of business imparts a sense of order as well as a broad overview; the successful operation of a large commercial enterprise is a thing of true beauty. Werner feels that he could convince his friend of this if only Wilhelm were willing to be more open. Wilhelm objects to the reduction of what he calls "the true sum total of life" to a series of columns and figures. And the praise of double-entry bookkeeping, as though it ranked among the greatest works of the human spirit, demonstrates to Wilhelm's satisfaction the extreme narrowness of Werner's outlook.[4] It seems that the two will never be able to see eye to eye; their beliefs are diametrically opposed. But the opposition here is not so lacking in subtlety as the literary form of the same debate from Wilhelm's pen. When Werner suggests that, were he to take a careful look, Wilhelm would discover that the businessman needs a versatile mind, he is not met with simple stubborn opposition. Wilhelm shows willingness to entertain the idea that his imminent journey might indeed open his eyes to the advantages of the situation

[2] Werner compares himself to the Venetians who made a profit by transporting the Crusaders by sea, without themselves engaging in any action to promote the cause. In 1453, when Constantinople was being besieged by the Turks, the Pope urged various monarchs and republics to raise a crusade; Venice was a government in which he placed hopes to no avail. The comparison works well within the context of the performance of *Gerusalemme liberata*, which tells its story against the background of the First Crusade.

[3] The olive branch was established as the symbol of peace by the biblical story of Noah's Ark in *Genesis* 8.11. The dove returns to the Ark carrying an olive branch and Noah knows by this that the flood waters have receded from the earth.

[4] The double-entry system of bookkeeping enables a business to know at any time the value of each item, how much of this value is owed to creditors and how much belongs to the business when cleared of debts. This method of bookkeeping began with the development of the commercial republics of Italy, and instruction manuals for bookkeeping were developed during the fifteenth century in various Italian cities.

his friend describes. The reader learns with surprise that the journey Wilhelm is about to undertake is in some way linked to the operation of the family business. It is not explicitly to be the realization of his much-discussed plan to set off to join a theater.

Werner is also not quite as rigid as first impressions suggested. He too inhabits the realm of the imagination, if only he could recognize this. What he prescribes for Wilhelm — visits to major trading centers and seaports — is unlikely to be an experience he has ever had himself (*MA* 723). At any rate, it certainly does not correspond to his normal way of life. Werner has learned from Wilhelm a spiritual way of looking at things and his speech becomes visionary at various points. He introduces a couple of poetic flourishes and adds an appeal to Wilhelm to engage his imagination in the same way. Werner is confident that his rhetoric, coupled with Wilhelm's forthcoming experiences, will ultimately persuade Wilhelm of the superiority of this position.

The lack of clarity about the purpose of Wilhelm's journey is not an isolated phenomenon. Not all incidents in Wilhelm's life that are ultimately relevant to the structure of the book are initially presented as decisive turning points for the hero (Pascal 24). Increasingly, Wilhelm will meet people and drift in and out of situations which do not appear significant. This singular brand of realism is typical for the type of development which Wilhelm undergoes. It is as though Goethe were drawing directly from life and unwilling to sacrifice any unexpected occurrences for the sake of an overall plan (Bruford 32). Several events seem unconnected and bewildering at the time, and only later does the reader learn that they have had an effect on Wilhelm. In fact, the ending of the novel is notorious for its failure to deliver a complete or satisfying resolution in Wilhelm.

Chapter Eleven

In Chapter Ten, Wilhelm was already packing for his journey; Chapter Eleven gives the background to these preparations: how the two fathers agreed to send Wilhelm on some business matters. Chapter Eleven is dominated by the narrator, who describes the different households and the fathers' attitudes. An exchange between the two fathers forms a counterpart to the conversation in the previous chapter between Wilhelm and Werner. The narrator also provides a fuller picture of Wilhelm's father and describes Wilhelm's state of mind as he anticipates his departure. Finally, Wilhelm, in a state of great excitement, goes to tell Mariane what has been planned and receives an ambiguous or, at best, noncommittal reaction.

The German wording expresses an intimate alliance between the narrator and the reader that is unfortunately lost in the English translation. Wilhelm and Werner are referred to as "*our* two friends," whereas the possessive is not used in the English version. The formulation seems to suggest that the narrator and the reader are operating at the same level — one is not better informed than the other. But since the narrator is the one who will now provide all the information, the suggestion is in fact purely illusory. However, by being called over to join the side of the narrator in this way, the reader is prevented from identifying too directly with Wilhelm's perspective; this seems to be the main objective of the narrator's pose.

The two fathers are united in their involvement in commerce and in their belief in its benefits, and yet in other ways they stand in contrast with one another, just as their sons do. The description of Wilhelm's father offers more evidence of the philistine leanings about which his son spoke so harshly in Chapter Two. He has cashed in the valuable family heirlooms, including works of art and antiques, and what he has replaced them with is all in the latest style. At the time, Wilhelm was arguing against the acquisition of these new furnishings; there was no mention of the inherited valuables that were sold. Wilhelm's point was that some things can be highly prized even though they have absolutely no monetary value, and he drew a parallel between the unnecessarily fine and ornate furnishings in the Meister house and the stage curtain in his beloved theater. The reader now learns more details about the objects selected for the house: they are practical, domestic items but not principally chosen for their utility. Wilhelm's father has seen to it that they are impressive and designed to exude an air of opulence. They seldom see any actual service, however, since entertaining guests is always so costly and disruptive. And so the silver cutlery and the fine dinner setting, instead of being symbols of elegant conviviality, are simply a display. These items belong in the realm of appearances; the household in general is described as a monotonous and cheerless place.

All these details give the reader more feeling for what impelled Wilhelm to turn his back on his father's sphere of influence. And yet the insights into the man himself reveal a much more appealing personality than anyone relying on Wilhelm's remarks alone would have considered possible. Wilhelm's father has a high view of his son's abilities. He also wishes fervently to be able to impart to his son the characteristics in which he felt himself to be lacking. In addition, his greatest desire is to leave behind something of value for his children. For all his rigid principles about the upbringing of children and despite his inability to express his affection for them, Wilhelm's father is a devoted and proud parent.

The narrator has given the reader some information to which Wilhelm has no access and which shows another side to his father.

Werner's experience of family life is the exact opposite of Wilhelm's. His father rewards himself for his day's work by sitting down to good food and drink in the company of as many family members and guests as possible. He sets great store by the quality of the meals and the wine to accompany them and seems oblivious both to the dishes on which they are served and to the chairs on which his guests must sit. The picture is of a generous man who cannot enjoy his food properly unless he is also enjoying the company of others. He is open-handed and genuinely hospitable; in this friendly atmosphere, while the guests enjoy their meal, the undistinguished dinner setting goes completely unremarked. The house itself is a contrast to the Meister establishment: it is dark and gloomy, and the father works in a small study at a very old desk. The reader already knows that, by contrast, the Meisters' house is new and very impressive.

The conversation between the two older men displays a masterly lightness of touch on Goethe's part. First, there is a wonderful irony in the fact that Wilhelm's father's thoughts about his son's future and Wilhelm's own thoughts are so disparate. By sending him out on his first business trip, the father imagines he is launching him in the family business, a direction he is destined to follow throughout his life. The reader already knows how differently Wilhelm feels about this matter. The second point is the subtly drawn psychological play Goethe sets up between the two fathers. Meister praises Werner *fils* to his father for all that he accomplished on undertaking a similar journey and makes a mildly critical prediction that his own son will not succeed in keeping down the costs of his own journey. The narrator now explains that Meister, who actually esteems his son's gifts very highly, was hoping that his friend would feel obliged to counteract this mild criticism by praising Wilhelm, and was disappointed when he did not.

When Wilhelm's father had sold his own father's art collections and made such purchases as he deemed desirable, he entrusted the remaining funds to his friend Werner *père* to invest. The reason for asking him to look after the matter was that Werner had a definite gift for successful speculation. In keeping with this knack for business, Werner also has a sound practical policy in relation to individuals: he is not prepared to trust a young man until he has proved his worth. One more indication of his practical resourcefulness is that Werner works out a deal for providing Wilhelm with a horse, through a payment-in-kind arrangement with a debtor.[1]

Wilhelm's view of the situation is that he is being offered precisely the opportunity he needs to carry out his plans. He will profit from a state of affairs not of his own making but to his benefit. For all his ambitious talk, Wilhelm has not contributed anything to what he sees as the realization of his private hopes. In fact, he more closely resembles a victim of circumstances than a young man about to set out on the path of his new calling. And here the narrator passes a moral judgment: Wilhelm feels no pricks of conscience, no qualms about accepting this commission and making use of resources put at his disposal, for his own, quite different, ends. In fact, his delusions lead him so far away from day-to-day reality that he even considers this opportunity as heaven-sent. Everything seems to be falling into place for him and he naively thinks his family would not see this as deception and would ultimately praise him for following his instincts. Wilhelm lacks the intuitiveness of the older generation.

As the hour approaches for Wilhelm to tell Mariane of this unexpected turn of events, his impatience mounts. The narrator, still in disapproving mode, compares him to a trick artist who knows he is capable of freeing himself from his prison chains and anticipates with joy the moment when he will deceive his unsuspecting jailer. In Wilhelm's imagination, he is already free as he leaves the pressures of his household behind. A succession of images passes before him, all fulfillments of his hopes and desires; only the cry of the watchman, perhaps heralding some sobering event, brings him down to earth.

Mariane's reaction to Wilhelm's news is a leaden anticlimax after the description of Wilhelm's own ecstatic feelings. He tells her about the journey; he asks for her hand in marriage and makes a discrete and gentle inquiry as to whether she might already be carrying his child. All this is met with silence on Mariane's part, except for sobs and sighs. Wilhelm, who is not as well informed as the reader, feels able to interpret Mariane's tears and kisses as a positive sign, although he would have liked a clearer reply. The reader, however, can add one more detail to the gradually forming picture of Mariane. To receive Wilhelm, she puts on the nightdress which came from Norberg — an act of duplicity to match

---

[1] In order to retrieve the horse he would need for his journey, Wilhelm had to travel by postchaise. A postchaise was a traveling carriage in use during the eighteenth and the first half of the nineteenth century. It was hired from stage to stage which also allowed for a change of horses. A man would be positioned or "posted" at each stage.

the one Wilhelm is embarking on. While Wilhelm takes advantage of his father's offer to pursue his own interests, Mariane accepts Norberg's gifts and uses them to enhance the time she spends with Wilhelm. The nightdress produces the desired effect; Wilhelm is enchanted, and feels blessed in his state of ignorance, while the narrator briefly joins forces with him to exclaim at Mariane's charms. But the reader feels a cold chill of fear for Mariane and the dangerous game she is playing.

Chapter Eleven, though brief, sets up important and enduring models. In the previous chapter, the opposing views presented by Wilhelm and Werner appeared not in simple opposition, but as though both positions, in varying degrees, were to be found within Wilhelm's own psychological makeup. The younger men are rather theoretical and idealistic, whereas their fathers, in this chapter, overcome their different dispositions in a conversation about practical arrangements. They are described as being of one mind as regards the advantages of their chosen profession. The basic oppositions, both here and in the previous chapter, together with their resolution, establish a pattern for Wilhelm's development. But the chapter ends with an unresolved issue involving Mariane and this too is a feature of the narrative as a whole. The diverging influences at work on Wilhelm also suggest that, contrary to his own views on the matter, Wilhelm may not be the master of his own fate. Many of the circumstances surrounding his departure are either not of his own making or are misinterpreted by him. Wilhelm thinks that his hopes are soon to be realized, indeed, that his own wishes are somehow in alignment with divine providence; the reader, however, knows that he is still languishing within the realm of imagination and delusion.

Chapter Twelve

Mariane is in a turmoil, the result both of Wilhelm's departure and of the unwelcome arrival of Norberg. Barbara tries to convince her to continue in this double existence. Mariane relates Wilhelm's clairvoyant dream in which a strange man saves Mariane from sliding into a swamp and Wilhelm is powerless to intervene. It is similar to a dream in Wieland's *Geschichte des Agathon* in which Agathon pursues the fleeing Psyche and eventually sinks down into a swamp (Book VI, 4). Agathon had disturbing thoughts before the dream and is upset on waking. Wilhelm, however, is unaware of Mariane's preoccupations and feels reassured by her when he wakes.

Barbara favors Norberg but she begins by praising Wilhelm, thus disguising her prejudice. Mariane acknowledges that Wilhelm's means are not adequate and, exhausted by trying to reach a decision, she will allow Barbara to formulate a plan. The principles of Barbara's plan accord with her pragmatic, even opportunistic personality. But the proposal is immoral and fraught with dangers. To make matters worse, Mariane suspects that she is going to have a baby.

This short chapter shows that the pressures of Mariane's life are, if anything, greater than Wilhelm's. In her case, the opposing forces threaten imminent catastrophe, so that some sort of resolution is urgently necessary. For Wilhelm, the main thing is to be allowed to follow his whims, free from the constraints of his family's expectations; Mariane's next step is crucial for her survival. Wilhelm's is a solution of sorts; he will agree to undertake a business trip but all the while will be intending to use it as an opportunity to pursue his theatrical interests. This dishonesty mirrors the dishonest solution Barbara proposes to Mariane, and in each case, the dilemma involves an issue of central importance.

When she makes the first suggestion that Mariane should keep two lovers, Barbara elicits no reaction. Mariane is taken up with thoughts of Wilhelm's dream. Instead of having Wilhelm relate the content of his own dream, Goethe places it in the mouth of Mariane, perhaps because she alone is well placed to interpret it. Mariane expresses regret that her carefully guarded secret has been revealed to Wilhelm in the dream, but this is a perspective only she could have. Wilhelm, it seems, was able to console himself in Mariane's proximity and in the reassuring reality of his present situation. He sees no signs of the dangers shown in the dream.

For Wilhelm, the dream presented a situation in which he felt acutely powerless to save Mariane. For Mariane, the main figure is the other man; her conscience forces her to concentrate on his presence. The reader knows that Wilhelm is inhibited by his position in society and that there is another man in Mariane's life. So for the reader, a third perspective presents itself: the image of Mariane sinking into a swamp is the new and arresting feature communicated by the dream. It seems to emphasize that a downward slide of Mariane's fortunes will be the outcome of her present dilemma.

After hearing the account of the dream, Barbara avoids commenting on it; instead, she steers the conversation back to the decision facing Mariane. This shift from dream to reality is described as a shift from poetry to prose. Prose, together with the negative connotations of its adjective *prosaic*, stands for reason, while poetry is the mode of expression for feeling and imagination (Schlaffer *Mythos*, 134–35). Even in Wilhelm's absence, these two factions are at war; in this case they are not at war within him, but he is still the occasion for their disagreement.

Goethe uses the image of a birdcatcher to describe Barbara's techniques. A birdcatcher uses a whistle to imitate the song of the bird and thus lures it into the spot where it will be caught in nets.[1] Barbara coaxes Mariane by praising Wilhelm in the words she likes to hear. The use of the whistle is the birdcatcher's main skill, but the net is an essential piece of equipment as well. Transferred to Mariane's situation, it implies that Barbara's proposal is a trap. And the proposal does not appear to have satisfied Mariane, who, despite her emotional state, periodically shows that she is well aware that Wilhelm lacks not only financial means but practical sense as well. She knows better than anyone else that the acting profession, which Wilhelm imagines is the right one for him, does not bring much financial reward. In fact, without Norberg's protection, she would be lost (Ratz 67).

Mariane is completely paralyzed by the competing claims of the heart and reason. In her exasperation, she asks Barbara to take the decision for her — it is more a cry of despair than a serious suggestion, the reader suspects. And then Mariane tries to influence Barbara's judgment by mentioning, in somewhat veiled terms, that she is probably already carrying Wilhelm's child. This revelation is designed to shift the moral balance in Wilhelm's favor. Barbara needs a moment to take in this latest piece of information, but then she takes up the methods of the birdcatcher once again. She speaks in the metaphor of the stage in putting forward the details of her solution. To begin with, she makes an unconscious reference to Wilhelm's allegorical poem when she claims to despair of young people who move from one extreme to another instead of trying to reconcile the two. At the same time, she is also describing Wilhelm's state of mind. But then Barbara places herself in the role of a theater director, a clear attempt to coerce Mariane into agreeing to the plan. Since Mariane is accustomed to carrying out the director's wishes when she performs on the stage, she may not be averse to allowing Barbara to organize her life. The methods of the theater can be used for practical ends and in this way imagination and reason are combined. According to this chillingly calculating plan, Wilhelm's child will find a rich provider in Norberg. Whereas Barbara expresses confidence in her ability to reconcile the opposing forces, the chapter ends with Mariane in despair of ever being able to do so. She cannot produce any practical alternative to Barbara's suggestion, but longs for the impossible: the ability to forget her situation.

---

[1] The birdcatcher would sell either birds to be roasted and served at table or songbirds to be kept in cages.

Chapter Thirteen

Wilhelm's expedition to fetch the horse is more eventful than he had anticipated. He is drawn into a drama in the household he is visiting. He hears how the stepdaughter has fallen in love with an actor and left home. Wilhelm is increasingly uncomfortable, partly because he is also planning to leave home with his beloved. The young man in question is an actor, and this does not recommend him to the girl's parents. Wilhelm hurries away, hoping to leave the signs and omens behind.

Unfortunately for Wilhelm, it proves impossible for him to avoid the situation. He comes across the sorry couple being conducted back to town to undergo a hearing in the courtroom. The scene is described in great detail: the narrator dwells on the officers' uniforms and weapons and the procession accompanying the cart which conveys the couple with about as much ceremony as one would expect for cattle being transported to market. The horrifying picture is somewhat alleviated by remarks which ridicule the pomposity of the various officials and the officious tone of the proceedings.

The parallels with his own situation cannot escape Wilhelm; he begins to take a real interest in the plight of these strangers, listens to their version of the events and circumstances and determines to try to help them. Wilhelm can easily picture himself and Mariane in a similar situation, which increases his determination to see the present situation resolved in a way likely to satisfy all parties concerned.

Wilhelm's experience of these events is taking place at the same time as the discussion between Mariane and Barbara in the previous chapter. Forced to confront a situation with so many features parallel to his own, Wilhelm begins to think more analytically about his relationship with Mariane. During their brief separation, both Wilhelm and Mariane are taking stock of the situation, Mariane out of practical necessity and Wilhelm because he is thrown into the path of two people who find themselves in circumstances similar to his own. But their respective deliberations are quite different. Mariane, conscious of an encroaching threat to her relationship with Wilhelm, cannot find any grounds to be hopeful of a happy outcome. Wilhelm thinks himself into the situation of the young couple who left home seeking happiness and wonders what the consequences might be if he and Mariane were to pursue a similar course of action. He pictures Mariane dealing with a court hearing and immediately romanticizes the scene. Mariane would make her confession with even more sincerity and in still finer words. His thoughts still have a dream-like quality; he has not yet turned them to practical questions.

Wilhelm is not blind to the signs of fate. On first hearing the story of the lovers from the stepmother of the girl — who condemns them in no uncertain terms — he feels embarrassed. It is as though she were condemning Wilhelm himself and his secret plans. The term "sibyl" is used to refer to the woman as though she were actually in a position to predict a black future for Wilhelm and Mariane.[1] Later on, when the young woman is giving an account of her situation at home, she paints an unsympathetic picture of her stepmother; the woman seems to represent the less pleasant overtones of the designation "sibyl" as well.

Wilhelm stays in that household for as short a time as possible and his feeling of discomfort persists as long as he is there. On meeting the lovers, however, he becomes transfixed and is impatient with anyone who appears to be trying to distract him from becoming involved with every stage of the lovers' journey and the subsequent legal procedures. He seems to be watching an absorbing play, one which bases its appeal on a convincing depiction of an entirely realistic dilemma.

The narrator contributes to the impression that Wilhelm's future life is being acted out before his eyes: the end of the chapter refers to "what usually happens only in plays and novels." The phrase describes the intensity of passion, generosity and strength of devotion displayed by the couple at the conclusion of their hearing. But it could also be taken to apply generally to a central theme of *Wilhelm Meister's Apprenticeship,* that is to say, the dialectical relations between reality and its representations, or the confusion between the real world and the world of the imagination. But it may also be the case that Goethe uses the observation to draw the reader's attention to echoes from other literary works. Whether or not this particular phrase acts as a pointer, the echoes are certainly detectable. The most obvious parallel with the general set-up in this chapter is to be found in the opening of L'Abbé Prévost's *Histoire du Chevalier des Grieux et de Manon Lescaut.*[2] Goethe adopts his generally sympathetic telling of the lovers' tale from L'Abbé Prévost; certain features of Manon and Des Grieux's story, such as the difference in social class, find themselves reproduced in Mariane and Wilhelm's situation (*FA* 1392).

---

[1] The term "sibyl" was also applied to the goddess of commerce in Wilhelm Meister's poem described in Chapter Eight. There it simply meant an old hag; here it means a prophetess.

[2] L'Abbé Prévost's *Histoire du Chevalier des Grieux et de Manon Lescaut,* written in 1731, relates a tragic story of two lovers, and Goethe was so taken with it that he planned at one time to incorporate it into the Gretchen tragedy in *Faust,* as he relates in *Dichtung und Wahrheit* I, 5 (*MA* 724).

The comparison between the present events and what normally occurs only in literature relates to a specific display of emotion and generosity by the lovers. This display leads Wilhelm to the abstract speculation that if emotions have to be kept secret, they become even more intense when forced out into the open. There is also a literary parallel that relates more closely to the scene between the lovers and to the speculation made by Wilhelm. The scene points again, most pleasingly, to Tasso's *La Gerusalemme liberata* (II, 14–54) and more specifically to the tale of Olindo and Sofronia, where love and generosity of spirit struggle with one another (*MA* 724–25).

In this chapter, the narrator appears to support Wilhelm's perspective. The events and Wilhelm's reactions to them are presented without any of the ironic and playfully critical remarks which the narrator sometimes directs against Wilhelm. The couple stand out as honest and sincere; they are the wronged party. The officials — actuary, magistrate, and clerk — appear to be a benighted group, a fact conveyed with touches of humor. The measures taken to ensure the secure transportation of the couple into custody are extreme and the interest among the bystanders is distasteful. Voyeurism among the would-be onlookers and a correspondingly killjoy attitude on the part of the actuary are set in contrast to the young lovers' sincerity and the purity of their love. They are portrayed as innocent, their condemnation coming at the hands of a society characterized by narrowness of vision.

This story is important enough to continue in Chapter Fourteen. The reader suspects that this is more than a mere interlude. For Wilhelm it is naturally of compelling interest. Not only is the couple's daring attempt at elopement close to what he has in mind for himself and Mariane, but the young man, Melina, is said to be a former actor.[3] Naturally, Wilhelm is all the more intrigued and wonders why he gave up his occupation. He is also impressed by the couple's comportment and the composed eloquence with which they state their respective cases. His romantic image results in a desire to help restore the couple to a position which he himself would consider ideal. They are possible models, in

---

[3] The derivation of the name Melina is given in *Wilhelm Meisters Theatrical Calling*. There, the actor has changed his name since he and Wilhelm last met; it used to be "Herr Pfefferkuchen." The literal sense of this name is "spice cake" and since this particular cake is sometimes also referred to as "honey cake," the actor made up a new name for himself based on the Latin word for "honey." By way of explaining why he needed to adopt a different name, Melina offers this insight: "Names have a great influence on the imagination of men" (*Theatrical Calling* 75).

his mind; they exemplify the realization of the dream he would like to bring about. But they can only be useful as models if their story proceeds along the precise lines which Wilhelm foresees for himself and Mariane. This is what prompts him to devote himself to bringing about a satisfactory resolution in what is, after all, a predicament involving complete strangers to whom he owes no obligation whatsoever.

Des Grieux and Manon stand as models for Melina and his beloved, and Melina and his beloved perform a similar function in Wilhelm's thinking. Their adventure takes on quite a different character when Wilhelm meets them face to face; it is no longer the scandalous affair he had heard about from the girl's stepmother. This is something like a rehearsal for his own plans and, seen in this light, it fits well with his short trip which is also a practice for the longer business journey which Wilhelm's father has planned for him.

Chapter Fourteen

Wilhelm has an urge to bring about a reconciliation. First, he reassures Melina by mentioning how he knows the girl's parents. Melina starts to think about the future need for employment. Unfortunately, the two young men are in fundamental disagreement over whether Melina ought to return to the stage. Wilhelm had not expected to have to convince an actor of the attractions of his profession. He argues that it is never a good idea to change one's direction in life without reason. This observation has the ring of something hastily formulated, without reflection. The two positions become more polarized. Wilhelm's praise of acting is increasingly poetic and Melina insists on the mundane practical difficulties: jealousy, favoritism, the fickle public, and financial uncertainty. Wilhelm ascribes Melina's view to a "grass is greener" attitude, and the reader is immediately aware of irony. Everything Wilhelm has so far revealed of himself demonstrates that this observation most aptly applies to him. Melina observes that Wilhelm has absolutely no experience of life on the stage.

Wilhelm's grandiloquence continues after the two have parted. He makes a long speech with many dramatic features and delivers it as though he were rehearsing for a public performance. The reader is also reminded of the conversation between Wilhelm and his friend Werner in Chapter Ten, in which two fundamentally different views about life and how to spend it are aired and found to be largely irreconcilable. On that occasion, Werner launched into a rhapsodic description of commerce in operation. But now it is Wilhelm who feels the need to deliver a speech, ostensibly addressed to Melina. The speech is impassioned and very dramatic, but when it comes to an end, the narrator introduces a touch of playful irony in the description of the actions which accompany the rhetoric. While expressing his inspiring thoughts and lofty exhortations, Wilhelm has been undressing and climbing into bed.

The remainder of the chapter describes Wilhelm's attempt to bring about a reconciliation by returning to the young woman's home and pleading with her parents to adopt a more favorable attitude towards the pair. The results are not crowned with success: the parents will agree to the marriage, but the daughter must forfeit her dowry and leave her father in charge of her inheritance for the time being. And there is absolutely no question of the father helping Melina by finding him a position. This suggestion meets with adamant opposition. In the meantime, Wilhelm has come to the view that Melina's attitude has rendered him unworthy to become an actor again. As a consequence, he argues very strongly in support of Melina's request, but to no avail. Right at the end, the narrator passes on a secret to the reader which explains the father's refusal to promote the interests of the couple. It emerges that his own wife had herself been attracted to Melina, and her husband now wants to ensure that the young man remain as far out of sight of his household as possible.

In response to Wilhelm's words in praise of acting, Melina observes that it is quite obvious from what he has said that Wilhelm has no first-hand experience of acting. This remark sets the tone for the chapter, in which Wilhelm shows a marked tendency to involve himself in matters he does not properly understand. Partly, he does this out of altruism and partly out of a fascination born of self-interest. He feels genuinely drawn to the unfortunate couple in their plight but he also wants to mold their fate to fit an image he has of his own future. Wilhelm has no doubts that his own priorities are the right ones and speaks with the assurance of a much older, more experienced man. Melina is also quite clear about what he wants, but he does not give voice to general statements about human nature or oppose Wilhelm directly. Rather, he tries to bring Wilhelm down to earth by mentioning some of the hardships an actor has to contend with. He has no wish to pursue such a difficult and uncertain career any further and asks Wilhelm to see if he can prevail upon the girl's father to help him find an alternative.

Wilhelm's initial agreement to this intervention is an act of bad faith. He is in fact agreeing to help Melina pursue a course of action of which he himself strongly disapproves. But after his long speech and a good night's sleep, Wilhelm has persuaded himself that there is no harm in helping Melina into a clerical position since he has shown himself unable to appreciate the nobler calling. In keeping with the less inspiring subject matter, Wilhelm's arguments are reported in a summarized form, rather than appearing as a direct quotation. Wilhelm's change in perspective is a result of a cherished ideal being thwarted: Melina does not live up to Wilhelm's image of an actor. He is evidently not cut out to become part of the movement Wilhelm visualizes, to found a national theater; Melina lacks vision. Such disappointments occur repeatedly throughout the novel and are an essential part of Wilhelm's formation. Again and again Wilhelm must suffer the disappointment of finding out that reality does not live up to his expectations (Irmscher 145).

Wilhelm's soliloquy is precipitated by what he sees as a very limited perspective on Melina's part. It introduces the first traces of a Shakespeare theme which will gradually grow in strength over the course of Book Two and culminate in Book Three. Shakespearean echoes ring out in some of the phrases Wilhelm declaims. He begins, "O, unhappy Melina, the misery that oppresses you, lies not in your profession but in yourself!" (Unglücklicher Melina, nicht in deinem Stande, sondern in dir liegt das Armselige, über das du nicht Herr werden kannst!) This is reminiscent in both tone and sentiment of Shakespeare's Julius Caesar declaring, "The fault, dear Brutus, is not in our stars / But in ourselves."[1] There are also echoes of the "All the world's a stage" speech from *As You Like It* in the schoolboy image Wilhelm uses. The German makes this clearer: the claim is that in Melina's view an actor considers roles the same way a schoolboy regards his homework. In the English translation, the schoolboy image is glossed over; the figure of the schoolboy is omitted and the phrase merely refers to "school assignments." But it seems clear that Goethe is employing phrases and images reminiscent of Shakespeare and preparing for the more direct encounter still to come.

Wilhelm seems to see Melina as belonging to the same school of thought as his friend Werner. He suggests that Melina sees nothing special in the acting profession and might as well sit at a desk all day, poring over ledgers. He lacks the feeling for life, emanating from the innermost self, that is necessary in order to overcome inconvenience and discomfort. Melina is also accused of never having felt a sense of "a conglomerate, inflammable whole" and the reader may well think back to a similar thought of Wilhelm's in reference to his experiences with the puppet theater. After watching the second puppet performance, Wilhelm catches a glimpse of what happens backstage, but this is still not enough. At the end of Chapter Four, Wilhelm describes himself as lacking "a sense of the enterprise as a whole."

All Wilhelm's high-minded theories about the stage and his analysis of Melina's unsuitability as an actor come to nothing in the end. Because Wilhelm is unable to persuade the parents of the girl to offer any

[1] William Shakespeare, *Julius Caesar* II, ii, ll. 139–40.

practical help to the couple, Melina is obliged to look for another theatrical troupe and thus return to his former way of life as an actor. The
narrator does not divulge Wilhelm's reaction to this painful irony. It
must have seemed very unfair to him that Melina should be obliged,
though unwilling, to pursue the profession that Wilhelm himself yearns
for but is hindered from pursuing.

Chapter Fifteen

The chapter opens with an exclamation about the joys of first love. Goethe
uses the image (omitted from the English translation) of a child producing
echoes, to encapsulate the absorbing passion Wilhelm feels for Mariane.
Wilhelm is oblivious to Mariane's less than robust response. Like the child
who takes simple pleasure in hearing his own voice echoed, Wilhelm is satisfied to be the main contributor in their conversations. Wilhelm is also
compared to a beggar who has given his riches to Mariane and now waits
for her to distribute alms. Wilhelm has chosen to ignore the danger signals.
A third image compares Mariane to sunshine in a landscape; for Wilhelm,
she transforms everything with her presence. Here again, there is a message
for the alert reader: Wilhelm's love for Mariane blinds him to the true state
of affairs. This chapter elaborates on the aspects of Mariane's life that
might have deterred Wilhelm from associating with her under any other
circumstances. The situation is brought to a head when Werner forces a
confrontation with Wilhelm on the subject of certain rumors he has heard.

Wilhelm's almost nightly visits to the theater have been spent standing
in the wings, with the director's permission. The angle was not ideal for a
good view of the performance, but Wilhelm was happy to stand beside the
cart which held the lights.[1] He breathed in the fumes from the tallow candles[2] and enjoyed the closeness to Mariane, especially when she gave him a
friendly look. The reader's initial impression, that the plays in which Mariane performed were not of very high caliber, is confirmed. However,
Mariane's presence can transform the scaffolding and lattice-work into a
form of paradise; the artificial props, fake waterfalls, cardboard rosebushes
and thatched cottage fronts conjure up a poetic pastoral world.[3] In Chap-

[1] Lights would have been mounted on a cart or wagon, kept in the wings, out
of sight of the audience. By moving this vehicle, a stage hand could alter the
angle of illumination.

[2] Tallow is a substance produced by melting the harder and less fusible kinds
of animal fat. It can be used for candles, soap and machine grease.

[3] Pastoral themes in all literary genres were particularly popular in Germany in the
first half of the eighteenth century. The peaceful state of nature acts as the setting

ter Three, Wilhelm had already alluded to pastoral performances on his puppet stage; this theme appears to adumbrate the seemingly idyllic but nonetheless hollow harmony between Wilhelm and Mariane.

The narrator comments that love is like a strong spice which gives flavor to the blandest of broths. Dancers appearing on the same stage with Mariane no longer seemed unattractive to Wilhelm, as they would when seen face to face. Mariane's room was another case in point. The extreme degree of disorder which reigned there formed a sharp contrast to the order and cleanliness which were the hallmark of the middle-class household Wilhelm was accustomed to at home. Not only were high standards of cleanliness in effect for the household in general, but Wilhelm was quite meticulous about the appearance of his own room. It was, in a word, theatrical. His bed curtains were arranged to lend the air of a throne and he kept a cloth for a turban, one for a sash, and even an old dagger on hand, so that he could practice tragic roles. He emulated actors of his imagination from days gone by, whose noble roles and fine costumes would have been reflected in the finest of sentiments in their private lives as well.

Two further observations about the state of Wilhelm's room are of interest. First, the narrator explains Wilhelm's liking for fine things as a quality he has inherited from his father. This suggests that when in Chapter Two Wilhelm vehemently opposes his father's desire to decorate the rooms at great expense, he is trying to downplay a similar inclination in himself. The second point is that Wilhelm has placed a coverlet on his table and arranged the objects on it with great care, so that the table has become a subject worthy of a Dutch still life painter. The motif of works of art and in particular of paintings is pivotal for the structure of the novel.

The description of Mariane's room which follows is beautifully presented. The narrator describes Wilhelm's initial shock at stepping from his own room, which nurtured his fantasy and noble sentiments, into Mariane's dressing room. The tone is set by the first group of objects mentioned: lightly discarded pieces of the actress's various disguises, all false and temporary. These are compared to the scales of a fish: glittering, but worthless once they have been scraped off. These objects lie around in disorder. Next mentioned are the materials used for personal cleanliness, still displaying traces indicating their use (one thinks of hair in brushes, grime on face cloths) and it is implied that they should really be stowed out of sight. There is an irony in the fact that the means to cleanliness are clearly displayed and are themselves covered in

---

for harmony and love. The pastoral topos dates back to Theocritus's *Idylls* and Virgil's *Bucolics* but reemerged into prominence in the European Renaissance.

powder and dust, like everything else in sight. A touch of humor accompanies the list of the other objects which make up the scene. The most unlikely things are juxtaposed, and Goethe produces a long and jumbled list so that form matches content; the parataxis reflects on the incongruity of the lovers' relationship as well (Dürr 103). The objects enjoy a brief anthropomorphosis when it is said that none of them takes any offense at being placed beside any other. Yet, even this room appears charming to Wilhelm because of its association with Mariane.

Wilhelm is prepared to see everything in a positive light. The fact that Mariane feels no compunction about leaving her underwear in view when Wilhelm is there indicates a welcome increase in their intimacy, in Wilhelm's present state of mind. But he finds the company of her fellow performers unsatisfactory. Just as when he met Melina, he feels that practitioners of the art do not appreciate what a noble calling it is. Their conversation is as banal and disorganized as the contents of Mariane's room. Last on the list of their topics is the only subject Wilhelm himself considers worth discussing, the influence of the theater on the cultural level of the nation, indeed of the world. By placing this after the petty gripes and gossip which form the actors' main preoccupation, Goethe shows how unimportant the question was for them. And by adding "the world" he inflates any possible claim and makes it unworthy of serious consideration.

Well into the chapter, the reader discovers that these are not the narrator's thoughts, but Wilhelm's. He is slowly traveling home on horseback after meeting Melina and making connections between Melina and other actors he has met through Mariane. On arriving home, Wilhelm finds his friend Werner waiting. Before revealing Werner's purpose, the narrator ensures that the type of friendship between these two young men is clearly explained. A profound but nonetheless productive difference of opinion exists between them and forms the basis of a surprisingly firm friendship. The two meet frequently, driven, it seems, by a strong desire to come to some sort of resolution of their differences. But recently, Werner has noticed that Wilhelm visits him less often and seems distracted. He has heard rumors about Wilhelm visiting an actress and accompanying her home from the theater. The reports about Mariane's character have not been encouraging; he has heard that she was nothing but a seductive gold digger.

The ground has already been prepared in two ways for Werner to dispel Wilhelm's romantic illusions. First, the reader learns that love has led Wilhelm to turn a blind eye to the less pleasing aspects of Mariane's situation. He is not unaware of them, and the reader knows he could not continue ignoring them indefinitely. Second, it is within the nature of Wilhelm and Werner's dialectical friendship that they will outwardly disagree on this matter, despite the bond that underlies their relationship. Werner conveys all that he has heard about Mariane with the best of intentions, but he leaves the conversation feeling like an unsuccessful dentist who has brought no benefits and only caused the patient pain. Wilhelm is also depressed by their conversation and seeks to obliterate the distorted image of Mariane by visiting his beloved in person.

The chapter ends with Wilhelm and Mariane taking simple pleasure in each other's company; Wilhelm enjoys a warm welcome and all his doubts about Mariane's commitment and her intentions are immediately dispelled. The description of their conversation is introduced by a commonplace: the narrator remarks that lovers experience tremendous pleasure in recalling the first occasions of their meeting, the first steps into the maze of love.[4] Mariane and Wilhelm indulge in these pleasures now and a childish squabble develops, in which each claims to have been the first to notice the other. The chapter ends as it begins, with a description of childish play. But the play at the end is not so innocent and straightforward; it is an escape tactic, an attempt to forget the unpleasant suggestions which Wilhelm has heard from Werner and has already passed on to Mariane. They are escaping into the past and the reader already knows that suits Mariane best of all, since it removes the necessity of coming to terms with what the immediate future will bring.

Chapter Sixteen

This short chapter comprises a letter from Wilhelm to Mariane, written just before departing on the journey that will separate them for some time. He asks Mariane for reassurances of her commitment to their relationship. Wilhelm is at pains to make clear how devoted he is to Mariane. He sometimes feels she does not fully understand this, as she does not reciprocate as fulsomely. He attributes this to Mariane's appealing modesty, but he senses something evasive in her response and so he makes a poetic proposal of marriage. He uses an indirect method of expression, as though Mariane might be frightened by straightforward wording.

---

[4] The "maze of love" is a reference to the title of a novel by Johann Gottfried Schnabel, published anonymously, in 1738. The title is *Der im Irr-Garten der Liebe herum taumelnde Cavalier. Oder Reise-und Liebes-Geschichte eines vornehmen Deutschen von Adel, Herrn von St.*** welcher nach vielen, sowohl auf Reisen, als auch bei anderen Gelegenheiten verübten Liebes-Exzessen, endlich erfahren müssen, wie der Himmel die Sünden der Jugend im Alter zu bestrafen pflegt.*

It is important to Wilhelm to put his words on paper and formulate them at a distance from his beloved. Only thus can he achieve the clarity which he seeks to establish between them. He feels the necessity to offer some sort of stable situation for their future and must therefore undertake the journey and be away from Mariane. Running parallel with this is the thought that he must make his concrete proposal of matrimony, but only from a distance. In both cases, separation is a necessary condition for the practical turn of events Wilhelm wants to establish.

There are plenty of tender outpourings in Wilhelm's letter but he also outlines his plan. He will approach a theater director of his acquaintance and establish a position for himself in his company. Mariane is to join him later. This is a further development of the plan he first formulated in Chapter Nine, to become an actor and even found a national theater (Gilli 200). The language of the earlier chapter is similarly poetic and visionary. About the success of his plan, Wilhelm has no doubts; he is confident that his own determination will bring about the desired results. But in relation to Mariane, there is a lingering doubt in his words. Mariane has not felt able to express her feelings openly and this has left Wilhelm slightly unsettled. Wilhelm is again keen to attribute this reticence to modesty (Chapter Three) and, far from being a deterrent, this quality in Mariane merely increases his ardor.

The letter is written in a spirit of supreme self-confidence. The first demonstration is that Wilhelm has noted Mariane's hesitation and ascribed it to an endearing feature of her personality. He certainly does not see it as an obstacle in the way of his plan to marry her before setting off on his journey. In any case, he considers marriage a mere formality in their situation.[1] Then, in relation to the acting world, Wilhelm has no doubt that his friend Serlo will welcome him to join the troupe of actors, merely on the basis of his expressed enthusiasm for the theater. Wilhelm is also completely convinced that his own acting technique far exceeds what the average professional has to offer audiences. He bases this latter conviction on the premise that a successful actor has to have some substance to offer; he idealizes the stage as being the place where noble words are offered to spiritually needy audiences. In addition, acting could be used to glorify both nature and God. Wilhelm experiences no apprehension about his

[1] Goethe includes a reference here to practices among knights. He is referring to medieval territories which were in effect ruled by knights, and where joining two people in matrimony was a simple matter without administrative consequences. In drawing this parallel, Wilhelm reminds the reader of his tendency to identify with the dashing heroes of fiction.

own gifts or about what fate has in store for him. He sees no need to fear the world or to doubt his own ability to provide for himself and Mariane.

Wilhelm appears to be almost in a trance as he writes his letter. As though in a dream, he experiences visions of Mariane's love and happiness and compares it to an endless dawn. In this state of mind, Wilhelm is able to meditate upon his love for Mariane, his vision for the German stage, and his own calling as though all three elements were somehow combined in an inspired divine plan. In this vein, Wilhelm refers to the quarrels between the theater and the church[2] — if his own lofty conception were to be realized, there would no longer be any cause for such differences. Actors would be noble people who saw it as their task to glorify God and nature. An important ingredient in all of this is love and when Wilhelm thinks in these terms, he visualizes himself and Mariane on the stage together, touching the hearts and souls of the audience with "heavenly delights." Love has the power, for Wilhelm, of elevating lovers above themselves and ennobling their every action.

Finally, Wilhelm tries to bring his letter to an end but is obviously reluctant to do so. There are still two more images that occur to him and they might help to describe the state of mind in which he finds himself. The first describes his feelings: it is as though a wheel were turning in his heart whose movements he is struggling to capture in words.[3] In contrast to the dynamism of this image is the sensation which Wilhelm goes on to describe, of being a prisoner in a cell, on the *qui vive* and filing away at his chains. The image of the wheel combines the idea of a swift succession of thoughts with the possibility of locomotion — Wilhelm is impatient to set out on his travels. The image of the prisoner counteracts this impatience and shows that Wilhelm is nevertheless conscious that he must make careful plans.

---

[2] The debates between the church and the stage have to do with the suggestion that the theater is capable of exercising an adverse moral effect on its audience. In 1769 Johann Melchior Goeze wrote a "Theologische Untersuchung der Sittlichkeit der heutigen Teutschen Schaubühne, wie auch der Frage, ob ein Geistlicher (. . .) die Schaubühne besuchen (. . .) und (. . .) verteidigen könne." Goeze's quarrel with Lessing ended with the Hamburg senate banning the publication of further contributions to the debate. Wilhelm's view is not only that the theater has no adverse effects, but that it can even exert a positive moral influence. Of interest is Schiller's speech of 1784 "Welche Verstärkung für Religion und Gesetze, wenn sie mit der Schaubühne in Bund treten (. . .)!" Further references can be found in Goethe's *Dichtung und Wahrheit*, Book 13, and in his 1815 essay "Über das deutsche Theater."

[3] The wheel is an image akin to the wheel of fortune; it expresses the relentlessness of change and succession (Gray 184).

Chapter Sixteen with its high-flown rhetoric ("Wrapped in the beloved cloak of night . . .") and idealized view of the theater shows Wilhelm making practical plans based on utter illusion. Wilhelm may well be at his most decisive, but his vision of acting as a sublime profession, coupled with his idolizing of Mariane, cause the reader to entertain serious doubts.

Chapter Seventeen

The letter that filled the previous chapter was not delivered after all. Mariane is again cooler towards Wilhelm and he leaves without handing it over, but snatches up a scarf of hers on his way out. Wilhelm is too restless to stay in; he changes clothes and goes out again. In the street, he is approached by a stranger who, it turns out, was an assessor and adviser for the man who bought the art collection from Wilhelm's father. The stranger remembers Wilhelm's favorite painting, of the ailing king's son, consumed with love for his father's new bride. The painting was not exceptional but the subject interested Wilhelm.

Wilhelm now sees that fate has allowed him to pursue his own route. The sale of the works of art led to the purchase of the new house, and the need for entertainment resulted in both his enthusiasm for the puppet theater and his passion for the theater (Ammerlahn 1978, 54). The conversation turns to the question of how the term "fate" ought to be understood, but the two speakers cannot agree.

Wilhelm returns via Mariane's house where he sits outside and dreams. He compares himself and Mariane to two magnetic compasses. Finally, Wilhelm turns for home but catches sight of an indistinct figure emerging from Mariane's doorway. The figure disappears into the streets and Wilhelm wonders if he imagined it. But he is uneasy, and the dawn, complete with cock crowing, finds him in distress. Wilhelm retrieves the scarf from his pocket. Out drops a slip of paper with a message betraying intimacy. The reader is left to imagine Wilhelm's reaction.

This last chapter, like the first one in the book, opens on a scene of waiting. In Chapter One, Barbara is waiting for Mariane so as to show her Norberg's presents. Now, Wilhelm is waiting for the day to end, so he can call on Mariane and give her his letter. He is excited about her reaction to the proposal contained in it and his feelings are so overwhelming when he sees her that he is at first unaware of her lackluster response. Wilhelm senses that this is not the moment to hand over the letter; the reader senses that this decision may be a part of the workings of fate, a subject soon to be discussed by Wilhelm and the stranger. Wilhelm is overtaken by restlessness; he goes home, but cannot stay put. Like an actor changing roles, he changes his outfit before going out again. It is as though he were conscious of having to give up the role of lover for a while. Both Wilhelm's change of clothes and the scarf he picks up tie in to the textile theme. Wilhelm's clothes become the costume the actor takes off when he steps out of a role. The scarf is one of those objects cast aside by Mariane and to be found scattered about her room but which, for Wilhelm, are transformed by their association with his beloved Mariane. Wilhelm's changing of clothes and his snatching up of the scarf are both influential in the subsequent course of events. Both serve to delay the resolution of the situation between the lovers. The changed suit of clothing symbolizes the changeability of human nature, of which acting is also an image; the scarf represents the beloved but also, because it was so easily discarded, suggests something left behind.

The account of the evening spent with the stranger is designed to intrigue the reader. The introduction of a stranger so soon after Wilhelm has spotted a figure emerging from Mariane's door is bound to be arresting. And the narrator declines to reveal the stranger's name, even though Wilhelm learns what it is; for once, Wilhelm is better informed. Their mutual introductions lead to the discussion of Wilhelm's grandfather's art collection, with which the stranger was well acquainted. The groups of objects in this collection are now listed in a way that appears to lend them significance. They include a variety of media: paintings, drawings, pieces in marble, bronze and stone as well as a coin collection. They were acquired in Italy and displayed with a great sense of artistry in the old Meister house.[1] Each individual group meets with the stranger's approval; the grandfather's taste and understanding of art earn high praise as well.

Wilhelm had felt very strongly drawn to one particular painting in his grandfather's collection.[2] It was not one of the better pieces in its execution, but that mattered little to him, either then or now. Rather, he was fascinated by the scene depicted in the painting.[3] Wilhelm sums up the

---

[1] The provenance of the art collection recalls Goethe's trip to Italy and relates to his own propensities as an art collector.

[2] Several plausible theories have been put forward to demonstrate which of the several pictorial versions of the ailing prince was the one Goethe had in mind. These include paintings by the Dutchman Gérard de Lairesse (1641–1711), by Antonio Belucci (1654–1726), by Andrea Celesti (1637–1706), and by Januarius Zinck (1739–1797).

[3] In stating that he is more interested in the subject matter than the artistic merits of a work of art, Wilhelm designates himself as a dilettante. Dilettantism was seen as a malaise of the period and came under fire from Goethe in his *Über den Dilettantismus* of 1799. The philosopher Immanuel Kant's *Kritik der Urteilskraft* (1790) provides the theoretical background, defining "pure taste" as free from the interest of emotional stimulus.

theme of the picture with very few words — despite the adult subject matter, he seems to associate the painting with his happy childhood, since it hung in a room in the house where the children could play. The story of the ailing prince in the picture dates back to Plutarch, who first told it. A Syrian king by the name of Seleukos (312–280 B.C.) has married for the second time.[4] His son from the first marriage falls in love with Stratonike, his father's young bride. The young man falls deathly ill, but the doctor is able to determine that his love for his stepmother is the cause; his pulse becomes more vigorous in her presence. The doctor, by putting a hypothetical situation to the father, brings him to see that the only method of saving his son is by giving up his own bride to him. The father agrees to this and thereby secures his son's life and happiness.

At this point, the reader can hardly be expected to detect the sustained symbolism of this picture or to relate it to Wilhelm's life. But both the stranger and the picture have reentered Wilhelm's life, the former in person, the latter through verbal reference, and there is sure to be significance in this apparent coincidence. In the meantime, it is possible to relate the picture to Wilhelm's current situation. Wilhelm himself speaks in an animated way about the poor prince having to hide his emotions and adds that he feels pity for the young woman who is bound by moral obligations to the wrong man. For Wilhelm in his present situation, the picture represents his own passion for Mariane which he must conceal from his family. For the reader, the situation of the young bride, as described by Wilhelm, is interesting because it runs parallel to Mariane's: she is morally bound to Norberg, but loves Wilhelm. The reader knows better than Wilhelm at this moment. Whereas Wilhelm thinks of himself as the love-sick son of the king, the reader suspects that he is actually better represented by Seleukos himself (Nolan 142). There have already been signals indicating that Wilhelm will have to renounce his love for Mariane and the letter he finds reveals to him the existence of another man.

The reader is better informed about Mariane's situation than Wilhelm is, but there is another reason why Wilhelm's interpretation of the painting is, at best, partial. The picture is of the scene of discovery; now that the cause of the prince's illness has been determined, his fortunes are on the point of changing. Wilhelm ignores this and concentrates on the young man's emotional state. The indelible impression made by the picture causes a subjective emotional reaction in Wilhelm and the stranger takes him to task for it.

---

[4] Plutarch (50–125 A.D.) was a Greek biographer and moral essayist. His *Parallel Lives of the Noble Greeks and Romans* provide much interesting historical detail without actually being a historical work.

The stranger and Wilhelm disagree on two points. The first has to do with judging a painting: Wilhelm is criticized for paying so little attention to objective judgment and concentrating instead on emotional effects. The stranger suggests that Wilhelm might have developed a more sophisticated taste for art if the collection had not been sold and he had been able to grow up among so many fine art pieces. Wilhelm is not capable of the aesthetic judgment his grandfather exercised.

The second, substantial point of disagreement concerns the concept of fate. The stranger suspects Wilhelm of identifying the dictates of his own emotions as the hand of fate. For him, the decisive factor is the use of reason. Wilhelm's judgment, by contrast, is always clouded by emotion and this is true both of his reaction to the painting and of his view of the workings of fate. He trusts excessively to chance and places his own whims and inclinations in the place that should be occupied by reason. This is not to say that the individual has no freedom in determining his destiny. The stranger uses the image of an artist who is given the raw material with which to mold something. The reference to the figure of an artist links the discussion of fate to the discussion of the painting. The lesson for Wilhelm is that it takes discipline and practice to make something artistic out of the raw material both with reference to art and in the art of living. The reader is reminded of the painting Wilhelm imagined himself creating at the end of Chapter Nine. Its misty background and indistinct figures are attributable to its inspiration: these are the colors of love and, from the stranger's point of view, they cannot produce a good painting.

After parting from the stranger, whose conversation has been filled with warnings against allowing emotions to play too large a part in life, Wilhelm immediately gives free rein to his own emotions. The scene outside Mariane's house shows him to be completely obsessed by Mariane and constantly longing for her presence. He oscillates between contentment, as he pictures Mariane sleeping, and the agitation of desire. In his peaceful state, his thoughts are like twilight spirits, but as desire takes the upper hand Wilhelm wishes he had his copy of her key with him. No doubt that, too, is in the pocket of the other coat. This mistake has tremendous dramatic implications: if he had opened the door with his key, he would have met the figure who left the house shortly afterwards. This narrow escape is another highly theatrical touch and the reader appreciates it all the more for being restored to the position of knowing more than Wilhelm does about who this figure could be.

Just before Wilhelm finds the letter from Norberg to Mariane, he is leaning, deep in thought in a corner. The details of this scene are especially important: dawn breaks, introducing the light of day to make clear the mysterious and shadowy events of the previous night. The cocks are crowing and heralding the theme of betrayal.[5] Wilhelm looks for the scarf as a way of reassuring himself and restoring his faith in his beloved, and finds a letter that must destroy the entire foundation for the future he had been building.

Norberg's letter stands in contrast to the one Wilhelm composed in the previous chapter. Wilhelm's letter had been tremendously broad in scope; he wrote unrestrainedly of the past and the future, of his love and of his aspirations, contributing a great deal to the reader's picture of him. Norberg's letter is restricted to the immediate past and the present; it is brief, frivolous, and makes a couple of rather obscure references. It tells the reader very little about any of the characters but is obviously crucial for the plot (Scholz 109–110). The first reference in the letter is biblical, and mentions the Witch of Endor, a woman with a prophetic gift. But Norberg simply uses it to make a negative comment about Mariane's clothing and appearance. Norberg likes to see Mariane in her white negligee, whereas Wilhelm loves her officer's uniform. The reference to the negligee recalls the first chapter when the parcel arrived containing the muslin for making it. The second reference — glossed in the English version — is to Iris, the Greek messenger of the gods. Norberg uses this image with a twist, making Barbara into the messenger of the devil.

[5] Peter's betrayal of Christ consisted of denying him three times before the cock could crow twice.

Book Two

Chapter One

AGAIN, THE CHAPTER opens with a commonplace: an individual seems worthy of interest and support only while striving towards some end. The goal itself is less important than the effort. When the enterprise is concluded, interest in the goal dwindles, especially if it ends in predictable failure. The narrator vows not to involve readers in Wilhelm's sufferings, but will rejoin him some years later, when he has taken up an occupation. Despite this resolve, the narrator indulges in some dramatic images to describe the stages of Wilhelm's emotional development.

The first image compares the sudden and overwhelming nature of Wilhelm's misfortune to the rapid devastation caused by the plague. Emotional disaster is compared with virulent physical disease. When the disease strikes a young and healthy body, its progress is accelerated. Wilhelm is similarly struck, without warning, by a completely debilitating grief. The course of his life so far is then compared to a firework that should have made a beautiful display in the sky but by accident catches fire too soon. Wilhelm's hopes and dreams, instead of soaring heavenward, have fizzled like the firecracker and begun spinning dangerously out of control. At this stage, no friend is capable of offering help and Wilhelm has grown numb.

The process of tracing the progress of grief returns again to a physical image, but rather a distasteful one. The claim is that a body can still be said to have life in some sense as long as decomposition is taking place. The forces which once gave life to the parts of the body are still working, in an effort to counteract the process of deterioration. This is similar to Wilhelm's period of recurring anguish which he welcomed, in a way, since the pain he experienced was a way of desperately holding on to what he had once had.

In this period, Werner, as a constant and loyal friend, takes part in protecting Wilhelm against his own inclinations. Finally Nature steps in and, converting literary image to reality, causes real illness to befall Wilhelm. This gives Wilhelm respite: the physical illness is treated with medication, while the patient receives the attention and devotion of family and friends. However, when the illness lifts, Wilhelm finds he has been granted a certain clarity of vision: he seems to be gazing into the abyss, the crater of a volcano, so profound has his suffering become.[1] He now blames himself for breaking off from his ceaseless grieving and longs to indulge once again in the tears and lamentation which had been his initial reaction.

In a counterpart to his earlier enjoyment in remembering the pleasures of childhood, Wilhelm now relives the high points of his happy times with Mariane, but it is only in order to provoke the kind of grief he feels he should still be suffering. His memories take him up to a height from which he can see more effectively into the abyss of the crater. In this way, Wilhelm tortures himself in the belief that he should always remain inconsolable.

In the face of such a detailed account of the physiological and psychological path of grief, it is well to remember the rather entertaining technique with which the narrator opens the chapter. An onlooker is no longer interested, it is claimed, when someone striving for a goal fails and gives up. Therefore, the narrator does not intend to entertain the reader with Wilhelm's sufferings beyond what is necessary to follow his story. But the whole of the chapter is then devoted to a detailed history of these sufferings. The reader can only deduce that this ample description nonetheless represents only a fraction of what Wilhelm actually undergoes.

Chapter Two

Wilhelm had felt destined to make his way in the theater — as an actor, but also as a poet. Now he turns a critical eye on his poetic compositions; they seem mere imitations of preexisting works, like a set exercise. Both form and content are uninspired. There is no hope of consolation in poetry or acting, so Wilhelm turns to work in the family

[1] Goethe had seen volcanic landscapes during his visit to Italy and had walked on Vesuvius. He took an interest in the opposing theories about the formation of the world which were based on whether volcanoes were formed by a sudden rupture or a slow process (Boyle 1992, 592).

business. His father and Werner are delighted, but Wilhelm is still prone to despondency. Even so, he thinks that fate is at work in his life. He decides to burn the keepsakes from Mariane along with his poems.[1] A string of beads, a scarf, and the poems remain when Werner interrupts. In the ensuing exchange each adopts an uncharacteristic position. Werner judges Wilhelm's action hasty, but Wilhelm insists his talent is mediocre. Poetic creation cannot be a hobby. He blames himself for having abandoned Mariane and the scene leaves Wilhelm sunk in sorrow and Werner in shock.

The previous chapter dwelt on Wilhelm's inclination to inflict pain on himself by thinking constantly of Mariane and his loss. Now he turns this tendency into savage criticism of himself, his pretensions, and finally his treatment of Mariane. And this time the gloomy account of this latest inward-looking exercise is relieved by the occasional commonplace and by Werner's presence. A commonplace makes the sort of observation that asks the reader to see Wilhelm as in some way representative of the human condition and detracts from the individual nature of his circumstances. One such example draws a parallel between the difficulty in turning away from a woman's love and the hardship involved in denying oneself the company of the muses.[2] Another concerns the understandable reluctance to face the truth and admit one's mistakes. Another remarks on the strange impressions created by the act of opening up a letter one has written, sealed with one's own seal, and sent off, and that has for some reason now returned.[3]

Both Werner's arguments and the commonplaces introduced by the narrator offer a more objective and practical viewpoint, calculated to weigh against the excessively subjective emotionalism in which Wilhelm persists. But it is ironic that Werner should be speaking in favor of poetry on this occasion. This is the same Werner who interrupted Wilhelm in Book One, Chapter Ten, when he was packing up his papers, books, and poems in preparation for his journey. That discussion focused on Wilhelm's allegorical poem "Jüngling am Scheideweg,"

---

[1] Goethe himself consigned some of his juvenilia to the flames, as he relates in *Dichtung und Wahrheit* Bk 8.

[2] The Muses were nine Greek goddesses of the liberal arts, daughters of Zeus and Mnemosyne. Though an ancient poet would invoke the muse to speak through him, references to the muses later come to be references simply to poetry or art.

[3] The letter would have been sealed with brittle sealing wax, melted in a candle flame and imprinted with a stamp or signet ring that bore the coat of arms or initials of the sender.

which, although it was brought to completion, earned only scorn from Werner. Werner foreshadows the later scene, exclaiming that Wilhelm should throw his poem in the fire!

Wilhelm realizes that his own poetic attempts are only imitations of the works of true poetic genius. In Book One, Chapter Ten, the narrator suggested that there was a certain lack of originality in Wilhelm's poetry; now, Wilhelm himself has achieved a similar insight. Then, he thought all poetic endeavor was laudable, even when it did not produce a completely polished product; now he declares that if ability does not accompany desire, the project has no merit whatsoever. In response to Werner, Wilhelm argues that poetry cannot be a part-time occupation and goes on to describe his exalted vision of the true poet. The poet soars free and bird-like above the earth, knows and experiences more than others, sees how to relate everything to the past and future, and provides comfort and advice to all. Wilhelm, who has renounced poetry for himself, is remarkably poetic at this moment. He contrasts animals working in the fields — oxen and dogs — with the poet in flight. Since poetry is associated with love in Wilhelm's mind, the poet's flight forms a thematic link with the wings of the imagination in Book One, Chapter Three and with the protective wings of love in Chapter Nine of the same book (Reiss 1951, 127–28).

Werner sees the contradiction in Wilhelm's wish to turn his back on poetry, about which he feels so much passion, and he says so. He makes pragmatic objections to Wilhelm's imagery, namely, that human beings are not built like birds and cannot simply fly south when winter comes. These objections restore the natural balance between Wilhelm and Werner by pointing out that Wilhelm is the more poetic soul while Werner has a more practical mind. Wilhelm shows the same thing by the way he warms to his subject; his renunciation of poetry amounts to an identification with the idealized portrayal of the poet he provides.[4]

Wilhelm's speeches are impassioned outbursts, but there is a certain logic to his position. He differentiates between real poets and ordinary people. On the one hand, imitation does not produce poetic talent and many have fallen by the wayside in pursuit of this course. A poet is completely devoted to his art and lives for nothing else. On the other hand, although poets understand emotion and know best how to repre-

---

[4] The opposing views of the poet have their basis in a very real eighteenth-century debate. Up until Friedrich Gottlieb Klopstock (1724–1803), poetry was practiced as a sideline to some other occupation. Wilhelm presents Klopstock's position here (see his *Kritische Dichtkunst* I, I) with a new and sublime view of the poetic craft and the position of the poet in society.

sent it, they are able to remain above the sufferings of the world. Wilhelm has always linked poetic inspiration with the passion he felt for Mariane, but he is incapable of the degree of detachment required in a poet. He confesses to Werner that he is still unable to banish the memory of his former joys or to recover from his misery at their loss. This emotional state does not accord with his definition of a poet; in fact it is diametrically opposed to it. According to Wilhelm, only ordinary mortals indulge in brooding and despair, whereas poets move quickly and gently between emotions. At the end of the chapter, Wilhelm is reduced to reviving all his conflicting thoughts about Mariane and trying to defend her before he descends into depression again. Once more, the reader recognizes much in this chapter which would have been effective on stage. After lively and passionate declamations, Wilhelm droops his head despairingly but dramatically to rest on the few remaining pages of verse, and the final tableau is a scene of reflective calm.

Chapter Three

Wilhelm undertakes the tasks of the world of business as a distraction: his feelings are waiting to lure him into a labyrinth.[1] He sets off on a business trip. The magnificent countryside he travels through improves Wilhelm's spirits and lugubrious thoughts recede. He recites a pastoral poem from "Il Pastor fido," as well as some of his own verses.[2] He imagines that the woods contain the characters and becomes more optimistic.

Wilhelm hears about a performance of a comedy in Hochdorf and is impressed that the production was organized by a businessman who encourages his workers to put on plays instead of playing cards, of which he strongly disapproves.[3] The preparations for the play are described in detail. The play is about two lovers trying to come between a girl and her guardian. In an epilogue the factory owner is honored on the occasion of his birthday. Wilhelm cannot resist offering the performers advice for the future.

---

[1] The labyrinth image originates with the Greek legend that tells how Theseus was able to enter the labyrinth, kill the Minotaur, and find his way back by means of a ball of thread which he had unraveled on his way in.

[2] "Il Pastor fido" (1589), a pastoral drama by Giovanni Battista (1538–1612), had a considerable vogue throughout Europe and was translated many times. Goethe read it in the original Italian.

[3] The objection to card playing refers to a religious opposition to gambling. The objection stems from the view that an individual's fortunes are divinely ordained and gambling is an attempt to counteract the divine will.

The scene of despair witnessed in Chapter Two appears to have been a recurring phenomenon. Wilhelm has found a way of dealing with it, at least on a temporary basis, and the solution satisfies his father as well because Wilhelm is more than competent at his work. This situation is reminiscent of the way Wilhelm had earlier managed to combine keeping his parents company at the dinner table with visits to the theater to see Mariane. And now, as then, Wilhelm's business journey is being planned.

The narrator fills in the background and then invites the reader to picture the scene, with Wilhelm riding through breathtaking countryside. Again the reader feels like a member of the audience at a play. But when Wilhelm himself is attending a performance, not much detail is given beyond the fact that the play is a type known as comedy of intrigue. Interestingly, however, the thumbnail sketch of the action — the girl with a guardian and the two lovers — echoes the situation with Mariane and Barbara, Wilhelm and Norberg.

It is certainly remarkable that Wilhelm should come upon a theatrical performance in the most unlikely of places. Wilhelm's labors at home — the bookkeeping and the business letters — occupy him but do not help him recover. He puts on a display which may convince his father and Werner, but the real beginnings of a recovery are provided by the journey with its new landscapes, situations, and people. Often in novels a journey provides the dramatic opportunity for such fortuitous chance encounters (Bakhtin 244).

The truly remarkable feature, which cannot have escaped Wilhelm's notice, is that in Hochdorf an alliance has been achieved between business and the theater. A factory owner with an interest in the arts must have seemed to him a most remarkable combination. In fact, the old man is something of an educator, wanting to regulate how his workers spend their spare time, and has devised a way of ensuring that they do not spend it at the card tables. He is not driven by any visionary view of the dramatic arts such as Wilhelm still harbors. For Wilhelm certainly has not abandoned his high ideas about the theater: he even speaks of the travelers as pilgrims on their way to the temple. And despite his recent feverish rantings, he has most certainly not given up hope of an acting career.

Not for the first time does the narrator encourage the reader in the impression that Wilhelm's progress traces, on one level, the history of the theater. Thus, this first performance has faults, but gains praise for its action and for its positive effect on the audience. Wilhelm finds the performance particularly attractive because it is beginning the task he visualizes for the theater, namely, the education of audiences in all parts of the country. These are unsophisticated people who do not know enough to refrain from smoking pipes during the performance and yet this is at least a step in the right direction.

A contrast is made between simple people and cultured ones, with a view to distinguishing their respective reactions to a play. The concept of "Bildung" is used here and three stages of education are identified: the least educated are satisfied to see action; the more cultured appreciate an appeal to the emotions, and the truly cultured want to have something to reflect on.[4]

The narrator relates the details of Wilhelm's business trip that are of interest to Wilhelm. Thus, just as his duties at home are enumerated without being described, so now Wilhelm's various calls on creditors are dealt with very summarily. In fact, some of these encounters must have provided a certain amount of excitement, as when Wilhelm was compelled to take the matter to the courts for a resolution. But the narrator hurries us through these and on into the next chapter, where another opportunity to meet some stage performers awaits.

Chapter Four

Wilhelm stops in a town for a break and finds a surprising amount of activity. A group of tightrope walkers, acrobats, and jugglers are preparing for a performance. Wilhelm considers moving on but, on an impulse, buys a bunch of flowers from a girl. A good-looking young woman appears at a window of an inn and a young boy asks Wilhelm for a flower for her. Wilhelm gives him the whole bouquet.

On the stairs to his room Wilhelm meets a strange-looking child dressed in a silk waistcoat with Spanish sleeves and puffed-out long trousers. He finally decides it is a girl. Then two young men are fencing on the landing and Wilhelm replaces one of them. In a procession to advertise the show Wilhelm sees the strange girl again. Wilhelm's fencing partner, Laertes, introduces him to the young woman at the window, Philine. She wears a black mantilla over a white negligee, and high-heeled slippers. They agree to go for a ride but Wilhelm wants to do his hair first. Philine flirtatiously insists on doing it for him and

---

[4] *Bildung* as a philosophical term came to the fore in the second half of the eighteenth century. It refers to an intellectual development, either in history or within an organism. In relation to *Wilhelm Meister* the term is restricted to the development of a personality to maturity through experience of the world (Ritter Vol. 1 Col. 924).

drapes his shoulders with her smock. Wilhelm uses her knife, inscribed "Remember me," to scrape the powder from his forehead, and she lets him keep it.[1]

At a mill, they watch an entertainment about a farmer and a miner. Wilhelm outlines his view of the theater. Philine cuts short the conversation by breaking into song. On the way back, she gives away her last coin, her hat, and kerchief to beggars. They watch the performance from Philine's window. Later, the strange child is brought up to the room. Her name is Mignon. Her father, "the big devil," is dead. She bows and speaks in broken German. Wilhelm is fascinated by her. Wilhelm, Laertes, and Philine arrange to go out again the next day, but Philine gives the men the slip. They catch up with her and she coquettishly compares the taste of their kisses. Laertes mentions the taste of wormwood.[2]

Wilhelm sees the leader of the company beating Mignon for refusing to perform the so-called egg dance. He accepts an offer to buy Mignon for the cost of her clothes. Mignon has meanwhile disappeared. Wilhelm muses about transmitting thoughts as though electrically through the medium of entertainment.[3]

Already in the previous chapter Wilhelm showed signs of recovering from the loss of Mariane. Chance circumstances seem designed to help him do so. Without going out of his way, Wilhelm is presented with the opportunity of attending an amateur performance of a comedy (Bahr 41). Now in this chapter, Wilhelm chooses the place where he will enjoy a few days' rest simply because it lies in a beautiful plain and he and his horse need to recover from the difficult mountain terrain. But this place, too, turns out to have much to offer of a theatrical nature. First, there is the group of acrobats and other entertainers, including the strange child, Mignon. Next, he makes the acquaintance of Philine and Laertes, who, by an interesting coincidence, have belonged to a now disbanded theatrical group. All these encounters symbolize and reawaken Wilhelm's interest in the stage. But Mariane stood for more than the acting profession and her sensual, romantic appeal is returning too, in the person of Philine. She dresses in feminine clothing — in fact, she wears a

[1] It was an eighteenth-century practice to apply powder to the hair when it was being styled. That is also the reason for the smock, which would protect the clothing from powder. The knife would have been used principally to remove a lady's face powder; Wilhelm makes use of it to remove some stray hair powder from his brow.

[2] Wormwood is a plant known for its bitter taste.

[3] Goethe was well versed in the contemporary scientific understanding of the energy produced by electricity.

dirtier version of Mariane's white negligee — and has a very alluring manner. The name Philine alone gives an indication of this: it comes from the Greek verb "philein" which means "to love."[4] Laertes also associates her with Eve, who committed the original sin by breaking her word, and this provides an echo of Mariane's loss of faith. The irony of the situation lies in the juxtaposition of Wilhelm's lament about losing Mariane with his evident immediate admiration for Philine. All aspects of Philine are reminiscent of Mariane: she is an actress, she is attractive, and she incorporates the very fickleness that Wilhelm has just been denouncing. Finally, she gives away a scarf and a hat, just as Mariane's scarf and beads fell into Wilhelm's hands. A certain degree of intuition is also suggested in the way the events are told. Wilhelm buys the flowers and rearranges them "lovingly." The German expression is "mit Liebhaberei" and it sets a definite tone which is lost in the English translation "with pleasure." It is just at this point that Philine sends her messenger to ask for one of the flowers.

This is a long chapter, full of action and new experiences. Wilhelm is treated to a showy, physical type of stage performance and he meets some remarkable people, the most remarkable of all being Mignon. As Mignon is so taciturn, her appearance strikes Wilhelm all the more. He cannot tell whether she is a boy or a girl at first and this has to do with the costume she wears. The clothes are masculine and exotic but they are very becoming on her. Especially interesting is the fact that she wears a silk vest — precisely what Mariane wore as part of her officer's uniform. Both Mariane and Mignon wear clothes which have an androgynous effect, so that this aspect of Mariane is revived by Mignon rather than by Philine. In Mignon's case, the name is further evidence of this sexual ambiguity. Her name is a French adjective which can be used of a boy or a girl; it refers to someone small and delicate and also carries an element of endearment. In addition — and this is especially pronounced in *Wilhelm's Theatrical Calling* — Goethe often refers to her by using a masculine or neuter pronoun. He is able to do this because he chooses neuter nouns, such as "Geschöpf," "Wesen," or "Kind," which has the effect of presenting her as sexually neutral (Ammerlahn 1968, 93). Laertes provides a brief contrast by his ironic assurance that another performer, Landrinette, was worthy of being and remaining a woman. Besides her clothing, which immediately identifies

[4] Philine is a name often used for dancers and courtesans in the literature of ancient Greece. Goethe probably knew the name from Aristophanes' comedy *The Clouds.*

her as a performer, certain theatrical gestures, such as the repeated bowing, are part of Mignon's behavior offstage as well.

When Philine first brings the strange child up to her room, she announces that she has brought the "mystery" or "puzzle" (Rätsel). This designation remains a very apt way of describing Mignon, even later on, when more is revealed about her. Even her brow is somehow secretive, in this description. She also has an unusual effect on Wilhelm, causing him to lapse into a sort of dream world, from which Philine has to wake him when Mignon leaves. It is as though contact with Mignon provides a stimulus for his poetic imagination so that he withdraws from his tangible, prosaic surroundings. Thoughts of Mignon seem to inspire Wilhelm, just as her presence did. At the close of the chapter, Wilhelm wonders whether the electrifying effect of the acrobats could be produced by a writer or by actors on stage. Philine and Laertes are not approachable or willing to speculate on this subject and Wilhelm now finds their company unsatisfying while he pines for the return of Mignon.

Much of what happens in this chapter is new and exciting for Wilhelm. But some of it also takes up themes introduced earlier. The clothing and textile theme and the masculine clothing worn by a female character are both important here, and for Wilhelm, the exposure to actors and performers of all types is perfectly timed to reawaken his earlier ambitions. The pair of acrobats, Narziss and Landrinette, remind the reader that Wilhelm visualized appearing on stage together with Mariane. At the mill, a group of musicians strike up with some songs in front of the building. Wilhelm must have been reminded of the musicians he paid to perform in front of Mariane's house on that fateful evening. The pantomime, in which the miner demonstrates the importance of mining to the farmer who fears for his field, elevates the miner to occupy a position superior to that of the unenlightened farmer. Truth is victorious over ignorance, in a move parallel to Wilhelm's belief that the theater can be used to enlighten the nation (Weiss 88). He now takes the opportunity of outlining this principle for the benefit of Philine and Laertes.

When the threesome return to Philine's room and watch the scaffolding being erected as a stage for the evening's show, the preparations are reminiscent of the steps in the construction of the puppet theater of Wilhelm's childhood, especially since carpets are part of the equipment. Then Philine's minor act of deception in arranging to go out with Wilhelm and Laertes and then going with two other men instead is a reminder of the shocking revelation that Wilhelm finds in the note addressed to Mariane. The theme of betrayal in love is certainly suggested once more by the song about the cuckoo which causes the unnamed acquaintance to depart.[5] Finally, the name Laertes is mentioned as though it were not the real name of this character, thus drawing attention to its appearance in *Hamlet* and so hinting again at the Shakespeare theme still to come.

Philine delivers a spontaneous speech against sentimentality in relation to nature. Nature is merely the setting for human activity in her view, and her speech is merely the opportunity to tease and flirt with her two listeners. Wilhelm takes up the theme, but in a less lighthearted way; his pronouncements are sententious and, as usual, he ends by drawing a parallel with drama theory. He announces that people are the most interesting thing in the world.[6] His criticism of those who set great store by the appearance of material things — gardens, buildings and clothing — is a clear demonstration that Wilhelm does not know himself well. The clothing of each person Wilhelm meets is usually described first and carries more weight with him than any physical features. This is especially noticeable when he is described as embracing not Mariane but the red uniform and the satin vest (Book One, Chapter One). There is, then, a certain justice in asking Wilhelm to pay for Mignon's clothes when he buys her freedom, rather than any sum which might be calculated as a fair price for Mignon herself.

Besides bringing Wilhelm into contact with dramatic performers, the chapter also contains scenes which could be described as rehearsals for Wilhelm. The first is the fencing scene in which Wilhelm, although he has had some instruction in the art, is easily defeated by Laertes. The next is the hour he spends dancing with Philine and Laertes. Again his partner, Philine on this occasion, is better at it than he is. Wilhelm needs more practice. Besides the rehearsal, there is also the off-the-cuff performance, in front of a large audience, in which he intervenes on Mignon's behalf and threatens the man from the acrobatic troupe. His

---

[5] Zeus seduced Hera in the form of a cuckoo. The bird lays its eggs in other birds' nests and its name is the basis of the term "cuckold."

[6] The formulation of this phrase in the German original, "der Mensch ist dem Menschen das Interessanteste," is reminiscent of the phrase made famous by Alexander Pope: "The proper study of mankind is man." It comes from Pope's *Essay on Man* (1733), but the sentiment can be found in earlier, particularly French thinkers such as Pierre Charron and Blaise Pascal (*FA* 1405).

gesture is violent and dramatic; he grabs the man by the throat. The words of his speech are desperate and marked by rhetorical hyperbole. At the end of the chapter, Wilhelm is alone, running through his plans for a future theater which would bring social benefits. The reader is reminded of Wilhelm's rehearsals of dramatic parts in the solitude of his room.

Chapter Five

Mignon reappears when the acrobats have left. She is conscious that money changed hands but vague about value. She is willing to serve and eager to learn. Mignon is uninformed about everyday things. For example, she wants to eradicate the make-up from her face and thinks that her cheeks, red from rubbing, simply need more washing. Wilhelm finds her intriguing, and Philine attractive, so he prolongs his stay and keeps up his fencing and dancing practice. Melina and his wife come looking for work. Wilhelm is delighted to meet them again, but Philine and Laertes dislike them. Melina also makes himself unpopular in the inn.

The only dialogue in this chapter comes at the beginning. Wilhelm and Laertes receive Mignon on her return, Wilhelm gently, Laertes with a mildly threatening tone. The price paid for Mignon becomes an issue. In Chapter Four, Wilhelm paid thirty talers;[1] now Laertes tells her it was one hundred ducats.[2] As talers were silver coins and ducats gold, Laertes is greatly exaggerating, as a way of impressing Mignon and guaranteeing her gratitude.

Mignon is rehearsing for a new role, that of a devoted serving girl. Wilhelm, too, continues to rehearse in the arts of fencing and dancing. He does this partly to justify tarrying in the enjoyable company of Philine but also because he is fascinated by Mignon's strangeness. But the picture is spoiled when dissension breaks out between the Melinas and Philine and Laertes. Jealousy is no doubt at the root of Philine's displeasure; despite minor faults, Madame Melina is cultured, intelligent, and likable, and men in particular seem to think so. In addition, she has a knack for finding a person's weak spot. The narrator is quite

[1] The name "Taler" was used from the end of the fifteenth century until the late nineteenth century to designate this silver coin. The name derives from an abbreviation of the name of a silver mine in Sankt Joachimsthal.

[2] Dukaten were gold coins originating in Venice. They became German currency in 1559 and were still used in Austria at the beginning of the twentieth century. The name comes from the Latin inscription on the back of the coin: "Sit tibi Christe datus quem tu regis iste ducatus." It is an appeal to Christ to be devoted to the place over which he rules.

precise about Madame Melina's faults, which concern her acting ability. She is forever practicing speeches, but she has no feel for the context as a whole. This reminds the reader of Wilhelm's feeling for what was lacking in his own development at the end of Book One, Chapter Four.

The narrator's voice comes through clearly in this chapter, and in the German original there is a direct intervention in the final paragraph. It is remarkable that the narrator does not mention Wilhelm's relation to the various tensions, but concentrates on the behavior by which Melina offended the innkeeper, and the qualities in Madame Melina that made Philine feel uncomfortable. Without giving any very clear impression of their physical appearances, the chapter contributes to the reader's insight into various characters.

Chapter Six

Melina wants to find out why the group of actors dispersed and what became of their props and costumes. They are stored and can be sold; Wilhelm goes with him to inspect them. Wilhelm feels attracted to these objects and Melina longs to buy the collection. He would put together a little play, and make enough money for food.

Melina is full of plans for establishing a theater and suggests Wilhelm come up with the necessary money. Wilhelm's conscience tells him that he has already stayed too long. However, he is loathe to leave Mignon, with her energetic movements, strange gestures, curious speech and willing nature. She sleeps on the floor, keeps herself and her clothes very clean, and attends Mass every morning. Melina pressures Wilhelm for financial help, and makes him uneasy. He starts a letter to Werner with an inaccurate account of events. On noticing that his paper already has writing on the other side, Wilhelm simply gives up.

The feelings aroused in Wilhelm by the sight of the costumes are connected with the puppet collection he had played with so happily as a child, as well as with the stories he acted out with his friends. The Turkish and heathen costumes relate to Tancred and Chlorinda, those of the Jew and the priest to the David and Goliath production. There is even the possibility of clothing a Hanswurst figure. Wilhelm tries to suppress these nostalgic feelings and the whole of this short chapter bears the stamp of his inner conflicts. He feels drawn to the costumes, but wants to resist their attraction. He does not like Melina's persistent requests for money, although he can certainly understand why Melina wants to buy the things. He feels an obligation towards his family and Werner, but cannot combine the world of business with the adventurous life he has been enjoying of late. Even his capacity for objectivity in his account seems to have disappeared. Objectivity belongs in business dealings; Wilhelm is following the lead of his imagination.

And then there is Mignon, who is gradually coming to occupy the place in Wilhelm's thoughts previously reserved for Mariane (MacLeod 102). His thoughts center on her as he tries to understand her strange ways. Her bodily movements, much more expressive than her words, draw attention to this strangeness; she is very supple and always seems to run or jump, rather than walk. When she disappears in Chapter Four, people say they have seen her on the rooftops. Like some kind of performing animal learning tricks, she works on a variety of greetings for different people, including different positionings of her arms. The exaggerated gesticulations she produces would be comic under other circumstances, but there is no such intent here (Steiner *Sprache,* 62). Her verbal communication is minimal and she speaks an idiosyncratic dialect of her own, made up of French, Italian, and German. In this, she represents the exact opposite of Wilhelm and the others; while they spend time on rehearsing theatrical oratory, she uses speech only with maximum economy and then in a curious, possibly even lyrical way. In an attempt to understand her better, Wilhelm even follows her to church early one morning and observes her praying, rosary in hand. Mignon's willingness to serve seems to be the only key to understanding her role. She wants to learn the rules of civilized society, whereas Wilhelm would like to leave these rules behind. Her foreign and bohemian ways fascinate him, but she has become dependent on the social stability which her new "owner" represents.

Chapter Seven

Philine recognizes an old actor friend whom she calls "the old pedant."[1] He is shabby, with a badly powdered wig, but Philine's affection for him is evident. The narrator observes that Philine takes equal pleasure in loving certain men and in taking advantage of others. Wilhelm recognizes two women and an older man as actors he has seen perform at home. The man played a blusterer, a character often encountered in real life.[2] The narrator observes that since doing good without a lot of

---

[1] The pedant is one of the stock characters coming from the Italian Commedia dell'arte. The same character is sometimes also referred as the doctor.

[2] The role of the old man was standard on the eighteenth-century German stage. A complete theater troupe would need to cover sixteen roles if they wanted to perform any contemporary German plays or Shakespeare.

fuss is natural to the German character, grace and style are often lacking. Wilhelm waits patiently to ask the old man for news of Mariane.

In an unpleasant scene Friedrich, a young, fair-haired man who waits on Philine, leaves her service asking rhetorically whether she imagines him incapable of leaving her, and Mignon takes over his duties. Wilhelm becomes agitated on hearing that the old man supported Mariane after the manager of the company fired her for being pregnant. He continued to send her money after she moved away, but she stopped writing to thank him.

The chapter introduces new characters to the reader. One of them Philine already knows and three of them are acquaintances of Wilhelm. This in itself is a technique which comes from the stage; if one of the players already on stage can hail a player stepping onto the stage for the first time, the audience instantly acquires the necessary information about the newcomer. In addition to being known personally by other characters, two of them are also stock characters, familiar to members of the audience. The pedant makes a fairly brief appearance here, but the narrator is able to underscore the facile quality of Philine's attentions, and her behavior towards the pedant provides a pretext for the remark.

The news about the theater in general is discouraging and would not seem to bode well for the group gathered together here, all of whom are in search of employment with a theater group. But whereas this report would ordinarily have set Wilhelm to brooding or delivering a discourse on the future of the theater, on this occasion he is far too preoccupied by his private thoughts to give the matter a moment's consideration.

In contrast to Philine's superficial frivolity, there are undercurrents of tension and suppressed emotion throughout the chapter. First, there is the uncomfortable scene when Friedrich refuses to lay the table for the visitors. This stubbornness goes unexplained except for the statement that he did not want his duties to extend beyond serving Philine herself. But the reader senses there is something lurking, unexpressed, beneath the surface. Was he jealous, and hiding an emotional attachment to her? His rhetorical question suggests that Friedrich is utterly dependent on her. Did he feel exploited? The reader is left to guess what could be behind it.

Wilhelm hears news of Mariane through a third party, the blusterer. This too is a dramatic technique used to heighten the suspense, done very effectively here. In the first instance, suspense is heightened because the listener, though keen to hear everything, cannot know for certain whether the third party is telling only facts or whether details have been edited in the telling, for whatever reason. This particular third party is certainly not neutral in his disposition towards the subject matter. And yet the emotions evoked in him by the mention of Mariane's name are as intense as those Wilhelm himself experiences. The man functions as a type of alter ego to Wilhelm. Both men hold on to a strong residual affection for Mariane and both harbor a feeling of having been shamelessly and inexplicably betrayed by her.

Further tension is produced by the irony of the situation. The man addresses Wilhelm on the subject of Mariane as though he were not well acquainted with her; he feels it necessary to explain that she has a very pleasing nature, hard to resist. Wilhelm, meanwhile, alternates agonizingly between wanting the old man to stop and eagerness to know more. Both men are at a loss to understand how ingratitude and betrayal could combine with such sweetness of spirit in one and the same person. Wilhelm does not of course permit himself to express any such views, but what he has heard is one more example of Werner's allegations about Mariane, hotly denied by Wilhelm. Now Wilhelm is even powerless to dispute the charge of wantonness leveled against Mariane, since he has had to accept evidence confirming it. This report, however, is tantalizingly inconclusive. At least Wilhelm has learned that Mariane was in fact expecting a baby, as he had suspected, but he is no wiser about her whereabouts or the fortunes of the baby. The man ends with a lament about the calculating nature of women who take advantage of men and leave them to suffer. The reader alone knows, of course, that it is Norberg who has most cause to complain about Mariane in these terms, since she was accepting his gifts and money despite being emotionally attached to Wilhelm.

All this emotion, both as expressed — in Philine's wild gestures, Friedrich's fit of pique, and the old man's tears — and as suppressed, principally by Wilhelm, contrasts with Mignon's inscrutability. In turn, her servile attitude and obedience to Wilhelm's wishes contrast with Friedrich's angry act of defiance.

Chapter Eight

Anyone can imagine Wilhelm's turmoil after this conversation. He feels partly responsible for Mariane's downfall and excuses her behavior. He is convinced that she was worthy of his love and and thinks sadly about her making her own way with the baby.

Mignon is waiting for him; she wants to perform the egg dance for him. She dances blindfolded, stepping among a number of eggs at precise intervals on a mat. A violinist accompanies her with the dance music, the fandango, while she plays the castanets.[1] Mignon completes the dance without

---

[1] The fandango is an old Spanish dance for two people who typically use castanets.

touching a single egg. The general effect is more ceremonial than graceful, but Wilhelm suddenly knows he wants to care for Mignon as a father. When he offers her a new suit of clothes, she says they must be his color.

Wilhelm is saddened by the news of Mariane. He feels he has wronged her, that she was deserving of his love; the thought of her trying to cope on her own fills him with sorrow. Without analyzing its cause, he even feels that her silence was somehow justified. With precise timing, Mignon steps onto the scene. It is as though she were meant to fill the gap created by the loss of Mariane. Her masculine clothing, her association with the stage, even her enigmatic and minimal communication make a thematic link to Mariane's reticence. Wilhelm's thoughts, no more substantial than recollected dreams, are replaced by the compelling presence before him.

The preparations for the egg dance demonstrate that artistic performance requires precision and care and plain hard work. Wilhelm's dreams of his own future as an actor are always very romantic; he dreams of having an electrifying effect on the audience, of conveying noble principles whose validity would instantly be acknowledged and embraced. But Mignon shows that the eggs have to be placed with exactly the right spacing in between, the violinist has to be coached, and the whole show has to be rehearsed until it is perfect. The fact that she wears a blindfold is a sign that she has learnt the steps until they have become automatic. It also prevents any eye contact between performer and onlooker. This is exactly the opposite of Wilhelm's ideal, where everything is measured by his relation to the audience.

The spectacle reflects features of Mignon's nature. It has a mechanical perfection; twice, her movements are compared to clockwork. She is wound up and runs her course, her energetic movements punctuated by the sharp and regular sounds of the castanets. It is not the sort of dance that leaves room for interpretation or for the sort of feminine grace often associated with dance. Mignon has gone about this just as she goes about learning her duties when waiting at table, and in both cases it is to please Wilhelm. The dance itself is strange, like Mignon. The castanet music suggests a Mediterranean culture, just as her speech does. There is a severity, a sharpness and dryness to the dance and it brings home to Wilhelm those very aspects of her character. Unable to act on his sympathy for Mariane, he transfers this sympathy to Mignon at this moment. And since Wilhelm cannot take responsibility for the child born to Mariane, of whose existence he has just heard, he converts his fascination for Mignon into fatherly love.

Mignon has steadfastly refused to perform the egg dance for the leader of the troupe. Now, she performs it for Wilhelm as a free-will offering. That she does so is a sign of her willingness to serve. The action is the same, whether it is required or freely undertaken, but Mignon is express-ing a determination to accept her destiny. The dance is like an image of that destiny; the hazards are all around and the individual progresses blindfolded through them. With skill and discipline, they can be avoided. Wilhelm is so completely drawn in to the performance that his thoughts of Mariane are dispelled and his emotions find their object in Mignon. His need for the theater and for the whole world of performance in general is now no longer entirely bound up with Mariane. For Mignon, the per-formance is a gift, a means of showing her devotion to Wilhelm.

The egg dance appears to be an isolated incident, merely to explain the earlier scene (Book Two, Chapter Four) when Mignon's refusal to per-form cost her her position. But it also brings to the surface the feelings Wilhelm has for her: fatherly, protective feelings. And it is no coincidence that he has just learned he is in all probability the father of some poor child destined to wander through life without the benefit of fatherly guid-ance. It takes little psychoanalytical theory to see that Wilhelm has been at least subliminally affected by the juxtaposition of these two events.

Cloth and clothing are significant at the end of this chapter and the link is made between what Mariane represented and the world that Mi-gnon comes from. When he offers to have some new clothing made for her, Mignon insists on the color she associates with Wilhelm — in part because she habitually manipulates her appearance to resemble that of a boy, providing a link to the male role played by Mariane on stage, but also as an outward sign of her commitment to Wilhelm. She will reflect his presence (Ammerlahn 1968, 105). She can express this in the gift of dance and in the color of her clothing, but not in words. It is an at-tempt to conform to her new surroundings and company, but because this clothing is to be modeled on men's, rather than women's style, it will be as forced as her unnatural gestures and will do nothing to de-tract from her strangeness.

Chapter Nine

Wilhelm dreams about Mariane and once again Mignon breaks in on his dream world, appearing the next morning with a tailor. The narra-tor explains that Wilhelm had worn the colors gray and blue ever since the loss of Mariane.

Wilhelm's dancing and fencing practice do not go well and Melina re-peats his request for money. Philine suggests an outing on the river. Laertes proposes an impromptu play, each person taking a standard character.[1] Wilhelm is enthusiastic: harmony and contentment do not for long accompany those who never dissemble, but never accompany those who always dissemble. From behind a mask, a real person can be revealed. Laertes and Madame Melina join in with repartee. The setting for the play is be a trade ship and they are meeting for the first time. They stop to pick up another passenger who is drawn into the game as a country clergyman. Wilhelm and the clergyman fall into conversation about the usefulness of such unwritten plays. Wilhelm hears the newcomer's views on natural talent, or genius.[2] Education is important: trust rather to human reason than to fate. Wilhelm objects to the view that lofty ideals must end in failure.

Wilhelm has even stronger objections to the apparently arbitrarily chosen example of a young man who becomes obsessed with puppet shows as a child. The day ends with forfeits and much merriment in which the stranger, or clergyman, takes full part.

Mignon's enthusiasm for the new clothing is plain; she loses no time in arranging everything. Through the colors she expresses her allegiance to Wilhelm — a sort of uniform which identifies her with him. She has also determined that the cloth should be cut in a style worn by boys. This intensifies her androgynous appearance. She becomes very forceful and the tailor has to agree to be quickly finished with the work. The new clothing also marks a complete break with her former life; Wilhelm paid her employer only what her clothes cost, and now those clothes are to be replaced.

Melina confirms the impression Wilhelm had formed of him from their first meeting, namely, that he was not suited to the noble calling of acting, but would be better working with figures. Melina incurs a heavy load of

---

[1] The parts the group chooses include conventional ones from the standard eighteenth-century repertoire: the Jew (dating from late in the century), the Tyrolean girl (an adaptation of the Columbine figure from the commedia dell'arte), and the good-natured old man.

[2] Genius or "Genie" is an important literary concept in the eighteenth century. Goethe's use of the term underwent some changes as he developed as a writer. During the Storm and Stress period, the "original genius" was the focal point and was conceived of as an individual resolved to throw over the existing social and aesthetic laws. This concept of genius included the productive ability to bring forth new ideas. Later, the genius is compared to the creative and organizing functions inherent in nature, forces which operate in accordance with nature's own rules. In his classical period, Goethe added the aspect of development to his nature-based model. The development of taste emerged from the study of the tradition, and the goal of the practical life became the ideal. Genius became more firmly grounded in a particular society and nation at a specific time period. The emphasis on the development of the individual's talents and character make it more practical than the amorphous and inspired Romantic model to which it stands opposed.

forfeits for his inadequate portrayal of a traveling Englishman. His primary concern is to acquire enough capital to found a company that can make money. The conversation between Wilhelm and the stranger belongs to the opposite end of the spectrum: instead of facts and figures, they discuss acting theory, the process of education, and the concept of fate. It is of course reminiscent of Wilhelm's earlier conversation, in Book One, Chapter Seventeen, also with a stranger, when there was a difference of opinion about fate. In fact this is a repetition and elaboration of that discussion (Storz 1953, 67). In both cases, an unknown man appears like some Greek or Germanic deity, and requires Wilhelm to think twice about the direction he is taking. The present stranger's uncanny divination of Wilhelm's early enthusiasm for puppets is also a suggestion of omniscience.

There is a connection between the two topics on which the clergyman gives his views. For actors, he strongly recommends exercises in which the script is not laid down, in which there is scope for a large degree of flexibility and individual freedom of expression.[3] On the question of fate, he warns Wilhelm against viewing the course of his life as preordained and suggests that the exercise of individual reason is a more reliable guide than trusting undeviatingly to some perceived higher plan. Chance occurrences are not to be trusted as indications of the future (Marahrens 162). Wilhelm's own view is that native genius would be sufficient to find a way out of any wrong turnings. However, he is reminded of the power exercised by the first impressions formed in childhood and the reader remembers Mariane's reluctance to reveal her own earliest impressions (Book One, Chapter Six; Graham 187).

Chapter Ten

The mysterious clergyman has disappeared without a word. Laertes and Wilhelm have a vague feeling of having seen him before. On the way back, Philine, to whose charms Wilhelm is becoming susceptible, suggests putting their songs together in a play.[4] The performance is held in Wilhelm's room and begins with a German play about medieval knights,

[3] At the basis of this discussion is the actual debate between Gottsched and Lessing about the usefulness of extempore drama. Gottsched was opposed to it, while Lessing championed it.

[4] The genre suggested here is the Singspiel, in which arias are joined together by spoken dialogue rather than recitative. It was a popular form of opera in eighteenth-century Germany and Goethe himself tried his hand at the Singspiel with *Claudine von Villa Bella* (1773) and *Erwin und Elmira* (1775). The genre culminated in Mozart's *Die Zauberflöte*.

a genre currently enjoying a vogue. The punch arrives between the second and third acts and the audience raises a glass as well. The play pleases everyone, particularly in the fifth act when the tyrant is defeated. Led by Melina, the audience joins in the ritual smashing of punch glasses. Things get out of hand and Wilhelm has to persuade them to leave.

The central topic of the chapter is the play, but it is remarkable how little the reader actually learns about it. The props and scenery are described as well as the salient features of the actors' costumes, the helmets and cuirasses for the men and the high, stiff collars for the ladies. But the costumes can only be imagined, because they are all still in storage. It is ironic that Wilhelm, who has for so long only been able to imagine himself acting, is now dependent upon his imagination for the costumes once again.

Goethe allows himself a little joke: in mentioning the plays about knights as a new and popular form, he is referring to his own play *Goetz von Berlichingen* (1773) which set this trend in motion and incidentally established Goethe's reputation.[5] This hint, together with the proclamations of national fervor, indicates again that Wilhelm's development runs parallel to the historical development of the German stage. Features of the production recapture moments from Wilhelm's past theatrical experience. His youthful enthusiasm for the story of Tancred and Chlorinda comes to mind, with the mention of armor and the defense of national pride. Then the fifth act is greeted with tremendous applause, just as the fifth act was always what attracted Wilhelm most in his reading and in his youthful productions of tragedies. The mention of a tyrant here reminds the reader of the second phase of puppet shows, when Wilhelm started using plays from the *Deutsche Schaubühne* collection and his King Saul puppet was transformed into the tyrant Chaumigrem (Book One, Chapter Six).

By means of these rather extreme circumstances, the individual characters are further developed. Laertes is portrayed as the calmest, most neutral member of the group. The narrator rarely misses an opportunity to cast Melina in a bad light, and Philine shows again how adept she is at drawing others in to providing her with entertainment. Wilhelm himself is very invigorated, but by his role in the play rather than by the drinking, and the scene of destruction seems to be a bad omen for the future success of theatrical enterprises of this little group.

---

[5] More references to *Goetz* follow. The gypsy scene is the same as Goethe uses in Act V of the play and a secret tribunal forms part of the same act (*FA* 1410). Goethe is quoting himself.

Chapter Eleven

Wilhelm discovers that his horse has been ill treated by Laertes, and is not likely to be useful now. He receives a greeting from Philine and wants to buy her something in return for the powder knife. He buys a hat and scarf and other objects he saw her throw to the beggars. Madame Melina warns him against Philine.

A harper arrives and they persuade him to sing and play his instrument. He sings a moving ballad in praise of song and singers and then of peace and harmony, also enmity and discord, the joy of reunion and the bitterness of indifference. His last song, "Was hör ich draußen vor dem Tor?" is given in the text. Philine sings too, but the narrator says no more about it, so as not to give the reader offense. Wilhelm praises the harper's technique, contrasting it with their own static poses on stage. Melina introduces the topic of money again. Wilhelm takes offense and goes outside.

The chapter begins uncertainly. Wilhelm shifts from one mood to another and the unsettled air continues during his conversation with Madame Melina. It is only with the appearance of the harper that he is able to rise above the minor irritations and larger tensions which are setting in among his companions. The discovery that his horse is unridable depresses Wilhelm, but the reader knows that he must at the same time be glad of a reason to postpone his departure for home and prolong his stay among the present company. The wave from Philine draws attention to her as a reason for his desire to stay on. The narrator intervenes while recounting Wilhelm's purchases with the observation that he did buy her more than the mere gift of one knife would warrant. There is an element of guilt in the phrasing, suggesting that Wilhelm is well aware of the danger in becoming too involved with Philine.

Whereas the time he spends with the group often ends in inconvenience or regrets, despite the euphoric heights he sometimes reaches, Wilhelm is wholly uplifted by the harper's performance. The new character will be an important one for the novel as a whole, but his immediate influence is also important; he gives the assembled company a focus. But it is only Wilhelm who reacts with such a wave of emotion; it is as though the harper's song had shown him the way out of his confused and indecisive state. Philine's reaction is completely typical of her; she welcomes the presence of the harper as a way of counteracting boredom. Melina's attitude is very negative: why should they be entertained by anyone else, when their own group included singers capable of making money? As usual, his primary interest is financial and Wilhelm's growing antipathy towards him is related to his own disliking for business. The harper has a harmonizing influence on the whole group, but for Wilhelm, the effect is immediate and overwhelming. Just as his strong and reciprocated bond with Mignon provides him with stability, so now the harper acts as a sort of anchor or protective spirit in this group of highly volatile and unstable people.

When Wilhelm delivers his poetic apology on the art of the singer, with its talk of birds and airy spirits, the reader recognizes the sentiments Wilhelm expressed to Werner in a completely different context (Book Two, Chapter Two). It is as though those earlier words, in which he even uses the image of the harp to complete his picture of a poet, were a preparation for the entrance of the harper (Keppel-Kriems 111). The harper comes as a re-embodiment of that ideal (*MA* 741). He unites the group with a sense of well being, but he fills Wilhelm, in particular, with inspiration. Wilhelm returns to his penchant for theoretical analysis and claims that this singer alone is more expressive than most actors. Laertes is equal to this with his remark that in singing one is given more help; the tempo and rhythm are provided, whereas an actor in a prose play is responsible for these himself.[1]

Curiously, the harper's physical appearance is described in some detail. He is bald, but has bushy eyebrows and a long white beard. The garment he wears is long and dark. The picture suggests age and wisdom and his preference for profound subject matter; he sings of sorrow and joy and of the essence of song. The contrast is then all the greater when he accedes to Philine's request and accompanies her in the song about the shepherd,[2] which is too vulgar to be mentioned further.[3] Wilhelm is evidently not impressed, although he concedes that Philine has talent. The altercation between them is a thinly disguised "pladoyer" for "Geschmack" (taste) to accompany "Genie" (inspiration).

This chapter contains the first of the songs to appear in the novel. The song itself is a fairly straightforward ballad, which first appeared in *Wilhelm Meisters Theatralische Sendung* in a slightly different version and underwent minor revisions once more before appearing as a sepa-

---

[1] Laertes' argument owes something to Karl Philip Moritz's "Versuch einer deutschen Prosodie," which differentiates in the matter of poetry between the "language of feelings" among the Ancients and the "language of thought" among Moderns (*MA* 742).

[2] A song with the same opening is also to be found in the Osterspaziergang scene in *Faust*.

[3] The narrator takes on a clear role as fictional editor of a manuscript here. The conceit is that the song was originally given in full, but the editor felt compelled to excise it. This pretense, which acts as an ironic guarantee of veracity, is very common in the eighteenth-century novel, and is particularly prominent in the novels of Wieland.

rate poem.[4] Before it is performed, there are suggestions of a mysterious air about both the singer and his songs. The vitality of his singing gives the listeners the impression that he might be composing the songs as he sings them. Then, when they ask him about the composer of the song, he answers evasively, adding that he has many more songs besides. He sings with feeling about human qualities and with bitterness about indifference, enmity, and strife. The group is transported by the sentiments and the melody combined.

The choice of song is strange; the reader may not find any immediate relevance to the setting in which it is performed (Kiess 101). It tells a story, set in medieval times, about a poet invited to sing to the king. He is offered the gift of a golden chain, but he refuses, accepting instead a glass of the best wine as sufficient payment. The harper sings as a narrator, telling the story in the third person; there is thus no scope for subjective feeling on the performer's part. Nevertheless, because he sings about a bard and because his whole appearance — long white beard, dark brown robe — creates an archaic effect, it is tempting to read the text of his song as self-referential (Schlaffer *Mythos,* 42–43). It is even possible to view the harper as a prose reincarnation of his own songs (Kiess 107). There are further parallels: in the song, the singer is alone at first and is then invited into the company. The song ends with a glass of wine and the harper, too, drinks one as soon as he has finished singing. The theme of the song is that company and entertainment are more valuable than gold and that the beauty of the song is itself the reward. It is a message from which Melina could certainly derive some benefit. He does indeed appear to admire the harper, at least initially, but his praise soon turns into unpleasant remarks about the harper's skills in persuading them to part with their money, which leads to the inevitable topic of the loan he had hoped to receive from Wilhelm. The result is that Wilhelm's spirits are as low at the end of the chapter as they were at the beginning.

The singer in the song requests that his listeners close their eyes while he sings and replace the enjoyment of their visible riches with an audible and thus more spiritual treasure. The imagery used to depict song is again related to birds, which reinforces the link to Wilhelm's speech in praise of poetry and the poet. The harper's entrance brings with it one

---

[4] The term "ballad" comes via French from the Latin "ballare," meaning "to dance." It originally meant a simple song to accompany a dance. Ballads later lost their association with dance, but kept their strong rhythm and easily identifiable rhyme patterns. The traditional ballad is transmitted orally and its authorship is anonymous.

more aspect of performance. And once again, this new figure is intriguing and mysterious. The group speculate about whether he could be a priest or a Jew; both of these are associated with an isolated position in society as well as with an uncommon spiritual dimension. In their failure to become integrated members of society and in their strangeness of manner and of physical appearance, Mignon and the harper both attract attention to themselves. But in both cases, it is Wilhelm who is most affected, and he takes more interest in these two characters than any of his companions do. Because the harper's ballad places a higher value on song than on material possessions, it appeals to Wilhelm's rejection of the world of trade and to his visionary relation to the arts.

Chapter Twelve

Philine wants to dissuade Wilhelm from leaving so that she will not be bored. She makes displays of intimacy, which cause Wilhelm embarrassment, and forces a promise to stay on a few more days. She switches to the familiar form of address and then back again to the formal pronoun in accusing Wilhelm of an unfeeling attitude.

Philine steps inside and Wilhelm, who is not as unresponsive as he led Philine to believe, follows her. Melina catches Wilhelm off guard and he finally agrees to the request for money. Next, Friedrich returns, determined to see Philine. Wilhelm goes to his room to find Mignon practicing writing. He feels too frustrated to help her. The chapter ends with the innkeeper talking to a man who is preparing for the arrival of his employer, a count, along with the countess and a prince.[1] Wilhelm realizes they are discussing him, and moves aside.

As in the previous chapter, this one opens with Wilhelm first despondent and then roused by an action of Philine's. But in this chapter the situation is a little more complicated: Wilhelm is embarrassed by her attentions and tries to ward her off. Philine eventually goes inside and it is as though the narrator had waited for her to withdraw in order to reveal that Wilhelm did not in fact respond to her as woodenly as it seemed. Beginning with this feature, the whole chapter is theatrical in structure. Philine goes offstage, as it were, and her pretext is that she needs to fetch some needlework to do when she returns. The implication is that Wilhelm is not a very entertaining companion. In fact, her absence is

---

[1] The prince's name is replaced by asterisks. This is a very common device in eighteenth-century novels and is designed to lend an air of authenticity to the story. The pretense is that this was a real person, whose anonymity must be protected.

planned and is essential, not only for the narrator's revelation, but also so that Wilhelm's instincts will be thwarted, first by Melina and then, more conclusively, by Friedrich. For Wilhelm in his present frame of mind, these encounters are annoying, but for the dramatic development the meeting with Melina, in particular, is crucial. The tension is skillfully heightened by Melina's appearance just at the moment when Wilhelm, attracted by Philine, but feeling guilty as well, has resolved to follow her. Because of these special circumstances, Wilhelm is impatient and agrees to Melina's request just to be rid of him. Friedrich's arrival, however, is an unexpected blow and there is nothing Wilhelm can do about it. Friedrich has every right to visit Philine, whereas Wilhelm has no desire to see her in company with anyone else. To make matters worse, Friedrich speaks in urgent tones of his need to see Philine and Wilhelm is evidently not only exasperated at the unfortunate timing of Friedrich's return, but is jealous of him as well. Wilhelm's plan has been stymied and he has only Mignon to console him.

It is easy to imagine all these exits and entrances taking place on stage and producing a steady increase in dramatic tension. They are followed by a vignette which adds to the reader's image of Mignon; she is clearly becoming ever more devoted to Wilhelm, but her efforts to improve herself are still an uphill struggle. Mignon has to work against a lack of coordination between her mind and her body. Wilhelm's dissatisfaction soon transfers itself to her; she reflects his moods. Even the disharmony between her body and mind is a reflection of the irresolute state into which Wilhelm has fallen (Gilby 140).

The chapter ends with a discussion that prepares the ground for a new dramatic possibility. Wilhelm has now been among a group of actors for some time and has already experienced their various limitations. He is moody and unresolved about his next step. Newcomers of a different social class may be able to provide him with more of a sense of direction. Here again, the scene is presented in such a way that it is easy to visualize on stage; two people are speaking confidentially at center stage, while the hero paces restlessly up and down to one side. Each new arrival has to be finely timed and a subtle balance is established between the individual temperaments.

Chapter Thirteen

Wilhelm finds the harper in a humble tavern. He listens in the doorway of the attic room to the old man repeating verses again and again in rhapsodic tones. The lines are sorrowful and his tears get in the way. The song, "Wer nie sein Brot mit Tränen aß," about the connection between sorrow and the heavenly powers, is reproduced. Wilhelm's tears flow as well. He steps into the room and urges the old man to continue. Wilhelm has noticed that the spoken word does not come easily to the harper. He sits beside him on the straw bed and expresses his envy at the harper's ability to overcome isolation in this way. In the song "Wer sich der Einsamkeit ergibt," the harper laments that true solitude in life is impossible, since suffering is a constant companion. Only in death are we free of grief and truly alone. The narrator compares their exchange to a meeting of spiritual seekers with alternations of readings, homilies, and hymns.

This chapter stands in complete contrast to the comings and goings of the previous one; here there are only two people and one setting. The emotions are only related and recollected, not directly provoked by any act. Besides the explicit comparison of the scene to a group of pietistic worshippers, there are other clearly perceptible echoes in this scene. Some dimensions reside in the setting, others in the content of the harper's songs, others still arise from the emerging picture of the harper himself.

The figure of the harper gains considerable depth in this chapter. When Wilhelm inquires after his whereabouts, he is directed to a humble tavern, where the harper sits on a bed of straw, in the attic chamber. These details are suggestive of stages in the life of Christ: those seeking the newborn Christ find him in the humblest of settings, the stable of an inn, with straw for his bed; later, those present at his last supper gather in the upper room. The suggestion of the harper as a Christ-figure is also apparent in that he himself suffers while singing of his sufferings, and Wilhelm derives relief from his own sorrows through the suffering which the harper has undergone. But perhaps more important is the image of the harper as a King David type, the figure who is commonly seen as a prefiguration of Christ. The harp is the instrument of King David the Psalmist, and the manner in which the harper intones his lines, repeating, sometimes reciting, very strongly suggests the psalms.[1]

The laments making up the songs reinforce this impression. The opening line of the first song bears a close resemblance to a line from Psalm 80:5: "Thou feedest them with the bread of tears; and givest them tears to drink in great measure" (*MA* 742). Wilhelm seeks the harper out because he senses that his songs will provide a release from

---

[1] Robert Lowth (1710–87) published an influential literary analysis of the Old Testament that was welcomed and further developed by Herder. His observations included an analysis of the Psalms which pointed out their parallel structure; the second half of each verse of the psalm reiterates or enlarges upon the first half.

his own sorrow and confusion. In this, the harper and Wilhelm are parallel to David and Saul in a scene related in the First Book of Samuel (16:3): "And it came to pass, when the evil spirit from God was upon Saul, that David took an harp, and played with his hand: so Saul was refreshed, and was well, and the evil spirit departed from him."

The harper's first song is quite different from the ballad heard earlier. There is no setting to provide a sense of a particular period, nor is the song about a particular individual. The theme establishes a link between individual destiny and the heavenly powers to whom the song is addressed. The poem consists of two stanzas, each of which contains a one-sentence statement. In each stanza, the first two lines begin with the same word and in each case it is a personal pronoun. Although the song is a lament, it does not simply take the form of an outcry, but presents a premise and conclusion in each stanza. It opens with a straightforward iambic line, but there are several points where variation in the basic pattern produces clashes. The first instance of this is in line 2, with the word "kummervollen," which gains tremendous power from its irregular beat. The second stanza needs to be scanned with a strong opening beat for each line, a complete deviation from the iambic structure. There are also several places where a caesura is required by the syntax or natural need for emphasis (Storz 1948/49, 51). The presence of these caesuras reminds the reader that the harper constantly interrupts his song with sobs. With the lines thus repeatedly broken, the beat markedly irregular, and the syntax occasionally unconventional or inverted, the form of the poem contributes a great deal to the force of its painful content. In their rhyme schemes, however, the two stanzas are completely predictable and regular. The circumstances in which the song is performed give some sense of a personal underlying grief and yet the song itself speaks in universal terms. Its theme is comfortless and offers no possibility of escape.

The first stanza begins with the universal individual and rises to reach the heavenly powers at the end of the last line. Again the three-syllable adjective "himmlischen" disrupts the metrical pattern and draws attention to itself in so doing. The pronoun "ihr," first introduced in this phrase, is repeated twice more in the second stanza, the bitter tone gaining in intensity with each repetition. The song is a brief statement; it requires no further elaboration, no examples or subjective comment.

Because the heavenly powers are referred to in the plural, it is also possible to relate the harper to a Homeric model of the bard. In Book Eight of the *Odyssey* a blind minstrel sings before the Phaiakians and their guest Odysseus, to the accompaniment of a harp. Odysseus asks him to sing the story of the wooden horse which housed the warriors who would overtake Troy. Odysseus is overcome with grief and his tears flow. The Phaiakians do not know who he is and ask why he should grieve, since, they say, the destruction of Troy was the work of the gods, and the deed was performed only so a song could be made about it. Like Odysseus, Wilhelm has a private grief which is triggered by the harper's sad song; in both instances, the gods are the cause of the suffering and the suffering is what makes the beauty of the song.

The second song is made up of three stanzas; the first two are four lines long, the third, eight. Again, a basic iambic structure provides the backdrop for repeated variations where natural stresses or emphases transgress against the regular pattern. The syntax and vocabulary are very simple and unassuming and although the rhyme scheme incorporates two patterns, the whole is undemanding. This is not to say that the song is plain or unadorned. Already the opening monosyllabic "Wer" goes against the iambic pattern and line 2 also starts with an exclamation which requires strong emphasis and forces a caesura after just one syllable. Line 3 is nicely divided in the middle between two parallel constructions that match each other completely; the only difference is provided by the extra vowel in the verb "liebt." The enjambment from this line to the next prepares the ground for the impact of the last word, "Pein."

The second stanza also has a strong opening and the whole stanza expresses a personal bitterness; the number of strongly stressed syllables drives home the point of this self-directed outburst. Between the end of the second stanza and the beginning of the third, a complete change of tone has taken place. The singer no longer speaks of himself; instead, there is a shift into imagery. Even the rhythm is lighter; the opening syllable is unstressed and the whole stanza conforms more closely to the dictates of iambic verse. There is a light, almost playful tone to the image of the lover trying to trick his beloved and catch her out in a dalliance; it is remarkably well chosen for Wilhelm as listener. And yet this lighthearted opening leads into the grim fate first suggested by the parallelism of lines 4 and 5. The sigh "Ach" follows, re-establishing the despairing tone of the first stanza. The import of the song admits of no ambiguity; the prominence of the words "Pein," "Qual," and "allein," supported by the rhyme scheme, bears this out (Storz 1948/49, 48).

The second song in this chapter is much more personal than the first. The harper is clearly identified as the lonely figure whose solitude is the subject of the song. Wilhelm's expression of envy for the harper has prompted the song: he speaks of the harper's good fortune in having the gift of song to counteract loneliness. But the harper paints a different and far more profound picture of the true nature of his solitude.[2]

The chapter ends with an extended intervention by the narrator. The conversation continued, the reader is told, with Wilhelm speaking and the harper expressing his agreement in the form of songs which gave rise to corresponding emotions and provided much scope for the imagination. To describe this kind of beneficial exchange, a comparison is introduced, and it extends almost to the end of the chapter. The scene is compared to a meeting of pious worshippers who wish to deepen their religious experience outside the official church. The leader of this group offers a sermon in sung form — the music helps to direct the words. Individual members of the assembly are then inspired to continue in turn in similar fashion. Well-known hymns combine with new ideas and, as was earlier observed about the harper's songs, they seem to have been composed at that moment. This new synthesis is of great benefit to the worshippers, just as the harper's technique does Wilhelm good. The reference is to the Pietist movement and to the combined sermon and hymn style recommended by one of its founders.[3]

The comparison suggested here is somewhat puzzling: two men alone in a room are compared to a whole community. The link between the two is provided by the similarity in their respective methods of weaving together new and familiar material and song with the spoken word. While the hopeless tone of the harper's song admits of no solution or escape, perhaps the membership in a community is being put forward as a possible temporary solace.

[2] The analysis of solitude was a favorite topic for contemporary popular philosophers. In particular, Johann Georg Zimmermann, a famous doctor whom Goethe knew well, wrote three treatises on the subject, between 1756 and 1785.

[3] Count Nikolaus Ludwig von Zinzendorf (1700–1760) led the branch of Pietism which later developed into Moravianism. He recommends sung sermons in the preface to a hymn book of 1735. The reference to Pietism is made more explicit in *Wilhelm Meisters Theatralische Sendung*, Book 4, chapter 13, with the use of the term "Herrnhuter," the group with which Zinzendorf joined in 1727.

Chapter Fourteen

Wilhelm hears that Philine has taken up with the count's stable master who is dining in her room. Melina arrives with the notary and Wilhelm has to honor his promise of a loan of three hundred talers. He hears terrible howling from downstairs and finds Friedrich in a rage. Friedrich in a jealous fit has thrown a casserole at Philine and her visitor and has been ejected. He now alternates between laughter and tears. Wilhelm remembers his own reaction when Friedrich called on Philine. Only decorum prevented him from reacting in such a violent way. Encouraged by Laertes, Friedrich challenges the stable master to a duel.[1] The stable master deals sensitively with Friedrich. They will use rapiers marked with chalk and whoever has fewer chalk marks will be treated to the best wine in town by the loser.[2] The stable master wins easily, while Philine watches with a lack of interest. Friedrich tells a fanciful version of his life, but the details are not given.

Wilhelm retreats to his room. He thinks back to his optimistic striving, realizes his lack of direction and is dissatisfied. He knows he should depart. Mignon comes to attend to his hair and dispel his thoughts.[3] His unhappiness affects her too. She reacts hysterically to his decision to leave (Krauss 331). In a scene of extreme tenderness they express mutual devotion to the strains of the harper's heartfelt songs.

Wilhelm is in a divided frame of mind at the beginning of the chapter, as indeed he has been for some time. The benefits of the brief interlude with the harper are immediately undermined by a succession of alarming and emotionally charged events. His jealousy and desire in relation to Philine are reinforced through Friedrich's experience and his reaction to it. But Wilhelm must contain these feelings. His reluctance to make a loan to Melina resurfaces, but he is powerless to do anything about that either. These events solidify his resolve to depart. No sooner has Wilhelm reached his decision than Mignon's entry and display of devotion reverse it.

At each stage, one of the characters is the agent of Wilhelm's change in mood. Philine has lived up to her reputation by paying amorous atten-

---

[1] A duel would normally settle a matter of honor and was fought between two individuals according to prearranged conditions. A printed code of conduct in relation to duels could be consulted. Debates about the ethics of duels did not arise until the end of the nineteenth century.

[2] A rapier is used for fencing and is thus designed not to inflict injury. It is tipped with a leather ball.

[3] Mignon was offering to roll up Wilhelm's hair in paper so that it would be curly the next morning.

tion to the third man that day. As her name suggests, Philine personifies the love instinct, untrammeled by moral considerations (Willoughby 302). For Wilhelm, she stands for the return of his capacity for love, which he had denied ever since parting from Mariane (Gilby 139). The narrator is explicit about the way in which Friedrich symbolizes part of Wilhelm's personality: he externalizes the desire and jealousy Wilhelm himself had felt a few hours earlier and Wilhelm is ashamed. The description of Friedrich as half boy and half man aligns him with Mignon, who is half boy and half girl. Friedrich is not adult enough to conform to society's norms and restrict the expression of his feelings. Mignon also struggles to conform but is cramped and unable to communicate her growing affection for Wilhelm. In the egg dance, her limbs seemed to move mechanically; now her embrace is compared to a lock springing open. Melina is important too; with his insistent demands for the money, he stirs up Wilhelm's antagonistic feelings for the mercantile life. All these warring influences are holding Wilhelm back from his ambition to pursue art in the form of the theater in a structured way.

The chapter is a complete contrast to the peace and harmony of the previous one; the scenes described here are wonderfully theatrical. Each exciting encounter is immediately succeeded by another with amazing speed. Friedrich's demonstrative nature would make for an exhilarating series of scenes on stage, especially when Philine and the stable master receive their meal in their laps. Then the challenge followed by the duel offers moments of supreme tension and finally, after the hysteria, everything subsides into a final tender scene with Mignon, and the curtains close. But despite the prominence of action and expression in this chapter, there is much suppressed thought and feeling as well. Wilhelm spends much of his time in introspective brooding, analyzing his inclinations, trying to come to a decision and merely observing others' behavior without intervening. Just as Mignon stands at the sidelines while Friedrich rages, so Wilhelm maintains his self-control, especially in the company of Philine, in order to give the appearance of detachment. But the contradictory tendencies in Friedrich, to laughter and tears, actually express the turbulent state of Wilhelm's soul. With her final outburst, Mignon, like Friedrich, gives vent to feelings on Wilhelm's behalf. Even so, her emotions are indicated more by the gestures and involuntary movements of her body than by words. The final scene, then, exemplifies once again the general structure of the chapter: external events and the actions of others come to express Wilhelm's inner thoughts and yearnings.

In a conversation which took place in 1814, Goethe maintained that he had written the whole of the *Lehrjahre* for the sake of Mignon. The scene which concludes this chapter gives some sense of why Mignon should be considered of central importance in the novel. So far, the reader has seen her strangeness and her mostly unsuccessful attempt to overcome it. There is also a constant conflict between body and mind, so that both speaking and writing cause her great difficulty. All her efforts to bring about change seem directed towards Wilhelm, and the desire to win his approval becomes increasingly clear. Less obvious are Wilhelm's reasons for becoming so attached to Mignon. Partly the attraction comes from the masculine side to her nature, which links her to Mariane dressed as an officer. But Wilhelm has sworn off romantic attachments and Mignon, for him, does not represent an erotic interest. Her presence is not dangerous, like Philine's. The fatherly love which arose in Wilhelm after the egg dance finds its explicit expression now.

Friedrich, in his rage, acts out Wilhelm's own feelings; this is fundamental to the experience of a spectator at the theater. But, in accordance with the Aristotelian theory of drama, there must also be the moment of release, of catharsis.[4] Wilhelm does not experience this moment, even when he retreats to his room alone. It is Mignon who enables him to experience catharsis in the face of the alarming physical display of her distress. Now Wilhelm's adoption of Mignon is made explicit and their language of address changes. At the beginning of the scene, she speaks to him as "Herr" or "Lord" (not simply "Master" as proposed in the English translation) and he replies "Liebes Geschöpf" or "Dear creature" (Hörisch 76). It is language which suggests a relationship between God and a part of His creation. By the end of the episode, they are using the terms "father" and "child." The formal declaration of the nature of their relationship has a double implication for the degree of intimacy between them. They become more intimate because Mignon no longer needs to consider Wilhelm as her lord and master, but a limit is also set. The taboo of incest would not allow erotic feelings between them (Hörisch 76).

The ending of this book reverses the situation at the end of the Book One (Hass 155). There, Wilhelm had severed his ties to Mariane and believed that in doing so he was cutting himself off from his dream of a future in the theater, to return to the bourgeois world of trade. Now, he has just formed a strong bond with Mignon and, through her, with a group of people whose way of life is the very opposite of that bourgeois world.

---

[4] Catharsis is a purgation of the emotions that Aristotle describes in his *Poetics* as one of the functions of tragedy.

Book Three

Chapter One

CHAPTER AND BOOK open with an unannounced song, "Kennst du das Land?" The singer is Mignon and the words are strange; Wilhelm translates them into German. Mignon is playing a zither that was among the reclaimed theater props.[1] She puts the song's question to Wilhelm, whether he knows the country described. He thinks of Italy and she asks him to take her there, out of the cold. Melina seems transformed by receiving the costumes and props — charming and grateful. He has secured an agreement with the others to form a troupe.

The count and countess arrive soon afterwards. Philine ingratiates herself with them. They regret that the actors are German rather than French but still want them to entertain the prince. The count advises them on posture, showing surprising expertise. The pedant catches his attention and Philine recommends Wilhelm for first lover. The countess catches his eye and the count engages them at the castle. Philine receives an English hat and a silk scarf from the countess who also singles out Wilhelm in her farewell.[2]

It is remarkable that the song should appear without any context. Both Wilhelm and the reader are in the dark at first. And the narrator keeps the reader waiting even longer, by first describing the events that took place earlier in the day. The fictional editor is also present here, since the song, it is said, was first translated by Wilhelm and then printed in German. Within a dramatic context, Mignon's performance reminds the reader of a Singspiel.

---

[1] A zither is an instrument with a wooden frame, flat sounding board, and between twenty-nine and forty-two strings made of metal. The player places it on the knees or lays it on a table.

[2] As the fashion of wearing very high wigs subsided in the 1770s, the wearing of hats became more practicable. A very large style of picture hat, trimmed with a large amount of ribbon, plumes, lace and flowers arrived on the European scene from England in the 1780s.

The song consists of three stanzas of similar structure; each opens with a question and ends with a wish or, in the case of the third stanza, an exhortation. The structure is very finely crafted: in each stanza the question "Kennst du . . ." is placed at the beginning and end of the first five lines and thus provides a frame around the verse formed by this question (Kiess 72). The repeated preposition "Dahin" occurs in the same position in each stanza, with matching punctuation. The final line of the first and second stanzas is almost identical, with only one word changed: "Geliebter" becomes "Beschützer" in the second. But the third stanza has a different form in the final line. The first half of the line is descriptive; a strong caesura divides the lines and lends great emphasis to the last phrase. This phrase combines the imperative form with a strong yearning tone and the most intimate form of address: the word "Vater." The triadic structure of the whole provides for a center of gravity that coincides with the mysterious question Mignon addresses to herself, "Was hat man dir, du armes Kind, getan?" This question stands out in isolation against the descriptive context and is the only specific and subjective line in the whole song (Kiess 73).

The rhythm at the beginning of each stanza is an inverted iamb, which gives impetus and movement to the opening before settling into a more regular five-beat line. The divided fifth line is again characterized by additional stressed syllables that gain even more prominence as the line is shorter. At the end of the fifth line, an enjambment leads smoothly in each stanza to the reinstatement of the regular iambic structure in the sixth and final line.

The first two stanzas describe the goal while the third contemplates the route which will lead there. Accordingly, the first two stanzas describe Mignon's desire, whereas the third makes a much more urgent suggestion. An idyllic landscape is painted in the first stanza. Nature is undisturbed; blossom, fruit, foliage, and trees are part of the peaceful setting under a blue sky while a light wind blows. These details evoke a calm setting somewhere in southern Europe, but there are also features which point beyond the mere description of Mediterranean countryside. The description is general, constructed from topoi; the mention of more specific features is reserved for the second stanza (Kiess 73). But the song, like the novel in general, is an amalgam of the realistic and the symbolic. The myrtle is associated with Venus and the laurel with Apollo; together they suggest the gods of antiquity; the picture taken as a whole is Arcadian (Keppel-Kriems 145).[3] The impossibility of blossom and fruit being present at the same time detracts from the realism of the picture (*FA* 1413).

The second stanza moves to a specific building within the countryside given in general terms in the first stanza. The architectural features — pillars, a hall, and statues — identify it as a temple,[4] strengthening the link with antiquity and the gods symbolized in the previous stanza. But a transition from idyllic countryside to the temple is characterized by the anguished question. The visit to the temple appears to have come about as a result of some form of suffering and the gods are now to be called upon for their help (Schlaffer *Mythos,* 162). The pathetic child is placed in overpowering surroundings: the grandeur of the hall, the dazzling richness of the chamber, the imposing pillars and the inscrutable effigies of the gods.

The third stanza presents a different landscape, more northerly in aspect. Calm does not reign here and the easy, gentle tone imparted by the breeze in the first stanza has been intensified. This stanza refers to the journey and the hardships imposed by a narrow path, poor visibility in mist, and an arduous climb through cliffs. Although the mule, a beast of burden, typically belongs in the warmer climate of the Mediterranean, it also functions as a symbol of sterility and thus contributes to the aridity of the present setting. On a more generally symbolic level, Goethe uses the mention of a mountain enveloped in cloud to suggest Mount Olympus and thus continue the allusion to the gods of antiquity. Further deviations from the realist pattern occur in this stanza, as the mythical dragon lurks in caves that the very ordinary mule must pass by. The dragon represents danger but can also be linked to ancient mythology as the symbol of the god Apollo (Schlaffer *Mythos,* 162).

Increasingly, the mood of the song seems to belie the apparent optimism conveyed both by the meter and by the depiction of paradise in the opening stanza. The second stanza already suggests some inhumane act and there is a threatening aspect to the marble statues. The third stanza, although it contains the most urgent invitation, also dwells on the difficulties of the crossing, producing an ultimate unresolved tension.

Mignon reveals that she has a talent for composition and singing, and it is noteworthy that she reveals it to Wilhelm. Indeed, the whole

[3] Arcadia refers to the district of Greece whose inhabitants were primitive and given to music and dancing. The term Arcadian suggests innocence and a pastoral setting.

[4] Goethe probably had a particular building in mind: Palladio's Villa Rotunda near Venice.

song is addressed to him. In the ensuing conversation Mignon is again better able to express herself in the context of an artistic performance than in ordinary conversation.[5] The exchange comes to an abrupt halt when she declines to answer the question about whether she had ever been to Italy (Kiess 128). Her medium of communication is poetry and dance; these artistic forms depend on the involvement of the listener, reader, or spectator as interpreter. And her initial designation as a "puzzle" seems increasingly apt. In her unusual use of words, she resembles the harper, whose songs alone provide explanation.

Melina shows a more sympathetic side in this chapter, softening the criticism of his practical bent. Now he appears to be efficient, a good organizer, no longer obsessed with financial gain to the exclusion of artistic considerations. The account of his fortunes concludes with the misfortune of his wife's pregnancy, which would prevent her from appearing on the stage. The subtle reminder of Mariane's expulsion from her acting company on the same grounds is certainly intentional.

The contact with the nobility will provide a perfect opportunity for the actors to start their work. For Wilhelm's development, it offers him exposure to a higher class of society, and he has great hopes from such an association. In the history of the development of German theater, which comes to the fore at various points in the narrative, this association represents the court theater, a stage prior to the establishment of the first national theater. The count himself expresses the long-lasting veneration for the French stage which hindered the founding of a German national theater.

Philine's behavior — partly feigned and certainly demonstrative — is designed to gain attention, although she is not as effective at this as the pedant, who is in no way seeking to draw attention to himself. Wilhelm, too, is successful at arousing the countess's interest, also without any expenditure of effort. Philine's reference to Wilhelm's suitability for the part of first lover is overlaid with ironic romantic suggestions, only some of which can be conscious on her part. The gift of

---

[5] Mignon embodies the issues of the eighteenth-century debates about the origins of language. Herder wrote his prizewinning essay "Über den Ursprung der Sprache" in 1772. It puts forward the theory that poetry was the original language, a view he shares with Johann Georg Hamann (1730–1788). In his *Aesthetica in Nuce* (1762), Hamann refers to poetry as the mother tongue of mankind. There were also questions surrounding the translation or adaptation of ancient oral poetry into modern language in written form. Contributors to these questions include Lessing and others engaged in translation, such as Wieland, Uz, and Voss.

clothing, in particular the scarf, ties in with the scarf Wilhelm had given to Philine before she turned her attention first to Friedrich and then to the stable master. It also leads back to the scarf which revealed to Wilhelm that Mariane was involved with another man.

The *frisson* when Wilhelm and the countess meet is revealed in a way suited to the stage, with an obvious shyness and an awkwardness in the countess's words and gestures. These understated signs are in their way just as expressive as Mignon's recent energetic display of emotion.

Chapter Two

The count sends the baron, an enthusiastic supporter of the German stage, to discuss details with the actors.[1] He pulls out a thick book, the script of a play he wrote himself and wants them to perform. They soon discover how long and uninspiring it is.

Melina mentions that Wilhelm writes plays as well, and Wilhelm produces some works which had miraculously escaped being burned. The baron assumes Wilhelm will come to the castle as well. Wilhelm sees a number of advantages: regaining the money owed to him, getting to know more of the world, and becoming better acquainted with the countess. His thoughts pour forth in an encomium on noble birth. Melina distributes the roles.

As the actors prepare for their move to the castle, Goethe takes the opportunity of indulging in ironic observations on human nature. His first target is the baron, whose accommodating stance and extreme affability are based on his own vanity.[2] He flatters the group of actors in every way he can think of, so that they will not be able to refuse to put on the play he himself has written. The play itself is described most humorously. The physical appearance of the script alone is daunting. A list of adjectives applied to the hero adds up to nothing more than the impression that it is an extremely conventional role.[3] The whole plot is given so summarily that one can only conclude that the play contains a large amount of superfluous material. Yet the reading of the play affords

[1] The higher nobility is distinguished from the lower nobility that dates back to the medieval knights. The highest title is "Fürst," then "Graf" and then "Baron."

[2] The best-known examples of these roles are in Lessing's "Emilia Galotti" and Schiller's "Kabale und Liebe."

[3] Goethe may have had an actual play in mind: "Medon oder die Rache des Weisen" (1767) by Christian August Clodius. Goethe did not have a very high opinion of the work.

those listening plenty of time to think about themselves. Their thoughts are also summarized with playful irony. Aesthetic principles are irrelevant; those who identify roles that would allow them to shine consider the play to be very good; the others conclude just the opposite.

Melina's ambitions for power and money are again displayed; his knack for arranging a favorable deal allows him to control the others by concealing some details (Schlechta 21). As director he runs roughshod over standards and artistic integrity. Both in the role of the courtier on stage and in his assumed role as director of the group, he gives himself airs. Wilhelm indulges in his first outburst of euphoria since Book One, Chapter Fourteen, when, after a conversation with Melina, he felt moved to deliver a speech describing his understanding of a true theatrical calling. His lack of actual experience on the stage did not prevent him declaiming on the subject on that occasion. Now his topic is the aristocratic life. His motives, however, are somewhat tainted. First, he sees that he has been presented with an opportunity to further his theatrical ambitions, and secondly, he is developing a romantic interest in the countess. He tries to convince himself that this association with the nobility will give him insight into life and art, but he is mostly impressed by the gracious manners of the count and countess. His impulses are actually much less elevated than he pretends in his declamation. And so when Wilhelm opens with his well-worn rhetorical device, the effect is more like a caricature than a sincere speech.

The theatrical enterprise is getting under way at last. At the same time, life seems to be imitating art. The accepted convention of the stage is that the actors are not who they claim to be. But in this chapter, the characters seem disposed to present themselves — offstage as well — as something other than they are. Motives are consciously misrepresented and abilities are exaggerated or overestimated. There is a discrepancy between objective reality and the individual perception of it. The reader recognizes that this established feature of Wilhelm's personality is encouraged by his current situation.

Chapter Three

Fewer carriages than anticipated arrive to take them to the castle. They long to reach the fairy castle of their dreams. Wilhelm tries unsuccessfully to find a room at the inn. Impolite servants at the castle redirect them to the old castle, which is locked. The stable master sends for Philine, and after a long delay, a servant opens the building. They have no furniture or food; an attempt to start a fire in a huge fireplace fills the room with smoke. Philine sends over a dish of fruit and sweets and invites Wilhelm to the new castle. Wilhelm has been avoiding Philine and refuses the invitation. Eventually they receive mattresses and messy leftover food.

This chapter contains a catalogue of disappointments, in which Nature seems to be in alignment with human indifference. The heavy rain storm is as unexpected as the offhand treatment the actors receive on their arrival. All the baron's promises of good food and fine lodging can be summed up by the experience of trying to light a fire in the palatial fireplace: the grandeur of the fireplace masks the fact that it no longer has any useful function, only a potentially harmful one for anyone who expects to put it to its intended purpose. The image of the count's castle as a fairy castle crumbles when the actors' whole experience is the exact opposite of what is supposed to happen in a fairy tale. They look up at the lit windows of the new castle, little suspecting that their own rooms will be not only unfurnished but also unlit (Braemer 170). The details of this cold reception follow in cruel sequence upon Wilhelm's exalted speech about the wonderful things one can accomplish with the advantage of high birth (Braemer 150–51). Goethe makes ironic use of Wilhelm's naïve idealism to insinuate this social critique into the novel.

Wilhelm was hesitant about joining the others in the previous chapter when the move to the castle was being discussed. He still feels as though he should maintain a certain degree of independence from them and now he looks for other quarters in order to maintain his distance. He is divided between his desire to be an actor and the knowledge that he does not in fact belong to this troupe (Minden 32). Of late, the group has been just as consumed by petty concerns as the actors associated with Mariane; Wilhelm, in his more sober moments, cannot help feeling disdain for them. The cycle of high hopes followed by disappointments, which began with Mariane, is becoming a characteristic of Wilhelm's life. The realities of the acting profession do not match up to his idealized views, and the behavior of the nobility does not meet his expectations either. The actors are more like traveling players in this chapter; they do not occupy a secure position in the employ of the nobility (Neumann 9–10).

Chapter Four

The count seems annoyed to discover how badly the actors have been treated. He takes a personal interest in each of them and makes a few jokes; the officers sent to rectify things take a great interest in the actresses. A man named Jarno accompanies the count. He seems well informed about the theater, deals with the prince's private business, and may even be his natural son. The baron warns Wilhelm against him, but Wilhelm feels drawn to him.

Melina tries to establish rules for behavior — to no avail. Wilhelm contributes to the construction of the stage, measuring[1] and ensuring that the perspective is correct.[2]

Disorder reigns among the actors; they begin behaving like children. The count, too, treats them like children and makes jokes to entertain them. Wilhelm's repeated attempts to disassociate himself from the actors is perhaps a little surprising in light of his long-held plans to become an actor or at least to join a theatrical company in some capacity. There are still signs of his bourgeois upbringing in Wilhelm's reactions to the current situation. The disorder that habitually follows in the wake of this group of actors is especially pronounced in this chapter. Disorder offends against the values inculcated in Wilhelm by his family household. Just as he could not altogether overlook the untidiness of Mariane's room, so now he does not feel he belongs to this troupe (Neumann 7). But the unsympathetic side to the actors is offset for Wilhelm by certain people at the castle: the count himself, who is clearly knowledgeable, Jarno, who also makes informed remarks, and the baron, who has a great interest in theater, albeit for the very personal reason that he wants to see his own work aired.

A new and intriguing character, Jarno, is introduced. His superior bearing, closeness to the prince, and knowledge of the world and of literature are bound to fascinate Wilhelm. Curiosity about Jarno is heightened by the baron's antipathy towards him and the suggestion that he may be a dangerous influence. The hint of illegitimacy is fascinating too and links him to other characters whose origins are unexplained or mysterious in some way. These begin with Mariane, who declined to reveal anything about her background and has now almost certainly given birth to an illegitimate child; Mignon's origins are obscure and she too avoids direct questions. In Jarno's case, however, an overlay of distinction puts an end to all questions. One of the first details about him is that he was not wearing a uniform; this sets him apart from the officers who took up with some of the actresses. It also con-

---

[1] Measuring was meant to ensure that the props and curtain would fit into the space provided. It would have been done with a flexible tape, as the German verb "abschnüren" makes clear. Metal tapes were not yet available.

[2] The point about perspective is to assure the count of the most favorable viewpoint. Goethe would have been well aware of techniques of perspective from his experience at the court theater in Weimar.

trasts with their behavior, which included disguising themselves. A further contrast emerges with Wilhelm's interest in Jarno. Wilhelm was attracted by Mariane, not least because of the officer's uniform she wore for the play. Jarno, on the other hand, is expressly not wearing an officer's uniform, contrary to expectation. Jarno impresses at once by his striking features and distinguished bearing alone.

Meanwhile, mayhem continues in the lodgings, and Melina is ineffectual in his efforts to control the troupe and their visitors. But order is established in the construction of the stage. Wilhelm contributes practical help with perspective and measuring; he alone is able to keep his eye on the artistic goal.

Chapter Five

Wilhelm is to meet the countess and read her something of his own composition; the baron suggests the epilogue. For Wilhelm, this is a tremendous opportunity: to read his work to someone outside a group of friends and without the aids to illusion available on stage. He sees it as a good omen. Wilhelm is to meet with the countess and one close friend.[1] Baroness von C** introduces him to the countess, but Philine is present as well. The countess is having her hair done, while Philine sings. Wilhelm is impatient and unable to enjoy the cup of chocolate and the rusk offered by the countess.[2] Further delays are caused by the count, some officers, and a peddler with his wares. When Wilhelm returns home after a frustrating hour, he discovers a lovely English wallet in his pocket and then the Moorish attendant of the countess brings him an embroidered vest.[3]

[1] The obvious dramatic possibilities of this scene seem to have provided the inspiration for the opening scene of Hugo von Hofmannsthal's libretto of *Der Rosenkavalier* (Bahr 71).

[2] The German "Zwieback" is dry and brittle through being baked twice, as the etymology of the word suggests. It would probably have been intended for dipping into the cup of chocolate.

[3] Moorish attendants in the European courts constituted a fashion dating back to the Renaissance. They often appear in paintings to provide a contrast to the much-admired white skin of the female subject. According to the terms of a treaty, the Dutch West Indian Company was charged with supplying young Africans to the Prussian court. Countess Karoline Henriette of Hesse-Darmstadt, the patroness of Goethe and Herder, had an African attendant (Debrunner 97).

The structure of this chapter repeats the pattern of events since the removal to the castle was first suggested. With encouragement from the baron, Wilhelm has high hopes for this opportunity to establish himself. Then, when the eagerly anticipated moment arrives, so many other events intervene that the promise is not in the end carried out. He will be called when the countess has a free morning, it is claimed, but during the morning chosen it would have been hard to fit in one more interruption. Wilhelm had been led to expect an intimate group of three, including himself, but the coming and going never ceases the whole time he is there. The sight of Philine makes his heart sink, not only because she recently displeased him, but also because she has clearly gained the countess' favor; she is performing for her at this very moment and that is something Wilhelm himself desperately wants the chance of doing. The hope of an intimate *tête à tête* vanishes completely when the count himself comes on the scene to discuss mundane matters, and when several officers follow, the picture is complete. Wilhelm has suffered a total reversal, in dramatic terms; he has been relegated from performer to spectator.

Wilhelm's disappointment is keen, partly because the baron had once again led him to expect more than he would receive. Then, throughout the scene, the tension mounts; Wilhelm thinks that if the hairdresser and Philine would only leave, his performance might begin. But he is repeatedly frustrated by every contribution to the busy atmosphere. It is not only the baron's fault for misleading him, however: Wilhelm himself is guilty of imagining the nobility to be a culturally enlightened, humane, and civilized class of society, by whom his own future success would be sealed. He has not learned the lesson of the previous disappointments, when the troupe was very shabbily treated and their hopes of luxurious lodgings and fine food dashed. Wilhelm's reading is the last thing on the countess's mind throughout this superbly staged comedy.

Goethe satirizes the elevated hair styles of the period by making it clear that the valet was a long time in completing the "construction" (Bau). And there is a great contrast between the cultured exchange Wilhelm had imagined and the empty conventions and petty concerns which actually form the chief occupations in the scene. The peddler's opening box after box of trinkets epitomizes the preoccupations of the morning. Wilhelm is being treated to the "levée" of a grand lady, such as were instituted by the French salons, only here the cultural element, the poetry reading, has been overlooked, leaving just the empty rituals. The mention of Philine leads back to the occasion on which Wilhelm had just met her and she insisted, in her flirtatious way, on styling his hair. The reader is also reminded of the scene in Book Two, Chapter Fourteen, when Mignon offers to roll up Wilhelm's hair into curls and there follows an emotional outpouring. In her case, the offer expresses true devotion to Wilhelm and her willingness to serve him. In the scene with the countess, on the other hand, hairstyling is carried out as a kind of public show, to impress onlookers with the finished product.

The first gift from the countess, the wallet, is given surreptitiously. The second, the embroidered vest, is delivered, but here again, the transaction lacks openness. Both gifts have something of the exotic about them; the wallet is not a domestic, but an English product, whereas the vest is brought by a very exotic servant. Given as well the French pretensions of the countess's chamber, it is perhaps not through these channels that a German national theater is likely to be established.

Chapter Six

The count wants a prologue performed to mark the arrival of the prince and to honor his heroic and humane highness. Personifications of his virtues are to sing his praises and decorate a bust of the prince with flowers and laurel. His initials and a coronet will shine out from this tableau. Melina will provide the verses and arrange everything with Wilhelm's help.

Wilhelm complains about the lack of artistic scope and wonders if the prince will be flattered by this display. The allegory will be farcical, as the actors have few costumes. But Wilhelm agrees to honor the enlightened prince. The baron is pleased with the plans but surprised at how little they resemble his outline. The count will have to be brought round by the ladies. Wilhelm enters the castle secretly and speaks with the ladies who are pleased with the plan, but insist on some allegorical content. Minerva should announce the arrival of the hero.[1] Wilhelm readily agrees to the bust with initials and coronet, since he is captivated by the countess's beauty. He even agrees to take on a role himself. His reluctance is overcome when the baroness describes this as a society theater.[2]

Wilhelm's experiences in this chapter form an extreme contrast to the disappointments of Chapter Five. The conflicting emotions with which he struggles in the first line of this chapter sum up this contrast; dejection and gratitude compete for the upper hand. But by the end of

[1] Minerva was the Roman goddess of war, wisdom, and all the liberal arts.

[2] A society theater is organized by amateurs and operates within a circumscribed group. Goethe himself established one soon after his arrival in Weimar (Flemming 45–69).

the chapter, things have improved considerably, as he is at last admitted to the presence of the countess in the seclusion of her chamber. The secrecy of this little adventure appeals to the ladies, and it also reminds Wilhelm of all those evenings when he used to arrange a rendezvous with Mariane. On those occasions as well, there was one other woman, Barbara, who knew about it, but Wilhelm concealed the relationship from his family and friends. A parallel situation now is bound to increase the atmosphere of romance.

The details of the production the count wants to see performed identify it as the kind of allegorical play, paying homage to an individual, which was current in Gottsched's time (*FA* 1416; Bahr 72). Wilhelm attended just such a production in Book Two, Chapter Three in the remote country setting, when the factory owner was eulogized on stage by his workers. Wilhelm objects to the genre; his own revised plans provide instead a narrative frame for the praise of the prince. His own view of the theater is that it has something to teach society; it is not society's tool (Borchmeyer 143). He does not oppose the principle of praising the prince, in fact he is honored to have the opportunity of doing so. Wilhelm's respect for the nobility remains intact, despite a number of setbacks. In fact, so strong is his admiration for the countess that he would have been prepared to give up all his aesthetic principles as well as all the details of this particular composition, if she had requested him to do so.

The countess is a somewhat remote figure; constantly accompanied by the baroness, who seems to protect her, she receives callers who come to pay their respects, but does not interact with them to any great degree. Rarely does she even speak directly (Ladendorf 48). Her feelings have to be deduced from her actions or transmitted through the baroness. Her motives for wishing to be involved with the theater are suspect; they have more to do with personal sympathies and exciting escapades than with aesthetic principles. The reader does not learn what her actual name is — part of Goethe's plan to expose and undermine the remote attitudes of the nobility is conveyed by the lack of personal names given to its representatives.

The narrator interrupts the scene in the countess's chamber to acquaint the reader with the details of Wilhelm's plan for the prologue. Wilhelm's approach to the task is less direct than the count had in mind — he has added a pastoral setting, some innocent entertainment, and plenty of action. Praise for the prince is thus placed in a context in which he is seen earning the praise. The children's game is not perhaps entirely innocent, as it involves usurping another's position; it presents a dream-like possibility for Wilhelm's relationship to the married countess.

Wilhelm's stated purpose for meeting with the ladies is to outline his plan and enlist their help in gaining the count's approval for the changes. Wilhelm's version has removed the allegories of virtues and the bust with initials and coronet. But far from convincing the ladies of the improvements, Wilhelm ends up agreeing to restore the bust, the initials of the prince, and the coronet, and to reintroduce an allegorical figure as well. By agreeing to his additions, the ladies have been able to insinuate these elements of the original back into the play. Wilhelm's feelings towards the countess and his respect for the nobility have made a subtle mockery of his aesthetic principles. On the other hand, the opportunity of discussing his plans with the countess in such an intimate setting has certainly boosted his spirits.

Chapter Seven

The action continues uninterrupted. Wilhelm has almost finished his work when he is called to the castle by the count. The baroness warns him to say very little about his play. The count is thinking about a costume for Minerva and consults several volumes, including the works of Monfaucon.[1] Surrounded by books, the count declares he has not found a true likeness. Would Wilhelm perhaps rather use Pallas, the goddess of the arts?[2] Wilhelm wants to preserve the double character of the goddess, since she will announce the arrival of a warrior. The baroness begins discussing garments; Minerva is to be played by the pregnant Madame Melina.

Mignon refuses to perform the egg dance; she does not intend to appear on stage anymore and begs Wilhelm not to appear either. But Wilhelm brushes her fears aside. Philine has gained the countess's favor and attracts attention from the men. By affecting a cool detachment, Philine finds all the weak spots of the company. The count wants to be present at a rehearsal, and has to be distracted from noticing how little of his script has remained. With the prince's arrival, the actors are ignored.

Wilhelm's enthusiasm for the arts always seems to have some kind of romantic implications. In Book One it became clear that his love for the theater was bound up with his passion for Mariane. Now he has the opportunity of composing and performing before an audience made up

---

[1] The work referred to is Bernard de Monfaucon's *L'Antiquité expliquée et representée en figures*, in fifteen volumes, which appeared between 1719 and 1724.

[2] The suggestion is that Minerva be replaced by the Greek goddess Pallas Athena, whose chief attributes are to do with warfare and victory, since the two are often compared.

of the nobility, but his enthusiasm for this sort of project waxes and wanes in accordance with the degree of favor he receives from the countess. The surreptitious visit to her chamber revives memories of his exciting nocturnal visits to Mariane.

Contact with members of the nobility is a drawing card for Wilhelm. He is willing to overlook folly to find favor in their eyes. In the previous chapter, he comes to the point of compromising his own poetic principles just to please the countess and the baroness. Towards the baroness he feels no romantic attraction; she forms part of the noble party into whose vicinity he is flattered to be invited. The count, who struck Wilhelm from the beginning as knowing a great deal about the theater, makes himself completely ridiculous in this chapter, with his dogged and fruitless search for the elusive ideal image of Minerva.

Jarno, still a shadowy figure at this stage, helps the count to look ludicrous by encouraging him in his quest. But he laughs, along with the others, at the count's implacability. And Jarno eventually joins forces with those who are planning to hoodwink the count while going against his expressed wishes in relation to the play. He also makes a strange, mysterious remark about some other court where intrigue is necessary.

The idea of incorporating Minerva into the prologue was suggested by the two ladies. But Wilhelm is able to agree to the proposal without further ado, since he has already sketched out some lines for Minerva to speak (Chapter Six). This shows that he went to the meeting in a spirit of compromise, but also that Minerva would be an acceptable allegorical figure. Now, in Chapter Seven, in the conversation with the count, Wilhelm speaks of the two natures Minerva displays. Suddenly, the theme becomes clear: Minerva is linked to Mariane, combining in her person the patron of the arts and the representative of war while Mariane embodies the theater but plays a military role on stage. For Wilhelm, both these facets of Mariane were attractive and now he is anxious to preserve both features of the Minerva/Athena cult.

Minerva is to be played by Madame Melina. It is hard to see this as anything other than a joke designed to undermine the whole occasion. Madame Melina is heavily pregnant and, as the German version makes clear, she is to play the part of the chaste goddess (Jungfrau). More satire arises from the arrangements for costumes: a dress from the countess's collection will be cut to suit Minerva, but the countess's maids are distressed. They had hoped to receive all the countess's cast-off dresses themselves.

The baroness obviously enjoys the clandestine way in which the whole affair is handled. Indeed the events are beginning to resemble a contemporary French comedy of intrigue ever more closely. Asides made to Wilhelm in the company of others, assignations under cover of night, adulation of the countess from an underling, and the plan to dupe the count all add up to a situation which could have been created by the pen of Beaumarchais.

A sobering moment comes with Mignon's refusal to perform and her warning to Wilhelm to stay away from acting. As usual, Mignon's words are cryptic, and therefore ominous, and the reader feels that Wilhelm ignores them at his peril. She tries to separate life from the theater, whereas for most of the other characters, the line between them grows increasingly indistinct. Philine, perhaps the clearest case in point, plays court jester to the countess and courtly damsel in front of everyone else. Philine is superficial, inconstant, and opportunistic, but there is nothing mysterious or sinister about her.

In the final paragraph, the picture of the nobility becomes clearer. The count, despite his interest in the rehearsal, has been delayed by other pressing matters. It dawns on him that this prologue is not in fact his own work. But all such questions are swept aside and the actors are completely banished from his mind with the approach of the really important matter: the arrival of the prince.

Chapter Eight

The prince arrives and all admire his combination of noble hero and debonair courtier.[1] The actors are to keep out of sight before the performance. It is a success, but is soon forgotten. Jarno sympathizes with Wilhelm for having to "play with empty nuts to gain empty nuts." The audience loses interest. The baron is still encouraging but admits that the prince's taste is for French theater, whereas Jarno favors English drama.

Wilhelm and the countess gaze with delight across the divide imposed by birth and station. The baroness is interested in Laertes, who becomes disillusioned at hearing the baroness compared to Circe.[2] The pedant is still the count's favorite; he has acquired a suit, watch and snuff box.[3] When the actors are invited to appear after dinner, they

---

[1] It is thought that Goethe modeled the character of the prince on Prince Heinrich von Preussen (1726–1802), who was the brother of Frederick the Great.

[2] Circe was a sorceress who welcomed newcomers to her island, but then changed them into pigs. Her tale is told in the tenth book of Homer's *Odyssey;* other sources include Ovid's *Metamorphoses*, Book Fourteen.

[3] Snuff is tobacco in powdered form which would be drawn in through the nostrils by inhaling swiftly. It was carried in a snuffbox and the snuff-taker might also make use of a snuff spoon.

seem not to notice that a pack of hunting dogs is being brought in as well. Wilhelm tries praising the French stage to the prince, to curry favor. He launches into a speech about Racine, thus preventing him from speaking to the next person as convention demands.

Jarno urges Wilhelm to read Shakespeare and lends him a couple of plays. The narrator observes that uncertainty often precedes a new stage in a person's development. A helping hand can be useful in reaching the destination. This applies to Wilhelm, for whom events do not always conform to expectations. Thinking about the positive effects of the nobility, he begins his reading of Shakespeare and is swept along by the poet's genius.

The prince, on his arrival, meets everyone's expectations — he really does embody the virtues for which he will receive praise in the prologue. Now that he is present in person, all the preparations that were building up to the performance are forgotten and nothing more is said about the potentially controversial aspects of Wilhelm's composition. The room in which the performance is to take place is described in more detail than the performance itself. It is decorated with ornate wallpapers from the previous century. The attention to wallpapers forms a subtle link with Wilhelm's father's house and with those wallpapers that came to sum up, in Wilhelm's mind, a certain bourgeois philistinism in relation to the theatrical arts. There is a suggestion here that an attitude that values trivialities and appearances more than substance is not exclusive to the bourgeoisie and can be found among the nobility as well (Minden 23). But the suggestion, along with the growing number of ironic observations about life at the castle, originates with the narrator. Wilhelm is not as perceptive about his surroundings and does not notice that the company is less culturally enlightened than he imagines them to be. He is disappointed at the rapidity with which the prologue is forgotten. There are hints that the acting could use some improvement. But there are several more indications that the actors' efforts are not taken seriously: undeserved applause gave them a false sense of their own importance; the prince attends the shows out of a feeling of obligation; Jarno prefers to play cards in the anteroom. In a kind of caricature of spectators at the theater, individual actors and actresses are invited for the honor of watching the count or countess prepare for the day. The final irony occurs when the actors achieve the particular distinction of being invited to appear as a group after dinner but have to compete against the distraction provided by a pack of hunting dogs. All these details show what Wilhelm and the other actors are not yet aware of: they are living in an illusion which is unlikely to last (Braemer 150).

Goethe uses Wilhelm's discussion of Racine as a social critique. Wilhelm is made to look foolish by following a tip for finding favor with the prince, since, not realizing that all discussions should be kept on a superficial level, he does not know that a lengthy analysis of Racine is socially unacceptable. The admiration for Racine comes as no surprise. The whole ritual at the castle is a provincial imitation of life at the French court (Borchmeyer 140). So anxious is he to pay the prince a compliment that Wilhelm does not notice he has transgressed social convention, which is far more important than anything he might have to say. This episode encapsulates the superficial pleasure-seeking which characterizes life at the castle; there seems to be little genuine interest in the art of acting, simply a desire to impress important visitors with an in-house theater (Martini 80).

The little adventure between the baroness and Laertes provides a further reinforcement of this point. She engages his affections merely so that she can indulge in some momentary titillation, and the revelation of her inconstancy is also a revelation about the general attitude at the castle. It is of a piece with the prince's inability to sustain an interest in the theatrical presentations. But the baron's unpitying description of Laertes's situation includes a reference to the gardens of the sorceress, which reminds the reader of Wilhelm's enthusiasm for Tasso's *Jerusalem Delivered* and the gardens of Armida (*FA* 1418).

Jarno, despite his double-edged comments, continues to impress Wilhelm.[4] His remark about hollow nuts is an expression of sympathy, flattering to Wilhelm, but it also contains an element of scorn by association. He insists that Wilhelm try reading Shakespeare, but speaks dismissively about the company he is keeping. Wilhelm would have liked a longer discussion with this interesting man and what the narrator presents in terms of a commonplace is actually an insight Wilhelm has gained by talking to Jarno. The image used by the narrator is of a man who falls into water when he is almost at his journey's end and needs a friend to help him out. This is compared to the state of uncertainty which precedes a new stage in an individual's intellectual development. In the present setting it relates to the occasional feelings of disappointment to which Wilhelm is subject and to the promise of a new world, which, through Jarno's intervention, may be discovered in Shakespeare.

Wilhelm and the countess continue to enjoy their escalating mutual attraction. But there are some features of their relationship that bear a

---

[4] Krehbiel suggests that Goethe's mixed reactions to Herder are reflected in Wilhelm's relationship with Jarno. It was Herder who introduced Goethe to Shakespeare.

resemblance to Wilhelm's passion for Mariane, and the reader hears an alarm bell sounding. When Wilhelm is on stage, the countess cannot take her eyes off him, just as Wilhelm used to gaze, entranced, at Mariane from the wings. The roles are reversed, but the phenomenon is the same. Infatuation makes them oblivious to their social differences, except for the fact that they refrain from displaying their affection openly. Wilhelm's secrecy about his love for Mariane also stems from a discrepancy in social class, but again the roles are reversed.

The previous chapter was almost entirely dedicated to the content of Wilhelm's prologue and to the intrigues needed to make it acceptable to the count. In Chapter Eight, on the other hand, there is no detailed description of anything the troupe presented on stage. Just as the initial aristocratic interest in a house theater seems to be waning, so the narrator steps back for a more distanced view. There are gradations of consciousness: Wilhelm does not possess the narrator's full awareness of the aristocrats' lack of true commitment to the actors, but he realizes by the end of the chapter that the way of the world is not exactly as he had imagined. The actors themselves still believe that they are the center of attraction for all visitors to the castle. The issues of the contemporary German theater are quite clearly represented in this chapter: the struggle to emerge from the stranglehold held by the French classical stage, the opposition to and then fascination with, Shakespeare, and the efforts, summed up in the baron, to have German works introduced and thus establish a national tradition.

Chapter Nine

It gradually becomes apparent that the baron favors certain members of the troupe, and exaggerated tales circulate about rivalry between the baron and other writers. A poem about this rivalry is handed around. Wilhelm claims that artistic genius is compatible with high birth. The count's theory is that it was written by the pedant, and this deepens the divisions. One night, the pedant is attacked, beaten, and covered in some kind of powder. The baron denies any part in it. Soon other activities take their attention, and the pedant has his come-uppance for wearing borrowed feathers.[1]

Wilhelm, immersed in Shakespeare, hears that a boy is being punished for breaking into the castle. The boy was wearing a wigmaker's

---

[1] The expression "borrowed feathers" refers to a fable of Aesop in which the crow dons feathers from other birds and gives itself airs, only to be made a mockery when its own dull plumage is revealed.

coat, and the powder might link him to the pedant's assailants. It turns out to be Friedrich. Wilhelm intervenes for his release and decides to take Friedrich in as the third member of the strange group he thinks of as his family.

The seeds of dissatisfaction with life in the castle become somewhat more visible now. The actors have, up till now, trusted the baron as their advocate and been prepared to overlook his vanity as well as the discomforts they have had to suffer on first arriving. Now his exercising of favoritism causes divisions among them. The poem contrasts the baron's situation with the poet's. It points out the discrepancy in social status and the differences in artistic ability. The first stanza expresses the speaker's envy for the trappings of high birth: the possession of lands, power, and steady income from taxes. The second stanza claims that the baron envies the speaker his innate intellectual gifts. The facetious solution proposed in the third stanza is that they both lay jealousy aside and accept what they are by birth. The speaker should not wish for a place among the titled and the baron should not expect a place on Mount Parnassus.[2] Criticism of the aristocracy, through the figure of the baron, has reached its polemical height (Braemer 151).

Although the poem is available in handwritten copies, its author remains unknown. This distinguishes it from the songs which appear in the novel; they are performed, and Mignon's ballad receives its written form only after Wilhelm has translated it. Other written documents also have something incomplete about them, some missing feature. First, there is the passionate letter in which Wilhelm describes to Mariane his plans for their future together. This letter could not be delivered. Then there is the note addressed to Mariane, which Wilhelm finds, but its author remains unknown to him. Finally, Wilhelm starts composing a letter to inform those at home about his progress on the journey, but finds this very difficult and is defeated by the task when he discovers he is using a sheet of paper that already has writing on the back.

Wilhelm delivers a speech suitable for the stage when he upbraids the group for taking such a pernicious delight in the poem. He himself is prepared to look on the baron with charity, especially since he has more than one reason to be grateful to him. The baron has arranged an entry into high society for him and has made possible some of Wilhelm's first acting engagements. Wilhelm also seems prepared to overlook the weaknesses of the baron's own dramatic composition and agrees to deliver the pompous speeches of the hero in the piece. This is all the more remarkable when one remembers how recently Wilhelm

[2] Mount Parnassus is a mountain in Greece, sacred to Apollo and the Muses.

expressed to the countess and the baroness his reluctance to take on any role. Indeed, the tenor of the speech he now delivers shows signs of his having been tainted by the lofty diction he was required to deliver on the stage. His speech is in defense of the baron, but it also makes a more general point about the future of German theater: unless class divisions can be abandoned, a national theater worthy of the name will never be established.

The story of the pedant's misfortunes, however, shows the nobility in a different light. Even Wilhelm, defender of the nobility, disapproves of the way the count makes fun of the baron. Just as the baron caused dissension by having favorites among the actors, now the count himself promotes the interests of his own favorite, the pedant, and causes him real harm. The account of the attack on the pedant emphasizes his coat in particular. Since it is a gift from the count, it is a symbol of unearned aristocratic favor, and there is justice served when it is soiled. The reaction of the other actors seems harsh, but the pedant's preferential treatment is completely undeserved, just as the aristocratic life of privilege is entirely unrelated to personal merit.

Injustice persists as the theme in the episode involving the boy who turns out to be Friedrich. He has been falsely accused of attacking the pedant, and the evidence rests with his coat. As it is a barber's coat, it will be liberally sprinkled with the same powder that has been mentioned as part of the preparation of Wilhelm's hairstyle. The pedant's coat serves to symbolize his undoing at the hands of the nobility, and now Friedrich's coat seems to be capable of condemning him also. The count's handling of the situation confirms the growing impression that he is keener on displays than on substance. He is more interested in the arrangements for the public flogging than on establishing for certain that the accused is guilty of the misdemeanor. The preparations for the flogging in the courtyard are parallel to the erection of the stage in the town square where Wilhelm first meets Philine and the others.

Hand in hand with injustice goes false pretense. The pedant's undoing lies with his failure to disabuse the count of his mistaken views: he does not deserve to be lionized as a talented poet and actor, but plays along and accepts what is offered. The story which gains Friedrich his release is also a fabrication, but since it will effect his escape from the clutches of the count, rather than increasing his favor with him, as in the case of the pedant, the actors can endorse it.

That Wilhelm should extend such a warm welcome to Friedrich is remarkable. At one time, they were rivals for Philine's attention; now Wilhelm invites him into his so-called family. This family is a strange collection; the other members are Mignon and the harper, and now

Friedrich is to make the third. The number three is emphasized, so that it is clear that Wilhelm does not count himself among them. The family has no mother, rather, Wilhelm is their protector. Mignon has already declared him to be her father, but the idea of the harper, an elderly man, standing in the same relation to Wilhelm gives an unstable basis to the whole (Hörisch 58).

Chapter Ten

The baroness approves of the countess's feelings for Wilhelm because she herself has attachments to men and feels the countess's disapproval. Philine hopes to regain favor in Wilhelm's eyes. The baroness makes a plan for Wilhelm to dress up as the count and enter his dressing room. She gives him a book to read, lights the Argand lamp,[1] and tells him to wait for the countess, who will be told that her husband has returned early from a trip. Instead of the countess, the count himself enters and immediately retreats. He really has returned early. Later on, the count even calls for Wilhelm to read a short story, which he does in a trembling voice.[2]

The baroness's habit of rapidly transferring her affections from one man to another is perfectly matched with her enjoyment of dressing up in a variety of disguises and mingling with the guests unnoticed. This is no doubt also behind her expressed readiness to act in one of the plays. But in a chapter dominated by the theme of costumes and disguises, it is notable that the countess now joins the other women, fictional and actual, in Wilhelm's life who choose to dress themselves as men (Bahr 77). Philine is not one of these, but her presence on this occasion is very important. The ease with which she takes the blame and the appealing way she shows readiness to change, taken together, make up a winning formula. However, the narrator observes crucially that it is Wilhelm's inexperience which leads him to trust Philine and believe her words to be sincere. A commonplace follows, which links the degree of apparent sincerity in an admission of guilt in inverse proportion to the ability to make any changes. For example, while Philine is perfectly capable of expressing remorse, she is absolutely incapable of changing.

---

[1] In 1782 the Swiss-born Aimé Argand made improvements to the design of the standard petroleum lamp, thereby increasing the intensity of the light given off.

[2] The German term "Novelle" had only recently been introduced into the German language. From the 1770s onwards, the word was adopted to refer to a short story. Goethe used the simple title *Novelle* in 1828 for a short story of his own.

Certain objects included in the preparation for Wilhelm's meeting with the countess serve to evoke his relationship to Mariane. The disguise Wilhelm puts on includes a silk dressing gown and a nightcap with a red ribbon. The dressing gown is the male version of the négligee;[3] Wilhelm has already been thinking of Mariane in her négligee and the reader remembers that both that garment and some ribbons were gifts from Norberg. Now in this anticipated moment of romantic confrontation, the ribbon is a reminder of those other clandestine meetings. Even the attention paid to the lamp, which the baroness herself lights and then extinguishes is a reminder of the nights Wilhelm would spend beside the lights in the theater when Mariane was performing. The difference now is that this whole operation has been staged; theater has entered real life. With the baroness as director, Wilhelm has been rehearsed in his part and helped into his costume. The two conspirators are both motivated by self-interest, although Wilhelm is less than fully committed to the plan. He does not want to go too far and neither does he wish to offend the countess. His ambivalence toward the countess can be extended to his attitude towards the aristocracy as a whole. Whereas the two ladies want to stage a scene which will actually draw the pair together, Wilhelm would much prefer that the scene remain an act. He has been persuaded to play the role but is not prepared for the role to become reality.

Wilhelm's mixed feelings of uncertainty and anticipation do not end when the door opens. Wilhelm does not know, and the narrator does not divulge, what goes through the count's mind, and what he thinks he sees, upon entering the room. The plan unravels with supreme irony. The pretence of the count's early return home becomes reality, and what he sees in the mirror is not his own reflection, but a fabricated *Doppelgänger*. Finally, in the last sentence, reality and illusion are once again confused: the count praises Wilhelm's tone when he reads, but it is real, not feigned emotion which causes his voice to tremble.

---

[3] The dressing gown and the négligee were loose but elegant garments worn at home but also suitable attire for receiving visitors (Yarwood 300).

Chapter Eleven

Wilhelm is overcome by enthusiasm for Shakespeare.[1] He creates characters who seem real; they are like functioning clocks made of crystal, their inner workings visible. Wilhelm is inspired to present something on stage to quench the thirst of the German public. Jarno advises him to make good use of his time and pursue an active life. He feels Wilhelm is ready for a change and mentions an advantageous opportunity, but he refers to the harper and Mignon in unflattering terms, which offends Wilhelm. At that moment, an officer rides up and greets them both. The officer mysteriously advises Wilhelm to follow Jarno's advice and then embraces him. Jarno then rides off with the officer. Wilhelm feels Jarno is incapable of true friendship. He even suspects him of writing the poem that caused the pedant so much suffering. Early one morning, Wilhelm sees a group of officers and actors applying a paste of chalk and water to their clothes to clean them.[2] He connects them with the attackers. He listens to the stories of how recruiting officers trick young men into enlisting, with false promises of excellent treatment.[3] Wilhelm thinks this must have been the opportunity Jarno had in mind.

Reading Shakespeare is a remarkable experience for Wilhelm. He refers to Shakespeare as some sort of heavenly spirit, sent to help human beings understand themselves. The plays he has read confirm all his own feelings about destiny and it is in this sense that he can exclaim, "They are not fictions!" They appeal to what he had always felt was true about human nature. The discovery of Shakespeare is like entering

---

[1] Wilhelm's enthusiasm for Shakespeare is couched in terms parallel to phrases from Herder's essay "Shakespeare" (1771). The sentiments are those of the Storm and Stress movement, as exemplified by Goethe's "Zum Schakespeares Tag" (1771), namely that Shakespeare's characters are taken from nature, a concept implying that human potential is fully realized. Shakespeare stood for a release from the classical rules of composition. The concept of "Genie" informs Shakespeare reception in Germany from Johann Georg *Hamann (Sokratische Denkwürdigkeiten* 1759) onwards.

[2] Chalk's astringent properties could be used to draw grease stains from the fabric. When the mixture and fabric had both dried, the residue would be brushed off.

[3] Armies in the eighteenth century were assembled through conscription, and controversies arose when recruiting officers crossed over into other states to conscript young men and take them back. Goethe himself was involved in opposing the plans of Frederick the Great to recruit for Prussia in Saxony-Weimar.

a new world; the characters created are lifelike and yet at the same time it is possible to see how they are constructed.

Wilhelm's enthusiasm has a familiar ring to it. It is a rehearsal, now in adult form, of his boyhood passion for the puppet theater. The awe he felt when first catching a glance of the puppets at rest, their joints and strings clearly visible, is similar to the sensation he now describes of being able to see what makes Shakespeare's characters work. When he was finally allowed to manipulate the puppets himself, Wilhelm felt that he was in a position to create a whole world, over which he would preside. And now he feels that to know Shakespeare is to enter a newly created world. Wilhelm is determined to transfer what he has read into his own life. He has reached one of those seemingly decisive stages when he thinks he sees the beckoning hand of fate. Through his reading of Shakespeare he will develop a new style of life, one which will have consequences for the nation as a whole. This is a grandiose ambition, expressed in imaginative, poetic language. The reader has by now come to recognize warning signals when Wilhelm delivers a speech of this type; subsequent developments usually uncover an irony embedded in the high-flown phrases (Gerth 108). Whether it is praise for Mariane, the vision of a national theater, or the outpouring of his idealized view of the aristocracy, the proposals contained in Wilhelm's ornamental speeches are rarely borne out by events. The narrator allows the reader to see that Wilhelm, in formulating his plans, is often deluded about what his true motives are.

The members of the nobility at the castle demonstrate at various points that they revere French classical drama and have little interest in German plays. Here again, Wilhelm's development runs parallel to the history of the stage in Germany. As a child he read Racine and Corneille, then placed his hopes in German productions and now he has overcome an initial prejudice against Shakespeare. His main objection to Shakespeare's plays was that they did not conform to the classical rules. But now that Wilhelm has read some, he embraces Shakespeare with the full ardor of the Storm and Stress movement.

Wilhelm chooses the example of a clock to express what he wants to say about Shakespeare's characters. This links the characters with the — literally mechanical — puppets. These are now the grown-up, living versions of those wooden representations. With the celebration of the poet as creator, the step has been taken from puppeteer to playwright. The image incidentally also conjures up the mechanical movements of Mignon's egg dance, which she executes as though she had been wound up like a clockwork toy.

Reading Shakespeare has made Wilhelm think about destiny and, reflecting on his own future, decide to take matters in hand. Jarno is there to offer him help; first he repeats his charge that Wilhelm is keeping company with a group of people who are unworthy of him. Next, he offers Wilhelm a way out and Wilhelm, simply as a result of the respect he feels for Jarno, reacts with gratitude. But the offer is so unclear as to be mysterious. Similarly mysterious is the warmth displayed by the other officer who appears on the scene. He sees fit to address Wilhelm, embrace him warmly like a trusted friend, and advise him. He reminds the reader of two earlier characters who appeared and disappeared in some unexplained way and went straight to the heart of the matter in their conversation. First, there is the stranger who starts speaking to Wilhelm about his grandfather's art collection and ends up discussing destiny, chance, and reason. Then there is the "country clergyman" who joins the boat trip and speaks to Wilhelm of education and destiny. None of these characters is given a name, each makes only a brief, cameo appearance, but manages to make a strong impression (Barner 90). And these strangers have a knack of passing dismaying judgment on some aspect of Wilhelm's existence. The first stranger criticizes the artistic execution of Wilhelm's favorite painting; the country clergyman dismisses puppet theaters as a silly pastime; and now Jarno, if not the nameless officer, makes wounding remarks about Mignon and the harper (Ammerlahn 1968, 106). The topic of destiny and the individual is of great interest to each of these individuals; it is also the most important question for Wilhelm and the aspect of Shakespeare's works from which he derives most profit.

Clothing is particularly emphasized in this chapter. Whereas those investigating the crime were prepared to condemn Friedrich on the strength of evidence deduced from the barber's powdery coat he was wearing, now Wilhelm sees fit to connect the officers with the attack, because he sees them applying chalk to their uniforms. In addition, Wilhelm comes to mistrust Jarno's motives in this chapter and tars the officer accompanying him with the same brush. Military uniforms then come to sum up an unreliable characteristic in the personality of the wearer. The reader cannot help thinking back to Wilhelm's attraction to Mariane in her officer's uniform and the bitterness of his subsequent sense of betrayal. The uniform ought to be a mark of discipline and integrity; the disappointment is all the greater when the wearer does not live up to this promise.

Wilhelm thinks he sees the way forward, but he is far from seeing clearly. He finds Jarno perplexing and, although willing to follow his rather ambiguous advice at first, turns against him completely when he makes cruel remarks about Mignon and the harper. Wilhelm's concluding thoughts are also ambiguous. He thanks his lucky stars for having avoided the trap of conscription set for him by Jarno, leaving out of consideration for the moment the kindness Jarno did him by lending him some Shakespeare plays to read. Having decided that the plan was to conscript him, he also thinks the unknown officer's embrace can be explained. But he does not formulate any such explanation in words. Finally, Wilhelm is in two minds about whether or not he wants the army to move on and what his feelings for the countess really are. Far from having achieved clarity of perception and purpose, inspired by Shakespeare, Wilhelm is as irresolute at the end of the chapter as he has ever been.

Chapter Twelve

The count is no longer either pedantic or imperious and asks for readings of a meditative nature. The baroness is afraid he is concealing a plan to have his revenge. She speaks to Jarno, with whom she is (discreetly) intimate. The baroness is promoting the mutual attraction between Wilhelm and the countess in order to make it less appropriate for the countess to reproach her for her own behavior.

Jarno says that the count must have thought he had seen a vision of himself, an omen of his impending death. He and the baroness start talking about premonitions, apparitions, and other similar topics, seeming skeptical. Finally the count warns Jarno, mentioning his own experience as evidence.

The army is to move on with the prince, and the count will move back into town. The actors will have to leave the castle. The countess asks Wilhelm to write out his plays for her. Wilhelm is asked to read to the ladies before a farewell dinner for the prince. Overcome by the countess's beauty, he reads poorly. Wilhelm thinks about how natural beauty can be enhanced by ornamentation and an interior monologue follows. He compares the countess with Minerva, the goddess who sprang fully armed from Jupiter's head; the goddess now before him appears to have stepped from a flower.[1]

---

[1] Minerva, the Roman goddess, is the equivalent to the Greek Athena. At Athena's birth she is said to have sprung fully armed from Zeus's head. A previous mention of the goddess occurred in Chapter Three when the count became obsessed with finding the best representation of Minerva in his library.

The countess offers Wilhelm a ring with a lock of her hair as a memento.[2] Philine compliments the countess and even suggests that the countess's heart does not belong to her husband. Wilhelm, meanwhile, has taken the countess's hand and notices his own initials on the clasp of a bracelet. Intending to kiss her hand, Wilhelm finds himself in an embrace with her instead. But fate parts them when, with a cry, the countess puts her hand to her heart.

Both the count and the countess are transformed in some way, as this chapter reports. The count's behavior since the unfortunate *Doppelgänger* episode has been completely unexpected. He seems to have undergone a complete metamorphosis, to have become, quite literally, a different person — in manner, interests, and behavior. The circumstances that brought about this change all belong to the realm of illusion and misunderstanding and yet they have produced a very real and, as it turns out, permanent transformation. The scene was staged in order to encourage certain feelings in the countess, and the count's absence was crucial to the plan. The charade of dressing Wilhelm up was never intended for the count's eyes; what the count saw was in fact not a person at all, but a reflection in the mirror; and his interpretation of the experience as a warning of his imminent demise arose from pure superstition (Neumann 63). He was even induced to reveal his experience to Jarno because Jarno and the baroness manipulated conversations to introduce certain topics and then pretended to adopt points of view they did not really hold.

The count's alteration has entirely to do with the inner man and his manner of interaction with others. He has abandoned his pedantic, officious, jocular, and tiresome "real self" for a meditative, withdrawn, and calm persona. The baroness naturally thinks that this must be an act and that the count will eventually launch into some plot to get his own back. She is bound to be suspicious because she knows how false is the foundation of this transformation. The countess, by contrast with her husband, has effected a stunning change which is concentrated in her outward appearance. And the impact that she makes on others is the opposite of that brought about by her husband's change. In her case, the aids to beauty do not seem artificial, they merely accentuate her natural beauty and make it all the more noticeable. For all her artificiality, she seems more real, whereas in her husband's case a genuine change of heart seems feigned. Unlike the count, for whom a momen-

---

[2] It was a common custom in the eighteenth century to encase a lock a hair in a piece of jewelry; often the hair had belonged to someone now deceased whom the wearer of the jewelry was mourning.

tary glance at a reflection was enough to change his life, Wilhelm feels the urge to look directly at the countess again and again, and she returns his gaze (Neumann 64). His speech in praise of artifice is an ironic reversal of the usual topos: praising a woman's beauty because it needs no embellishment. Wilhelm's rhetorical technique is somewhat wanting as well. He uses Minerva as an *exemplum,* comparing the countess to this goddess of war. The comparison is ludicrous, since the only point Wilhelm wishes to make is that the countess seems divine. None of the specific attributes of Minerva are appropriate to the countess.

The baroness and Jarno are in league; Philine works on her own. All three are bent on furthering the attraction between the countess and Wilhelm. The baroness is operating out of self-interest, but Philine's need is more straightforward. She likes to have fun and her carefree ways ignore all constraints imposed by society. Thus, Philine is not daunted by the countess's exalted position in society and makes blunt remarks to her. Her heavy hint that the countess should make her a gift is not a sign of acquisitiveness; Philine is distinguished by her marked indifference to material possessions; she can as easily cast them aside as accumulate them (Ladendorf 101). Like a stage director, she makes suggestions to Wilhelm about how he should conduct himself and instructs him to kneel on the other side of the countess and take her other hand. She also insinuates, without much subtlety, that someone other than her husband has a special place in the countess's heart. The lack of fine feeling in Philine's method nevertheless guarantees her a much greater degree of success; it is she who brings the pair together.

Jarno and the baroness enjoy themselves as well, but their fun begins in fear. The baroness is afraid that she will come to regret her role in the accidental transformation of the count. Their actions are sinister by comparison with Philine's and the results range further than they intend. Philine observes a perfectly obvious mutual attraction between Wilhelm and the countess and makes arrangements to facilitate a little fling. The baroness and Jarno operate by stealth and pretense. The scornful manner in which they speak of the count shows that their public display of respect for him is a sham. Not for the first time, the reader detects a critique of the nobility. Both the baroness and Philine are women who enjoy the company of men and fly in the face of conventional morality. But there is something slightly sordid about the way that the baroness tries to undermine the countess's purer soul, so that she is compromised and less able to criticize others. The baroness's plan to dress up Wilhelm failed in its real purpose; ironically, she comes much closer to achieving her end when she tells the countess the whole story than when she persuades Wilhelm to appear in a disguise. Merely by relating events, the baroness sets in motion the change of heart in the countess which is a necessary prerequisite for any increase in intimacy with Wilhelm (Hass 161).

Some of the countess's items of jewelry have a strong symbolic function. She gives Wilhelm a ring containing her hair and he is keen to interpret this gesture correctly. A gift of a lock of her hair is highly significant: the hair is a part of her self. It signifies her readiness to give herself to Wilhelm. A medallion bearing an image of her husband acts a reminder that there is an impediment to her relationship with Wilhelm. This contributes to a hovering atmosphere of tension and ambiguity. The moment of their coming together in complete privacy is actually occasioned by the prince's departure, which in turn triggers the count's departure, and so the moment of their union quickly becomes their moment of separation. The question about whether the initials on the clasp represent Wilhelm's name or not remains unresolved; the reason for the countess's cry is left unexplained at the close of this book.

Clothing has been an important element in recent events. When Wilhelm puts on the count's clothing he displays his positive attitude towards the aristocracy. The fact that the countess never even sees Wilhelm in her husband's clothing is symbolic of the impossibility of their relationship. The action involved in changing garments has been significant ever since Mariane introduced the theme in Book One. In a similar act, Wilhelm exchanged his own coat for Philine's hairdressing jacket just prior to embarking on a bohemian lifestyle. In this chapter, the countess's finery attracts him because he finds almost everything about the aristocracy attractive, and the countess's ornate appearance at this last meeting sums it up for him.

Wilhelm's efforts as a playwright and performer have been encouraged during the time spent in the castle. The baron was partly responsible for this, and he had his own reasons. In this chapter, Wilhelm is immensely pleased to have been asked to make a copy of his plays for the countess to keep. The narrator shifts gear at this point to designate Wilhelm's reaction as typical of any young author whose work is not yet in print. The work of producing a fair copy transports him back to the golden age before the printing press, when, the narrator wryly comments, only worthwhile manuscripts were preserved. However, the narrator issues a warning: the act of writing it out does not guarantee that the manuscript is a great work of art. The reader gathers that the romantic interest of the countess has led Wilhelm to overestimate his own talents. Wilhelm's indifference to the mistakes he makes while reading to the countess reinforces the conclusion that romantic involvement can distort aesthetic judgment.

Book Four

Chapter One

LAERTES POSES MEDITATIVELY at the window. Until recently, the army had been camped in the field, and Laertes regrets the passage of time. Philine comments maliciously on how unattractive Madame Melina looks in pregnancy. The baron passes on the count's compliments and hands Wilhelm a bag of gold coins.[1] Eventually Wilhelm accepts the money, feeling less guilty towards his family whom he has neglected. The baron wonders why a valuable object is more acceptable than a sum of money. He tells about a poet who produced some works that pleased the monarch. A messenger was sent to inquire if he would prefer a jewel as payment or money. The poet replied that he had a right to accept money from someone who had taken so much from his subjects.

Wilhelm thinks with satisfaction of his talent and of the good fortune which has accompanied him. He writes to his family of his healthy financial situation, the favor he has been shown by the aristocracy, his ability to attract women, his large circle of acquaintance, his own development, both physical and mental, and his hopes for the future. The finished product is comparable to a fata morgana.[2] Wilhelm's enthusiasm arises from the example of the noble soldiers, from Shakespeare, and from the countess's kiss. The actors are packing, and Wilhelm discovers that Ma-

---

[1] A letter from Schiller to Goethe dated February 22, 1795, expresses reservations about the first version of this episode. In the original, the money had come from the countess, and Schiller felt it was not proper for the gift to be offered or accepted, in light of their relationship. Goethe subsequently reduced the involvement of the countess to her part in the construction of the bag (Bahr 89).

[2] Fata morgana is an Italian expression that was adopted into German usage in the eighteenth century. It is entirely possible that Goethe here introduces it into German for the first time. It refers to a type of mirage commonly occurring in the Strait of Messina. Although a natural phenomenon, it is ascribed to the fairy (*fata*) by the name of Morgana. In Arthurian legend, Morgana is the sister of Arthur and a pupil of Merlin.

dame Melina has used his suitcase and that his money is at the bottom of it. Unwillingly, he has to put his things into Philine's case.

Melina wishes Mignon and the harper would adopt a more professional appearance. Philine remarks that if the harper were clean shaven, he would have to attach his beard to a string to wear it on stage. The count actually thinks the beard is false and approves of the harper's habit of wearing it all the time. The harper believes he brings bad luck, but Wilhelm is opposed to letting him leave. Based on the song "Ihm färbt der Morgensonne Licht," Wilhelm thinks the harper is burdening himself with the memory of some accidental misdeed.

As might be expected at the start of a new book, the scene is quite different from the one with which the previous book closed. There the reader was left with a puzzling incident, but it is evidently not to be explained yet. The theme of departures and leave-taking is suggested at the beginning of the chapter, with Laertes's musings prompted by the sight of an empty field where the army had camped. It continues with the gift the baron brings from the departing count and countess, and finally Wilhelm and the actors pack their belongings in preparation for the move. Philine makes her presence felt, first by cheering Laertes with the suggestion of a turn about the dance floor but then by mocking Madame Melina behind her back. She persuades Laertes to dance, but cannot cajole Wilhelm. He is still keen on maintaining his distance from her and dislikes her offer to pack his clothes in her suitcase.

Whereas in Book Three the action takes place exclusively in the present and there is no opportunity to look back and recapitulate, Wilhelm now has leisure to think about his obligations to his family. The idea arises because of Mignon, who takes an interest in his family members and asks him to tell her about them. Once again, Wilhelm relates details about his childhood and background to a young woman of whom he is very fond. The evenings spent with Mariane talking about the puppet theater are recapitulated, with variations. Mignon shares some characteristics with Mariane, including an unwillingness to divulge any personal details and a habit of wearing masculine clothing. This repetition of events and reappearance of characters happens, in varying degrees of clarity, throughout the novel. Sometimes it is the merest suggestion of something similar; at other times the characters themselves are aware of having seen a person or an object before (Storz 1976, 192–93).

Although everyone in this chapter is moving on, Wilhelm evidently has no thought of returning home. The letter he writes to his family is remarkable in that it provides so little in the way of precise information. The hazy picture he paints in the letter is an illusion, and shows how unclear he is both about his future and about the stability of his present lifestyle. The mirage described here echoes the picture Wilhelm painted in his imagination in Book One, where the haziness was a sign that the character of his relationship with Mariane was largely supplied by his own imagination (Reiss 1951, 117).

Wilhelm is also spurred to write home by receiving the bag of gold coins. Attention is drawn to the bag itself, and the reader remembers the English wallet that Wilhelm received from the countess after his disappointing visit to her chamber. Wilhelm tells the baron that he is troubled by the implications of accepting the money. However, Goethe mockingly depicts Wilhelm counting the coins as soon as he receives them. The refusal was simply a pretense and an attempt to portray himself, through the adoption of this polite etiquette, as belonging to a class closer to the nobility, one not dependent upon payment for services. Although paid for his contribution to the entertainment provided by the actors at the castle, Wilhelm still sees himself as separate from the actors with whom he is associated.

What exactly is the nature of Wilhelm's objection to receiving the money? He has an exalted view of the arts, and had imagined that, at the castle, he would have his first opportunity to show off his talents before a discriminating and cultivated audience. He was briefly discouraged on the occasion when the countess's hairdresser took up so much of her attention that there was no time left for him to read to her. Hairdressers are paid for their services, but actors and playwrights, in Wilhelm's view, are on quite another footing. They operate in a different realm and he would like this difference to be recognized. As he expressed it in his speech to Werner (Book Two, Chapter Two), the poetic art is free from the law of gravity which applies to everyday life; it is free to glide above the earth. The poet ought not to be expected to take up a trade. The offer of money establishes poetry's dependence on society and is, theoretically at least, unwelcome. But in accepting the money, Wilhelm makes reference to a higher sense of duty; in fact, he considers the world of trade in which his father is involved as considerably less worthy of esteem than the acting world he himself has entered.

Considering the position he took with the baron, Wilhelm's gloating over the gold coins is unseemly. But there is more to it. Wilhelm wants to demonstrate to his father that he has used his talent and has not simply been wasting his time. This is an allusion to the biblical parable of the talents.[3] In the parable, the slothful servant restores to his

---

[3] The story is told in Matthew 25: 14–30. A talent was a considerable amount of money, the largest unit of monetary measure used in the New Testament.

master the original amount he was given. Like the slothful servant, Wilhelm has restored to him, after the frivolity and futility of his recent adventures, the amount of money with which he set out. Goethe plays with the material so as to deliver a more ironic effect. In the parable, it is the Lord who travels abroad and the slothful servant who refuses (through fear) to add to the single talent he has been given. Wilhelm, by contrast, is the one who does the traveling in Goethe's version and who has restored to him the same amount of money he squandered. Goethe uses the parable to make a beautifully ironic comment on the bourgeois conception of the value of money.

Philine's story about the count is told to entertain the company and mock the count, yet the dramatic principle she ascribes to the count is not without its point.[4] For Wilhelm, at any rate, the identification with fictional heroes makes up most of what he likes to call his talent for acting. Right from the early days of his interest in acting, Wilhelm was preoccupied with the characters beyond their life in the puppet theater or on stage. He kept articles of clothing in his room that he could use to complete the illusion when he practiced his speeches, and when hurrying to meet his lover, he had literary lovers in mind.

Dramatic touches punctuate the chapter. Laertes strikes a pose as he stands at the window, meditating on the transitory nature of human endeavor.[5] Philine's need for entertainment comes through when she dances and sings, unaccompanied. The contrast between Wilhelm's noble refusal to take the proffered bag of money and his jubilant haste in counting the coins as soon as the baron has turned his back could be enacted in a very amusing way on stage. The harper's dark warnings are all the more striking because he is normally very economical with the spoken word. His song is separate from the chapter, since it is quoted by Wilhelm from memory. It is reproduced at the end of the chapter and its solemnity contrasts with Philine's singing at the beginning, the words of her song not being worth repeating.

The exchange between the baron and Wilhelm occupies the central position and makes up the largest portion of this chapter. It marks the break from the life led at the castle and effects a parting from the aris-

---

Although Luther uses the translation "Zentner," the English has preserved, in the word "talents," the basis of the pun which identifies economic wealth with the fullness of human potential.

[4] The Count's views are in fact a version of what Goethe himself outlines in his rules for actors (*FA* 1421).

[5] The lament about the transitoriness of human endeavor dominated the baroque period of German literature. It is usually referred to as the vanitas concept.

tocracy. But it also revives an unresolved aspect of Wilhelm's psychological make-up: the tension between his dreams and ambitions and the way of life, associated with his father, in which making money is the prime object. For all his confidence in his own strengths, Wilhelm is forced to recognize his financial dependency. And self-confidence is also the only encouragement he has to offer as reassurance for the harper. Each has a presentiment of his own destiny, but for the time being, Wilhelm's is dominant.

Chapter Two

Wilhelm is happy to share a name with Shakespeare; he has now discovered Prince Hal, with whom he identifies, since he, too, takes pleasure in the company of people below his own social status.[1] He designs a new outfit for himself — practical, but with flourishes — that includes a sash and Mariane's scarf. Philine asks for a lock of his hair, as it has been cut. Acting like Prince Hal, Wilhelm is uninhibited about such a request. But Philine is lying in wait for Wilhelm; he will need a good guardian spirit.

Wilhelm explains to the actors that those endowed with riches from birth are sometimes unable to recognize talent unaccompanied by opulence. One should pity the nobility, since immediate experience and sincere friendship are denied to them. An aristocrat can easily influence people; others have to work harder and therefore value friendship and devotion more highly. Wilhelm points to examples of truly devoted servants in Shakespeare. A person of noble birth cannot act as a true friend.

They perform a fashionable but now forgotten play, and Wilhelm stresses the importance of working together. If acting were as difficult as tight-rope walking, only the truly accomplished would dare to appear on stage. Everyone agrees, since each person is confident of being among the talented group. They agree to work together more closely and do not want a director with absolute power. The director should be voted in, with advisors forming a senate. Melina agrees to suspend his directorship and Wilhelm is elected.

Melina, in the first paragraph of the chapter, is nothing if not consistent. His miserliness contrasts with Wilhelm's plans to spend his own recently acquired money. Goethe uses a wonderfully ironic touch when

[1] Prince Hal, or as he is called in the German, Prince Harry, is the Prince of Wales in Shakespeare's *Henry IV* Parts I and II. He conducts a riotous lifestyle in the company of Falstaff and his friends. On being crowned Henry V, he coldly turns his back on his old companions.

he shows how quickly Wilhelm forgets his noble obligations to his family. But he also prepares the ground for the lordly speeches Wilhelm will soon deliver. The claim that only ordinary people, among whom Wilhelm counts himself, are capable of true devotion, becomes positively comic when viewed in the light of his own inconstancy. His lack of self-knowledge in this regard is further supported by the narrator's observation that Wilhelm's identification with Prince Hal allowed him to persist in his self-deception. A hidden irony lies in the fact that, in the end, Prince Hal is the complete opposite of a model of loyalty.

Because Wilhelm feels that the character of Prince Hal expresses his own circumstances, he wants to adopt a style of clothing that will demonstrate his present bohemian way of life. In fact, in doing so, he is not far removed from the count's opinion of what it takes to make a good actor. In designing a new outward appearance for himself, Wilhelm seems to be acting, if not living a role in his everyday life. Interestingly, the last time he did this was the time he impersonated the count. Wilhelm's unwaveringly high regard for the nobility makes it obvious that on that occasion he was acting out a desire to be assimilated into the aristocratic class. Furthermore, he believes in outward appearance as a true indicator of inner worth (Irmscher 141). Now that he has decided to be like Prince Hal, he is acting out the life of a bohemian. In both cases, the reader easily detects, as Wilhelm does not, the discrepancy between his true nature and the role he is playing. The count's view of the acting profession is inextricably bound up with his own mode of existence. Life at the castle is all to do with appearance; it consists of nothing else and this is why the count is taken in by the sight of Wilhelm, disguised and reflected in a mirror (Schlaffer *Mythos,* 89). Wilhelm, on the other hand, is not summed up by his appearance, but rather, the roles he adopts are more or less unsuccessful but necessary attempts to find his true being (Schlaffer *Mythos,* 82).

Of Wilhelm's new costume, the first garment mentioned is a vest, which evokes both the one Mariane continued to wear after her stage appearance and the embroidered vest Wilhelm received from the countess after he had been summoned to her room but never given the opportunity to read to her. The next item of note is the sash that he bought for himself — it was not simply something he found among the actors' costumes. This evokes the clothing Wilhelm collected and used to dress in when rehearsing speeches in his bedroom. The alteration made to his collar gave it the appearance of an ancient style, vaguely reminiscent of some of his early reading. The material chosen for the added pieces is muslin, the same material Norberg sent to Mariane in the parcel that arrives in the first chapter of the novel. The totemic significance of these elements is perhaps a matter for the individual interpreter, but the silk scarf that had belonged to Mariane is an explicit and tangible link. There is no mention at this stage of Wilhelm's feelings as he tied this object around his neck — whether he knotted it with nonchalance or with reverence for Mariane's memory. But because he is so self-consciously creating his own image, the scarf suggests the importance of the relationship with Mariane as a stage in his development.

The ladies heartily approve of Wilhelm's change of image. This may be a superficial judgment, or it may tie in with Wilhelm's reasons for bringing about the change. The eclectic ensemble is intended to make Wilhelm appear as belonging to the troupe. Despite his earlier attempts to keep separate from them, he now participates fully in the actors' plans, and the outfit reflects this involvement. At the same time, the components call up moments from his past, his experiences, and his reading. In this way they typify a clear structural phenomenon of the novel as a whole: Wilhelm's forward progress is marked by reprise. Set against the basic forward motion are recollections of experiences, objects seen before, and characters dimly remembered from a past encounter (Storz 1976, 191–92). And now Philine asks for a lock of Wilhelm's hair, thereby claiming for herself the same degree of intimacy expressed by the countess's gift of a ring containing woven strands of her own hair.

Wilhelm's change of wardrobe goes together with a change in behavior, but this does not mean that he has made a clear-cut decision and will now side with the actors when they lampoon the aristocracy. With an authoritative air, he defends their former benefactors against the actors' complaints. In the position he adopts, Wilhelm shows his own life to be something of a contradiction. He disassociates himself from the tendency at the castle of judging people by their title, rank, or clothing and yet Wilhelm himself plans his new outfit so that people will judge him in just this way. His moving words on the subject of loyalty among the low-born imply that he counts himself among this group. And yet he has demonstrated loyalty neither to his own family nor to the group of actors, with his intermittent efforts to maintain a distance from them.

Inspired by examples found in Shakespeare, Wilhelm expands on the loyalty of servants to their masters.[2] It is no accident that Mignon, who

---

[2] Commentators agree on three examples of devoted servants in Shakespeare's plays: Pisanio in *Cymbeline,* the Fool in *King Lear,* Adam in *As you like it.* To these may be added Tranio in *The Taming of the Shrew* and the maid in *Romeo and Juliet.*

is completely devoted to serving Wilhelm, has just come over to embrace him when Wilhelm starts on this topic. Giving her a perfunctory pat on the head, Wilhelm continues, overlooking the flesh and blood example of loyalty beside him in favor of literary characters. The reader now discovers that the satirical touches Goethe employed to show the folly and superficiality of life at the castle have not escaped some of the actors either. Wilhelm's interlocutor speaks of the favoritism, the lack of true aesthetic appreciation, and the almost decadent tendency among the aristocrats to applaud the absurd and ignore high quality.

Wilhelm's unconcern about providing food is ludicrous in its lack of appreciation for his companions' situation; they do not, after all, have the bourgeois background on which he himself can rely. But his final point is well taken: the group needs to make plans to stand on its own feet. The image of schoolchildren which he uses to emphasize this point is a subtle pastiche of Shakespeare's unwilling schoolboy in *As You Like It*.[3] Art, in the form of the impromptu play, restores harmony to the group and allows Goethe to make a disparaging remark about contemporary playwrights.

All Wilhelm's speeches in this chapter appear to be preparing the ground for his election as the first director of the troupe. He has enlightened the others about the psychological make-up of the aristocracy and now he shows his understanding of how important cooperation is for a dramatic production. The speech leads logically to the adoption of a constitution for the group, based on the model of a republic.[4] According to the new arrangements, female members of the group would also have a voice and the entire tendency is away from the autocratic directorship of Melina. Melina's attitude is described with some degree of cynicism.

[3] The speech which begins "All the world's a stage . . ." contains the lines:

> And then the whining schoolboy, with his satchel,
> And shining morning face, creeping like snail
> Unwillingly to school.

[4] The proposed model is said to be the best for good people like themselves. This formulation suggests Montesquieu's *Esprit des Lois* (1748) III, 3, where virtue is referred to as the driving force behind a republic. Goethe is not offering political theory, but simply reiterating ideas current at the time in the aftermath of the French Revolution. Kant's essay *Perpetual Theory. A Philosophical Sketch* (1795) states that a republic ensures freedom for all citizens, dependence of all upon a single common legislation, and legal equality for all. There were precedents for this type of constitution among theaters at the time, in Vienna and Mannheim.

One or two hints in this description of events seem to suggest that the idealism which moved the actors to join together in a new spirit of community is not destined to last. Some of the actors are clearly misguided in thinking they possess the requisite skill to succeed. Melina's agreement to step aside as director is only temporary; as usual, he is motivated by self-interest. Finally, the narrator describes the measures taken to introduce the new arrangements as games and ironically remarks that the actors have indulged themselves with the thought that they are pioneers for the German stage.

Chapter Three

Wilhelm offers more advice about the production of a play. He stresses the differences between the audience's attitude and the actor's. The audience may pass immediate judgment on a performance, but the actor must work hard at the text and try to understand its author. Wilhelm admits to having made the mistake of deciding the merit of Shakespeare's *Hamlet* based on the role of the eponymous hero and his soliloquies.[1] He also took the burden of Hamlet's melancholy on himself, practically becoming one with the fictional character. He was unable to regain the sense of the whole, but then searched for clues to Hamlet's character, to see what he would have been like if his father had not been killed. A sketch of his findings follows.

Hamlet was born into a regal family; this determined his early influences. He was educated in the concept of right and of princely duties and virtues and was determined to fulfill his role as ruler. His love for Ophelia arose from duty, more than from strong passion. He valued honesty and friendship. He was discriminating in the arts, abhorred tastelessness, and worked against hatred. Hamlet was detached but straightforward and balanced activity with leisure. His mood, rather than his heart, determined his joy. A good companion, Hamlet was flexible, modest, and thoughtful. He could forgive an insult, but never a serious infraction against justice.

Wilhelm now proposes that the group reread the play together and see if his views can be sustained. They all like Wilhelm's way of entering the mind of the author.

---

[1] Goethe took on the position of theater director in Weimar in 1791; in 1792 he produced *Hamlet*. It had been preceded by other German productions: as early as 1772/73, there was a production in Vienna and in 1776/77 Friedrich Ludwig Schroeder produced it in Hamburg.

Wilhelm's fascination with roles in Shakespeare continues. In view of his attraction to the nobility it is not surprising that he is drawn to the role of a prince. In the previous phase, he allowed himself to act out the part of Prince Hal in his daily life and to imagine his fellow actors as resembling the prince's companions. The identification and imitation are taken on lightly; it is a way of permitting himself some enjoyment with his companions while still maintaining a certain aloof detachment from them. The narrator speaks plainly about Wilhelm's tendency to self-delusion; with splendid irony, the very moment when Wilhelm identifies himself with the prince is when his self-delusion is most marked (Wuthenow 82). But the tone is quite different here. In the case of Hamlet, Wilhelm now insists that he should not have identified with the role; instead, he stands back from the text and analyzes Hamlet's character with a view to reproducing it when playing the part. The reader may look on this as a self-analysis, but from Wilhelm's point of view, it is a step forward in his development as an actor.

Just as Wilhelm so often seems incapable of analyzing himself accurately, so now, in his determination to maintain a distance, he becomes blind to the similarities between himself and Hamlet. Certain hints have already prepared the reader for this moment: the name Laertes is also the name of Hamlet's rival, for example. The theme of the ailing king's son, with whom Wilhelm identifies, can be applied to Hamlet as well (Bonds 102–3). Both Hamlet and Wilhelm have a talent for soliloquy. Other parallels between Hamlet and Wilhelm are revealed in subsequent chapters. But here Wilhelm is less concerned with Hamlet as an individual than with general principles for actors. His own acknowledged fault in identifying too closely with Hamlet's sufferings is mentioned in order to demonstrate the importance of considering the play as an entity (Bahr 92). Having concentrated his efforts on the hero of the piece, he found that elements in the rest of the text did not fit in with his conception. An understanding of the context of the whole has been a conscious need of Wilhelm's ever since his puppet theater days.[2] The process recommended by Wilhelm as a way out of this difficulty is to try understanding the mind of the author. In fact, Wilhelm has teased out a character study of Hamlet and a history of his development up to the point where the play takes over. Since the novel as a whole is

[2] In 1771 Goethe delivered a speech in honor of Shakespeare, "Zum Shakespeares-Tag." In it he describes the same immediate positive reaction which Wilhelm felt on beginning to read Shakespeare's plays. Goethe isolates the main point of the plays as the clash between the freedom of the individual will and the unchanging direction of the whole.

about Wilhelm's development, this parallel history of an individual cannot fail to be of interest (Bahr 93).

Enthusiasm for Shakespeare formed a significant moment in the history of German theater and Wilhelm's attitude is a reflection of this phenomenon. The availability of Shakespeare's plays allowed for Germany's liberation from the classical French stage. Goethe himself fell prey to Shakespeare's influence, and as Hamlet made almost as great an impact on society as Werther had, this tremendously popular play was the logical choice for inclusion in the novel. Yet Goethe's interest in including *Hamlet* had less to do with Shakespeare's mode of composition than with the personality of the hero (Gundolf 317).

Chapter Four

Laertes becomes the object of desire of a lady of property, but reacts coldly. Philine tells Wilhelm of the unpleasant experience that turned Laertes against women. At eighteen, he had joined a theater group and fallen in love with a girl of fourteen who was about to depart with her father. Laertes offered to marry her. While he was rehearsing, after one night of married bliss, she cuckolded him. He challenged the lover and the girl's father and received a serious wound. Father and daughter departed, leaving Laertes doubly wounded. He was treated by an incompetent surgeon and emerged with black teeth and running eyes.[1]

Melina announces the departure for the next day and Wilhelm decides to spend money on a better carriage. Unfortunately, their route will take them past a detachment of hostile soldiers. Wilhelm does not think they should change the plans, and his view prevails. On the second day, Wilhelm, Laertes, Friedrich, the harper, and Mignon go ahead on foot to a hilltop where they want to rest. Wilhelm's appearance causes surprise, Mignon carries a knife and wears a hat with Mariane's necklace. Friedrich carries Laertes's gun and the harper carries only a walking stick. They find the spot very attractive, with fine views.

Laertes's adventure with the lady of status resembles in some ways the liaison between Wilhelm and the countess. Laertes's coldness towards her is unlike Wilhelm's attitude, but it allows Philine to reveal Laertes's distressing earlier experience. Features of this story, as well, reproduce events in Wilhelm's life. Like Mariane, the girl in this story

[1] The treatment which caused these side effects was not for the flesh wound, but for venereal disease, which he had contracted from his bride. This is the meaning of the reference to the "double wound." The inexpert surgeon had given Laertes an overdose of mercury (*MA* 754).

was associated with an acting troupe. Laertes is thrown over in favor of an older man; in Wilhelm's case one can also assume that Norberg, the usurper, is older and more established than Wilhelm.

In telling Laertes's story, Philine is subtly appealing to Wilhelm. She cannot know about Mariane, but she would like to know why he continues to resist her flirtatiousness. As had happened before, discussion of seating in the carriage brings out the most salient or worst characteristics in the members of the group. The constitutional discussion also allows for a typical reaction on the part of each individual; they play out caricatures of themselves. However, in view of the democratic method employed, it is ironic that Wilhelm, as director, should so easily bend the others to his will. He argues from authority, saying that those in the know consider reports of hostile troops in the area to be exaggerated. In addition, this is a route outlined by the count and one for which their papers are made out.[2] To this, Wilhelm adds pragmatic arguments: the original route is much shorter than the proposed detour and would therefore incur fewer costs along the way.

The weapons with which they equip themselves are as varied as the individual members of the group. They include knives with double blades, intended for deer hunting, a musket, and pistols. The party that goes ahead on foot presents a motley picture in physical appearance, age, and equipment. Mignon is particularly notable; she has not stayed with the women, but has insisted on being allowed to carry her dagger and join the men. But an incongruous note is struck by the necklace adorning her hat. Combined with the hunting knife, it reinforces her androgynous nature and, through the association with Mariane, appears to be a statement of claim to Wilhelm's affections. Like an embodiment of Aphrodite, the goddess of the hunt and of love, she proudly strides alongside the others (MacLeod 102). Whereas Mignon has adopted additional symbolic objects, the harper has set out without his identifying instrument, the harp.

This short chapter sees the actors making some progress along their chosen route. It begins with the story of an adventure and ends with an idyllic scene in which the travelers reach a classic *locus amoenus* in which to rest and refresh themselves.[3] A gentle wooded slope, a group of

[2] It would have been necessary to show official papers when crossing the border of any of the numerous small principalities of which the country consisted in Goethe's day.

[3] A *locus amoenus* is a literary topos common to pastoral poetry both ancient and modern. It consists of a fictional landscape composed of standard elements including a meadow, flowers, a brook, a particular tree or group of trees, and sometimes birds.

beech trees, and a brook, combined with the distant view, contribute to the perfection of the place. The natural beauty of the spot belies the tension in the air. There is the threat of danger and Wilhelm has taken on the responsibility, on behalf of the whole group, of ignoring it. The peaceful natural scene masks the hardships visible in the distance, in the form of hills still to be crossed. On a corresponding human level, Wilhelm's reassuring words minimize the dangers of persisting along the chosen route. The advance party shows every sign of being at one with the world as they undertake their climb: Wilhelm is brisk and contented, Laertes is whistling, and the harper is the picture of peace. They are not even especially well armed: there is no mention of Wilhelm or Laertes bearing a weapon, Friedrich is carrying a gun belonging to someone else, with which he would not be familiar, and the harper carries only a walking stick. The reader does not actually know more than Wilhelm at this moment, but certain details point to a possible change in fortune ahead.

Chapter Five

Everyone is pleasantly influenced by the beautiful surroundings; they envy those whose profession allows them to spend their lives in the open air, especially gypsies.[1] The actors gather in groups in the shade. With their strange assortment of costumes and weapons, they make a picturesque and romantic scene. Wilhelm imagines himself the leader of a migrant colony and later he and Laertes start to fence, trying to make the final duel in *Hamlet* more convincing.

Suddenly a shot rings out, followed by another, and armed men rush over to the coaches. Wilhelm and Laertes drop their rapiers and take up pistols. They demand an explanation of the attackers, but receive only laconic musket fire by reply. Another group of robbers descends upon them and, although Wilhelm and Laertes defend themselves, Wilhelm loses consciousness. He has been shot in the chest by the left arm and struck by a saber on the head. He is to learn of the rest of the attack only from others' accounts.

When Wilhelm comes to, he is lying in Philine's lap, while Mignon looks on anxiously with blood-stained hair. He learns that he and Laertes were the only ones injured. Mignon had tried to stop his bleeding with her hair; it is now bound with Philine's scarf. Philine had managed to save her suitcase, but several open cases were lying in the

---

[1] Gypsies are also presented in a romantic light in Goethe's *Götz von Berlichingen*, Act 5.

meadow. Everyone had hurried to the nearest village. The harper had left his damaged instrument against a tree and gone in search of a surgeon to treat Wilhelm.

The gravity of this experience is repeatedly undermined by touches of irony in the juxtaposition and in the recounting of events. First, Wilhelm and Laertes are fencing, but they are doing so in order to prepare for a play — a group of spectators is already watching — and the intention is to make it seem as though their conflict was in earnest. With the attack, their pretense becomes a reality; what was practice for the stage turns into a rehearsal for real life; blunt rapiers are exchanged for more effective weapons.

The romantic atmosphere of the beautiful place, which spread an air of contentment over the group, is destroyed by the attack and even the physical beauty of the setting has been marred by the detritus of the ransacked belongings. The attack on Wilhelm includes a blow from a saber that splits his hat, thus destroying a part of his carefully constructed costume. When he awakes, he first notices his blood-stained clothes, seemingly of more immediate concern than the pain in his body. Wilhelm and Laertes are the only two who show bravery in the event, but they also make an error of judgment early on in asking the robbers to explain themselves in words. The narrator describes the response as "laconic" musket shots, making Laertes and Wilhelm look rather foolish.

An attack is a favorite component of the eighteenth-century adventure novel and this one has been well prepared.[2] The group is warned of potential danger on this route, although in the form of the army rather than of robbers. They express fears while discussing whether to alter their route. The beauty of the countryside ensures that they are all relaxed and contented, so that they can be caught off guard when the attack comes. The hero's temporary loss of consciousness is also a literary motif and effective dramatic device; it allows for a quick transition in the narrative and introduces variation in the narrative technique when the hero learns of the intervening events.[3] When Wilhelm awakes, it is to an almost surreal vision, with two guardian angels and a scene of destruction replacing the idyllic setting and merry company.

Mignon's hair has become blood-stained as a result of her self-sacrifice — an act that recalls, most appropriately, a scene from Tasso's *Jerusalem Delivered*, in which Erminia, finding nothing else to hand,

---

[2] The attack motif occurs in Wieland's *Don Sylvio* and *Geschichte des Agathon* and Friedrich Nicolai's *Sebaldus Nothanker*.

[3] Faust is just waking from his sleep at the opening of *Faust II*, where he finds himself in remarkably different surroundings.

uses her hair on Tancred's wound, to stop the bleeding.[4] Wilhelm's amazed reaction to finding himself alone with Philine and Mignon draws attention to these two companions (Neumann *Liebe* 50). Mignon, in her masculine clothing, shows a devotion towards Wilhelm unsullied by self-interest or romantic scheming. Philine, on the other hand, is utterly feminine and epitomizes sexual desire; all Wilhelm's attempts to avoid her have been in vain, as this scene makes clear.

The chapter takes place within the play of forces of illusion and reality (Hass 167–68). The narrator speaks for Wilhelm in describing the beautiful scene in poetic terms, and imbuing the whole with a romantic air. In his imagination, Wilhelm sees himself as the leader of this nomadic tribe; what he fails to acknowledge is that, as their self-styled leader, he alone is responsible for bringing them on this dangerous route. Then the fencing is an attempt to imitate reality more closely, while at the same time the fencing partners imagine themselves to be fictional characters in *Hamlet*. Their imitative play spills over into reality. And the attack itself is as well prepared and makes as much dramatic impact as anything a playwright might have produced.

Philine has obviously taken advantage of the situation to increase her level of intimacy with Wilhelm and a symbol of this is provided by her scarf, which she gives up for binding Wilhelm's wound. But she is also binding him to her by engineering a feeling of obligation for all the care she has provided. The final vignette is of the harp, damaged and leaning on a tree while its devoted owner goes for help on Wilhelm's behalf. The damaged harp stands out as a sad statement, in contrast with the earlier merriment. In keeping with Wilhelm's vision of himself leading a tribe, this detail is an ironic reminder of Psalm 137, which tells of the Babylonian captivity of the Israelites. They are depicted weeping by the waters of Babylon; unable to sing the Lord's song in a strange land, they hang their harps upon the willows.

[4] The scene also recalls a biblical scene: the devotion of the woman, sometimes identified as Mary Magdalene, who used her hair to dry Jesus' feet.

Chapter Six

After a long wait, a woman appears, mounted on a white horse. This "lovely Amazon" is accompanied by an older man, grooms, servants, and a troupe of hussars.[1] She rides over and inquires after the wounded man, lying in the lap of this frivolous Samaritan woman.[2] Philine cannot claim him as her husband, but uses a tone that irritates Wilhelm when describing him as a good friend. Wilhelm is very taken by this newcomer. She seems noble, charming, and sympathetic. Her form is concealed under a wide coat, cut for a man. She leads a man from one of the carriages to Wilhelm's side. His box and instrument case identify him as a surgeon and he declares that the wounds are not dangerous.

The woman expresses concern, but suggests also that her party are somehow to blame.

Meanwhile, Philine kisses the woman's hand. Wilhelm feels that Philine is unworthy to touch such a noble person. She addresses her companion as "Uncle," removes her coat, and lays it over Wilhelm. He is taken aback by the beauty she reveals and has a vision of rays of glowing light surrounding the woman's head and body. The surgeon uses a little pressure to remove the bullet, and Wilhelm faints, losing sight of the saint.

This chapter is generally regarded as pivotal: it introduces the figure of the "lovely Amazon" and it constitutes the mid-point of Wilhelm's progress (*HA* 1424). Tension and fear are increasing at the beginning of the chapter, as the three presumably await the return of the harper. Instead of the harper, they are pleasantly surprised by the arrival of the beautiful woman mounted on a white horse. This figure is an ironic inversion of the conventional knight in shining armor; a woman appears on a white steed and comes to the aid of a handsome young man in distress. The reversal is reinforced by the style of clothing she has adopted: she wears a man's coat and is referred to as the "beautiful Amazon." Indeed, she is known only by this sobriquet for some time to come.

The Amazon's entry into the narrative draws on a number of recurrent themes. This new character shares with Mariane and Mignon an androgynous aspect, reflected in her clothing. A further link to Mariane is provided by the sounds of horses and carriages that announce the Ama-

---

[1] The concept of the beautiful Amazon arose in conjunction with a review by Goethe of an anonymous work with the title *Bekenntnisse einer schönen Seele, von ihr selbst geschrieben* (1806).

[2] The reference is to the biblical story of the good Samaritan who stopped to help a wounded traveler by the wayside (Luke 10: 33–35).

zon's arrival. Similarly, Mariane's return home was eagerly anticipated by Barbara, listening for the sound of the carriages, on the first page of the novel. Wilhelm is transfixed by the sight of the Amazon, to the point where the sight of her is the only anesthetic he needs during his treatment (Larrett 37). The reader remembers how he used to gaze, transported, at Mariane while she performed on stage. Mignon too had the same effect on him when they first met in Philine's rooms: so fascinating did he find her, that Wilhelm became unaware of his surroundings.

By the end of the chapter, the Amazon's transfiguration is complete: the initial image of a knight is further embellished when she appears to Wilhelm in a vision, as a saint, with light surrounding and emanating from her. Wilhelm's reflection that Philine should not even touch the woman is a sign of her unworthiness thrown into relief through juxtaposition with a superior being. It also calls to mind the biblical account of the resurrected Christ, who told Mary Magdalene not to touch him. This detail, then, prepares the ground for the saintly designation and appearance of this new character at the end of the chapter. Her act of charity in giving up her coat to Wilhelm aligns the beautiful Amazon with the legend of Saint Martin as well (*HA* 746). But it also brings to mind the image of the Muse removing her veil in Wilhelm's adolescent poem and the coat can also be seen as the mantle of poetry (Larrett 37). The Amazon's role is thus also comparable to that of the goddess Minerva, as she appears in the prologue in honor of the prince performed in the castle (Schlaffer *Mythos*, 85). In that story, country folk come under attack and Minerva intervenes on their behalf. With Wilhelm seeing himself as the leader of the country troupe, the Amazon's complex person reflects the twin qualities bestowed on Minerva by mythology (Schings 1984, 175 n. 27).

The situation also brings to mind two of Wilhelm's early experiences. First, there is a reference to the figure of Chlorinda in Tasso's *La Gerusalemme liberata*. There, the connection between love and wounds is introduced, and a woman is clothed like a man and referred to as an Amazon. There are also links to the painting of the ailing prince, especially since Wilhelm, now lying wounded, has just been playing the part of, and identifying with, Prince Hamlet. Like Stratonike in the painting, the Amazon leans over Wilhelm, her beautiful face a picture of sympathy. In the painting, tension arises from the rivalry between father and son. Here there is tension as well and it is Wilhelm himself who encourages the reader to compare Philine and the newcomer, so that they, too, appear as rivals (Neumann *Liebe*, 47). Even the doctor from the painting is present, with his bag of instruments (Schings *Symbolik*, 165).

Philine annoys Wilhelm in this chapter, in spite of her kind act in caring for him. Her describing them as very good friends is irksome because it suggests intimacy. It also recollects her earlier behavior when she kissed him out in the street, which is when his antipathy begins. When Philine rises to kiss the hand of the Amazon, she repeats the action last performed on the countess, just before leaving her alone with Wilhelm. And Philine again makes an unfavorable impression. The link with the countess can also be seen in one other detail. The Amazon finds it hard to tear herself away from the sight of Wilhelm; one remembers the countess having eyes only for Wilhelm when he was on stage.

The pleasant hilltop meadow has become the stage for two very dramatic entrances. In the last chapter, the robbers broke in on the scene, creating havoc; here, a surreal and beautiful rescuer emerged just as suddenly from the bushes. The drama of this chapter, together with the numerous threads connecting the episode with other events and themes, contributes to its sense of special importance.[3]

Chapter Seven

The surgeon departs and the harper arrives. Some peasants construct a stretcher from twigs and boughs to carry Wilhelm. The harper pensively carries his damaged instrument, Philine's case is dragged along, Mignon dashes in front and casts longing glances back at Wilhelm. Wilhelm thinks the coat imparts an electrical warmth to his body. They arrive at the inn to find the actors disgruntled. They are packed into one small room while Madame Melina is in labor in another. They blame Wilhelm for advising them to take the dangerous route. The huntsman from the Amazon's party goes in search of other accommodation for the supposed married couple.

During his absence, the malcontents describe and exaggerate their losses, taking a perverse pleasure in seeing Wilhelm wounded. They resent Philine for saving her suitcase by shamelessly insinuating herself into the good graces of the leader of the marauders. She does not reply to the charge but simply clicks the locks of her suitcase.

---

[3] Ammerlahn lends emphasis to this view by pointing out that the chapter also occupies a central physical position, if one leaves Book Six out of the calculation (Schings *Symbolik*, 141).

Wilhelm comes round from his swoon to find that he has returned to a world in which practicalities are the most urgent consideration. The procession to the village is described in detail, including the arrangements for transporting Wilhelm and what each person carries. Meanwhile, Wilhelm himself is protected from all such concerns and inhabits a realm of his own. When they arrive at the inn to a hostile reception, there is no mention of Wilhelm's response to the accusations. The coat has kept him warm with a kind of electrical charge that affects him in a positive way, both physically and spiritually (Bahr 96). He dwells on the moment when the coat slipped from the beautiful Amazon's shoulders and in his mind's eye the surreal picture of the rays of light around her constantly repeats itself. He inhabits a quite different sphere at this moment, one in which his physical and spiritual needs have been met, for the time being at least, and he is indifferent to the needs of others. The discomfort of the others at the inn is of no concern to him. Even the narrator promotes this attitude with reference to Madame Melina's situation. She is close to being delivered of a child and there are ironic biblical echoes of the circumstances in which Christ was born. The couple is traveling; the inn is overcrowded; provision and accommodation are inadequate. And yet very little attention is drawn to the event; the others' resentments and Wilhelm's indifference form the largest part of the chapter.

Philine's plan to attach herself to Wilhelm has made some progress; she has succeeded in giving the huntsman the impression that they are married and therefore need to have a room together. But she has attracted criticism from the other actors: they resent the fact that she suffered so little from the attack as a result of the calculating use of her charms.

Morale by the end of this chapter is low, at least among the troupe members. It contrasts strongly with the heights of enjoyment they reached just prior to the attack. It also contrasts with the mood induced in Wilhelm by the beautiful Amazon's intervention. She has left a member of her party behind to ensure that Wilhelm is well cared for, and he takes on the task conscientiously, but again this is of secondary importance for Wilhelm. The Amazon's coat has a healing and protective function, as well as serving to keep the memory of the remarkable woman in the forefront of Wilhelm's mind. It protects Wilhelm from physical discomfort and cold, but it also makes him impervious to the chorus of insults aimed at him. In possession of this talisman, he has no pressing physical needs and his mind is elsewhere.

Chapter Eight

Wilhelm is weak and dreamy from loss of blood. Eventually he is able to raise his bandaged head and defend himself against the repeated and unjust criticisms with a speech. He sympathizes with the others but recalls their previous expressions of gratitude to him. The only reaction is a further rehearsal of their woes and losses. Melina is almost demented, and the situation worsens with the announcement that his wife's baby is stillborn. Wilhelm, divided between pity and irritation, launches into a second speech. He reminds them that the costumes and props are his loss, since Melina has never repaid him. In a grand gesture, he releases Melina from the debt. The laments begin again about Wilhelm and Philine and her suitcase, enviably intact. Wilhelm offers to share his belongings from the suitcase. Philine reminds Wilhelm that he will need money for his medical treatment. Wilhelm holds out his hand but no-one takes it; they are far from reconciled. The chapter closes with Philine, a study in insouciance, sitting on her case, cracking nuts.

Chaos reigns in this chapter. Wilhelm has been transported from a idyllic tableau, in which three women have been concerned with his comfort, to a scene where he cannot seem to make anyone take any notice of his injuries at all. Wilhelm considers his companions petty: they fail to show any sympathy towards him and insist on moaning about their own losses. His idealist views about the noble character of actors have been seriously undermined. Yet, despite this unpleasant insight into their characters, he feels a moral obligation to stay with them, because of the attack, and to support them a while longer (Hass 169).

Among all the losses, there is a cruel irony in the fact that the announcement of the stillbirth hardly even seems to register. The stillbirth is a grim symbol of the abortive attempt to form a company of actors who could work together. But this crucial moment of birth and death simply becomes one more in a series of mistakes.

Just as inappropriate as the petty complaints is Wilhelm's attempt to improve the actors by a speech delivered from a propped-up position in his bed of pain. His imagined role as the inspired and respected leader of a migrant colony seems almost comical now. He feels the injustice of the recriminations and is handicapped by his injury. Wilhelm has stepped from the role of charismatic leader to that of sacrificial lamb. And the suggestion made by the beautiful Amazon, that he suffered for their sake, intensifies this impression (Schings 1985, 205). The uplifting and ethereal image of the beautiful Amazon could not be more remote from the actual setting and circumstances of this chapter.

Chapter Nine

Philine and Wilhelm are to lodge with the local parson. Wilhelm's wound has opened up and been bleeding and he has developed a fever. Philine and the harper keep watch alternately but Mignon, despite her best intentions, falls asleep in the corner. Wilhelm has somewhat recovered by morning and learns that the beautiful Amazon had gone away from her estate to escape the war. The surgeon declares, after examination, that Wilhelm's wounds are not dangerous but that he needs rest.

The huntsman has left some money and paid the parson. Wilhelm is grateful towards Philine, but asks her to leave; he finds her presence disturbing. She laughs and asks why it should bother him that she is fond of him. The patient's condition improves, more due to nature than to any intervention by the surgeon.[1] Wilhelm thinks of Chlorinda and the ailing prince in the painting. He wonders if these dreams are signs of a forthcoming destiny, like seeds sprinkled by the hand of fate. He recalls the Amazon's voice and envies Philine, who kissed her hand. The episode becomes dream-like; only the coat connects Wilhelm's memory with reality. Wilhelm takes particular care of the coat; it sums up all his longing.

Wilhelm's fever, like his earlier loss of consciousness, is another sign of a transition to different surroundings. In this chapter, his thoughts are completely taken up with his experience of the beautiful Amazon. His mind transforms her memory and remembered gestures into a vision. But two features in this chapter counterbalance this tendency. The first is that Wilhelm learns a few facts about this woman: that she has an estate which she had to leave because of the war; that the man accompanying her was her uncle; and that she had left money to cover the costs incurred by Wilhelm's convalescence.[2] The second tangible evidence of her real and physical presence is the coat, which Wilhelm dons each morning with fetishistic enthusiasm. The saintly and healing qualities of the beautiful Amazon also seem to inhere in her coat (Irmscher 168). Dream world and reality alternate throughout this short chapter. The movement of these two spheres culminates in the rhetorical question Wilhelm poses: he asks whether the visions of youth and dreams are not the seeds that will someday bear fruit to be enjoyed. With this question, Wilhelm seems to recognize something the reader already knows: it belongs to the fun-

[1] The surgeon's lack of skill is not so very remarkable when one remembers that surgeons were really only glorified barbers in Goethe's day.

[2] The factor of the war, first introduced in Book Three, Chapter Eleven, is the Seven Years' War, which lasted from 1756 to 1763 (Blackall 1989, 376).

damental structure of the novel and a strong feature of his own life. In this insightful moment, he conjectures that childhood experiences grow into future directions, that images from books and paintings recur in later life, that connections between persons and clothing become ever clearer through recurrence (Neumann *Liebe*, 50). But the reader has learned caution: Wilhelm has repeatedly believed he could see the hand of fate guiding him, at times when the reader was well aware that Wilhelm's wishes and desires were not allowing him to discern the truth of the situation (Schlaffer *Mythos*, 86).

The emphasis on early impressions first arose with Wilhelm's question of Mariane about her earliest memories. The motif was reiterated when the stranger joined the party on the river and engaged Wilhelm in conversation. And now the two instances of early impressions confirmed by later experiences are those of Chlorinda in *La Gerusalemme liberata* and of the painting of the ailing prince. Tancred, too, was visited by a shimmering vision of his beloved. Light from heaven surrounds her face and enhances her charming gestures (*MA* 759).

Philine, always the actress, plays the part of Wilhelm's wife. He finds this unbearably irritating, despite a grudging feeling of gratitude towards her. He tries to buy her off with the gift of his gold watch in her suitcase. In response, she changes to the role of mother and addresses him in the familiar form, saying she knows what is best for him, as though he were a child (Hass 169).[3] But she soon returns to her coquettish self, and draws on her experience of ungrateful men. She ends with question "If I love you, what is that to you?" Her question, within the context of her short speech, combines emotion and indifference. With this formula, she keeps the memory of *Hamlet* alive, bringing to mind the hero's question "What's Hecuba to him?" This is Hamlet's reaction to the feigned and exaggerated emotion displayed by the actor performing in the play within the play.[4] When she asks this question, Philine reveals an aspect of her character that is not simply superficial (Lukács 1968, 54). It shows as well that in the transition from *Wilhelm Meister's Theatrical Calling* to

[3] The "du" form would not have been used by married couples in Goethe's time. Philine is therefore not at this moment furthering the impression that she and Wilhelm are a married couple.

[4] Philine's question also emerges from the fact that Goethe was intensively reading Spinoza when he first formulated these events for *Wilhelm Meister's Theatrical Calling*. The sentiment reflects a tenet to be found in Spinoza's *Ethics*, and it is among the lines of which Goethe was particularly fond. Spinoza warns whoever loves God, not to demand that God reciprocate that love (Spinoza, *Ethics, Demonstrated with Geometrical Order (1674)*V, 19; MA 756).

Wilhelm Meister's Apprenticeship her personality has acquired depth and resonance. For all her flightiness, Philine never becomes dispirited. Now, she shows herself capable of dogged self-denial in her very domestic devotion. Despite Wilhelm's irritation at her attempt to pass herself off as his wife, there is no suggestion of self-interest in her generous determination to nurse him back to health.

The chapter does not recount any action and yet there is plenty of motion, principally within Wilhelm's thoughts. To begin with, he succumbs to a fever. Having recovered from this, he is determined to proceed with carrying out his plans. He wants his dreams to become reality. The beautiful Amazon combines dream and reality for Wilhelm. Because she seems dreamlike, he clings to her coat. And he imagines her as the embodiment of the fictional Chlorinda. The vision and the fever, the simultaneity, as it seems to him, of present and past, the confluence of the saintly woman, Chlorinda, and the scene in the painting all nevertheless help Wilhelm to remember his plans more clearly.

Chapter Ten

Laertes pays Wilhelm a visit; he is unaware of the unpleasant scene at the inn and has recovered from his losses. Wilhelm hears entertaining anecdotes from him about the others. Laertes is critical of Madame Melina because her sole regret at the loss of her baby girl was in not being able to christen her with the name Mechthilde. Melina, it now appears, has possessed plenty of money all along and has not really needed to borrow from Wilhelm. Laertes is anxious to depart the next day and asks Wilhelm for an introduction to his friend Serlo, the director.[1]

Mignon reveals that her arm is sprained; she had tried to defend Wilhelm and been flung aside by the attackers. She did not want to involve the surgeon, who still thinks she is a boy. She is unhappy because Philine will take over the provision of Wilhelm's needs. One morning Wilhelm finds Philine asleep, draped across his bed, and finds her attractive. The actors make their requests for recommendations and traveling money. Wilhelm repeats his wish that Philine return to the company. Philine desires the return of Friedrich, who has been missing since the scene in the woods. The next morning, however, Philine is gone. Wilhelm finds he misses Philine now. Mignon steps in to attend to Wilhelm's needs.

---

[1] The character of Serlo is commonly considered to be based on the director of the Hamburg Theater, Friedrich Ludwig Schroeder (1744–1816).

Wilhelm's recovery is reflected in a chapter markedly lacking in dream sequences; he is no longer subject to feverish delusions. Instead of conjuring up the image of the beautiful Amazon, Wilhelm is entertained by stories of the quirky and small-minded behavior of the group of actors. Laertes's story about Madame Melina refers back to the occasion in Book Two, Chapter Ten when the actors ran through a play about German medieval knights and were all touched with patriotic fervor. The revelation about her husband's duplicity is a less entertaining tale, serving to bring Wilhelm down to earth to confront the mundane practical demands of his fellows.

The discovery of Mignon's injury, incurred in an attempt to protect Wilhelm, demonstrates her stoicism and propensity for self-sacrifice. She proves herself perfectly capable of caring for Wilhelm as selflessly as Philine has done. And her determination to appear as a boy even overrides her need for medical attention. The strength of her emotions rises to the surface in the description of her jealousy when she has to hold back while Philine dominates the scene. Upon being liberated, Mignon shows extreme willingness to assume her former role of attending upon Wilhelm.

Philine has indeed managed to ingratiate herself with Wilhelm by her kindness. And he even feels dangerously attracted to her, against his better judgment, when he sees her sleeping on his bed. And yet, all along, he has felt uncomfortable about accepting Philine's kindnesses, and so feels emotional conflict. Eventually, it is Philine herself who prevents any increase in his feelings for her, by leaving as soon as Wilhelm no longer needs her help.

Wilhelm's injury had two main effects. First, it isolates him from the rest of the company and signals a serious break in the spirit of cooperation required to continue as a company. The ironic side effect of this isolation is utter dependence on those who take care of him (Steer 13). This tension shows in Wilhelm's mixed feelings about Philine. The second effect is the tendency to dream, enhanced by the onset of fever. For Wilhelm, as for the ailing prince in the painting, the process of healing is intimately connected to the woman on whom his dreams are focused.

A sign of Wilhelm's increasing readiness for reintegration into society is that Laertes comes armed with more or less entertaining stories about various members of the company. This narrative bridges the distance between Wilhelm and his companions. The reader remembers Wilhelm's attempts to forge a stronger bond with Mariane by sharing an account of his childhood with her. The other event Wilhelm now hears about is Mignon's foolhardy attempt to protect him with a knife during the attack. Her resultant injury is both physical and psychological; her inability to care for Wilhelm wounds her as badly as the damage to her arm.

Wilhelm's physical healing is also an emotional healing. His suffering at the loss of Mariane has long prevented him from indulging in sensual attraction. Now he feels attracted to Philine, although it is actually under the influence of the beautiful Amazon that his emotional energies find their release (Gilby 146–47). With the departure of Philine, Mignon once again steps forward to nurse Wilhelm back to health. Similarly, Mignon first entered his life and had a positive effect on him when he had suffered emotional upheaval as well as physical illness at the loss of Mariane (Ammerlahn 1981, 25).

Chapter Eleven

The recovering patient is determined to follow his plan from now on. He wants to find and thank the Amazon for her help and then travel to his friend Serlo, the director, to see if he can place any of the actors with him. Wilhelm also wants to conclude his father's business.

Wilhelm's desire to see the beautiful Amazon grows stronger and stronger. He sends the harper to make investigations, but in vain. The harper has to return — not wanting to be taken for a Jewish spy[1] — without any olive branch to offer.[2] Wilhelm deduces that the robbers had meant to attack the Amazon's party and knew they would have valuables. It also occurs to him that she resembles the countess. The resemblance extends to their handwriting: he has found a note addressed to the Amazon's uncle in the pocket of the coat. Wilhelm is in a state of dreamy longing. Mignon and the harper sing a duet, "Nur wer die Sehnsucht kennt," that is fully consonant with his feelings. They sing of longing and suffering, and of separation from joy.

The chapter opens with Wilhelm full of plans and optimism and ends with hopelessness and longing. It begins with concrete plans and ends with dreams. His fruitless research into the family and home of the beautiful Amazon ends mysteriously. Yet it is suitable that this ethereal being is difficult to trace. Just as she disappeared when Wilhelm swooned, so, now, she has departed without being observed by anyone in the area.

---

[1] Beards were not common in the eighteenth century and were all but exclusively worn by Jews. At the harper's first appearance in Book Two, Chapter Eleven, there is speculation about whether he might be a Jew.

[2] As mentioned above, in the biblical story of Noah's Ark, the olive branch was brought back to the Ark by a dove and was taken as proof that the waters had receded from the land (Genesis 8: 8–11).

Wilhelm has now worked out that the Amazon's party was actually the robbers' target and that he and the actors were attacked by mistake. Ironically, the robbers apparently had considerable information about the direction of travel and the likely holdings of the Amazon's party, while Wilhelm is unable to find out anything at all about her. He is reduced to examining and analyzing the handwriting in a note that may not even have been written by the beautiful Amazon. The handwriting expresses a harmony that he also associates with the writer's person. The resemblance to the countess is rather fanciful and yet there are certain parallels. Both women are of a higher social station than Wilhelm and his companions, both take an active interest in Wilhelm's welfare, both are beautiful. In neither case does the reader gain any precise details about physical features, but both women gaze at Wilhelm in an intense and sympathetic manner. All Wilhelm's determination to make a fresh start has been sapped away by such thoughts, memories, and longing, and his passions are further encouraged by the song.

In *Wilhelm Meister's Theatrical Calling* it is Mignon alone who sings the song. Here, she is joined by the harper and the song is aptly called an "irregular" duet. Both Mignon and the harper have a strange and even mysterious air; they are not given to communicating in the usual way. It is thus quite appropriate that they should join together to sing a mournful song that reveals little about the cause for the sorrow.

The shape of the song is given by two joined stanzas of six lines each and the remarkably monotonous rhyme scheme consisting of an a-b rhyme throughout. This repetitive rhyme lends emphasis to the repeated experience of the singer whose subjective suffering is more real than the objectivity of the world (*HA* 749). The whole is framed, or rather formed into a circle, by the repetition of the first two lines at the end. The lament has no resolution, so that the repeated lines lead back to suggest an endless repetition. The rhythm is more notable for its clashes than for its adherence to a basic iambic structure. Strong caesuras, emphasis on the opening syllables, audible anapests, and dactyls combine forces to establish this as highly irregular verse. The curiosity of the verse form reflects the strangeness of its singers. The stanzas are perceptible as distinct and yet appear joined together as a kind of symbol for Mignon and the harper.

The two lines forming the frame open with a heavily stressed syllable immediately followed by a strong caesura, as does line seven, which opens the second stanza. The effect is of a step being taken, but haltingly. It is as though the emotion of the opening syllable must first subside before the thought to follow can be expressed (Storz 1949, 42). When it does follow, there is a remarkable lack of impact; the calmer rhythm and the repetitive rhyme express the powerlessness of the individual in the situation.

The climax of the song comes with the word "Eingeweide" in line ten. There is a sudden halt and a shift from concentration on the breadth of the distance separating the singer from the beloved to a focus on the physical sensations experienced by the singer.[3] Longing gives way to dizziness and a burning in the bowels (Kramer 239). The word "Eingeweide" itself was in fairly common usage in Goethe's day, but the echo from the language of the Old Testament is nonetheless discernible. Job and the Psalmist both refer to bowels burning, and Job's reference to God is expressed in a formula similar to line seven of the song (Keppel-Kriems 116).[4] The biblical reference links the harper with the ancient legendary figure of the bard or psalmist. But it is also a factual physical description of suffering and suppressed desire.

The juxtaposition of the song allows it to apply to Wilhelm's situation as well as to the secret, inexpressible sorrows of Mignon and the harper. The harper's habit is to start singing, unannounced, behind a closed door, and here again, the song is a background comment on Wilhelm's despondent state. It also contributes to the drama of the situation; it is as though the singers are expressing Wilhelm's thoughts by performing the song offstage (Storz 1949, 43).

Chapter Twelve

Wilhelm is unsettled and filled with longing. He needs to move on, but does not know where to go. The threads of his fate are tangled. The sound of a horse or carriage makes him start, hoping for good news. He spends his time thinking over the past. He is troubled by his failure as leader of the troupe. The narrator observes that self-regard exaggerates a person's virtues and faults. The first step in repaying the others might be achieved if he set off to join Serlo. Mignon and the harper go with him.

Wilhelm is looking for some indication from that force which he thinks of as his fate. But there are no clear signals, primarily because he is undecided in himself. Wilhelm has a tendency to elevate his inclinations to the objective level of fate; he deludes himself into thinking that the pursuit of his desires is preordained. But at the beginning of the

[3] The abruptness of this climactic change is exactly reproduced by Schubert in his solo setting of the song.

[4] In Job 16: 19, the line is, "und der mich kennt, ist in der Höhe."

chapter, he is not sure what it is that he desires. That he is looking for a sign from some external source indicates an evolving view of fate and the individual. In connection with Mariane, Wilhelm viewed fate as a solemn destiny, one that did not originate in himself (Marahrens 146). Now that he is directionless, Wilhelm finds himself desiring to see Mariane again. At first, this appears to be a curious development, occurring so soon after he has been smitten by the beautiful Amazon, and without having had any opportunity to pursue this acquaintance further. The desire for Mariane is in effect a desire to revert to that former belief in fate as a force which enters the individual's life, unbidden, from time to time. And the wish to see Werner is, similarly, a feeble wish that the concerns of his father's business would once again take over and control his life. For Wilhelm has arrived at a consciousness of his own guilt in relation to the attack on the actors. He feels responsible and remorseful in a way that his self-absorption has not allowed before.

Wilhelm has fallen into a depression in which his feelings of guilt are becoming increasingly strong. This is not the first time he has been strongly affected, both mentally and physically, by a traumatic experience. The loss of Mariane brought about a more severe version of this psychological ailment; on that occasion, it was the business trip that offered Wilhelm a way out. Now, he is again looking for a chance or a sign of destiny to help him move forward. His recognition that fate may not simply be born of his own desires, together with his almost morbid willingness to shoulder guilt, indicate that he has taken a step in the development of his subjective consciousness (Schings, *Pathologie,* 44).

The opening paragraph describes Wilhelm's restlessness, a state caused by the lack of information about how to find the beautiful Amazon. He becomes prey to a series of desires, wishing for a horse, or wings. Both these wishes indicate that he needs to be in motion, even if he does not know which direction to take. But in the imagery used to describe the workings of his individual fate, complications and obstructions are the dominant features. The threads are tangled and inextricably knotted; he feels the need to untie or cut them. This imagery fits in with the recurring emphasis on cloth and clothing and the people associated with them. So Wilhelm's restlessness and indecision also stem from the need to cut ties. The first person to introduce the textile theme was Mariane; Wilhelm would like to be free of her memory. But no sooner does this become clear than he feels a desire to see her again. His thoughts about Mariane are as unstable as his whole state of mind at the moment. Similarly, Philine is associated with certain textiles — scarves, for example, and a negligee — and in this way she holds an appeal similar to Mariane's. But Wilhelm is constantly struggling with conflicting feelings towards Philine. He oscillates between attraction and disapproval.

Amidst feelings of uncertainty and indecision, Wilhelm gives up waiting for events to take place, gathers his two reliable "family" members together, and sets off in a definite direction.

Chapter Thirteen

Wilhelm receives a warm though hesitant welcome from Serlo, who senses a distant attitude in Wilhelm's letter recommending Melina's troupe. It is as though Serlo were a distinguished person, to whom one could recommend weak actors with a clear conscience. Serlo does not think he can use them. Wilhelm wants to defend them but is to be interrupted by Aurelie, Serlo's sister.[1] They have a pleasant conversation, and Wilhelm overlooks the slight anxiety in her face. He enjoys being among knowledgeable and professional people. Inevitably, Shakespeare's plays come under discussion. Serlo wants to produce *Hamlet* and play Polonius. Once someone is found for the part of Hamlet, there will be no trouble finding an Ophelia, he says jokingly. Aurelie looks displeased but Wilhelm fails to notice.

Serlo listens to Wilhelm's interpretation of a prince who has gradually developed an inclination to carry on after his father's death. Deprived of expectations by his uncle, Hamlet becomes depressed. He feels his status is reduced and acts like a surly servant. His mother's marriage is a second blow. His sadness and meditative frame of mind are not his innate disposition. In Wilhelm's view the key to the play is that a grave responsibility is set onto the shoulders of someone to whom such actions do not come naturally. He compares Hamlet to an oak tree set in a pot meant for flowers; the roots break through and the pot falls apart.

Serlo's welcoming words, as well as containing a cynical view of the aristocracy, are tinged with criticism of his old friend. Indeed, his question as to whether Wilhelm's love for the theater is still as strong as before seems, in retrospect, to be meant ironically (Hass 171). Wilhelm appears to be the same and yet his letters show that he has changed in some respects. He is finally in the company of someone who has an equally high regard for the acting profession. But now Wilhelm's lack of frankness has been exposed: he has promoted the interests of actors

[1] Aurelie is generally considered to be based on the stepsister of Schroeder, a gifted actress by the name Charlotte Ackermann (1758–1775). At the young age of seventeen, she collapsed and died after a performance on stage.

in whom he himself has been disappointed. By way of explanation, Serlo uses the term "fate," pointing out that as a theater director, his fate is inextricably linked to public opinion. This conception of fate is much more pragmatic than Wilhelm's.

Wilhelm has not acted in good faith: he has betrayed his friendship with Serlo by recommending actors who do not meet his own idealistic requirements. He had tried to appease the actors, who felt that Wilhelm was largely responsible for their misfortune, and had succumbed to their point of view to a certain extent. His decision to journey to Serlo now stands in ironic contrast with the lofty ideals behind his first dreams of taking up the acting profession. The reader has no prior knowledge of Serlo, but it is clear that in earlier days he and Wilhelm shared the same views of the acting profession as a noble one. Serlo now enters the story and acts as a kind of yardstick: when measured against Serlo's views, the changes in Wilhelm's attitudes come into focus. So it now becomes evident that Wilhelm is content to make do with actors who do not share his vision. This is a different kind of pragmatic compromise from the one Serlo has adopted. For Serlo, a compromise has to be made with the theater-going public. In his view, the director's fate is determined by the public's approval. By contrast, the reader may recall Wilhelm's plan to educate the public taste and so influence the path of German theater.

It is indeed a stroke of fate that interrupts this slightly unpleasant conversation. The subsequent lively discussion about all aspects of the theater and then all topics of mutual interest is as therapeutic for Wilhelm's spirit as the long rest was for his injured body. For once he is not delivering a speech without any hope of an exchange of views. For all their potential disagreements, Wilhelm and Serlo are of one mind about the merits of Shakespeare's plays and both are eager to discuss and collaborate in the production of *Hamlet*.

Wilhelm now has an opportunity to continue expanding on his views about the role of Hamlet and how it should be played. In Chapter Three of this book, he related how his own interpretation of Hamlet's character had undergone changes. At first he had tried to identify with the prince, but then he went on to analyze Hamlet's personality, using whatever hints he could find about the method of the prince's upbringing and formation. He emphasized the importance, for an actor, of seeing a particular role in the context of the play as a whole. Now, in the presence of Serlo and Aurelie, Wilhelm penetrates Hamlet's psychological make-up further still.

It is already evident that in concentrating so directly on Hamlet, his upbringing, motivation, and character traits, Wilhelm is also engaged in self-analysis. In settling on an explanation and justification for Hamlet's initial deliberations and subsequent actions, he is also attempting to settle the direction of his own life. Here Wilhelm's inclination to identify with fictional figures reaches its height. Hamlet and Wilhelm share a problematic relationship to the outside world. And Wilhelm views the Hamlet figure as a paradigm of the individual's conflict with fate.[2] His ongoing attempt at self-analysis repeatedly leads Wilhelm to posit a role model. The direction in which fate will lead Wilhelm should, he feels, be circumscribed by exemplary characters whom he would like to emulate. What began with David's valor in the Old Testament story of David and Goliath and proceeded to Tancred's noble deeds has now culminated in Hamlet worship. In the previous stage of his Shakespeare enthusiasm Wilhelm had taken pleasure in noticing features of Prince Hal's dissolute behavior that resembled his own. Indeed, his Hamlet interpretation seems to have been influenced by the perspective he gained from reading about the fate of Prince Hal. Prince Hal was uneasy about succeeding to the throne, but was subsequently able to adopt a notably regal indifference to his former companions. So, now, Wilhelm sees Hamlet as having to resign himself to his fate and steel himself for action in a similar way.

In view of the crucial importance of this opportunity for Wilhelm and in view of its pivotal function within the fictional confines of the novel, it is ironic that Wilhelm's view of *Hamlet* should have had such influence on the contemporary world of letters. A. W. Schlegel first adopted the interpretation and Coleridge then propagated it in England (Mueller 198). It is also clear that Goethe himself was drawing on his own reading and dramatic experience of *Hamlet* in his position as theater director to the court in Weimar, as well as his acquaintance with Schroeder, when he formulated this interpretation. But the reader should not hastily conclude that Wilhelm's interpretation of the character of Hamlet was actually the same as Goethe's. Neither should one assume that in using Hamlet as a way of analyzing himself, Wilhelm imagines himself to be precisely like Hamlet in every respect (Bonds 103).

Wilhelm's meeting with Serlo and Aurelie provides an opportunity for some social comment. Serlo's remark about the aristocracy shows the positive and negative side of the theater's relationship to that stratum of society. On the one hand, with a satirical stroke, Goethe depicts Serlo as being slightly offended at being treated as an undiscerning

---

[2] In his essay *Zum Shakespeares-Tag* Goethe refers to this basic conflict between the individual will and the ineluctable path of fate as the fulcrum of all Shakespeare's plays.

aristocrat. On the other hand the complete dependence of actors on the patronage of the nobility is very clear.

The reader notices that Wilhelm has relaxed his high aesthetic standards to some extent, but there is also an indication that his character remains unaltered. The portrait of Aurelie is still imprecise in this chapter, so that her unexplained displeasure at the remark about Ophelia is all the more noticeable for its isolation. But Wilhelm is so taken up with his own elaboration of the character of Hamlet that he fails to notice Aurelie's reaction. Here he again displays that same tendency to become oblivious to his audience that had earlier prevented him from noticing that Mariane had slept through his account of his childhood.

Chapter Fourteen

Serlo insists on the importance of a love of music for anyone who wants to be a success on stage. An actor ought to submit the prose of the text to musical influences, and learn to deliver lines rhythmically.

Aurelie draws Wilhelm into a discussion of Ophelia. He sees her as uncomplicated, sensual, and passionate. Her passions determine her outlook to the point of danger, and her father and brother warn her of this. Aurelie tells the story of Ophelia, in heartfelt and poetic words, but Wilhelm fails to sense that some personal tragedy informs her interest. Aurelie's eyes fill with tears as she alludes to her brother's lack of sympathy. Wilhelm's sincere words are unable to stop her tears. Surprisingly, Serlo and Philine enter. Philine is restrained only until the others leave the room, then prances and giggles. She has worked out that Aurelie must have had an affair with, and been abandoned by, a nobleman. This would explain the good-looking three-year-old boy. Philine dismisses both her and Serlo as fools. She teasingly reiterates her old claim that she is in love with Wilhelm. Nevertheless, she urges him to pursue Aurelie and asks him not to spoil her chances with Serlo.

The chapter combines a number of features that may remind the reader of the theater. It begins with the entrances of several characters, and continues with a tragic outburst on the part of Aurelie during which two more characters, Serlo and Philine, intervene. Each of them provides an unwelcome interruption, for separate reasons. Aurelie finds her brother's presence disturbing; he interrupts her precisely at the moment when she is opening up to someone prepared to listen to her with sympathy. Wilhelm finds Philine's presence disturbing for the usual reason that she enjoys manipulating people, playing them off against each other, and arranging romances. It is almost as though there were stage directions instructing Serlo and Aurelie when to depart, so that Aurelie's tragedy can turn into Philine's comedy. Even Philine's theory about Aurelie's romantic history is a technique employed on the stage, whereby one character's remarks obliquely introduce someone who is about to make an appearance.

Wilhelm's speech about Hamlet has been interrupted, as the first sentence makes clear, by a musical performance. This evokes the structure of a Singspiel, a popular art form in Goethe's day, in which dialogue and song alternate. The chapter concludes with Philine providing what is essentially a summary of a Lustspiel, the dramatic form that suits Philine's outlook on life best of all (Reiss 1981, 135–36). Now that Wilhelm is in the company of knowledgeable, discerning, and above all experienced actors, this environment becomes clear: a whole spectrum of dramatic forms is enacted within the novel.

The narrative technique reflects the theater setting but it offers practical tips for actors as well. Serlo's theory of the benefits an actor can derive from music are a case in point. He represents the discipline of the dramatic art, and the people who are summoned to appear each week and perform before him are referred to as virtuosos: they have mastered and finely tuned the technique of the art form. Serlo's sister, on the other hand, represents the passion of drama, and brother and sister do not see eye to eye. Aurelie's companionship is as rewarding for Wilhelm as Serlo's because they are both experienced and well informed and this qualifies her for the status of true friendship, without the ironic overtones that so often accompany the term as it is used in the novel (Ladendorf 66). Her conversation is distinct from that of other female characters in the work, because it is just as likely to turn to an account of her sorrows as it is to focus on the analysis of a role in the play. She clearly identifies her own life story — as yet incompletely revealed — with that of the long-suffering Ophelia.

When Wilhelm first meets Aurelie, he is oblivious of her reaction to Serlo's remark about Ophelia. During the more intense conversation between Wilhelm and Aurelie, Wilhelm shows a similar insensitivity to the rawness of the emotions on display. Wilhelm, for all his acute analysis of the characters in drama, has never yet shown himself to be very perceptive in relation to people (Bonds 105). In this respect he stands in direct contrast to Aurelie whose sensitivity and depth in turn form a striking contrast to Philine's frivolity. Indeed, this scene would seem to suggest that the women cannot even bear each other's presence.

The information Philine provides is incomplete and her promise of more to come ensures continuity from this chapter to the next. She also piques Wilhelm's and the reader's interests with her speculations about Aurelie's life, even though her detective work may be as faulty and wanting as her romantic scenario is superficial. She makes clear that she already belongs in the little society made up by Serlo's troupe. In a sense this is a recurrence of the situation at the castle where Philine contrived to find her way into the favors of the countess and thus enjoyed privileges denied to the other actors. But a theater group represents the other side of the coin from the social group at the castle — they are at once more knowledgeable about the theater and less able to realize their endeavors successfully.

Chapter Fifteen

Philine has invited the actors to breakfast. They are all in good spirits, having been plied with chocolate.[1] Philine assures them there are still avenues open: she will influence the director to hire them on. The chocolate and Philine's encouraging words effect a general improvement in their view of her. When they have left, Wilhelm discovers that she would actually like them all except Laertes to leave as soon as possible. Philine tries to persuade Wilhelm to take on a role. He is divided: tempted by her flattering words, troubled by the thought that his family might be concerned about him, yet reluctant to find out if this is so.

That evening, Wilhelm is impressed by a production. Serlo's performance is arresting; his inner equilibrium spreads to the audience; his ability to disguise his art is a joy to behold.[2] Aurelie, too, puts on a moving performance to great applause. A few days later, Aurelie sends for Wilhelm. She seems feverish and wants to confide in him. Wilhelm notices the little boy, with his golden shining curls. Aurelie regrets that her sorrows inhibit her from truly appreciating him.

Aurelie tells Wilhelm her story. She lost her mother at an early age and grew up with an aunt who was a poor moral example. Aurelie now rings for an attendant to remove the boy. An elderly woman appears with a scarf tied round her face: it seems she has a toothache. To break an awkward silence, Wilhelm opens a copy of *Hamlet*. Serlo enters and points out the play's weaknesses. Wilhelm praises Hamlet for following

---

[1] The habit of drinking chocolate and the word itself originate with the Aztec Indians. In the 1500s, Spanish explorers learned of the drink, which was served cold and unsweetened among the upper classes. They took to sweetening it and serving it hot. Its popularity spread from Spain to the other courts of Europe; as the cocoa bean was very expensive it became the fashion to reserve chocolate as a drink for royal guests.

[2] Ancient poetic handbooks recommend that the artist strive to conceal the artistry; the illusion of ease is part of the art.

the dictates of his heart; although the hero himself does not formulate a plan from the beginning, the play presents one.[3] The evil influence of a misdeed spreads to include the innocent, and good deeds bring benefits to wrongdoers. Not even a spirit can deter the workings of fate, and in the end, all perish, good and bad alike. Serlo observes that Wilhelm assigns a higher role to the poet than to fate.

In the opening scene of this chapter, Philine appears in her main role — as temptress. She is buying her way back into the favors of the other actors; the sweet chocolate is washing away their resentments. Her scheme extends to flattery of Wilhelm and she dangles in front of him a prize which he does not confess to wanting. The narrator lets the reader know what Wilhelm cannot admit to himself. Having spent some time thinking about his obligations to his family, he puts off all decisions in favor of the immediate gratification of attending an evening's performance of a play. This brief moral dilemma follows directly on Philine's suggestion that Wilhelm should go on stage. Her flattering remarks revive the fundamental struggle within Wilhelm: the formation he received from his upbringing in a civilized merchant household stands opposed to the bohemian world of the stage to which he feels strongly attracted.

The play is a most rewarding experience and Wilhelm's first opportunity of watching a production by a group not obliged to travel, and working from a fixed stage (Bahr 103). Ironically, whereas Philine encourages Wilhelm to learn the craft of acting, Serlo will not permit him to see the production in its rehearsal stage. It is as though he prefers Wilhelm to think of himself as a member of the audience rather than learning practical points about the art of acting. The reader may think here of Wilhelm's boyhood experiences with the puppet theater: at first he was strictly forbidden to know anything of what went on behind the stage or how the puppets were manipulated. The mixture of awe and disillusion which Wilhelm felt on first catching a glimpse of the wonders behind the puppet stage resurfaces in his present refusal to admit to a strong desire to act on Serlo's stage.

The narrator concentrates completely on the performers, in particular Serlo and his sister. Serlo is impressively controlled and entertaining; Aurelie succeeds brilliantly in moving the audience. He represents comedy, whereas she epitomizes tragedy. The plot of the play is not recounted nor does the reader learn what type of play it is. Aurelie's performance appeals to the audience's emotions, which is

---

[3] This view parallels Polonius's renowned assertion about Hamlet: "Though this be madness, yet there is method in't" (*Hamlet* II, ii, 206).

particularly fitting, since the young woman herself is a prey to her emotions. In fact she lives at an emotional pitch where there is little to distinguish life from performance. The physical weakness to which she succumbs is a result of an emotional trauma from which she cannot recover. She does not yet fully reveal the nature of her past experiences in this chapter, but the weakness of her constitution is apparent.

Her narrative is twice interrupted by other characters, a delay tactic not unfamiliar to the world of drama. First, Aurelie is distracted when she notices that Wilhelm's attention has been drawn to the little boy. Like Philine, Wilhelm is immediately attracted to the child. Then, when Aurelie has launched into her narrative, the boy creates a disturbance and his nurse has to be called. The old woman makes the briefest of appearances and yet the reader learns, curiously, that she has a cloth tied around her jaw because of a toothache and that this makes her voice sound muffled. Such precision is surprising when one considers the brief nature of her appearance.

The chapter sees Wilhelm move from the company of Philine to the company of Aurelie, and the contrast between the two women could not be more complete (Lösch 33). Philine is a superficial, fun-loving schemer, irresistible and exasperating. Aurelie has more substance, but she is depressive, cynical, and vulnerable. Philine delights in the company of men and is inconstant with her favors. Aurelie seems made for the role of tragic heroine and yet this role may be too uncomfortably close to real life for her to accept it. The reader begins to understand why she was displeased by her brother's remark about Ophelia.

Aurelie is overcome with sorrow and unable to continue. She cannot find the words to complete her story in real life, where there is no script provided. Any chance she might have to resume the thread is lost when she and Wilhelm are again interrupted, this time by Serlo. But just before Serlo enters, Wilhelm picks up a book as a way of overcoming the silence. This Shakespeare edition, opened at *Hamlet,* is obviously the stage prop that allows the discussion to return to Wilhelm's interpretation of that play.

In between interruptions, Aurelie manages to tell Wilhelm something about her upbringing and how it has affected her way of regarding men. She clearly values Wilhelm's friendship all the more in light of her very negative view of men in general. In response to her diatribe and lament, the narrator notes that Wilhelm can think of nothing either particular or general to say. The narrator is indulging in two-fold irony here: first, Wilhelm is accepted as a confidante and is keen to fulfill this function, but when the first occasion arises, he has absolutely no resources to draw on from his general knowledge of human nature, nothing to offer by way of consolation. The next level of irony explains why: Wilhelm is just as guilty of inconstancy and arrogance as the other men Aurelie could name.

Wilhelm's interpretation of *Hamlet* extends over a number of chapters, just as his account of his childhood did. But now he has a female listener who is attentive and props herself up on her pillow to promote this alert state of mind. His opening words describe the qualities traditionally found in an admired hero, including strength of purpose and single-mindedness. He dismisses the approach of historians and philosophers.[4] Then he puts forward an interpretation that tries to encompass the difficult inconsistencies of Hamlet's nature; at the same time, Wilhelm has tailored it to satisfy his own needs (Gundolf 319). It accords with Wilhelm's view of his own life as prearranged by fatal forces whose workings he is mostly unable to glimpse (Braemer 163). In Hamlet's case, the play and its momentum determine the hero's actions and the hero himself has no plan.[5] The presence of evil and good in the unfolding of events is relegated to a position of secondary importance; there is no exact correlation between evil-doers and punishment or the innocent and reward. Fate itself determines all and the efforts of the individual hero are by no means guaranteed success (Wertheim 64).

Wilhelm sees Hamlet as a hero who, when thrown into a situation where he has to act, follows the dictates of his passions and achieves his goal. He distinguishes the play from the protagonist, maintaining that, although Hamlet did not set out with a plan, the events of the play imposed one on him. The appearance of the ghost is in vain and other circumstances are also powerless to bring about any resolution without direction from the hand of fate. Fate ordains that both the just and the unjust perish at the end.

Serlo's succinct objection to the latest installment of Wilhelm's *Hamlet* interpretation accuses him of elevating the poet to a position which is normally occupied by providence. What he describes is the view which sees the poet as a god; it is a view held by members of the

---

[4] Aristotle's *Poetics* ascribes more truth to the works of poets than to historical works.

[5] The Shakespearean corpus in general offered a more natural model which German playwrights could look to in their attempt to emerge from the domination of the classical French stage. But *Hamlet* in particular enjoyed a special status in the writings of Georg Christoph Lichtenberg, Christian Garve, and the Schlegel brothers. The interpretation of Hamlet's character offered here by Wilhelm played a catalytic role in the debate which drew the Schlegels' support and opposition from Ludwig Tieck and Friedrich Theodor Vischer.

Sturm und Drang movement who pictured the poet reproducing the outside world as an inner world. Thus the stages of Shakespeare worship through which the German world of letters passed are retraced from the particular perspective of the development of Wilhelm Meister (Gundolf 319). Serlo's objection to Wilhelm's outline of the play is based on the view that the play's concept should reflect and accord with the creation of Nature by a benevolent creator. The playwright should not usurp the role of divine providence; rather, this poetic creation should be a smaller version of the divine plan in which all things turn out for the best.[6]

Chapter Sixteen

Aurelie has reread the part of Ophelia and wants to play it, but feels the songs ought to be melancholy ballads. Wilhelm insists that they are unconscious expressions of innocent desire. His speech is interrupted by Serlo snatching up an object and hurrying out with it. Aurelie pursues him and grabs one end of the object — a dagger. Aurelie addresses the dagger, apologizing for not guarding it better, and kisses the blade. Serlo storms out and Aurelie resumes the discussion of Ophelia; she praises Wilhelm's understanding of Shakespeare but adds that he has virtually no understanding of real people. Wilhelm is aware of his lack of maturity. He asks for help in acquiring an understanding of particular individuals. Aurelie remembers being idealistic and patriotic when she first went on the stage. She describes being pursued by men in whom she had no interest. Her distaste for them became a distaste for the German nation. Aurelie tells how she agreed to marry a man who helped in the theater. When he fell ill, she cared for him, but meanwhile, she had made a new acquaintance that transformed her life. Aurelie pauses and Mignon enters, carrying an atlas. She asks strange questions in broken German, showing how difficult she finds learning. Only on the zither can she express herself. Mignon has taken to greeting Wilhelm with a passionate kiss, causing him embarrassment. He realizes she is maturing and becoming restless, and only enjoys the company of the boy, Felix. Now Aurelie wants to continue and asks Mignon to leave. She tells Wilhelm more about her lover, Lothar. They

---

[6] Lessing develops this view in his *Hamburgische Dramaturgie*, section 79.

met when he had recently returned from service in America.[1] She was slightly wary of his success with women, but he took an interest in her husband's situation and recommended a doctor. She was attracted to him both emotionally and intellectually. After her husband's death, his presence in her life embellished everything.

Under Aurelie's influence, the discussion of *Hamlet* now centers on the person of Ophelia. Aurelie's willingness to play the part of Ophelia is not a good sign. It is evident that her thoughts about the role do not arise from the same source as her brother's light-hearted remark in Chapter Thirteen, but, rather, from a deep-seated affinity with Ophelia. Her question about Ophelia's songs and whether they are out of character indicates a dangerous wish to identify her own situation with that of the tragic heroine. She pictures herself as incurably melancholy, but in full possession of her senses, and would prefer to convert the role of Ophelia to conform to her own self-image. But Wilhelm has his interpretation ready to hand and explains why Ophelia's songs must speak of her latent passions. In his enthusiasm, he expounds his views without any hesitation or curiosity about Aurelie's interest in the role. This brief exchange is an example of the very phenomenon Aurelie identified in him in the previous chapter. Wilhelm can analyze a literary type, the wronged lover, more easily than he can understand what moves the young woman in front of him.

The melodramatic scene involving Serlo, Aurelie, and the dagger shows that Serlo, for all his apparent lack of sympathy for his sister, at least senses her dangerous tendencies and acts upon them. The scene has all the dramatic features most effective on stage. Serlo pounces and Aurelie throws herself in his path; they struggle, and the blade of the dagger is brandished. In a gesture of defeat, Serlo casts the sheath to the ground. The reader is reminded that both brother and sister are accomplished actors and they know how to heighten the drama of their lives off-stage as well. The dagger lying on Aurelie's dressing-table also recalls the powder knife, with its inscription, that Philine gave to Wilhelm. In each case, the knife in a woman's possession symbolizes danger, but in different ways. Philine herself is dangerous, as Wilhelm knows. She causes distress to any man who becomes emotionally dependent upon her. Aurelie's dagger is more than a domestic implement and it suggests her self-destructive nature, reinforced by her brother's alert reaction.

---

[1] The reference is to the War of American Independence. Aurelie's lover would have served with the troops under the command of General Marquis de Lafayette (1757–1834) in North America.

To Serlo's fury, Aurelie goes on to talk of the dagger as a talisman, an object with magical powers that would bring her luck. Such perverse reasoning in the face of Serlo's obvious fears effects a realignment in the way the reader sees Aurelie. Her wild thoughts make her seem like the mad Ophelia from whom she initially wanted to preserve a distance. Indeed, Serlo, in his exasperation, claims that such talk will drive him crazy — surely not an accidental choice of words. A further sign of the growing kinship between Aurelie and the character of Ophelia is that after the excitement of this scene, Aurelie has decided to accept Wilhelm's point of view. She will uphold the author's original intention, although she insists that she is unlike Ophelia in this regard. Aurelie's analysis of Wilhelm's shortcomings is not only accurate, but also reveals something of her own principles. What she admires in Wilhelm is his capacity for sensitive analysis of a play, a capacity not arising from any breadth of experience of the world. Her own ability as an actress, on the other hand, is and must be based on her depth of experience. Wilhelm's lack of insight into the people he meets stands out in contrast to Aurelie's perceptiveness. She sums up Wilhelm's strengths and weaknesses on a short acquaintance, which she is able to do because she recognizes in him a stage she has already gone through. In relating her experiences to him, Aurelie is trying to make good the lack of worldliness she perceives in Wilhelm (Bruford 46).

Aurelie softens her criticism of Wilhelm by telling him that he will be able to learn how to develop the judgment he lacks and that he already has fullness of heart, an attribute that could not be acquired. She uses the image of a plant: Wilhelm's naiveté is like a protective covering for the bud which is his heart and the covering should not be removed too soon. This image is reminiscent of the oak tree to which Wilhelm compared Hamlet. The oak tree bursts through the small pot; Wilhelm, on the other hand, is not ready to discard his protective husk.

Much of Aurelie's story runs parallel to Wilhelm's dreams. Aurelie describes her days as an idealistic actress, and her ideals are very similar to those that moved Wilhelm to his idea of establishing a national theater. She was distressed at finding that so many male members of the audience had less than elevated views about her; it is ironic that her interlocutor is an example of a man whose admiration for an actress (Mariane) was converted into a romantic liaison. There are other parallels to Wilhelm's life: both Wilhelm's beloved Mariane and Aurelie's unnamed lover are rumored to be experienced in love; both Wilhelm and Aurelie are torn between a reverence for the theater and a disdain for those involved in it; both have experienced the life-enhancing effect of love (*FA* 1420).

More productive perhaps than these faint suggestions of a link to Mariane is the juxtaposition of Aurelie and Mignon in the present chapter. Just when Aurelie begins to lose her conversational thread she allows Mignon to come in. Mignon stands for the exact opposite of loquaciousness and her difficulty with words is reiterated at this point. Her restlessness is mentioned as well and it seems that her bodily movements mime the emotional unrest of which Aurelie speaks. As Aurelie loses sight of her narrative direction, Mignon is poring over the words and maps in an atlas (Koch 409).

Just before Aurelie breaks off from her narrative she describes how close her new relationship was and, although she is no longer speaking hysterically, the reader knows that this is not the end of the tale.

Chapter Seventeen

Wilhelm has finally called on his business contacts and fetched his letters. He is relieved to find that his father's letters are quite mild in tone. Wilhelm sends a reply, promising a detailed journal of his travels. But he is in the same situation as when, as a child, he stood on stage without a script. He has not been observing his surroundings and could only write about his thoughts and emotions.

Laertes is able to help. Laertes loves company and spends a great deal of time in coffee-houses and taverns.[1] His favorite reading matter is travel books, and he has become knowledgeable about the world. Laertes can put together a fictitious account of Wilhelm's travels if Wilhelm tells him the route. He will provide details and population statistics or invent the numbers. He will invent princes more or less praiseworthy, famous people, and a love affair with a naive and wholesome girl. The result will be a delight for Wilhelm's parents. Meanwhile, Wilhelm continues to attend the theater, enjoy the company of Serlo and Aurelie, and expand his horizons.

The chapter begins with Wilhelm in a state of apprehension. Not only does he fear a reprimand from his father for neglecting to carry out his business, but he is also aware that he has neglected his own development and that his family might perceive how immature he has remained. This consciousness may well be due to the influence of Aurelie; although mostly absent from this chapter, she had pointed out Wilhelm's unobservant attitude towards other people, and this same

[1] The eighteenth century was the heyday of the coffee house. An establishment noted for highbrow conversation, it became the gathering place for the literary intelligentsia.

character trait is behind his inattention to his surroundings on the journey. The pace here is much calmer than the feverish, restless tempo of the previous chapter (Irmscher 145). To some extent, this is a response to Wilhelm's great relief at not having had to face reprimands from his father. Instead of a tortured and emotional account from Aurelie, the chapter presents the amusing prospect of a fabricated traveler's tale. Since traveler's tales were a common and popular genre in the eighteenth century, Goethe is evidently making fun of writers who present the reader with exaggerated and invented accounts of far-off lands in the guise of nonfiction.[2]

Although this chapter also provides an intermission in the discussion of *Hamlet,* the play lingers on in the name of Wilhelm's friend Laertes. Laertes is different from Wilhelm's old friend Werner in that he does not try to persuade Wilhelm to change his ways. Instead of trying to convert Wilhelm to another point of view, Laertes becomes Wilhelm's accomplice, devoting his imagination and energy to helping Wilhelm create a written account of his travels. This will make up for Wilhelm's negligence in failing to keep any record of his progress. In both his business trip and his own private inner journey, Wilhelm really has nothing to show. And the narrator makes this shortcoming quite explicit by comparing his present situation with the occasion when, as a boy, Wilhelm was embarrassed by a lack of script when he appeared on his makeshift stage. The reader recalls that Wilhelm vowed, at the time, never to be caught in such a situation again. There is irony in this parallel, but there is also a severe judgment: Wilhelm has not yet grown out of his childish dreams. This is the real reason for his low spirits at the beginning of the chapter. What Laertes offers is no solution; it cannot replace the immediate and unfeigned experience of the world that Wilhelm lacks (Selbmann 73). Laertes produces an artifice, the sources for which are only documents and not first-hand observation. Nevertheless, Wilhelm is restored to equilibrium at the end of the chapter.

The minor crisis at the beginning of the chapter was born of Wilhelm's old inability to distinguish between appearance and reality. In retrospect, it also seems to stem from the home truths he heard from Aurelie in the previous chapter. Here again, his indecision is clear as he suffers from the tension created by the opposing worlds of commerce

---

[2] Travel literature has a long tradition, beginning with Homer's *Odyssey.* Authentic and fictitious accounts of journeys have alternated with parody and satirical travel stories both in ancient and in modern times. Eighteenth-century German examples include *Reise um die Welt* by Georg Forster (1778–1780) and Goethe's diary of his visit to Italy (1786).

and the theater. Wilhelm's existence is based in theory, imagination, enthusiasm, and dreams. Luckily for him, Laertes is not only a good actor, he has a more practical gift which can now be put to good use.

Chapter Eighteen

Wilhelm hears Serlo's story. Unlike Aurelie, Serlo is not given to confiding, nor does he like to speak in continuous narrative. He was born into the theater and appeared on the stage even as a toddler. Sporting wings, he played Cupid; as Harlequin, he crawled out of an egg. His father believed children's concentration was improved by beatings, just as small boys are beaten at the spot where a marker is erected, to help them remember. Serlo grew to be a gifted actor and soon left behind both his father and the harsh treatment.

He first arrived at a monastery where the Shrove Tuesday carnival was under threat, following the death of the organizer.[1] Serlo took on the role of the angel Gabriel, appeared in the Mysteries,[2] and finally had the part of the Savior. After playing a trick on some of the soldiers, Serlo moved on. He joined a group known as the Children of Joy, who believed that irrational enjoyment is part of human make-up. At the carnival, their display of the vices and virtues was more instructive than that of the church.[3] Although well received by this company, Serlo became restless and set off. He saw routine performances of plays, with unimaginative, moralizing content, and knew what to improve. He earned his way by putting on plays during his travels. He could transform a garden or room and had a wonderful effect on his audiences. Serlo adopted a natural acting style and yet he was always dissembling. When he seemed transported, he was actually observing his audience closely. He was proud of increasing his influence over the audience by slow degrees. Serlo was sent from one court to another with letters of introduction and enjoyed many adventures, but was close to no one. He imitated outward appearances and manners. Temperament, talent,

---

[1] The days leading up to Ash Wednesday are a time for masked processions and costume balls, especially in the south of Germany.

[2] The Mystery plays dealt with events of biblical history or with the lives of the saints. They were performed by members of religious and professional guilds, often on a Feast Day, such as Corpus Christi.

[3] Parallel to the Mystery plays were the Morality plays. These offered a more individual, ethical perspective, concentrating on the Christian's need to confront morality and Judgment. They were performed by itinerant groups of professional actors.

and lifestyle combined to make him a first-class actor, whereas in life he became more secretive and increasingly anxious.

The narrator intervenes to postpone telling the remainder of Serlo's adventures. But there is one final observation: Serlo adopts an ironic tone, plays the sophist, and avoids serious and sincere conversation.[4] This manner is particularly pronounced when Wilhelm makes a speech. Wilhelm's analysis of art is in earnest; he tries to mount universal theories on his preformed concepts. Serlo is quite different: invariably light-hearted and evasive — and yet Wilhelm and Serlo enjoy each other's company.

Serlo's story is not told in the first person, by Serlo himself, although it is implied that he provided the details for the account. This abrupt change in narrative form points to the difference in character between Serlo and Aurelie. Because Serlo is disinclined to be open or expansive, the narrator has to step in and speak on his behalf. But Aurelie speaks passionately and directly of her own experiences. In Serlo's case, the narrator has pieced together the parts of his life and presented them as an anecdote, without dramatic setting or interruptions from either the narrator or the other characters. Serlo's own method of communicating is said to be disjointed and lacking in narrative continuity. This is the first hint that much of Serlo's account is a subtle comment on Wilhelm's own haphazard and directionless journey (Hass 172). Serlo's experiences also resemble Wilhelm's in tracing the history of the contemporary theater (Neumann 19). Thus, once again, the reader observes the novel's tendency to circle back and reprise earlier events as part of the process of moving forward.

Just as parts of Aurelie's life story reflected Wilhelm's ambitious dreams of founding a national theater, so, now, Serlo's adventures also incorporate some elements that run parallel to Wilhelm's life in the theater. Wilhelm showed promise as a young boy, first when he took charge of the puppet theater and later when he organized a group of friends into a drama group. Serlo's talent for the stage was recognized and nurtured even before he could walk. Wilhelm showed talent as a child for transforming ordinary objects into props, and whatever room was available to him into a stage. Serlo, as an adult, showed the same type of aptitude. Both boys suffered from excessively strict fathers who based the upbringing of a child on very severe principles, and both set out to gain independence, using the theater as a means of survival and escape. Wilhelm's first puppet performance told the Old Testament

[4] The Sophists were rhetoricians in ancient Greece for whom eloquence and persuasion were of far greater importance than sincerity.

story of David and Goliath. Serlo's first independent appearances were biblical too — commemorations of New Testament events.

Serlo had worked his way to becoming an accomplished actor by taking the route of experience. But one important detail distinguishes him from Wilhelm: Serlo was born into the theater; it is in his blood. Both his appearances on stage and the performances he directs display his truly artistic talent, whereas Wilhelm's opinion of his own gifts is based on little more than his own imagination and wishes.

Aurelie's relationship to the part of Ophelia seems too dangerously close to her own very personal emotional experiences. In addition, she related how her performances on stage had been inspired by a romantic relationship. Her artistry is always an intensely personal matter. But Serlo has trained himself to maintain a distance from people, to observe and use them simply as types, models to imitate; he sees other people as raw material for the promotion of his acting career. In addition, his pranks and his dislike of serious conversational topics confirm him as representative of comedy, in opposition to Aurelie's tragic persona. And it is easy to see how Aurelie could have formed a view of her brother as unfeeling and lacking in sympathy for her situation. There is no danger that Serlo will pour out his emotions on the stage, but the disadvantage is that he exercises the same control in daily life: he is guarded, hides behind a mask of cynicism, and lacks openness. It is interesting that Wilhelm and Serlo should have formed such a close relationship, since their ways are so different. Perhaps the only quality they share is the self-absorption which makes Wilhelm so unobservant of his surroundings and Serlo so detached. But whereas Wilhelm merely harbors thoughts of playing Hamlet, Serlo exceeds him in vainglory by feeling intense personal satisfaction at being cast in the role of Christ.

The tale of Serlo's life is told from a definite perspective. Repeated use of irony leaves the reader in no doubt as to how to judge each situation. The father's idea of discipline is presented in a ridiculous light; there is a sly remark about the impression Serlo, as the Archangel Gabriel, made on the girl playing Mary; the story of the soldiers' punishment is told entirely at their expense, and the use of the name "Children of Joy" is also ironically intended. Although the narration is in the third person, the ironic remarks are usually made to the detriment of persons other than Serlo, so that the emphasis, if not the actual authorial voice, appears to be his.

Chapter Nineteen

While Wilhelm enjoys himself, the actors from Melina's troupe are dissatisfied. Serlo has the actors repeat lines and parts regularly, even after the first performance, and draws out the potential of seemingly average players. He helps them feel the effect of rhythm in verse. Serlo is planning to use Melina's troupe to ward off a revolution threatening his own company. Suddenly, he asks Wilhelm to join his troupe and bring the others with him. Wilhelm asks how Serlo's opinion of the actors has altered and why his own presence makes a difference. Serlo tells him an actor in his troupe might leave in protest and take others with him. If so, Serlo could replace them with the pedant, Laertes, and Frau Melina who are all capable of improvement.

Wilhelm, meanwhile, has unexpectedly begun to see some point in his father's interests. Laertes has helped him appreciate the town as the center of commercial activity. Wilhelm thinks of his youthful poem about the two muses, and now the muse of commerce is not so distasteful, or the muse of the arts so glorious. The choice is between his newfound interest in business, and the acting career he has dreamt of. He wonders if his love for the theater made him fall in love with Mariane or if it was the other way round. Feeling indecisive, he goes to call on Aurelie.

The chapter opens with a contrast between Wilhelm's contentment with his situation and the actors' resentment born of uncertainty. By the end of the chapter, Wilhelm is no longer simply content: he is plagued with indecision and uncertainty. Whereas the actors are in need of some means of livelihood, Wilhelm finds himself unable to decide between two concrete and available options; his circumstances are situated on quite a different plane.

Details about Serlo show him to be an accomplished and skillful director with a keen eye for dramatic potential and a talent for furthering it. But what he proposes to Wilhelm is risky. Wilhelm had periodically asked about the actors' chances of employment, no doubt as a way of appeasing his own conscience. However, when Serlo makes such an unexpected offer, Wilhelm does not immediately trust him and so Serlo is forced to reveal his hand. Wilhelm's guarded reaction is indicative of a new degree of maturity in his personality. A comparison with events at the castle brings out this change more clearly. There, Wilhelm was tremendously flattered by the baron's offer to play in front of nobility and he was taken in by apparent signs of favor. Wilhelm was blind to the dismissive treatment and the superior and philistine attitudes towards the group. Whereas at that time he was naïve and unsuspecting, now, faced with Serlo's attractive proposal, Wilhelm is more cautious.

Once more, Wilhelm finds himself at the crossroads, and he is not alone. On the side of commerce, ironically enough, there stands Laertes, the actor. He has helped Wilhelm to appreciate an involvement in the mechanics of the city and the world of trade; he has encouraged him to engage his powers of observation. But the project which has engendered Wilhelm's new insights is pure fiction; it does not constitute a stable foundation. On the side of the arts there is Serlo with his offer, which ought to be irresistible, since it is in effect the fulfillment of Wilhelm's dreams. And yet Wilhelm is uneasy, suspicious of Serlo's motives, and fearful that the offer is not genuine. And so the factors influencing the two sides of Wilhelm's dilemma, both of which he considers concrete possibilities, actually display signs of instability.

The change in Wilhelm is not so extreme as to prevent him from indulging in his old habit of soliloquizing. In his speech he contrasts his own inner feeling of being called to a way of life with his notion of fate, and he examines both of these phenomena in his attempt to analyze his hesitation. The scope of Wilhelm's unanswered questions ranges from particular events in his life to elements of human nature. He wonders whether Mariane was too great a factor in his interest in the theater and whether it is human nature to step backwards when confronted with the realization of one's hopes and dreams. Finally, he asks himself why he does not simply welcome the opportunity to pay off his debt to the actors, for whom he still feels a responsibility.

As though he were on stage, Wilhelm debates his future and wonders which way to turn. For the reader, however, this speech is reminiscent of Hamlet's dilemma, and Wilhelm's dramatic stance and declamation point towards his decision to step onto the stage. The narrator rounds off the chapter with what amounts to a stage direction, as Wilhelm makes his exit.

Chapter Twenty

Aurelie seems peaceful. She is determined to go on stage the next day, but speaks of the pain caused by applause. The audience actually applauds the expression of her suffering. She is exhausted from memorizing and rehearsing and her life is constantly revolving. She ascribes part of her trouble to her serious German temperament. Wilhelm speaks metaphorically of her dagger, urging her to stop sharpening it and using it against herself. She curses love as a waste of time and exclaims that no man could appreciate a woman who gives up her natural pride and reserve and dedicates her whole existence to him.

Wilhelm is included in Aurelie's bitter complaints against men. She distracts herself by rehearsing a role, which, she says, is difficult to separate from one's self. She is torn between reason and emotion, and to stave off insanity, she gives her emotions free rein. She is in love, she declares, and wants to die. Wilhelm recognizes that Aurelie's situation is partly due to temperament and partly to circumstances. He suggests that she was fated to fall for an unfaithful lover and compares her situation to his own with Mariane. He was destined to burden and perhaps even destroy Mariane. Aurelie asks Wilhelm to swear he has never betrayed a woman or used flattery to get his way. He solemnly proposes to resist any such inclination, so moved is he by her lament.

Aurelie displays both wildness and indifference and steps back from Wilhelm's proffered hand. Wilhelm assures her that he knows what he is promising. Suddenly, Aurelie cuts Wilhelm's hand with her dagger. She cries that men need to be hurt, to help them remember, but then rushes to bandage the hand. She begs Wilhelm's forgiveness. When asked for an explanation of her act, she gives no answer, but simply motions Wilhelm to be quiet.

Aurelie's position, languidly outstretched on the bed, contradicts her emotional state. She quickly becomes quite hysterical and even violent. It is not simply bitterness against her unfaithful lover that gives rise to her desperation. She is aware that the distinction between life and art has collapsed, that applause for her performances on the stage causes her anguish because it is close to being a comment on the painful events of her life. Despite Aurelie's disturbance, she is capable of acute analysis of her own behavior. She knows that the habit of throwing herself into rehearsing dramatic roles that she is never going to perform is the expression of a desire to turn her back on her true condition, one she sees as hopeless. She speaks of the difficulty of gaining distance from oneself and knows that her life-like and convincing performances delight the audience, while she herself experiences a crisis of authenticity. The audience applauds what it takes for feigned emotion; in fact it is genuine emotion that she has been unable to keep from taking over her performance. This lack of distance is most dangerous for her. Insofar as Aurelie succeeds in standing back to assess her situation, she moves immediately to a general level. Thus, her serious temperament is ascribed to her nationality: she suffers because she is German. And her lover's attitude is taken to be typical for all men. Wilhelm tries to persuade her that he is an exception, that he does not fit her cynical description, but Aurelie cannot accept that any individual man should deviate from the pattern. In this violent and literally dramatic scene, actually rehearsed in the earlier scene involving Serlo, Wilhelm must receive the cut on behalf of all men.

Wilhelm's sympathetic reactions in this chapter demonstrate true concern about Aurelie's destructive temperament. But he also finds a way of drawing a parallel with his own state of affairs. As he sees it, Aurelie's love story presents a mirror image of his relationship with Mariane, but the lesson he has to learn relates to his feeling for the theater and how this relates to Mariane. In each character Wilhelm meets within the theater, there are aspects of the theatrical life that he has not taken into account in his dreams of entering the theater himself. In Aurelie he has found an intelligent and discerning actress, who has held the same beliefs and ideals Wilhelm now holds, but who is nonetheless being destroyed by her incapacity to separate her dramatic from her emotional life.

Wilhelm consistently views the life of the individual guided by the hand of fate and offers this insight to Aurelie as an explanation for the course of her life. She, however, sees human nature, divided along the lines of nationality and gender, as the main factor in determining events. When she strikes out at Wilhelm she is demonstrating their fundamental differences. Significantly, the wound cuts across his lifeline. Her stroke is a show of strength and a warning of her ability to impinge on what fate has ordained for Wilhelm. Aurelie seems to feel relief as soon as she has wounded Wilhelm and grows immediately calmer. Her role instantly changes from attacker to healer. The possession of the dagger is important to her and its use provides occasional stability. Her will to continue life, seen in her determination to continuing acting, is achieved through the consoling presence of the dagger, the means of ending it (Steer 14).

Book Five

Chapter One

AURELIE, HAVING INFLICTED Wilhelm's wound, insists on treating it — with embarrassing ceremony. Felix reacts to her strangeness by misbehaving. He drinks straight from the bottle and dispenses with a plate. He prefers his nurse to Aurelie, but unfortunately the nurse is ill, so Mignon is Felix's only companion. She teaches him songs and imparts her idiosyncratic interest in maps to him. She will not perform on stage, but enjoys learning and singing. Serlo encourages Mignon and the harper; he believes in exposing oneself to beauty and perfection.[1]

A letter arrives announcing the death of Wilhelm's father. The narrator observes that a sudden occurrence can find one unprepared. In a sense, Wilhelm is free but he still lacks experience. He resolves to collect useful points from conversations and reading, but abandons his natural ways. He is confused by Aurelie's bitterness, Laertes's scorn, and Jarno's harsh judgments. Serlo wants to give the company a new form, with Wilhelm as a member. A letter from Werner helps him make up his mind.

The narrator forges a link between the wounds Wilhelm had previously suffered and the cut hand he now has. This link also joins Aurelie to the other two women who, respectively, insisted on the prerogative of taking care of Wilhelm: Philine and Mignon. Aurelie's readiness to nurse him follows the logic of penance and is a kind of apology for her violent act. But when Philine supported Wilhelm in her lap after the attack in the woods, it was out of a proprietorial desire to claim him, and indeed she pretends for some time that he is her husband. And when Mignon fiercely insists on taking over after Philine leaves the pastor's house, it is one more expression of her devotion to her master.

---

[1] Goethe expressed a similar principle in a letter to Kanzler v. Müller dated May 30, 1814. Daily readings of the Bible or Homer are also mentioned in his list.

Aurelie claimed to have recovered from her fit of rage, but yet her behavior still shows signs of imbalance. She uses both traditional methods of dressing a wound and procedures that smack of magic, and rejects any suggestion that her patient might need a doctor. It is not made clear whether Aurelie's methods are effective; instead, the reader learns that her influence on Felix is less than salutary. Her strange speeches embarrass Wilhelm, and Felix shrinks from close contact with her. Mignon does not try to look after Wilhelm; she takes over the care of Felix from Aurelie and from the nurse. This is a role Mignon is prepared to play, but she will not set foot on the stage, nor is she prepared to watch others do so.

Mignon's whole being was in tune with Nature from the start and her responses are unmediated by social codes. Her objection to acting has nothing to do with having to learn a part, but with separating herself from that natural state. So, in this chapter, she is happy to learn poems and songs, but she recites or sings them unannounced, without preamble, and with her own curious intonation. Her refusal to repeat the egg dance, and her desire to wash off stage makeup both point to her preference for a natural appearance (Mayer 74).

Werner's announcement of Wilhelm's father's death puts a sudden obstacle in the way of the enjoyable and beneficial pastimes available in Serlo's entourage. For it is evident that Serlo's recipe for self-improvement offers Wilhelm precisely the kind of education he feels he needs. It is like a dramatic change of scene on stage, forcing the hero to face a situation he would rather ignore. A general observation provided by the narrator assesses this as the most dangerous type of situation, because one is completely unprepared for it. Wilhelm, whose one desire was to leave home and be free of his father's control, is left rudderless. He tries to compile a sort of anthology of useful insights and principles, but this is a feeble literary effort when placed alongside the polished product of his own energies combined with those of Laertes. Instead of helping him find the right direction, this practice sends him along all sorts of different paths in a disorganized way.

Serlo saw with greater clarity than Wilhelm how to turn the death of Wilhelm's father to advantage. He knew that his father's disapproval hampered Wilhelm and that he might now be more open to suggestion. Indirectly, through agents, he increased the pressure on Wilhelm to go on the stage. But it was not Serlo's encouragement, in the end, which helped Wilhelm to make a decision, but rather, ironically enough, Werner's proposal that he take the other route.

Chapter Two

Werner's letter states that the best policy is to carry on with one's work. Wilhelm's father's death has brought a change in the business. Werner has become engaged to Wilhelm's sister and they will live in Werner's house. The big house is to be sold, and the money invested. Werner advises Wilhelm not to collect works of art and luxury items. Werner wants to enjoy his family and make money but have few possessions. Husband and wife should wear the latest style, which can be peddled when it is no longer modish.[1]

Werner praises Wilhelm for his report: aside from a few mathematical slips, it was impressive. With the money realized from the sale of the house Werner now plans to purchase an estate in sequestration.[2] Wilhelm would ultimately supervise the improvements. Wilhelm dislikes the praise for his fabricated report and the bourgeois ideal described by Werner. Wilhelm is still convinced of the benefits of the theater and plans his reply.

The letter opens with a commonplace that, despite its general applicability, is nevertheless very pertinent to Werner's purposes: In the face of an eventuality such as a death, one's best recourse is to continue working. Other chapters have opened with similar comments provided by the narrator, but as this is Werner's own observation, it can the more easily be formulated and used in a self-serving way.

Wilhelm's own reaction to his father's death does not show much filial affection, but Werner's response is positively mercenary. He emerges as the counterpart to Serlo, who tries to profit from Wilhelm's father's death by enticing Wilhelm onto the stage, now that paternal control had gone from his life. Having briefly mentioned small scale profiteering by others, Werner self-confidently outlines his own complete manipulation of the situation. His description of the ideal life is curiously contradictory: the ability to make money is the central aim and interest, but one's style of life should not visibly reflect commercial success. There should be no display in terms of quantity, only of quality. Whatever Wilhelm found disagreeable in his father's values can be found in Werner's letter, only in a more grotesquely exaggerated form. Even worn-out clothes can be turned to a profit and there is a wonderful irony in the picture of a well-to-do woman dealing with and behaving like a poor peddler.

---

[1] A peddler is a traveling merchant who carries around a pack of goods for sale.

[2] Sequestration of a property occurs when the owner is unable to pay outstanding debts. In effect, the property is confiscated until financial matters are settled and it can be put on the market.

Werner's letter offends in many ways. He expresses admiration for Wilhelm's knowledge, but cannot resist mentioning small errors of calculation. To this subtle assertion of his own superiority he adds the presumption of speaking on behalf of Wilhelm's father, as though he also had the authority to determine what was best for Wilhelm. Despite his supposed alliance with Wilhelm's father, Werner feels free to criticize him and his father before him for their luxurious tastes. Using a metaphor, he appeals to Wilhelm not to inherit such habits, but never mentions Wilhelm's literal inheritance or concedes any authority to Wilhelm in decisions about its disposal.

Both the style and content of the letter are double-edged. In his praise of Wilhelm, Werner successfully embeds a criticism. His scorn for the accumulation of goods rings hollow in the light of his enthusiastic anticipation of the proceeds from their sale. He chooses the example of a ring as an extreme demonstration of his principles but the reader remembers what strong sentimental value such objects can have for Wilhelm when they are associated with Mariane or the countess. The same point could be made in relation to Wilhelm's grandfather's art collection: it is ironic that Werner should dismiss this collection on the grounds that it gave no pleasure to anyone except the one person who owned the objects (Hass 179). For Wilhelm, as the reader knows, those objects, in particular the painting of the ailing king's son, continue to hold a tremendous significance, even years after they had passed to another owner. And it was the same philistine attitude in his father that Wilhelm so deeply regretted when the collection was sold. Werner is not yet Wilhelm's brother-in-law and yet he treats him like a younger brother and even addresses him as "Brüderchen."

The death of his father has released Wilhelm from his feelings of guilt and obligation. And yet, strangely, he has recently begun to reassess his hostility towards the world of trade and this makes him hesitate to turn his back on it completely. Thus his father's death does not simply bring with it the expected liberation; once again Wilhelm is conscious of standing back at the crossroads. This letter, which praises the life of a merchant so highly, has a decidedly opposite effect on Wilhelm — and the narrator explicitly refers to this irony. There is a further irony in the play between fact and fiction. Wilhelm's enthusiasm for trade was founded on a fiction he had constructed with Laertes. Werner believes the fiction, is influenced by it and acts upon it. He offers Wilhelm a substantial opportunity and Wilhelm has the chance to develop his interest, founded on pretense, into a reality. A further aspect of this opportunity, however, is that it involves an estate that has yet to be purchased; this undermines the concrete nature of the profitable future Werner is laying before Wilhelm. The choices as presented to Wilhelm are not as clear-cut as they seem. Serlo's motives for urging Wilhelm to join his troupe are tinged with self-interest. Nevertheless, Wilhelm decides to reject Werner's plan by return of post and take the other route.

Chapter Three

Wilhelm's letter to Werner occupies most of this chapter. He admires Werner's letter but may do the opposite of everything Werner suggests. Wilhelm rejects Werner's aims: accumulation of property and light-hearted enjoyment. He reveals that his travel report was fabricated and he is not interested in mineral production. What use would it be, since his soul would still be full of slag?[1] He could not organize an estate with his own being in disorder.

Wilhelm's plan is to develop as a whole person and he asks Werner to take his letter seriously. He analyzes the differences between the nobility and the middle classes. A member of the German nobility can pursue personal development, whereas the middle classes are left to their own resources. But in working to provide an income and in developing the mind, the profession becomes all important and the personality is neglected.[2]

Wilhelm is aiming at the harmony normally reserved for the nobility. He has improved his self-presentation and cuts an impressive figure in society, though the path to becoming a public person is difficult.[3]

---

[1] Slag is the scum or dross thrown off in the process of melting metals. Goethe used a more extended form of the same image in a letter to Friedrich Jacobi, dated Nov. 17, 1782. Both formulation and sentiment are reminiscent of a biblical passage at Matthew 16: 26: "For what is a man profited, if he shall gain the whole world, and lose his own soul?'"

[2] The characterization of these social classes is borrowed from the work of a popular writer, Christian Garve. Similarities to his essay *Ueber die Maxime Rochefoucaults: Das bürgerliche Air verliehrt sich zuweilen bey der Armee, niehmals am Hofe* would have been recognized by Goethe's contemporaries. Schiller reduces Garve's discussion to a formula in his essay "Über die notwendigen Grenzen beim Gebrauch schöner Formen." He writes there that the burgher works and the nobleman represents.

[3] A public person is one involved in affairs of the state. Wilhelm would be automatically barred from such a position because he had not been born into the nobility. The concept of person, as used by Wilhelm in this chapter, suggests as well the original Latin sense of the mask or role adopted by an actor (*MA* 768).

Wilhelm expects Werner to recognize that he could realize all his goals in the theater, where a cultivated person can shine. He also announces that he is changing his name, as "Meister" makes him feel ashamed. Wilhelm and the rest of the group sign on as actors. Only Laertes expresses his gratitude towards Wilhelm; the others feel beholden to Philine. At the moment of signing the contract, Wilhelm thinks back to the Amazon on her white horse, her face and body glowing. Wilhelm signs in a daze, but Mignon tries to prevent him.

Wilhelm exaggerates when, agreeing with the narrator's judgment, he compliments Werner on the style of his letter; in fact, his own is better expressed. Some aspects of their mutual differences, both in character and in principle, show through in their contrasting styles. Wilhelm is wont to analyze and describe, in broad strokes, the theories he holds pertaining to society and the individual; Werner is satisfied to extol the virtues of his own lifestyle and, in a comradely way, expects Wilhelm to find everything he proposes acceptable. Wilhelm is more conscious of the differences between them and treats these as openly and frankly as he does the fabrication of his report.

Wilhelm justifies his desire to become an actor by contrasting two social classes and identifying the essential characteristics of each. Using this pattern, he likens the position of an actor to that of a nobleman. The first reason for doing so is that an actor does not participate in the life of the middle classes and is free from the burden of labor. Furthermore, the nobleman needs only to concentrate on appearances, since in him, person and personality coincide (Wilkinson/Willoughby 103). The actor does not in fact exercise a choice: the whole acting profession revolves around appearing, and actors are released from the usual middle class restraints (Saine 65). In fact, Wilhelm is talking of two different concepts: one, the self-representation of the nobility; the other, aesthetic representation (Borchmeyer 25). Both stand in opposition to the middle-class work ethic, but this does not mean that the two are synonymous or interchangeable. Since, according to Wilhelm's analysis, the ability to achieve the balance and inner formation he seeks is not available to the middle classes, but is exclusive to the nobility, the next best method of achieving this goal is to become an actor.

The reader now discovers the principle underlying Wilhelm's initial, theoretical esteem for nobility and sees why Wilhelm clung so tenaciously to this admiration, despite the disappointments at the castle. It becomes clear why he found it so distasteful when the actors lampooned their erstwhile benefactors in an extempore play. Despite all indications that those he encountered were shallow, fickle, and anything

but elevated, Wilhelm needed to believe that members of the aristocracy conformed to his view of them.

What Wilhelm seeks is an inner development, not simply the external appearance of one. Once this becomes evident, his remarks about
Werner's letter can be seen to contribute to the dichotomy. Although
he considers Werner's letter well expressed, Wilhelm completely disagrees with its contents. The outer and the inner are set in contrast.
Wilhelm rejects the middle-class notion that faculties should be developed so that they can be put to use. And yet, in describing his development so far, he tells Werner only about external aspects, that is to
say, his physical exercises — fencing and dancing practice — and the
improvements in his voice and presentation (Saine 65). He would like
to step across the boundary line that restricts the sphere of influence of
the burgher and to appear publicly in front of a wider circle. This is the
result of his long-held view that the time is ripe for the establishment of
a national theater and that he is destined to found it. But this view is
not particularly compatible with his idealized view of the nobility, since,
at the castle, Wilhelm learned that the aristocrats' views on the theater
were in fact very conventional, if not reactionary. And in dedicating his
efforts to crossing over the boundaries set in front of him by the structure of society, Wilhelm is implicitly suggesting that social categories
need to undergo change (Hahn 172).

In attempting to use involvement in the theater to achieve a state
denied him by birth, Wilhelm is also bypassing the goal he first sets
himself in this letter: that of becoming a public person. Clearly this is a
reaction against Werner's narrow horizons, which are restricted to
moneymaking and the sphere of one's own family. It is also a revolt
both against Werner's opposition to art and against the way he simply
takes it for granted that collections of art and artifacts are no longer desirable. However, it is ironic that Wilhelm should choose the theater as
a replacement for the unattainable state of nobility, since the theater
was never the preserve of the nobility. And although a movement away
from the patronage of the nobility in the direction of independence is
progress, Wilhelm fails to see this. He regressively characterizes his entry into a bohemian realm as a step closer to the aristocratic status
(Blessin 1979, 16). Yet his views, if misguided, are at least consistent;
the elevation of the arts began with the youthful poem — referred to
more recently again — where the muse of poetry is represented as a
noble and beautiful figure and the muse of commerce an unattractive
and busy old woman (Borchmeyer 23–24).

Wilhelm's stance derives partly from the freedom imparted to him by
his father's death. He is now able to reject the bourgeois life and its prin-

ciples and follow his more artistic inclinations. But what he leaves out of his account is his obvious dependence on the financial stability that his father's commerce and speculation provide (Janz 329). The irony becomes still more complex here, since Wilhelm has replaced the nobility's patronage of the arts by a dependence on the largesse of bourgeois capitalists. At the same time, he wishes to have the freedom to develop his faculties, a freedom he associates with the aristocratic class.

Having explained to Werner how he plans to free himself from the constraints imposed upon him by birth, Wilhelm now proposes to change his name. The connotations of the name "Meister" are unwelcome, since they imply a mastery that he does not feel he possesses. The irony here is that only a member of the middle classes would ever be inclined to think in terms of the categories of apprenticeship and mastery. In this way, Wilhelm demonstrates that he is still caught up in the middle-class social system (*FA* 1438).

After such a long period of hesitation, Wilhelm finally makes his decision precipitously. Werner's letter provoked this decisiveness, as the narrator observes, and yet Wilhelm's doubts about taking up acting have been simply swept aside. The first difficulty is that he will now have to continue working with the mediocre group of actors who have not yet resolved their resentments against him. Misguidedly, they choose to express to Philine their gratitude for the new contracts, rather than thanking Wilhelm. The very next sentence describes Wilhelm's vision of the Amazon as arising from an inexplicable thought process. The mention of gratitude and of Philine certainly contributed to Wilhelm's train of thought. But there is a further connection: signing the contract will allow Wilhelm to fulfill his lifelong hopes and dreams, and the latest object of his dreams, the beautiful Amazon, appears to him at that precise moment.

Because Wilhelm signs under a false name, and because Mignon tries to prevent him from signing at all, there seems to be a subtle suggestion that Wilhelm's decision is not destined to be an uncomplicated realization of the plan he had formulated so long ago. The false name indicates that Wilhelm is adopting a false persona. In her customary wordless way, Mignon communicates an intuitive feeling that Wilhelm is about to take a step in the wrong direction.

Chapter Four

Wilhelm wants to use the unabridged *Hamlet*, but Serlo disagrees. Wilhelm's relationship to Shakespeare is compared to a lover blind to flaws in his beloved. Serlo has no respect for the unity of a work of art.

They adopt botanical metaphors: Serlo speaks of separating the wheat from the chaff, but for Wilhelm the parts of a plant belong together. Serlo insists that guests be served golden apples in silver baskets — not the whole tree.[1] Finally, Serlo suggests that Wilhelm edit the play and combine some of the characters. He points to the lack of resources and the audience's preferences. Wilhelm feels Serlo is already refusing to honor the terms of their contract.

Wilhelm soon decides that Shakespeare was led astray by his sources. Serlo, stagily arrayed on a couch, listens. The main characters cannot be improved but circumstances that brought them together must be emphasized. This includes the troubles in Norway and the war with Fortinbras, Horatio's return from Wittenberg, Hamlet's capture by pirates and the death of the courtiers because of the Uriah letter.[2] These details, essential for a novel, are destructive and misleading in a play. Serlo is enthusiastic about Wilhelm's changes because the audience will not have to use their imaginations. He urges Wilhelm to set to work and prepare the text.

The chapter goes straight to the heart of the controversy between Serlo and Wilhelm and this runs parallel to actual developments in the German theater in Goethe's day. Wilhelm's enthusiasm for Shakespeare reflects the views of the followers of the *Sturm und Drang* movement. Shakespeare's more spontaneous outlook was embraced as an antidote to the dominance of the static, classical French stage. The botanical vocabulary adopted by both Serlo and Wilhelm was commonly used to express the association of Shakespeare with Nature.[3] Wilhelm's view at the beginning of the chapter is that Shakespeare's plays should not be cut because they are an organic whole. Serlo represents the more pragmatic point of view: the play must be shaped to fit the circumstances.[4] By the end of the chapter, Wilhelm has already outlined his own ideas for editing *Hamlet*. This is an unusually rapid change of heart for him;

---

[1] The image of the golden apples is taken from the Old Testament book of Proverbs 25:11, where the reference is also to the appropriate use of words: "A word fitly spoken is like apples of gold in settings of silver."

[2] The expression "Uriah letter" originates with the Old Testament. Uriah, the leader of David's army, was the bearer of a letter that would send him to his death (2 Samuel 11: 14–17).

[3] Herder, for example, uses the analogy of a plant when describing Shakespeare's plays in his essay "Shakespear."

[4] It was common to edit Shakespeare for the German stage. Schroeder, on whom Serlo is based, edited and then reedited *Hamlet* in 1778 for production in Hamburg (Krogmann 30).

his sudden willingness to cooperate with Serlo is a mark of his new allegiance with the troupe and shows the same tendency to precipitous decisions as when he agreed to sign the contract.

Wilhelm moves quickly from utter opposition to editing Shakespeare to a willingness to perform the deed himself. This is a decisive undermining of his idealized conception of life in the theater. He is immediately accommodating himself to the practical exigencies that drive Serlo's every decision. Here again, it seems, is a sign that Wilhelm is making a mistake when he takes this decisive step; Wilhelm himself is the first one to suggest it when he speaks of having signed the contract in error.

The comparison of Wilhelm's love of Shakespeare with the uncritical devotion of a besotted lover serves as a reminder of Wilhelm's passion for Mariane and for the theater. Certainly Wilhelm's present attitude has lost the pure and theoretical aspect it had in those heady days. And Serlo's prediction is that Wilhelm will only become more hardened and practical in his approach to art.

Wilhelm, on returning from his work on the *Hamlet* text, announces that he has edited it in a way that Shakespeare himself would have approved. This position again echoes a contemporary aesthetic debate, which centered on the issue of originality. Imitations and translations were defended on the grounds of having been undertaken in the spirit of the original author.[5] In effect, Wilhelm has adopted a critical position towards his beloved Shakespeare, suggesting both that his single-mindedness and his sources for the legend are to blame for the unwieldiness of the play. It is an ironic paradox that, despite embracing Shakespeare for his fidelity to Nature, Wilhelm now proposes to streamline the action of the play to fit into one unifying concept (Guthke 228–29). Such unity is only too reminiscent of the unity of action, which, together with unity of time and unity of place, provides the three unities required by the French classical stage. Wilhelm stresses the importance of the graveyard scene and then mentions that he is unwilling to alter the number of deaths at the end of the play. This remark alludes to a contemporary practice of allowing Hamlet, at the very least, to survive.[6]

By way of justifying his editorial decisions, Wilhelm claims that some incidents in the play undermine its unity and would be more suitable material for a novel. And when he sketches his new, streamlined version of *Hamlet,* the tables are turned: the scene depicted is deliber-

[5] In a farce with the title "Götter, Helden und Wieland" (1774), Goethe ridiculed Wieland for making such a claim in relation to his updated version of Euripides' *Alceste.*

[6] Schroeder allowed both Hamlet and Laertes to live (*MA* 773).

ately made to resemble a theatrical experience. Serlo, as a member of the audience, settles himself into his seat, Wilhelm delivers his monologue, and Serlo applauds at the end. The German word "Beifall," which can mean approval or applause, has obviously been chosen with this overall illusion of the theater in mind.

Chapter Five

Wilhelm has been translating *Hamlet,* consulting Wieland's version, and supplying missing passages.[1] The final version is approved by Serlo, especially the inclusion of events which elevate the whole beyond a domestic falling-out. Some of the roles are already set: Serlo as Polonius, Aurelie as Ophelia, Laertes as his namesake, and a recent arrival as Horatio. The roles of the king and the ghost have yet to be filled. Serlo wants to combine Rosencrantz and Guildenstern, but Wilhelm protests that these two represent a whole society. Philine is delighted to be cast as the duchess in the play-within-a-play and is confident of demonstrating her quick transfer of emotions. Aurelie's displeasure is evident.

Serlo teasingly suggests a ballet, to allow Philine to show off her legs and dainty feet on the smaller stage.[2] Philine removes her slippers, a gift from the countess. Serlo praises the sound they make, especially joyful for a bachelor. In a moment of hyperbole, he prefers the clicking sound of slippers to a series of literary topoi: nightingales' song, bubbling brooks, or the whistling wind. Offended by their flirting, Aurelie leaves.

The chapter lurches from serious discussions of a theoretical nature to practical considerations for the production and finally to incidents of pure frivolity. Although it ends with a light-hearted, staged comic scene, the chapter begins with an account of Wilhelm's work on the translation and textual manipulation that result in the version of the *Hamlet* script to be used in the forthcoming production. Not only has Wilhelm reconciled himself to the idea of embellishing Shakespeare's

---

[1] In 1766, Wieland published his translations of twenty-two of Shakespeare's plays into prose. They are not now considered among his most successful translations: Wieland omits some passages, and renders others inaccurately. Led by Herder, Goethe was critical of Wieland's efforts in his *Rede zum Shakespeares-Tag* (1771). However, on Wieland's death, Goethe acknowledged the benefit he had bestowed in translating these plays and thus giving his own nation an insight into Shakespeare's world (*Zum brüderlichen Andenken Wielands,* 1813).

[2] The smaller theater is the one on which the play-within-the-play was performed.

original along the lines he had described, he also supplements Wieland's translation where it is lacking. Nevertheless, Wilhelm suffers some pangs of guilt because he is doing damage to Shakespeare's text and, since this point is not resolved, the reader is left with an uneasy feeling about the whole undertaking.

Serlo's remarks are closely linked with actual events and movements current within the theater. He is pleased that Wilhelm has been able to maintain just enough of the events external to the main action of *Hamlet* and so prevent the play from becoming too domestic — a very real threat, since productions were apt to tame Shakespeare and shape his characters in a guise more familiar to an eighteenth-century German audience (Guthke 229). Then later, when he suggests collapsing Rosencrantz and Guildenstern into one, he is articulating the very practice adopted by Schröder in dropping Rosencrantz altogether (*MA* 774). But his suggestion is vehemently rejected by Wilhelm, who, at this point, is defending the inviolability of the text on the grounds that these two characters are a true representation of natural human traits. His defense is delivered in an overblown, theatrical idiom, but Serlo is nevertheless convinced.

Because there is always the potential for a dramatic disagreement between Wilhelm and Serlo, it is all the more surprising that they are able to convince each other of an opposed point of view at several junctures, both in this and in the previous chapter. Serlo is interested in simplifying the plot in order to reduce expenses; Wilhelm wants to make it more coherent and comprehensible. And yet they are also capable of lapsing into contradiction with their own principles. The contradiction inherent in praising the natural effect of Shakespeare and then rendering the play in a more rounded, polished form is the first of these instances. The domestication issue is another. In Serlo's view, the grandeur of the circumstances must be maintained, so that the play does not resemble the story of an ordinary family. But then both agree that too much concentration on sea-voyages would have an alienating effect on German audiences. This rather patronizing observation urges precisely the sort of domestication Serlo has just dismissed. Wilhelm himself embodies a contradiction: he has radically altered the text by now and yet he violently objects to the idea of cutting out one character.

There is something verging on the ominous about the alignment of characters in the novel with roles in the play. The coincidence of Laertes's name lends an air of unreality to the whole arrangement. In addition, it suggests that Laertes is where he belongs, whereas Wilhelm, with his false name, is still not cast in the right role in life. The authoritarian air Serlo adopts suits him to the role of Polonius, but for

Aurelie to be given the part of Ophelia without further discussion is surely a dangerous decision.

Aurelie's antipathy towards Philine is made evident in this chapter. Philine's coquettishness is a consistent trait and the reference to the sound of her slippers is an attribute that serves as an allusion to Venus, goddess of love (Schlaffer *Mythos,* 139). The narrative detail that the slippers had belonged to the countess carries the suggestion of an erotic symbol, since Philine had acted as matchmaker between Wilhelm and the countess (Hass 183). Serlo encourages Philine to continue the banter, confirming Aurelie's view of Serlo's character and his inability to sympathize with her own situation. Wilhelm's reaction to this scene is notably absent from the details provided by the narrator at this point. The scene is staged for public consumption and might have been taken from a romantic comedy, with Aurelie as a dissatisfied member of the audience. When she stands to leave at the end of the chapter, the reader again has the sensation of the curtain being drawn over the scene.

Chapter Six

Serlo and Wilhelm continue their conversation about the cast and wonder whether to ask the prompter to take on a role. The prompter is prevented from acting by his rough voice and stiff bearing but Serlo admires his ability to distinguish between declamation and recitation.[1] Delighted, Wilhelm declares that he would be perfect for the speech about the rugged Pyrrhus, an important passage to preserve in the script.

Wilhelm then analyzes the twofold function of the play-within-the-play. The death of Priam is so emotionally declaimed that the prince is moved and his resolve stiffened. This prepares for the short play directed at the king, his stepfather. Serlo will ask the prompter to fill in at the rehearsal. There is still no one to play the ghost.

Wilhelm receives an anonymous note, addressed to his assumed name. The writer uses the first person plural, suggesting that the note is from a group of people. Wilhelm is praised and informed that the ghost will appear when needed. Serlo is concerned about the letter, but Aurelie thinks it is a joke of Serlo's. Wilhelm has influenced Serlo to talk about art. The narrator might disclose their discussions later, and observes that Germans like to give an account of what they do.

Serlo enjoys planning how to play Polonius. Aurelie is not optimistic about her role. She doubts whether she can break free from the feelings

---

[1] Goethe's "Regeln für Schauspieler" contain rules for recitation and declamation in paragraphs 18–30.

that drove Ophelia mad. Wilhelm will realize his wish to play Hamlet although convinced that he bears no resemblance to him. Serlo thinks the actor should adapt, but the role can be made to fit too. Wilhelm thinks Hamlet would have been blue-eyed and blond, being Danish, and also plump, based on the line, "He's fat and scant of breath."

The discussion about including the prompter in the cast gives rise to a further instance of indecision and inconsistency in the continuing discussions between Serlo and Wilhelm. The man is declared unsuited by nature to the stage and yet this is not an end to it. Serlo and Wilhelm plan to coax and trick him into taking on a part, even though they also know that his emotional response to the lines is sure to be misplaced. This curious — and persistent — exchange can have only one explanation. It sheds light on Wilhelm's own situation: he is forcing himself to enter the life of an actor, despite his recurring misgivings. There is already unease created in the reader's mind by the fact that Wilhelm had to sign the contract under an assumed name and now the doubts about the prompter's suitability have an unsettling effect on Wilhelm's situation as well.

The ghost poses a problem for Wilhelm and Serlo — they cannot decide which player would be most suited to the part. Again, the inability to reach a decision is significant: it reflects the irresolute nature of Wilhelm himself. The role of the ghost in the play is to inform Hamlet of his uncle's treachery and thus determine the entire course of the play. From beyond the grave, Hamlet's father is watching over his son and informing him of potential dangers. In receiving the mysterious note, Wilhelm, too, learns that some unseen persons are keeping an eye on his progress and that they are in a position to determine events. The writers' vague mention of a decision obliquely picks up the theme of the choice to be made at a crossroads.

The narrator involves himself more directly here than in recent chapters. The ironic and self-deprecating remark about Germans liking to justify what they are doing is of passing amusement and can be seen, in the context of Wilhelm and Serlo's discussions, as an example of domesticating a text. The narrator also informs the reader that Wilhelm had been keeping a record during these conversations, but that the contents of his notes would not be revealed until later. The readership is even divided, by an artifice, into those who might be interested in such matters and those who would not. That Wilhelm should have been taking notes is not altogether a good sign. When he was last engaged in such an activity, in the first chapter of the present book, we were told that his confusion was merely compounded by his inability to discriminate between useful and irrelevant detail.

In Wilhelm's deliberations, Serlo has taken over the practical side. With financial considerations governing many of his decisions, he has come to replace the figure of Werner, who previously kept Wilhelm's flights of fancy in check. Like Serlo, Werner did not remain unaffected by Wilhelm's point of view and tried to be sympathetic, within limits. And now the reader learns that Serlo, under Wilhelm's influence, began to talk in more theoretical ways about art.

The letter Wilhelm receives picks up an already existing theme involving letters, received by Wilhelm, which have an influence on his development. It begins with Norberg's note, which was not intended for Wilhelm, but seemed to have been placed in his hands by fate — it was certainly instrumental in determining his next move. The letter from Werner after Wilhelm's father's death was equally determinative, although unintentionally so. Now this latest letter is mysterious on all counts: its provenance is unexplained, its writer is unidentified, and its message is cryptic. But the effect now is to reintroduce doubts. Serlo himself takes it very seriously and becomes irresolute in his plans for the play. However, his mood rapidly alters when he sees how well the old actors are performing and how promising the new ones seem to be. His mood is also much improved by the obvious enjoyment he derives from his role as Polonius.

Wilhelm's relation to *Hamlet* is by no means clear yet. At first, with his tree analogy, he maintained that the play was an organic whole and not to be tampered with. Then he agreed to cut the script, streamlining it along the lines of his own character sketch of the protagonist. He seems to be tailoring the play in order to allow the parallels between himself and Hamlet to emerge more clearly (Blackall 1965, 60). But now, with his remarks about physiognomy, Wilhelm again distances himself from this identification. His concerns about physical discrepancies between himself and the character he plays, and the basis on which he comes to his conclusions about Hamlet's appearance, are surprisingly frivolous, considering they come after a period of intense involvement with the text. Wilhelm cannot come to a decision about whether he wants to project himself into the figure of Hamlet or not.

Aurelie's disposition is again the opposite of her brother's. Whereas he overflows with confidence and eagerness, she has severe doubts about her own suitability for the part of Ophelia. The nature of her doubts is different from the principle informing Wilhelm's misgivings. While his thoughts centered on the physical disparities between himself and Hamlet, Aurelie thinks in terms of attitude. But even while pointing to the differences, she alludes to the dangerous similarities: Aurelie recognizes that she too is capable of losing her wits under duress. Her instincts in relation to Hamlet are more accurate than Wilhelm's: she rejects the notion that Hamlet is fat.[2] The conversation comes to a close with Aurelie placing more emphasis on the players' enjoyment than the author's intentions. The whole chapter has the feel of a nervous and excited group of actors conversing behind the scenes and expressing immediate reactions rather than reflected theories.

Chapter Seven

This chapter opens with a discussion of the differences between a play and a novel: both genres depict human nature and action. In one, dialogue predominates and in the other, narration, but some plays are novels in dialogue and could even be written in epistolary form. A novel deals with sentiments and events; in drama, the emphasis is on characters and deeds. A novel proceeds slowly, held back by the protagonist's sentiments; in drama, the main character compels the action towards its resolution. The hero of a novel is passive; a dramatic hero active and effective. Various protagonists from English novels "retard" the action, and fashion events according to their own ideas.[1] In drama, the hero fashions nothing. In a novel, chance has a role to play, while fate is confined to drama. The discussion returns to Hamlet, a man of thoughts rather than actions, yet fate drives both hero and play to a tragic end.

Wilhelm stresses the importance of the reading rehearsal. Serlo says actors talking about studying are like freemasons talking about work.[2] He compliments Wilhelm on his efforts, but fears the actors will disappoint him. It is easy to stimulate the imagination, but there is no guarantee that creativity will result. Actors often simply play themselves. For

[2] Shakespeare commentators are now agreed that the reference to Hamlet as "fat" is in fact intended to mean that he is sweating (Dover Wilson 255)

---

[1] The main characters of three novels by Samuel Richardson: Grandison, Clarissa, and Pamela, are mentioned, as well as the Vicar of Wakefield from the Oliver Goldsmith's novel, and Henry Fielding's Tom Jones.

[2] Freemasons are members of a secret fraternity, united in lodges. Their events are largely social and they undertake to assist one another. Goethe joined a masonic lodge in Weimar in 1780 and remained a member, at least in name, for the rest of his life. However, a letter he wrote in 1789 attests to his reservations about the ritualistic excesses of secret societies (Neumann 78).

Serlo, the worst situation arises when an actor claims to understand the spirit without being fully acquainted with the letter.[3]

Although the chapter comprises a conversation, the first half is not in reported speech, but is presented by the narrator. The results of the conversation are summarized in unbroken narrative. And when Serlo begins to outline his views, it is again a virtually unbroken speech. Such a style imparts the character of a discourse to what purports to be a dialogue. This feature is less surprising when one remembers that this exchange is largely based on Goethe's "Über epische und dramatische Dichtung" — itself the summary of an exchange between Goethe and Schiller.

The chapter bears some resemblance to other recent chapters containing theoretical discussions about Hamlet and related questions. But whereas on those occasions Wilhelm was offering a highly personal interpretation with practical repercussions for the players and the actual production of the play, here the discussion is more purely theoretical. The topic of the debate sets the genres of novel and drama on an equal footing, by no means taken for granted in discussions among Goethe's contemporaries, many of whom still viewed the novel as a poor relation to poetry.[4] Attempts to categorize the novel as either "epic" or "dramatic" were typical for this period. Here, however, the novel is discussed on its own terms.

Two theoretical literary hybrids are mentioned: a play which is simply a novel set in direct speech, and a play which consisted of nothing but letters. Goethe may have had some example in mind for the first possibility; it is tempting to think that for the second he envisaged his own *Werther* being produced as a play. Goethe identifies a failure of the modern era: writers no longer stay within the strict demarcations separating epic from drama. In a letter to Schiller, he criticizes writers who trespass onto another's territory merely in order to please the audience.[5] The standpoint of the first contribution to the theory of the novel in Germany, Christian Friedrich von Blanckenburg's *Versuch über den Roman* (1774), is that the novel should be modeled on drama. But in the present conversation between Wilhelm and Serlo, Aristotle's *Poetics* are more clearly in evidence, with the distinction laid out in chapter six between character and thoughts (*MA* 776). However, Aristotle

---

[3] This is an echo of St Paul's Second Epistle to the Corinthians (3:6): "Who also hath made us able ministers of the new testament; not of the letter, but of the spirit: for the letter killeth, but the spirit giveth life."

[4] In his essay "Über naive und sentimentalische Dichtung," Schiller describes the novelist as a "half brother" of the poet, implying a degree of inferiority.

[5] The letter is dated Dec. 23, 1797.

places character as well as thoughts within both the dramatic and epic genres, whereas Goethe divides them here, assigning characters to drama and thoughts to the novel (Blackall 1976, 80–82). When the principles articulated in this discussion are applied to *Hamlet,* however, it is not possible to maintain these distinctions too rigidly. The play has something of the breadth of a novel about it. In conformity with the Aristotelian view, the theory outlined here has obvious relevance not only for *Hamlet,* but also for the *Wilhelm Meister* novel itself. Chance plays a large part in the events of Wilhelm's life so far, and yet he insists on believing that he is led by the hand of fate, so that there is a continuing tension between fate and the individual will. And here, too, lies the basis of Wilhelm's problematic identification with Hamlet: it is necessary for Wilhelm to believe in a plan for the play, despite his conviction that the hero himself has no such plan. Wilhelm's innate fatalism prevents him from seeing Hamlet in any other light (Diamond 94–95).

The theoretical outlook of the beginning of the chapter is not yet completely abandoned when Wilhelm starts to make his plans for the rehearsal. He now draws a parallel between a musical and a dramatic performance, comparing what is required by way of preparation for each and drawing parallels between them. Wilhelm has evidently come to share Serlo's high regard for musical performance as a way of perfecting one's aesthetic sensibilities. However, Serlo fears that Wilhelm is bound for disappointment and he gives his own view of the typical misconceptions actors have about their roles and how to counteract them. So the chapter that begins with a poetic theory ends with practical tips for training actors — a matter with which Goethe was also very well acquainted.

Chapter Eight

Wilhelm arrives for rehearsal and is surprised by memories of the props when Mariane performed, the sun shining in on her bosom, just as it is shining now. He thinks back to the moment when she first declared her love for him and promised him a night of bliss. Two friends of the theater arrive, one particularly devoted to Madame Melina, the other generally attached to the company. They are easily transported, and able to overlook small faults, but make helpful comments on the posture, costumes, and delivery of the actors. They predict this company will bring about a new beginning for German theater.

The narrator ends the chapter with a threefold observation: human beings like to reach their ends in their own ways; it is difficult to convince them of what is self-evident; it is not easy to persuade ambitious people that, to achieve their goals, they should start at the beginning.

Wilhelm's recollections of Mariane on the stage remind the reader that his enthusiasm for the theater was in large part aroused by her presence and influence. In those happy days, the inexpert props and scenery were transformed into something real because of their association with Mariane; now Wilhelm overlooks the fact that the props they are currently using are no better, because they have brought these happy memories to mind. Real sunshine streaming in on the artificial props produces the unlikely dream that Mariane might soon appear. This dream is already undermined for the reader before the actors arrive and disturb Wilhelm: the narrator points out that what gave rise to Wilhelm's musings was simply a set of the standard decorations routinely used for epilogues in theater companies all over Germany.

The two amateur theater critics introduced in this chapter are embodiments of two of Goethe's essays: "Regeln für Schauspieler" and "Schema über den Dilettantismus," compiled together with Schiller (Bahr 125; *MA* 778). This, plus the fact that they are never given names, makes them appear stylized. In contrast, the theme of love for a woman mingled with love for the theater flows over from the opening paragraph. There is an understated suggestion of a dalliance between one of these men and Madame Melina, a hint reinforced by the ambiguous word "Liebhaber," meaning both "amateur" and "lover."

Although they are not professionals, the two critics exercise a beneficial influence on the company. They are most highly valued not for their theoretical views, but for their practical hints. Their appearance on the scene is fortuitously timed for Wilhelm, since he has exhausted the possible approaches to the structure of *Hamlet* through theoretical discussion. He needs now to translate his views into practice, on the stage. He, more than anyone, needs some practical pointers prior to his first appearance.

The visiting critics are allowed free access to all parts of the theater, including the dressing rooms, and this license is reflected in the broad-ranging array of advice they are able to offer. Some of their views, such as the one prohibiting the taking of snuff during rehearsals, seem to be based on superstition or false association rather than reason, but even this type of discipline is likely to have a beneficial effect. The narrator presents them in an increasingly positive light; their understanding of what is required for a good performance far exceeds what the actors themselves, who after all, have some experience to draw on, have ever imagined.

The narrator's conclusions have the effect of removing the veil of illusion. It is as though the reader is now being advised to consider the latter part of the chapter as something which does not properly belong in the narrative frame: these events were simply examples, and their interpretation is now being laid out.

Chapter Nine

In discussions with Serlo, Wilhelm's views sometimes prevail. He wants Hamlet to mingle with the courtiers at first. In the scene between Hamlet and his mother, Wilhelm wants the portraits life-sized, placed beside the main door, so that the painting of the old king fully resembles the ghost as he leaves. As Hamlet looks at the ghost, the queen looks at the painting.

Serlo tries to persuade Wilhelm that Hamlet should be allowed to survive at the end of the play but Wilhelm insists that the structure demands the hero's demise, while Serlo pleads on behalf of the public's preferences. But Wilhelm compares the situation to one in which a man who is chronically ill cannot be saved; the doctor is powerless against the course of Nature. He distinguishes between the feelings the audience want to have and those that they ought to have. Serlo points out that the audience is paying, but Wilhelm says they should not be treated like children, from whom it is easy to take money. They should gradually acquire aesthetic taste and will then invest their money willingly. The public should be flattered and enlightened as one flatters a much-loved child, not as one flatters refined and rich people and so perpetuates their faults. Wilhelm and Serlo discuss whether the play can now be left untouched. The narrator undertakes to present to readers who are interested an account of this new version of *Hamlet*.

The two characters who contributed so much to the previous chapter are no longer present; they have been replaced by Wilhelm and Serlo. And whereas the theater critics seemed to be largely of one mind and capable of working together, Wilhelm and Serlo proceed by means of dialogue and debate. Wilhelm is at first concerned with the visual effect made by Hamlet at the beginning. The scene he describes reflects his own analysis of Hamlet's personality: he is unremarkable at first but when provoked by his stepfather's presumption, he takes on the central role. The second idea concerns the paintings, and Wilhelm insists that they be life-size, in contrast to the current practice for stage productions in the eighteenth century, which made use of miniatures for the paintings (*MA* 778). Wilhelm wants to produce an optical illusion by making portrait and apparition resemble one another in size and dress as closely as possible. The viewer would note that while Hamlet watches the ghost's movements, his mother, unable to see the ghost, is transfixed by a portrait of the same man. The reader, meanwhile, is reminded of the scene in the castle when Wilhelm is dressed as the count. Wilhelm sees the count in the mirror and the count catches sight of Wilhelm's reflected image, and takes him for an apparition. This experience has a transforming effect on the count just as this parallel situation will have an impact on the audience.

The question regarding Hamlet's death is, as Wilhelm rightly insists, crucial to Shakespeare's tragedy. The issue was raised earlier, in Chapter Four of this book, when Wilhelm insisted on preserving the four deaths at the end of the play. Now the reader is able to assess Serlo's position, which has more to do with his concern for the audience's approval than with the integrity of Shakespeare's play. Serlo represents the same viewpoint as the director in the "Vorspiel auf dem Theater" in *Faust*. There the director debates with an actor and a poet, each of whom presents an individual perspective on what is of paramount importance in a play. The director's overriding concern is with the public's pleasure as this relates to consequent income for the company. Wilhelm, despite his present interest in the mechanics of the production, still dwells on the idealism of his national theater concept and responds to Serlo on a far less practical level. He is determined to maintain his goal to educate the theater-going public and to train their powers of aesthetic discernment.

This brief chapter forms part of the preparations for the performance of *Hamlet*. Practical details of the staging are discussed, but much larger questions are aired as well. Serlo and Wilhelm discuss the extent to which the play should be made to conform to the public's preferences, and Wilhelm returns to his initial lofty ideals. The narrator is an insistent presence here and adopts the role of editor, bringing the conversation to an end and suggesting that it might be continued in due course. The dialogue is thus interrupted and the effect is again similar to watching a play, with the curtain falling at the end of a scene.

Chapter Ten

The rehearsal is over, but the portraits are not ready yet and the ghost has not appeared. Wilhelm assures Serlo that the ghost will materialize. Philine and Wilhelm disagree about rehearsal time, comparing it with preparations for a banquet. Wilhelm's view is that their play will have some incalculable and lingering effect on the audience. Philine complains that Hamlet's finest remark — she would not say which it was — has been cut from the text. As they are about to leave, she sings a song in praise of the night and departs with a clattering of heels.

Aurelie mentions a cut on Philine's forehead that she finds repellent and decides that Philine should be avoided. She is scornful of her brother for finding her attractive and suspects Wilhelm of similar feelings. Wilhelm defends Philine's character, while conceding that she is frivolous. Aurelie and Wilhelm nearly have an argument, but Aurelie bids him goodnight, calling him her "bird of paradise." By way of explanation, she mentions that these birds have no feet and hover in the air, feeding on ether. But she immediately discounts this as fairy tale fiction.

While undressing, Wilhelm notices Philine's slippers by his bed, and the curtains seem to move. A feeling that he takes for irritation makes him catch his breath. When he calls out there is no reply and a thorough but fruitless search of the room follows. The narrator makes an ironic remark and then posits an evil genius, who observes Wilhelm playing with the slippers all night. Serlo has to wake him in the morning for rehearsal.

The calm confidence with which Wilhelm discusses the ghost's anticipated appearance contrasts with his intense involvement in details of staging in the previous chapter. The practical considerations trouble him more than the prospect of what might be termed a supernatural visitation. Even though the assumption has to be that he and Serlo are awaiting the arrival of a flesh and blood actor, the means of communication was so mysterious that Wilhelm now refers to him, only half ironically, in terms that speak of superstition.

The fact that the portraits are also not yet ready is conceivably a further obstacle to the ghost's arrival. The importance of paintings is a theme already introduced at the mention of Wilhelm's favorite picture of the ailing king's son in Book One. Since his painted likeness is not yet on display, it would be futile for the ghost to appear now, as he could not have the overwhelming effect for which the scene is designed. This link is more superstitious than reasoned, but the whole exchange takes place within this idiom. Wilhelm completes the conversation by making one more superstitious claim: that the ghost might be dissuaded from materializing if the actors express any doubts.

Philine then introduces an analogy between an audience at the theater and guests at a banquet. Although their appetites are satisfied, it is in their nature to complain about some detail or other which then assumes a disproportionate significance.[1] Wilhelm latches onto Philine's image and elaborates on it until he has painted a vast network of unseen connections about which he holds forth at some length. This style of rhetoric has already emerged as a characteristic of Wilhelm's, but the subject matter is perhaps surprising in this context. Wilhelm would like the others to think about the stages that precede the moment when a

---

[1] The analogy between presenting a play and preparing a meal is also used in the Vorspiel auf dem Theater of *Faust I*. There, the director recommends ignoring the rules of unity in a play; if one presents a ragout of small pieces, everyone will find something pleasing in it (l.97–100).

sumptuous banquet is placed on the table. His speech is reminiscent both of Werner's encomium to the world of trade in Book One and of his own fabricated traveler's observations assembled with Laertes's help in Book Four. Wilhelm considers all the effort justified, even though the pleasure it provides is ephemeral. In his view, something remains when the immediate pleasure recedes. In applying this tenet to their own theatrical enterprise, Wilhelm is again reiterating the principle of educating the audience, an aim he feels should inform the establishment of a future national theater.

Philine immediately dismisses Wilhelm's words and goes on to make an intriguing criticism of the way the script was edited for the production. She claims that Hamlet's best thought has been left out of the text. She refuses to explain, but is clearly referring to Hamlet's line in Act III, 2, "That's a fair thought to lie between maid's legs"(Bahr 127; *MA* 779). In her coquettish way, she first teases Serlo and then prepares the way for her suggestive song and for the next stage of her campaign to make an amorous conquest of Wilhelm. The reader remembers that Philine's name itself expresses her erotic and amoral nature (Willoughby 302). Her song, "Singet nicht in Trauertönen," reinforces this theme and she begins to sing while Wilhelm and Serlo are still trying to solve the puzzle.

This is the only song sung by Philine for which the words are given; as usual, Wilhelm is present during the singing. The song provides relief from the long hours of rehearsal and the equally long discussions about arrangements and still-outstanding concerns. Philine wants to cast dramatic theory aside and replace it with the pleasures of the senses, but her song does not address these concerns or relate to any aspect of the *Hamlet* production. However, there may be an echo of Hamlet's words when he describes his speech as "phrases of sorrow" in the first scene of Act Five (*MA* 779). Philine's song is a *carpe diem* call to turn away from the worries of the moment and indulge in some straightforward pleasures.[2] The mention of "sorrowful tones" with which she begins her song may be conceived as a reference to the earlier, mournful songs of the harper, for instance, rather than to any present circumstance. The contrast between her songs and those sung by Mignon and the harper could not be greater. Where they sing of past, dark experience, she sings of present and future joys. Where they sing

---

[2] "Carpe diem" literally means "harvest the day" and is the theme of poems which exhort the reader to take advantage of youth, since time flies. The phrase come from the last line of Horace's *Odes* 1.11 and was taken up by the German Anacreontic poets.

of the inescapable forces of fate, she urges temporary and free participation in the pleasures of the hour.

Philine's song is meant for Wilhelm, and with its praise of night's pleasures and playful rejection of the day, it is bound to evoke the joys Wilhelm shared with Mariane. It also arouses in him a degree of interest in Philine, as becomes increasingly clear throughout this chapter. Aurelie now steps in as a foil to Philine, pleading with Wilhelm to look at and assess her objectively. But her own reaction is unbalanced and lacking in reasoned judgment; she goes as far as to interpret the scar on Philine's forehead as a version of the mark of Cain, a sign that Philine is dangerous and should be avoided. She also uses the occasion to condemn men for falling for a woman like Philine, who has no character, and Wilhelm takes up the term "character" when he defends Philine. The present discord between Wilhelm and Aurelie is reflected in their diverging usages of this word. Aurelie means that there is no stable core to Philine, no integrity, while Wilhelm is thinking neutrally — and more charitably — of her disposition, or personality. Wilhelm's defense of Philine is ambiguous; it is not wholehearted or unreserved. He recognizes and finds distasteful her habit of willfully offending against society's standards, but knows that there is no malice or bitterness in her. This lack of coherence weakens his position and renders suspect his rejection of the idea that he has romantic feelings towards Philine. It is because Wilhelm cannot find it in himself to condemn Philine unequivocally that he is plagued by uncertainty later that night in his room.

Aurelie who, unlike Philine, is a woman of convoluted emotional complexity, speaks in riddles and contradictions. She calls Wilhelm a bird of paradise.[3] Her characterization of this type of bird as having no feet and feeding off air alone is the only explanation she will give. It is not the first time that Wilhelm's more imaginative aspects have been described in terms of a bird (Reiss 1951, 127–32). Then, having employed an image, Aurelie diminishes its force by using the term fairy tale, thus discounting the validity of the term of comparison. Her second leave-taking is also less than straightforward, although this time it may not be so conscious on her part. But when Aurelie wishes Wilhelm sweet dreams, and does so only in a qualified way by introducing the element of luck into her phrase, there is a hidden irony in her words of which the reader soon becomes aware.

---

[3] From Zedler and Campe one can learn that the belief in a footless bird was actually based on the local inhabitants' habit of removing the birds' feet (*FA* 1444).

These two women and their respective influences cause a division in Wilhelm. Aurelie has been unjust; he has no reason to censure Philine and believes that a romantic involvement with her is the furthest thing from his mind. Again, the reader perceives the dramatic irony. Philine's slippers are now featured for the second time. On the previous occasion, their provenance and association with the countess and the coquettish way Philine uses them to entice Serlo combine to establish them as an erotic motif. In the meantime, under the influence of the theater critics, the actors have received advice about wearing the same shoes in the rehearsal and the performance. Philine's slippers, then, first rehearse and then become the symbol of her custom of flouting convention.

The narrator communicates a considerable amount of information about Wilhelm's state of mind at the end of this chapter, mostly through innuendo and irony. First, the illusion of movement in the bed curtains appears to have been suggested by association with the slippers. And here already is an instance of the kind of dream one could have, with luck, as Aurelie expresses it in her goodnight wish. But the theme of bed curtains also ties in with the stage curtains: Wilhelm's thwarted anticipation in this scene is a sign that the theater curtain conceals disappointments on occasion as well. The narrator makes fun of Wilhelm by suggesting that he did not recognize the feeling that overcame him — no doubt one of rising passion — and misidentified it as irritation.[4]

Wilhelm addresses the absent Philine, imploring her to leave his room, and he warns that they might otherwise become the talk of the household. The word he uses is again "Märchen," the same term Aurelie used to discount popular belief about the physical characteristics of the bird of paradise. The primary meaning, for Wilhelm, has to do with avoiding scandal, but the secondary meaning, which involves the falsity of the account, is implied as well. Wilhelm tenaciously clings to his contention that he is not interested in any amorous involvement with Philine. His heartfelt words delivered to an empty room make Wilhelm into an actor rehearsing a part, and when he begins his thorough search for Philine, his actions have something of the exaggerated nature of an actor's gestures. When the reader remembers how he used to dress up and practice speeches in his bedroom, Wilhelm's present behavior seems to be a parody of the youthful ideal he harbored then. The testimony of the evil genius, which follows, strengthens the symbolic power of the slippers. It also makes the reader wonder whether the slippers have been provided for what amounts to a rehearsal and will re-

---

[4] This amusing narrative intervention, which prepares both the reader and Wilhelm for events to follow, is unfortunately lost from Blackall's translation.

appear in the same setting, together with their wearer, when it is time for the actual performance.

In this chapter, the main theme, pleasure, is introduced by Philine. She begins by speaking about the ephemeral nature of theatrical performances, in an attempt to lighten the atmosphere and divert Serlo and Wilhelm from their preoccupation with details. Her image of the banquet shifts the emphasis to culinary pleasures and then her song introduces the pleasures of lovemaking as a topic. There ensues an indirect struggle between the two women seeking to influence Wilhelm. Aurelie is only able to express her displeasure, principally with Philine, and is no match for the hedonist Philine's onslaught with its multipronged attack. Philine's plan for Wilhelm has had an effect by the end of the chapter: she has succeeded in preoccupying him, and has disrupted his sleep to the point where his devotion to the theater may well be undermined.

Chapter Eleven

Wilhelm is getting dressed in a hurry, aided by the women. He takes one last look in the mirror just as a voice announces the arrival of the ghost. He hurries onto the stage and hears Horatio's last words, delivered in a state of confusion.[1] When the drop curtain rises,[2] Wilhelm sees a full house. Horatio remarks that the ghost is like a devil in armor. Wilhelm sees two tall men in the wings, clad in white robes with hoods; he is quite unnerved and feels his delivery is suffering. Wilhelm is rooted to the spot by the sight of the noble figure of the ghost in heavy armor. He addresses him haltingly, which suits the scene well. The translated text is close to the original here and the words express fear and surprise. The effect produces tremendous applause.

The ghost turns suddenly, and Hamlet is standing a little too close to it. Through the visor Wilhelm sees deep-set eyes and a well-formed nose. The ghost declares itself to be the ghost of his father and Wilhelm steps back in fright. The voice reminds Wilhelm of his own father's. Wilhelm is beset by feelings and memories, curiosity and fear. At last, the ghost sinks down under a light gray veil that seems to rise up mysteriously like mist. Then Hamlet's friends return and swear upon the sword. The old

---

[1] Horatio's speech is in fact an addition to the text, provided by Wilhelm.

[2] The drop curtain is an unframed canvas backcloth that was rolled up on a bottom roller. This distinguished it from the type of curtain that could be drawn away to the sides.

mole keeps urging them to swear and a flame appears from below each time.[3] The play continues successfully and without interruption.

When it actually comes to the performance, despite all the preparations, Wilhelm is caught off guard and has left himself insufficient time to dress with the proper care. This is surprising, considering the long hours he spent in discussion with Serlo, the care he took in editing the text, and the attention he devoted to polishing his technique during rehearsals. The women descend on him, fussing and adjusting, each laying claim to separate components of his costume. Philine and Aurelie have already vied for his attention verbally in the previous chapter, and now the competition is transferred to his appearance. Ironically, Wilhelm has spent long hours rehearsing ways of fabricating the desired effect on stage, but when it comes to the performance itself, he speaks in favor of a natural look, merely because expediency demands it. The women insist that his costume must be properly adjusted; they lay great emphasis on his appearance for the stage. The reader is reminded that Wilhelm's affection for Mariane was especially strong when she was wearing her stage costume. A measure of the change in Wilhelm is the fact that he has now adopted a *laissez faire* attitude towards his own costume; he had deplored just such indifference to detail among Mariane's fellow actors, suggesting that in the meantime he has acquired a sense of the actual life of an actor, as opposed to an idealized version.

The chapter is constructed like a fabric, woven out of strands pertaining to real life and strands which belong to the theater and the world of semblance. The confusion between the spheres of imagination and fact, so often apparent in Wilhelm, reaches a climax here. Wilhelm's defense of untidiness, on the grounds that it is more true to life for the character he is portraying, is the first instance of this. But the main contributor to this interplay between appearance and reality is the figure of the ghost. The actor who plays the ghost turns up just as unexpectedly in real life as he does within the context of the play. This unsettling situation causes Wilhelm to deliver his lines without the customary polished ease, but this actually makes for a more convincing and lifelike performance, and the members of the audience show their appreciation of this. No amount of artistic talent could have produced this degree of verisimilitude.

There is another issue that runs in tandem with the question about the relation between reality and dramatic portrayal and this arises from the script of the play. The reader is told that in the passage containing Hamlet's speech addressed to the ghost, Wilhelm stayed very close to

---

[3] Hamlet addresses his father's ghost below the stage as "old mole" (I, 5).

the original when preparing the text. The narrator approves of this, since only the original version can express the required surprise, shock, and fear. This observation is of a piece with the repeated experience that Wilhelm's actual fear was more effective on stage than a feigned version of it. Just so, Wilhelm realizes that a close facsimile of the original version of the speech is more expressive than any adapted version he might have produced.[4]

The climax of the production is the ghost's revelation of its own identity. For Wilhelm, this pronouncement has an immediate and literal effect: although he does not know who the actor is, and although he knows that his own father is dead, he seems to recognize his father's voice when the ghost speaks. At this moment the confusion between Wilhelm the actor and the role he is playing is at its most intense. It is not a simple matter of Wilhelm's inclination to identify with the character (Blessin 1975, 202; Diamond 92) or of the normative effect the role has on him (Mueller 199). It is not even an example of the claim — as yet to be made — that Wilhelm is unable to play a character whom he does not in some sense resemble. It is more a matter of confusion and internal conflict within Wilhelm. Goethe reinforces this confusion in a number of ways: first, he has the narrator enumerate the assortment of forces at work in Wilhelm at this moment, which include emotions and memories, curiosity, fear, and shame. Another device, which runs throughout the account of the play, is to refer to the main character sometimes as Hamlet and sometimes as Wilhelm. Again, the effect is one of confusion rather than of a successful and complete identification between the actor and his part. The uncertainty comes through once more when Wilhelm is described as constantly shifting position during the ghost's speech; he is a prey to indecision and embarrassment, and is at once both attentive and distracted. Nowhere is there a sense of a good fit between Wilhelm and the role of Hamlet. There is no suggestion that he either plays the part to perfection or that he has been taken over by it. The overriding impression is of an uncertain oscillation between life inside the theater and life outside it.

The ghost's descent is partially obscured by a mist-like rising veil of gauze. This detail revives the theme of veils and scarves which associates the intriguing theater curtain with the enticing scarf which, as part of a woman's wardrobe, can conceal, reveal, or be discarded in careless abandon. The woven texture of the fabric also reproduces the network of

---

[4] In fact, the German translation diverges quite significantly from the English phrase, "a questionable shape." Goethe's word for "questionable" is "ehrwürdig," and is simply adopted from Wieland's translation (Bahr 128).

characters and the mesh between the spheres of appearance and reality. The final sign of the ghost's presence is the flickering flame seen from below each time the group shifts its position. No indication is given as to whether this is a special effect planned beforehand or an inexplicable phenomenon emanating from the mysterious figure. This combination of acting and reacting, of the rehearsed and the spontaneous meets with general approval, as the concluding paragraph makes clear: both the audience and the actors themselves are satisfied with the performance.

Chapter Twelve

At the end of the *Hamlet* performance, the narrator describes the tumultuous applause for Horatio and the delight of the actors as they rise from their graves. The audience wants a repeat of the same play.[1] Serlo is jubilant and keen to begin the celebration. The actors will eat together in their costumes. A room, decorated for the purpose, looks like a garden in one half and a colonnade in the other. The two self-styled theater critics are full of praise for the prompter's Pyrrhus, Hamlet and Laertes's fencing, Ophelia's mourning, and especially Polonius. The absent ghost's performance is also praised, and Madame Melina convinces everyone that she could not see the apparition.

The children and the harper enter, in procession, playing instruments and singing. They are given food and sweet wine. Mignon plays her tambourine more and more wildly. Serlo warns them against taking over the ghost's chair but Mignon has no fear: he is her uncle, she says. The narrator observes that this relates to her earlier reference to her father as the "big devil." The company suspects Serlo of knowing something about the ghost.

The children put on an act like Pulcinello puppets, but Mignon flies out of control.[2] She begins flinging her limbs in all directions like a Maenad.[3] Others try the types of games that involve touching hands with the next person at the table. Madame Melina does not conceal her affection for Wilhelm. As Wilhelm is accompanying Aurelie away from the banquet, he finds the ghost's veil and is surprised by an attack from Mignon, who bites him. Wilhelm goes straight to bed where he hears a

[1] An actor would step in front of the curtain at the end of a performance to announce which play would be performed on the next occasion.

[2] Pulcinello is the clown figure from the comedia dell'arte.

[3] Maenads were the frenzied female followers of Bacchus, the god of wine.

noise and thinks of the ghost. But he finds himself in a woman's embrace and has no strength to resist.

With a light-handed comic touch, the chapter opens just as the curtain closes at the end of the *Hamlet* performance. Goethe continues in whimsical mood by referring to the four princely corpses suddenly springing to their feet. Serlo wants to prolong the euphoric moment and discourages the others from discussing any serious topics that evening. So theatrical illusion effortlessly spills over into ordinary life. The narrator still calls the characters by their stage names at the start of the banquet, and their agreement to dine in their costumes allows the general mood to persist. But the costumes and the fact that the improvised banqueting hall is also decked out just like a stage combine to promote an unreal atmosphere that manifests itself in various ways. The ambience in the room is enhanced by the use of lights — just as stage lighting is crucial for a performance — and fragrant smoke fills the room. This is in keeping with the mist-like veil that, together with the small flames, added a thrilling dimension to the ghost's appearance on stage.

On the basis of their initial behavior, the narrator compares the company to royal spirits. Then the spirit, or ghost, himself, receives praise in his absence, specifically for the marvelous way he succeeded in combining truth and illusion. This statement can serve as a motto for the rest of the evening. The mixture of truth and illusion, of acting and conducting life as usual sets its stamp on Madame Melina, with her show of affection for Wilhelm; on Mignon, in her wild cavorting, her intriguing remarks, and the manic biting episode; on the various impromptu entertainers, including Serlo, the master of illusion on this occasion; and on the impressionable Wilhelm, whose first thought on hearing a sound in his room is of the fully armed ghost. The erosion of the boundary line between illusion and reality also prepares the ground for the discovery of the ghost's veil, a tangible link with this unexplained apparition, and for the strange question of the identity of Wilhelm's companion for the night.

Unresolved mystery accompanies the appearance of Wilhelm's visitor, but Goethe does in fact prepare the ground for the theme involving eroticism. He does so in ways that are evidently more apparent to the reader than to Wilhelm, as his initial reaction shows: Wilhelm is not expecting an amorous, but rather a ghostly encounter. It is Mignon who introduces abandoned frenzy to the banquet scene, and to compare her to a Maenad is to suggest the ecstasy of the female followers of both Bacchus, the god of wine, and, more significantly, of Priapus, the god of sensuality. Even the musical instrument Mignon plays — not the zither on this occasion, but the tambourine — is associated with courting (*MA* 780). The bite inflicted on Wilhelm expresses both frenzy and sexual passion, and it too harks back to the cultic practices in mankind's infancy (Schlaffer *Mythos*, 82). The bite is a frustrated expression of Mignon's inarticulateness, but it is unclear whether she feels jealousy at Aurelie's presence or whether the urge rises up from some deeper spring. In her representation of eroticism and in her androgynous appearance, Mignon is first of all a reminder for Wilhelm of Mariane and his love for her. But then, using a very different image, Goethe once again compares Mignon to a mechanical puppet in this chapter, using the image first applied to her in the egg dance scene. When regarded as a puppet, Mignon sums up the happiest moments of Wilhelm's childhood (Irmscher 154). These two elements — sensual love and childish pleasure — express the contradictory nature that is Mignon's. They demonstrate the coexistence within her of the child and the adult and because both parts hold such significance for Wilhelm, the reader can see how it is that he holds her so dear.

In keeping with the main theme that shows how easily theatrical illusion can spread into everyday life, the leitmotif of the veil reemerges. Associated with other textiles, such as stage curtains, theatrical costumes, Mariane's scarf, and the coat worn by the beautiful Amazon, the veil again emphasizes the thin line between the real and the illusory. The ghost's participation in the play is shrouded in mystery and his performance has an uncanny feel to it, as though it were the result of some sort of spiritual communication. The veil itself makes no small contribution to this effect: it is so insubstantial that the most apt comparison is with mist. And yet, ironically, it is this least substantial element of the ghost's appearance that remains behind to give concrete evidence of his presence.

The veil also forms part of the erotic element of this chapter, not literally, but metaphorically. Uncertainty surrounds the identity of the person who shares Wilhelm's bed that night; it as though the figure were shrouded in a veil, through which some features were discernible, but complete recognition was not possible (Schlaffer *Gattungspoetik*, 208).

The chapter depicts a decisively triumphant success on the stage and a very lively banquet to follow. Emotions are high and unequivocal expression is given to them. And yet several elements remain unresolved at best, while others are opaque or even positively misleading.

Chapter Thirteen

Wilhelm is disturbed at the memory of his unknown visitor: it might have been Philine, but he is unsure. His door is not bolted and he cannot remember if he locked it. The ghost's veil, lying on his bed, has a message sewn into it: "For the first and last time! Flee, young man, flee!" Mignon seems to have physically grown overnight, and is more restrained. Only Wilhelm's good habits get him through the rehearsal. The narrator notes that practice and custom fill the gaps left by genius and mood. A career should not be celebrated at its instigation, but when something is accomplished. A wedding, too, should begin in an atmosphere not of celebration, but of calm and sanguine humility. Wilhelm shows the veil to the others and they assume the ghost will not return. Philine whispers to Wilhelm that she needs to retrieve her slippers and Wilhelm's suspicions appear confirmed. The narrator agrees, slyly adding that it is impossible to know why Wilhelm had any other theory.

Mignon charges in to Wilhelm to announce that there is a fire. Aurelie bursts out of her room and passes Felix to Wilhelm who gives him over to the harper's care. But then, alerted by Mignon that the harper is mad and trying to kill Felix, Wilhelm rushes down the stairs to find Felix lying by a lit woodpile. He rescues the boy but cannot extinguish the flames. Wilhelm is relieved that Felix and Mignon are safe. Mignon addresses him as "Meister." Serlo is keen to start rehearsals again for *Hamlet,* with the actors in new parts. The church authorities want the theater to close after this act of God, but Serlo insists on recouping his losses, and it is a tremendous success. The chapter ends with a focus on the pedant: the narrator remarks on the strange way he has succeeded in his role. The count had predicted great things for him, and Philine advises him to be humble.

The narrative continues the next morning without interruption. But the transition to this chapter is also strengthened by the reappearance of the ghost's scarf; with its sinister embroidered warning, it binds the curious events of the previous chapter with the disastrous ones related here. Wilhelm still suffers from a degree of confusion brought on partly by intoxication. But there is also the lingering mystery surrounding the identity of the ghost and now the narrator adds to this Wilhelm's uncertainty about his nocturnal visitor. A number of details contribute to the general lack of clarity: Wilhelm does not know with whom he exchanged passionate caresses the night before; he finds the door to his room unbolted and cannot actually remember drawing it across as usual; he discovers the ghost's veil spread out on his bed, but is unsure whether he laid it there himself. Finally, not only has Mignon's behavior altered — her very appearance and physical stature seem to have changed overnight.

In the communication of these details, the narrator provides no help for the reader, divulging nothing beyond Wilhelm's perplexed state of mind. But soon after this, the narrator becomes more prominent, offering a commonplace observation in the paragraph describing the rehearsal. The narrator advocates discipline and experience as essential components of any art, as these can fill in the empty places where genius and temperament are wanting. Initially, this remark sheds a positive light on Wilhelm, since his good habits help him perform better in the rehearsal than others — who were still recovering from the night before — could manage. But the remark is double-edged, because it simultaneously passes an ultimate judgment on Wilhelm's innate abilities, and that judgment is certainly negative. Nor does the narrative intervention end here. The next contribution is lengthier and has to do with the role of celebration. If one is embarking on a state or profession and expecting it to last for an extended period of one's life, it is inappropriate to celebrate at the beginning — far better to celebrate a successful completion. This piece of advice has something like the force of superstition, as though precipitate rejoicing were a bad omen for the future. This fits in well with Wilhelm's other recent strange experiences, in particular with the advice sewn into the veil, but it also sounds suspiciously like a death knell for Wilhelm's acting career.

The narrative technique becomes positively intrusive with the clear hint from Philine that it was she who crept into Wilhelm's bed. Once again, her slippers suggest an erotic motif, but the narrator sets Philine's debonair confidence against Wilhelm's obtuseness. In a disloyal move, the narrator turns on Wilhelm, stating that his obtuseness in this matter is beyond comprehension.

In the light of both the stunning success of the opening night, and of the strange events associated with this performance, the boredom of the actors at the prospect of playing *Hamlet* again forms an ironic interlude. The actors' lack of interest and the triviality of the day's pursuits stand in strong contrast to Wilhelm's own adventures. He tries to alleviate the mood and stimulate the interest of the company by showing them the veil. The motto on the ghost's veil recalls the inscription on the powder knife Wilhelm received from Philine. And this is indeed the appropriate stage at which to bring that earlier inscription to mind, since Wilhelm is preoccupied with thoughts of Philine when he awakes. But the advice to Wilhelm to flee can be seen first as a warning of the threat of fire, but then also as an order to leave the stage.

Again there is the curious suggestion that Serlo is acquainted in some way with the ghost's intentions, but the motto on the veil is declared inexplicable. The reader, however, is reminded of the moment when Wilhelm signed the contract with Serlo, and Mignon tried to prevent him from doing so, by pulling at his sleeve. That silent gesture is now reiterated in needlework, the sign that a tension within Wilhelm, which began at the subconscious level, is taking on a concrete form (Irmscher 169). His outward actions do not betray signs of this tension, but periodic allusions to episodes that undermine Wilhelm's confidence in himself as an actor plant doubts in the reader's mind. Much less subtle is the cynical rhetorical question: "How could Serlo agree with someone who seemed to want to deprive him of the best actor in his company?" This portrays Serlo as the self-interested director whose main concern is to keep a good actor working for him.

The traumatic outbreak of fire and the events that occur during the blaze are highly symbolic (Gilby 148). The world Wilhelm had built up in his imagination has gone up in flames. Even though the actors manage to stage another production following the fire, the message for Wilhelm is graphic and undeniable. At first, he does not take in the gravity of the situation, but then Wilhelm realizes the urgency of trying to preserve lives. It is as though the changes in his reaction in these few moments were representations of his own development in capsule form.

Two images from the tradition are clearly discernible in the story of the fire. As the harper prepares to end Felix's life, his gestures, his knife, and the fire he lights all point to the biblical precedent of Abraham and Isaac (Krauss 341–42; Keppel-Kriems 119).[1] The fact that Wilhelm does not directly witness the scene, but hears about it secondhand is a further indication that the events are patterned after a model, in this case, a biblical text. The second image is of Wilhelm leading the harper and Felix out of the fire to safety. Here the picture of Aeneas, helping his father Anchises and son Ascanius to escape from the flames of burning Troy, comes to mind.[2]

With Virgilian and biblical overtones and with a Shakespearean finale, Goethe has almost compressed the literary heritage of the Western tradition into one chapter. And yet the effect on Wilhelm is to turn his attention to other things: he now directs his energies to his human companions, rather than to artistic endeavors. This tendency begins with the night of sensual pleasure, in which Wilhelm lays aside the vow of abstinence he made in honor of Mariane (Gilby 147). Then he becomes aware of renewed and strong affection for Felix and Mignon, engendered by the narrow escape from the fire, and his reaction to the harper's deed is one of concern rather than censure. Wilhelm now knows that his little group of protégés is dearer to him than he had realized and he again vows to dedicate himself to their protection. Both

---

[1] See Genesis 22: 1–13.

[2] Virgil has Aeneas relate the events in *Aeneid*, Book II, l.700–30.

Philine and Serlo, on the other hand, are reassuringly unchanged: Philine is a teasing coquette and Serlo a shrewd opportunist.

Mignon's attitude towards Wilhelm has become more distant and she even seems to have grown. The fact that she addresses him as "Master," or perhaps by his name, Meister, is surely significant, and the narrator draws attention to it. It is less warm than "Father," which was her most recent way of addressing him. But besides being his actual name, it suggests mastery. Mignon rarely utters anything more than a cryptic phrase and so the reader is left to deduce what kind of mastery applies to Wilhelm at this point. Mignon does not use this name in connection with Wilhelm's dramatic performance, and indeed she has already demonstrated misgivings about his involvement in Serlo's troupe. She addresses him as "Master" three times in this chapter: once when asking him to save the building from the fire, again when asking him to save Felix from the harper, and finally when he has succeeded and they are all safe. The implied meaning is that Wilhelm has earned his title through these feats of bravery, he has succeeded in the practical, social context, as distinct from success on the stage (Ammerlahn 1993, 6).

Chapter Fourteen

Wilhelm has to accommodate everyone after the fire, and he takes over the garden pavilion with Felix and Mignon. Philine's attitude has unsettled Wilhelm: she avoids him, then whispers something inaudible. He is divided between disinclination and desire. Wilhelm fears that the harper may have set the fire and is relieved to learn that it broke out in another house. Sitting in the garden, he hears the harper singing sadly. Only the last verse of this lament, "An die Türen will ich schleichen," survives in the text. The harper wants to flee, but Wilhelm explains that he would bring suspicion on himself. Wilhelm manages to force him to enter the pavilion, where they have a remarkable conversation, the contents of which the narrator chooses not to divulge.

The dispersal of the actors to other quarters as a result of the fire is a signal that the group itself may soon be forced to part company in a professional sense as well. Wilhelm's comfortable and surprisingly domestic set-up, isolated with the two children in the pavilion, together with his concern for the welfare of the harper, emphasizes the increasing importance of Wilhelm's "family." His thoughts about the harper are mistaken and, taken with his previous troubled and inaccurate thoughts about the identity of his nocturnal visitor, add up to a confused state of mind. While his physical comfort has been amply provided for, Wilhelm's emotional life is in a state of upheaval. The fire has done more than to dislodge him from his room; it has unseated him emotionally as well, and undermined his confidence. He cannot fathom Philine or her intentions, and now, tellingly, he cannot even make out her words. The chapter is dominated by Wilhelm's thoughts; the narrator even blames Wilhelm's faulty memory for the fact that only the last verse of the harper's song has been printed.

Wilhelm is wrong about the harper on two points: he did not in fact set the fire and he did not perish in its flames. These form the last in a series of misjudgments — about Philine, Mignon, the ghost, and the severity of the fire. For the reader, the signs are clearer: the fact that the fire destroyed Wilhelm's door indicates that he will not be residing with the actors much longer; the burnt slippers signal an end to Philine's mischievous amorous tricks.

Whereas Wilhelm is disorientated, the harper's song marks the singer as close to insanity. This single verse (which, incidentally, does not appear in *Wilhelm Meister's Theatrical Calling*) derives its melancholy tone from the profound lack of understanding between the singer and the rest of the world. Loneliness is again the harper's theme, but, in contrast to his other songs, this one is composed in a regular and popular form — a four-beat, trochaic line. The coincidence of a return to a regular strophic form with the onset of insanity has evoked comparison with the later Hölderlin, who strove to conform ever more closely to the poetic norms (*HA* 764) as his mental capacities deteriorated.[1] Storz suggests an apt comparison with the songs of the mad Ophelia and this is particularly appropriate given the context of the recent *Hamlet* production. In both the harper's song and in Ophelia's ditties, there is an absence both of consolation and of the need for consolation (Storz 1949, 50).

Unlike Hölderlin's translations, in which he attempts to mould the German poetic diction on the pattern of Greek verse, this song uses a rhythm that arises naturally from German intonation. The choice of the trochee here, in preference to the iamb, imparts a naive rhythm to the verse, and this is most evocative of children's chants. Another property of the trochee is its rapid tempo; it is an inherently joyous, dancing beat. This works against the melancholy content of the song, but it also emphasizes the naïve aspect and introduces a bittersweet tension to the whole, counteracting what might otherwise have been oppressive regularity.

The rhyme scheme is simple and confined, which is to say that a preponderance of words deriving from the same stem is further supported by assonance (Dürr/Krause 195). Goethe chooses vocabulary to emphasize

---

[1] This is especially evident in the translations from Sophocles, Pindar, and Euripides, in which Hölderlin took pains to adhere as closely as possible to features of the original, including the word order (Harrison 298).

the childlike impression as well: the harper means to be "still" (quiet) and "sittsam" (demure) like a well-behaved child. In accepting food, he unquestioningly trusts the "pious" hand that offers it, just as a child confidently relies on an adult for nourishment. In this way, three aspects of the song — rhythm, tone, and diction — contribute to Wilhelm's basis for imagining himself the head of a family that includes the harper. Despite his advanced years, the harper displays several childlike features that suit him for inclusion with the youngsters under Wilhelm's protection.

The song describes a way of life in resigned tones and the only outward display of emotion is attributed to others, those who pity the harper. The harper himself, in this song, is indifferent to emotion and does not even understand what could provoke sorrow in his benefactors. The last two lines, which speak of tears, are the only ones that depart from the happier tempo: the caesura in the last line brings the song slowly to a halt. But despite the quiet closing, there is no peace to be found here. The last line, with the single tear on the brim of the void (Storz 50), expresses the singer's lack of comprehension, which is allowed to linger, unresolved. The substituted word "was" (what), for "warum"(why), although perfectly acceptable usage, nevertheless strikes an unnatural note when it appears in the form of an indirect question, and the singer of this phrase appears all the more unconventional, even mentally disturbed, because of it.

The chapter ends with a description first of the harper's attempt to escape from the garden by climbing over the espalier[2] — again an activity favored by children — and then of Wilhelm's attempt to pacify the old man. The narrator takes over the scene, effectively drawing the curtain over it, so as to spare the reader from having to be exposed to the fears and disjointed ideas expressed in this exchange. And so the narrator, who up until this point has been providing the reader with privileged information about the workings of Wilhelm's mind, suddenly adopts a change in policy, allowing Wilhelm to conduct his conversation with the harper behind the scenes. Their parting stands in contrast to the moment they first met in Book Two, Chapter Thirteen (Fick 237). That scene was also introduced by a song, but both it and the ensuing conversation brought the two characters together. Here, both song and discussion express the breakdown in communication and mutual understanding.

---

[2] An espalier is a lattice work of wood against which fruit trees can be trained to grow.

Chapter Fifteen

Laertes knows of a country parson who might have a good effect on the harper. Wilhelm reaches an agreement and the parson takes him in. His harp was lost in the fire, so the harper takes a replacement with him. Aurelie is unsuccessful in persuading Mignon to adopt a feminine style of dress. Performances continue, with Wilhelm frequently in the audience. He hears various reactions and three amusing examples are given. In the first, what sounds like satisfaction with the play is in fact self-satisfaction. In the second, the speaker mistakes Wilhelm for Laertes. A third speaker tempers his praise by mentioning that a ribbon was protruding from Wilhelm's vest.

Serlo and Wilhelm visit Philine one evening and find her in the arms of a young officer in a red and white uniform. She claims it is a woman friend in disguise and Wilhelm thinks of Mariane. Philine coaxes them to guess her name in three tries. She promises to send word in the morning, if her friend will receive Wilhelm, but when he returns the next day, they have gone. Laertes thinks it might have been Friedrich. Wilhelm hires another of Laertes's acquaintances to pursue them.

This chapter contains some important and decisive events and yet it has been largely ignored by commentators. Structurally, too, it is worthy of attention because it is a good example of the simultaneous cyclical and forward motions of the work as a whole. So, with the harper's departure, the reader is reminded of his arrival; with the uninformed reactions of the public in the theater, one thinks again of Wilhelm's vision of educating the public by means of the stage, and with the departure of Philine and the suggested presence of Mariane departing with her, Wilhelm himself is transported back to the world of Book One.

The fragmented, emotional, and disconnected conversation between Wilhelm and the harper at the end of the last chapter had left Wilhelm with the strong impression that the harper needed the kind of help that he himself was unable to provide. The ever resourceful Laertes now comes forward with a plan that consoles Wilhelm and leaves him feeling optimistic that the harper's spiritual wounds and rifts can be healed.

The harper has been strongly affected by the fire; his standard themes of isolation and foreboding take over completely and set him apart from the rest of society. The loss of his harp is symbolic of his exile from the society of his companions, as it calls to mind the Babylonian exile and lament which make up Psalm 137. Mignon, on the other hand, despite Wilhelm's recent impression that she has changed, is unaltered in her view of herself. She still insists on having masculine clothes to wear.

The figure of the country parson is a recurring theme, like that of the scarf or veil, the knife, the inscription, and all the other instances of leitmotifs and connections between disparate elements (Blackall 1976, 124–25). A country parson joins the actors on their boating trip, and Philine and Wilhelm find lodgings with a country parson after the attack, when Wilhelm is recovering from his wounds. The character is not described in any detail and never introduces an overtly religious aspect to the story, but exudes a beneficial spirituality.

The chapter began in tragic mode with Wilhelm taking leave from the harper, but then a comic element enters with the reactions to the *Hamlet* production. What is amusingly referred to as an act of heroism involves a member of the audience stubbornly wearing a hat throughout the performance; this reveals a philistinism more deeply rooted in audiences than Wilhelm had suspected. The second instance is based on the speaker's having confused Laertes and Wilhelm. This might have been an understandable mistake, based on a superficial resemblance, but the narrator makes it clear that the resemblance is not so great after all, which leaves neither the reader nor Wilhelm in any doubt that it was Wilhelm's performance that was being condemned. The third speaker really meant to praise Wilhelm in the scene with Hamlet and his mother, but noted that one small detail of clothing had ruined the whole effect. Just as this scene was ruined, so now the praise with which the speaker began is rendered invalid by the mention of this distracting detail. Wilhelm is downcast by what he hears while sitting among the audience, and even more upset by the events staged by Philine, which occupy the rest of the chapter.

Philine's performance in her rooms is definitely more skillful than what Wilhelm had managed on stage. For Wilhelm, the sight of the officer's uniform alone is enough to produce a strong reaction, a passionate declaration of love sent via a go-between. And Philine, the arch-temptress, knows precisely how much to reveal and how much to conceal. Like a sorceress in one of the Grimms' fairy tales, she allows her visitors three guesses at the name of her friend; indeed, by the end of the chapter, the narrator actually uses the word "Märchen" to refer to Philine's story. Philine provides a very subtle hint when she urges that her friend be protected from an unexpected encounter with a former lover: to meet a ghost would be preferable to that! With this allusion to the unexplained and unidentified ghost who appeared for the *Hamlet* production, Philine suggests that there is acting involved now as well.

The situation provokes an extreme reaction in Wilhelm, to the great surprise of the other two. Philine's act gives rise to a heartfelt outpouring of emotion from Wilhelm, whose love for Mariane has welled up again. But by an ironic twist, this impassioned speech might as well be a performance for the stage, since it is not directed to the object of his affections, but as it were by proxy, to Philine, and the report that Mariane is present is spurious at best. Wilhelm has made himself look foolish and the reader realizes that he is neither able to shine on stage nor to conduct himself as the occasion dictates in real life. That night, Wilhelm is again restless as he used to be before, while in the throes of passion. He is waiting for a note from Philine, to let him know when he can call; this too is reminiscent of the notes passed between him and Mariane and of their secretly arranged meetings in her room. But Wilhelm's present restlessness is based on a fiction, the note from Philine is never written, and when he arrives at her rooms, Wilhelm realizes that the two have departed without leaving any word. The final parallel with the events of Book One is thus a cruel ironic twist: then, Wilhelm left Mariane without a word of explanation; now he himself has to undergo the same treatment. And in both cases, the action is influenced by a figure glimpsed but not completely identified or understood.

It is significant that so much of this chapter is imprinted by the suggestion of drama, that dramatic effects should be heightened just when the troupe is undergoing a crisis in its existence. There is the alternating effect of tragedy and comedy produced by the harper's farewell and the audience's blunt remarks, then by Philine's masterful game of illusion involving the mysterious young officer whose presence is visible only as a uniform, or costume, and then by Mignon's reiterated determination to continue her own illusion by means of her masculine guise. The chapter begins and ends with a dramatic exit — the harper's and Philine's — as though they are going offstage. A frame for the whole is provided by the practical and resourceful Laertes, who knows what to do about the harper at the beginning and then brings Wilhelm down to earth at the end by suggesting that the young officer was in fact Friedrich. His influence on Wilhelm is persuasive enough to dissuade Wilhelm from setting off in pursuit of Philine and her companion, and in this way he prevents a third exit. In the stories of both departing characters, the harper and Philine, there are still matters left unresolved, which suggests that they will step back onto the stage at some point in the future.

The narrator makes two direct interventions. First, when Wilhelm is taken for Laertes, the narrator confuses the issue by claiming that there is in fact a resemblance between the two, but then adds that it is a very remote resemblance. This intensifies the sting of the criticism of Wilhelm's performance. In the second intervention, the narrator addresses the reader in a conspiratorial manner, with the invitation to imagine how restless a night Wilhelm spent after the scene at Philine's place. This too takes the reader back to the restless nights of Book One, when Wilhelm was awaiting a response from Mariane. With its implicit negative assessment of Wilhelm's dreams for the theater both on the national and the personal level, and with its various backward glances, this penultimate chapter has the function of beginning to take stock before a new book begins.

Chapter Sixteen

Philine lingers in the others' thoughts: the women are glad she is gone, while the men miss her. Serlo had meanwhile become romantically involved with Elmire, a girl with a tremendous appetite. Serlo believes that theater should not reflect the endless variety of Nature before a national taste is established. Both society and the theater need limits. The group is divided into supporters of the French and the English stage. When they read French plays, Aurelie leaves the room because her faithless lover switched from German to French in his final letters.

The troupe is satisfied but not for long. Serlo encourages Wilhelm and Aurelie's friendship; they could start running the theater. The public is losing interest and Aurelie's disdain and Serlo's critical stance are well known. The mood deteriorates and Wilhelm fails to restore order. Wilhelm visits the harper, who is giving harp lessons. The pastor stresses the benefit of an occupation. He wants the harper to give up his cowl and beard. Wilhelm is alarmed to hear of a nobleman who became melancholic when someone impersonated him, and who then joined the Moravian brethren. His wife was wounded by a brooch during an embrace with the impostor. The doctor visits Aurelie, who is suffering from a self-induced fever. He will send her an inspiring manuscript written by a woman who found religious sentiment beneficial in her weak condition.

Melina criticizes Wilhelm's management. He suggests Serlo perform amidst mediocre players and employ the others in an opera.[1] Serlo and Melina are hostile towards Wilhelm and Aurelie. The company per-

---

[1] With the Singspiel, a greatly favored form in the eighteenth century, theater and opera were combined. But as opera made increasing demands for professionalism on the part of the singer, there arose a need to keep the two genres separate.

forms *Emilie Galotti*[2] and Wilhelm, as the prince, discusses the difference between noble and aristocratic. Serlo says aristocratic behavior should not be all formality and pride, but the player should avoid vulgarity. A noble man can relax for a moment; the nobleman never can. In art, the hardest things need the lightest touch. To play an aristocrat, one has to be aristocratic.

Serlo criticizes Aurelie for pouring her sorrows into the role. She storms outside, returning with a fever. Aurelie hands Wilhelm a letter for her former lover. Wilhelm reads the manuscript sent to her by the doctor. Then one morning he finds her dead. Wilhelm will deliver Aurelie's message and speak severely to her former lover. Mignon packs the ghost's veil and asks for Mariane's necklace. Melina will take over the theater and his wife will care for the children. Felix asks Wilhelm to bring him back a father. The narrator closes with a poem, "Heiß mich nicht reden, heiß mich schweigen," which Mignon has recited before.

The chapter contains two significant events: the death of Aurelie and Wilhelm's departure. But besides these major events there are also some minor reversals and inconsistencies. The perception of Philine's departure is one of these: at first she is not much missed, but then later the actors realize that she had been a beneficial influence in a variety of ways. As an actress, just as in life, she was not in the habit of exercising responsibility or taking anything very seriously (Kieferstein 51). There also seem to be conflicting forces at work within Serlo. Having tried to promote thoughts of matrimony between Wilhelm and his sister, he is then persuaded by Melina to turn against Wilhelm, and finally offers Wilhelm some friendly and very helpful advice about his acting. At the beginning of the chapter, Serlo's remarks bear the stamp of optimism, but then both the management of the theater company and the public's assessment of it are described as being in a state of decline, and yet the production of *Emilia Galotti* seems destined to be a great success. The most compressed and therefore most striking instance of this contradictory state of affairs occurs within the confines of a single sentence. After Serlo has urged the actors to exercise restraint on the stage, the narrator observes that they are more or less in agreement and disagreement about his views. This observation is surely ironical and points, ultimately, to the impossibility of any sort of resolution (Blackall 1976, 123). All these changeable elements underscore a growing in-

---

[2] *Emilia Galotti*, a tragedy by G. E. Lessing, in five acts, first performed in 1772, was a tremendous success. Goethe also mentions the play in his novel *The Sorrows of Young Werther* (1774), in which Werther leaves a copy of *Emilia Galotti* open on his desk when he commits suicide.

stability, both within the troupe and in Wilhelm's personal outlook. A further discordant note is provided by the coincidence of comic and tragic components: the young and attractive Elmire's healthy gluttony is offset by Aurelie's frailty, self-induced fever, and death.

Serlo's suggestions for improvement are aimed at restricting the disorderly, natural style of acting. Only with the imposition of limits can the public's taste be properly formed. This point of view resembles the spirit behind Goethe's "Regeln für Schauspieler" (Bahr 130), where he discourages spitting and the use of handkerchiefs on stage. It also introduces the aesthetic discussion about the relative merits of the more structured classical French theater and the freer, more natural English style. Serlo is the champion of order, both as regards individual performances and in his preference for the French style of play. In this, he joins forces with Wilhelm the producer, who was eager to introduce more order, and with the parson who explains his methods for restoring the mentally deranged to sanity (Blackall 1965, 63). The need for order establishes itself in opposition to disorder in its various guises: the madness of the harper, Aurelie's overwrought mood and actions, Wilhelm's lack of resolution.

This chapter displays tension between stylized and natural theater, between theater and life. First comes the distinction between Philine as an actress and as a personality. Then Serlo draws a parallel between the need for limits in the theater and the need for the same sort of restraints in a society. But the tension reaches crisis point with Aurelie. Her antipathy towards the French language is based on her inability to separate the sophisticated aesthetic entity that is the language of the stage from the tongue in which the wounding words were written by her lover.[3] More serious still is her inability to separate art from life, acting from living, as her performance in the role of Countess Orsina demonstrates. She is preoccupied with thoughts of the past, and acting is her substitute for life in the present (Blackwell 1965, 63).[4] Another instance arises in Serlo's advice for playing the role of an aristocrat. He formulates the dictum that one needs to be aristocratic in order to play the part convincingly; in other words, there should be no distinction

[3] Aurelie's point of view reflects Herder's remarks in *Journal meiner Reise im Jahr 1769,* in which he associates French with elegance, gallantry, and show, in contrast to the German of the Storm and Stress writers, which expresses true feeling.

[4] The circumstances of Aurelie's demise are based on the fate of Charlotte Ackermann, even including the detail of her dislike of the French language (Krogmann 51).

between art and life. But, ironically, when Serlo and Melina, both well acquainted with the theater, try to keep their plans secret from Wilhelm and Aurelie, they cannot summon the requisite acting skill to disguise their intentions.

The most ironic example of art being closely linked to life is provided by Wilhelm. While listening to an entertaining story by the doctor, Wilhelm suddenly discovers that he himself has lived through the events now being recounted. This experience takes him back to life at the castle and his dalliance with the countess, just as, in the previous chapter, he had been reminded, by Philine's little act, of his relationship with Mariane. These two reminders of past romance stand in contrast to Serlo's failed attempt to convert Wilhelm's friendship with Aurelie into something more serious.

In treating his two patients, the harper and Aurelie, the doctor employs different methods, but these share the basic principle, widely held in discussion among Goethe's contemporaries, that a cure must be based on treatment of both the physical and the psychological (*FA* 1445–46). The harper's main therapy, which is to cure him of exaggerated feelings of isolation and foreboding, is practical activity that benefits others. For Aurelie, who is displaying signs of physical sickliness, a more contemplative method is recommended: reading and discussion. The religious slant of her prescribed reading material suggests an alliance between the doctor and the parson, which reflects again the two-pronged approach to treatment of the ailing (Steer 19).

The narrator and Wilhelm can both see that all is not well with the theater group. The public is tiring of the well-known actors and favoring the younger, less experienced ones; Melina and Serlo are engaged in intrigues, Wilhelm feels that his efforts as producer are going unrewarded, and the narrator sees this deterioration and inability to cope with change as typical for any enterprise built on cooperation. The narrator offers the analogies with a kingdom, a circle of friends, or an army. All of these can attain a state of perfection built on working together, and yet this stable moment is not destined to last, because circumstances and personnel are both subject to change. The departure of Philine had its effect, as did Wilhelm's temporary absence.

Mignon's poem expresses both longing and foreboding. Its iambic metre, naturally akin to speech patterns in prose, is unobtrusive, but a remarkable tension stretches from beginning to end of the poem. The first line is divided by a strong caesura, each half being introduced by a stressed syllable clashing with the natural word stress. This imparts urgency to Mignon's request, while the caesura anticipates the silence of which she speaks. So the initial tension is between speech and silence.

The third line looks into Mignon's innermost being, while the fourth pits the massive force of fate against her individuality.

The second stanza remarks on the inevitability of natural forces and cycles, by way of contrast with the unnatural constraints of Mignon's existence. The dependable sequence of night and day is reinforced by enjambment at the end of the first line: the first line flows inevitably into the second. The metre also proceeds with uninterrupted regularity.

The third stanza moves from the realm of nature back to mankind. The first two lines express a general behavioral pattern which, line three makes clear, is denied to Mignon. Line four, the grand finale, builds up to a climax with the word "Gott" and a light caesura separates this word from the second half of the line, which then fades away, ending on an unstressed syllable. Again, the reader feels that a scene on the stage has come to an end.

Book Six

"Confessions of a Beautiful Soul"[1]

BOOK FIVE ENDS with Mignon's autobiographical poem, and Book Six is autobiographical throughout. It is a reproduction of the original manuscript Aurelie received from the physician who recommended reading material of a religious bent for patients suffering from a terminal condition. It is the work of a female friend of the doctor's who has since died, and he himself had decided on the title for it.

The writer relates that at the age of eight she was afflicted by a hemorrhage, and forced to rely on the resources of feeling and memory. The nine-month convalescence greatly shaped her character. Her main entertainment came from books, stories, and objects. Her mother read from the Bible, her father brought objects from nature, and her aunt read her love stories. On recovering, she spurned toys and longed for living things, in particular a pet lamb. At first, reading provided her consolation, especially pious love stories like *The Christian German Hercules.*[2] Her mother ensured that the Bible was among her reading matter and she also gained the accomplishments of cooking, drawing, speaking French, and dancing.

At a ball, she acquired two admirers, brothers, and liked them both equally. When the older brother fell ill, her sympathy for him resulted

---

[1] The term "beautiful soul" has its origins in Plato's dialogues *Phaedrus* and *Symposium* and in Plotinus. Wieland characterizes the term in his *Geschichte des Agathon* and devotes an essay in the *Teutscher Merkur* to the subject "Was ist eine schöne Seele?"

[2] The book referred to is by Andreas Heinrich Bucholtz (1607–1671), *Des Christlichen Teutschen Gross-Fürsten Herkules und der böhmischen königlichen Fräulein Valiska Wundergeschichte* (1659). It was intended for the nobility and gentry and contains edifying discourses. The other book, which the narrator mentions as her favorite, is by Anton Ulrich, Herzog von Braunschweig. *Die römische Octavia* (1677–1707) presents an aristocratic ideal through the medium of twenty-seven pairs of lovers in six volumes.

in the younger brother's jealousy. She prayed with passion for her friend's recovery but her French teacher urged caution, since virtue is vulnerable to the onslaught of passion. Eventually this relationship faded, and both brothers died.

Events at court made life exciting for the young woman, now fully restored to health. Her religious and literary interests became less important, but still she maintained a distance from the young men who showed an interest in her. With one young man, Narziss, she enjoyed several interesting conversations despite his narcissistic tendencies. Narziss did not show a romantic interest in her but encouraged the literary interests she was concealing because of prejudices against learned women.[3]

One evening Narziss was given a forfeit of whispering something pleasing into the ear of each person present.[4] One man thought Narziss had been too forward with his wife, attacked him with a dagger, and inflicted a serious head wound. The writer sent for a doctor and comforted the wounded man, trying to restore him with wine while the doctor attended to the wound. The experience transformed her feelings into love, and a similar change occurred in Narziss. Her mother warned her that he might be mistaking gratitude for love.

The writer abandoned her superficial pursuits and looked to her spiritual well being again. Narziss, on recovering, visited the household regularly, showing signs, but not speaking of his tenderness for her. She was troubled by this, but not capable of appealing to God again. She expected protection from God, but it was like a prince ignoring a courtier who expects benevolence.

Finally, Narziss asked her to marry him once his position became stable. She imposed certain conditions before finally agreeing. Immediately, relations between them improved: a fiancé is preferable to both a suitor and a husband. However, Narziss's moral stance was different from her own and she felt he only paid lip service to her position. She turned to God again, though still not in the right spirit. Narziss was the reason for everything she did and she felt isolated in society. Eventually she returned to God, but Narziss did not understand.

Narziss held that women should conceal their learning, but also praised her in public for her intellect. He attracted the attention of a man at the court, and they engaged in lively debates. Eventually, she

[3] The name Narziss or Narcissus comes from Greek mythology. Narcissus was a beautiful youth who fell in love with his own reflection in a pool and consequently pined away and died.

[4] Forfeits is a party game in which the player has to surrender something and win it back by performing some ludicrous task.

joined in, and submitted an essay in French and some poems. This pleased the count, who in turn praised Narziss in a poem. Another count and his family moved into town, adopting Narziss and his fiancée as family members.

After a year, a position opened, but, despite his fiancée's prayers, Narziss failed to gain it. This disappointment made him suffer, while the writer found consolation from God. But such consolation was only forthcoming when her own soul was in good order, not when she was involved in unworthy activities. She was torn between wanting to give up their frivolous but all-consuming social life and reluctance to upset Narziss.

Eventually she decided in favor of the good and pure over the merely attractive, and relations with Narziss cooled. To her family she insisted on the right to act in accordance with her convictions, caring nothing for contrary opinions.

Narziss now ceased to visit, although her affection for him did not diminish, and in a note she asked why he was staying away. His reply struck her as evasive and wordy. When he again asked for her hand in marriage, on condition that she change her outlook, she refused.

The writer no longer had to conceal her piety and her enjoyment of nature and the arts, and gained a group of new friends. She joined a movement among the nobility concerned with the health of the soul, and was now drawn more closely in to the same count's family who had welcomed her with Narziss before.

A stepbrother of her father's had lost his wife and son and was in possession of a good-sized fortune. He was an agreeable man; but the narrator was well aware that he had no sympathy for her convictions. He wanted to arrange a marriage for the youngest daughter of the family and for the narrator a position as canoness.[5] The sister was established as a lady-in-waiting at a nearby court, and the narrator accompanied her there. Having engaged fully in the life of the court, she suffered another hemorrhage on returning home and decided to renounce the life of society. Both her parents now fell ill but physical frailty prevented her from caring for them. She saw this as a test of faith. God's presence was a constant source of comfort and she needed no theological system.

She did, regrettably, encounter a system among the Pietists at Halle.[6] They compelled members to recognize their sins and see in punishment an intimation of Hell. She could not subscribe to this pi-

[5] A canoness here is a lay position in the Lutheran church.

[6] The Pietists were a religious movement within Protestantism that laid particular emphasis on the personal nature of the worshipper's relationship with Christ.

ety, preferring a benevolent, not a wrathful God. Her calm confidence kept her from fear, which she did not see as part of religious conviction. But she still had no concept of sin.

The narrator compares her life to a diet, which has good, but not lasting, effects. Eventually, she unwisely became involved in another relationship. She sought guidance through prayer and encountered no objections. The man, Philo, had been of great help to her father, whose strength was failing.[7] He became a friend of the family and particularly of the narrator herself. Her family's warnings did not deter her from the relationship.

Philo was not dissimilar to Narziss, but had been influenced by a religious education. He told her about the members of high society and his own affairs. Eventually he revealed something of his difficult circumstances. She compared him to the hero of Wieland's *Agathon*,[8] who has to pay dearly for his education, and she suffered on his behalf. She too could easily have placed herself in dangerous circumstances: she became aware of being capable of sin. She still felt secure and wanted only to be rid of this consciousness. The possibility of sin had always been present and she compared herself to King David, who was favored by God and yet lusted after Bathsheba.[9]

The writer poses a rhetorical question about morality: must one fall prey to sin at least once, to know how to avoid temptation? Conventional morality was not helpful. The songs of David showed that sinfulness was part of his make-up, but that he prayed for release. She returned to the belief in the power of the blood of Christ to wash away sin. Finally she knew the word of God as the means of redemption. Christ had to pass through the trials of earthly life to regain the heights. She prayed for faith and, suddenly, felt sure she had received it. It was an intense feeling but not peculiar to her. No longer was she content with intermittent feelings of this kind, but seemed to have grown wings to rise above her troubles. Her family could not explain her joyfulness. Now she regretted being persuaded by circumstances to disclose the secret.

The writer analyzes imagery in relation to God: images supplement the strength of the believer through mediation, but they may impede

---

[7] The name Philo, like the name Philine, comes from the Greek verb meaning "to love."

[8] The hero of Christoph Martin Wieland's novel *Geschichte des Agathon* receives an education from Delphic priests, but one of them arranges for his seduction. Agathon is desolate on discovering that the woman is a courtesan.

[9] The Old Testament story of King David and Bathsheba, a story of seduction and murder, is told in 2 Samuel 11.

the true vision of higher things. She still listened to sermons, but felt they remained on the surface. Philo showed her a Pietist hymnbook, and, despite initial skepticism about the views of Count Zinzendorf, its founder, she found some hymns appealing.[10] She read additional works and came to appreciate the count's methods. The story of her spiritual development moved Philo deeply and she thought he was undergoing a conversion. She cared for her aging father and studied these works at home. Meanwhile, relations with Philo had become rather less open.

The writer felt it necessary to conceal her Pietist sympaties from her own court preacher who had previously been disappointed by a courtier's conversion to Pietism. More or less by accident, she became part of a group of worshippers, of whom this courtier was a member. She tried to speak to them of the ultimate meanings, which their expressions did not capture. Eventually the court preacher heard about this movement among his flock and took great offense. Amid bitter debates, the narrator managed to maintain neutrality, still respecting the court preacher. God settled the dispute by calling him to the higher realm.

Meanwhile, the writer's uncle had arranged a suitor and dowry for her sister. The wedding took place at the uncle's splendid but not ostentatious castle. The ceremony itself pleased her and everything seemed to be in harmony — the architecture was as tasteful as the banquet and the company was well entertained. The uncle's home provided a feast for the senses. The sight of so many works of art made the writer reflect on the pleasures of art and delights of nature.

In conversation, the writer noticed that her uncle took her principles into consideration. He esteemed the ability to control and form objects and circumstances, either on a spiritual level, or on the level of the senses. He admired her ability to pursue a goal steadfastly. Both agreed that sacrifices are required in the pursuit of higher aspirations but that an appetite for culture needs to be controlled by a serious attitude. The uncle liked people who had priorities among their various pursuits and explained that he had often endured offers from people who promised him the company of a Sisyphus or the Danaids but had no real conception of poetry.[11]

---

[10] Nikolaus Ludwig von Zinzendorf (1700–1760) was the founder of the Pietistic community.

[11] The Danaids, the fifty daughters of Danaus, killed their suitors and had to scoop up water in the Underworld as punishment. Sisyphus, as King of Corinth, conducted his affairs without principle and was condemned endlessly to roll a marble block uphill after it had rolled back down again.

They discussed the paintings and he made her aware of the artists' technical difficulties. As she was inclined to interpret the moral impact of the subject matter, her uncle saw that moral development accompanies the cultivation of the senses. She recognized the tastelessness of some of her favorite hymns.

Together, she and Philo met a physician who showed them the collection of natural specimens in cases on the walls. The doctor was interested in her religious views and appreciative of her uncle's preservation of items pointing to a view of the unity of human nature.

The uncle planned to sign over his various properties to the bride and her future children. When most of the guests had gone, the choir, which had performed at the wedding, returned for another performance. This contrasted with the lusty but inexpert hymn singing the writer was used to but was not showy concert music either. She was inspired by the harmony of these voices. Before leaving, she received the cross of her order, attached to a large diamond. The uncle tried to maintain his influence on his niece by sending her works of art on loan. She, however, soon reverted to paying more attention to moral content than artistic execution.

Meanwhile, her other sister, still single, was taking care of the household and their elderly father, but she now fell ill and died. This loss affected both the writer, whose own health troubles returned, and her married sister, who had a miscarriage. But soon the writer's prayers were answered and her sister was expecting a child again. The sister and her husband did not see eye to eye, but the writer mediated between them and improved matters. The sister gave birth to a son and the elderly father would not be deterred from traveling to see the child. He was inspired by the baptism, both looking forward to the child's future and to the realm of the afterlife. On his return home, a fever set in, but he expressed quiet confidence in the face of death. The writer was inspired by his serenity.

After her father's death, the writer enjoyed renewing friendships. She returned to the Pietist community, but did not find what she expected there. Meanwhile, the married sister gave birth to a daughter and there was pleasure in planning her upbringing. The sister's husband was less pleased when a second daughter, not a son, followed the next year. The writer worked on bringing her soul closer to God. She felt as though the soul were thinking separately from the body, and knew the past and future. It could see the body torn like a garment, while the true self lived on. The physician she had met at her uncle's redirected her attention to the objects of nature and she was then able to see God in them.

The sister's husband died in a riding accident and his wife also died, after giving birth to a boy. The writer had strong sympathy for the four children, but felt powerless to help them and was relieved when the uncle provided for their upbringing. She compared each child with portraits of their forbears to see which each resembled. The eldest son was like his paternal grandfather and had inherited his interest in weaponry. With the eldest daughter she felt the strongest bond and admired her balanced and charitable nature. The girl, Natalie, was always sorting through her aunt's wardrobe for unwanted garments and refashioning them for the children of poor families. The writer noticed, however, that her niece had no need for dependence on a higher being. The younger sister loved to dress in fine clothes and the writer was pleased to think of her possessions being distributed among her late sister's children.

The writer was not consulted about the upbringing of the children, possibly because her uncle wanted to discourage them from meditation and the search for communion with God. A French Abbot convinced the uncle that the course of education should be determined by a child's natural inclinations. These should be pursued and wrong turns could still be rectified. Her misgivings about this method were based on her need to attribute her own continual progress to something higher than her self. This insight was not being granted to the children.

The basis of the "Confessions of a Beautiful Soul" is an autobiographical manuscript from the hand of a cousin and close friend of Goethe's mother, Susanna Katharina von Klettenberg. The document came to Goethe's attention while he himself was confined to bed as the result of a hemorrhage, and von Klettenberg's visits were important to him. He derived great benefit and consolation from the company of von Klettenberg and she even influenced him to take the first steps towards joining the Pietist movement. Thus, not only does Goethe model the narrator on an actual woman of his acquaintance, but he begins the account with her confinement to bed after a hemorrhage, thus reflecting the parallel incident in his own life (Boyle 2000, 340). In Pietist terminology, the state of sinful temptation is referred to as sickness, so that the writer's need for convalescence at the starting point of the Confessions provides the first image.

Within the novel, these are the memoirs of a character who has no other role and is not even granted a name. The "Confessions" represent the fulcrum on which the earlier version of the novel, *Wilhelm Meister's Theatrical Calling,* is balanced when Goethe extends it to form the final work. The structure and form of Book Six are radically different from those encountered in the other books. This is a continuous narrative, with no division into chapters. The narrative voice speaks in the first person now, rather than in the third person in which practically the whole of the rest of the novel is written. The other portions, such as Wilhelm's childhood reminiscences, and Aurelie's story of betrayal in love, which are related in the first person, are much more tightly integrated into the story. The content of this book is very personal and introspective — no longer does the reader learn of events and journeys, but instead, thoughts, secrets, and, above all, feelings fill the pages.

In terms of the overall structure, critics see it as an interruption in the narrative, which slows down the momentum of events, in accordance with Goethe's designation of the novel in contradistinction to drama (Bahr 136). It is also regarded as an additional account of individual development, which reflects and runs parallel to the main one, Wilhelm's own development (*FA* 1448). The evaluation of the religious perspective of Book Six is vexing: is the life of contemplation, communion with the Creator, and moral introspection offered as something positive, even an ideal (Becker-Cantarino, Swales) or is it presented in an ironic, parodic, and therefore critical light (Norton, Strack)? Alternatively, these two interpretations need not be mutually contradictory and can instead be identified as coexisting, albeit performing different functions, within the Confessions (Beharriell). The positive features then become a tribute to Susanna von Klettenberg while the negative elements are an expression of skepticism towards organized forms of the Christian religion.

Goethe's contemporaries debated whether or not he had taken up a preexisting manuscript and simply introduced a minimum of minor alterations. Nowadays, this question seems less pressing, and, in any case, too difficult to determine. It is commonly assumed that Goethe modified the manuscript to suit his own ends. Accordingly, the practice adopted by some commentators, of naming the unnamed narrator Susanna (Beharriell, Sjögren) appears to beg the question and is therefore avoided here.

The insertion of a fictional autobiographical interlude was a favorite device of eighteenth-century European novelists, and appears most notably in Christoph Martin Wieland's *Geschichte des Agathon* (1767).[12] There are earlier models too. The religious, confessional nature of the insertion points to the *Confessions* of Saint Augustine (397–98), rather than to the more closely contemporary *Confessions* (1765–70) of Jean-Jacques Rousseau (*MA* 785). Both these writers also use the term

---

[12] The narrator of Book Six herself refers to Agathon (see note 8). An earlier novel that employs the same technique is Johann Gottfried Schnabel's *Insel Felsenburg* (1731–1743).

"beautiful soul," Rousseau in his novel *Julie, ou la Nouvelle Héloise* (1761; *FA* 1449–55). The combination of natural virtue, beauty of character, and grace outlined in Schiller's essay "Über Anmut und Würde" (1793) describes the "beautiful soul" in terms that contribute something to Goethe's depiction of her here in Book Six. Yet the narrator is a composite character who owes as much to Wieland's ironic use of the term as she does to the more serious-minded Schiller.

Goethe prepares the way for the insertion of the Confessions by mentioning, in the last chapter of Book Five, the doctor's request that Wilhelm read to Aurelie from this manuscript. The narrator adds that the reader will be able to judge the effect this had on her after becoming acquainted with the text in the next book. This is perhaps a somewhat artificial and flimsy link, but it is reinforced at the end of the chapter by Mignon's poem, the precise placement of which is also not particularly well grounded or explained (Boyle 2000, 339). Mignon's themes are secrecy, and the desire to reveal her innermost thoughts and feelings. Against this she posits a strong sense of moral obligation that, because it contrasts starkly with the realm of nature in the second stanza, must be seen as unnatural. In the third and final stanza, compassion and love are denied in the name of this mystery, whose disclosure would have to be divinely ordained. The secrecy, the isolation from society and companionship, the presence of the divine, and the inclination towards inwardness are all elements that return in Book Six.

The first event in the life of the beautiful soul is a hemorrhage. This clearly exemplifies Goethe's practice of contributing his own experiences to his works of fiction, but it also functions as a religious symbol. Bleeding and the resultant loss of physical strength are the preconditions for the narrator's introspection and heightened sentiment; the hemorrhage marks the start of her more cerebral path of development, but there is an obvious Christian motif here too. Suffering and loss of blood in the service of a greater good apply both to the individual life of the narrator and to the Christian understanding of Christ's suffering. On yet another level, the bleeding has to do with female sexuality, and the nine-month confinement to bed is symbolic of the period of gestation after which a new, more spiritual being will emerge (Staiger, 142).

The parallels with the account of Wilhelm's childhood are many (Boyle 2000, 343). The first are suggested by the narrator's means of entertainment: puppets and books are brought to her bedside, and her mother reads her stories from the Bible. Both the writer of this manuscript and the narrator of the novel as a whole use biblical allusion as part of their standard idiom. The titles of favorite books during the childhood of both the beautiful soul and of Wilhelm are explicitly mentioned. The beautiful soul's father encouraged her to develop an inquiring mind, while her aunt read her romances and stimulated her fancy to the point where she confused the products of her imagination with reality. Again, stages of Wilhelm's early life come to mind, particularly the episodes in which his overactive imagination misleads him. Here, however, the perspective is a moral one, as the phrase "Prince of this World" is used to characterize the aunt's more secular contributions to her niece's reading list.[13] And the mention of her communion with the Invisible Being sets the narrator definitively apart from Wilhelm. For Wilhelm, passion for the theater has taken the place of the quest for religious faith.

On her recovery, the narrator has but one wish — for a pet lamb. She traces this back to one of the fairy tales her aunt had read to her, in which a lamb, kindly treated by the heroine, turns out to be an enchanted prince, but this attribution is simply a smoke screen for the Christian symbol for Christ: the lamb of God. The juxtaposition of a childish tale with Christian imagery, and the emphasis on wounds and blood in this book give substance to the view that Goethe wished to expose some aspects of Christian worship as sentimental and distasteful. Although Goethe had been drawn to and actually joined the Pietist movement, this was some twenty-five years earlier and he had had time to gain a critical distance by the time he was writing the novel.

The tension now arising between the parents, brought about by their daughter's reading habits, is reminiscent of the differences between Wilhelm's parents on the subject of the theater. The narrator's mother insists that the Bible be part of her reading matter and the young Wilhelm's first puppet show has a biblical theme. The narrator's father tries to appease the stricter mother, while still keeping his daughter entertained. In Wilhelm's household, the roles were reversed, but the dynamic was the same. And while Wilhelm had his head in the clouds, fancying himself in the roles of various heroes in books, the narrator of the Confessions, by contrast, is eagerly accumulating practical knowledge and experience.

Into the most worldly of pursuits, religious symbolism infiltrates. The narrator enjoys dancing and the company of two young men, who are brothers. What decides her in favor of one over the other is an event involving his suffering and her show of compassion. She refers to him now as the lamb she had longed for, and relates that the experience led her to look inward and devote herself to prayer. This episode establishes a pattern in which her relations with men are associated with

[13] The phrase is Martin Luther's name for the devil.

injury or suffering, and lead not to lifelong companionship, but to her renewed isolation and introspection.

Based on what his pupil writes as an exercise in French prose, the French tutor sees fit to deliver a lecture to her on the perils of loose morals. She had hoped to make her account appear fictional and innocent, by inserting the names Phyllis and Damon, standard names from Rococo pastoral verse (Bahr 147). Pastoral genres had also made their way into Wilhelm's puppet repertoire. The adoption of fictional names is a standard idiom in the Confessions: the names Narziss and Philo are allegorical, and later on the narrator draws a comparison with Agathon, the eponymous hero of Wieland's novel.[14] This habit, taken together with phrases which link real people with the lambs or handsome princes in books, imparts both a fictional and a didactic flavoring to the book, and militates against the view that these pages are essentially the work of Susanna von Klettenberg.

The figure of the French tutor and self-styled mentor allows Goethe to introduce a criticism of the eighteenth-century concept of virtue and triggers some rather distracting speculation among commentators. His eagerness to disclose to his pupil the distasteful aspects of human sexuality points to an unhealthy obsession on his part (Beharriell 50). But, alarming though his warnings may have been, the tutor's effect on his pupil's subsequent development should not be overrated. Her independence of spirit is merely strengthened by her various encounters with men.

The narrator associates dissolute periods of her life, when she is caught up in a social whirl, under the influence of people who lack depth and substance, with a neglect of her reading habits. On reflection, she realizes something Wilhelm failed to see during his period among the nobility — that courtiers are completely lacking in culture. Although she participated in a flurry of activity, and although she no longer spent time in prayer and meditation, the beautiful soul cast a critical eye over the company.[15] Because most of them seemed superficial to her, the young man referred to as Narziss stood out as knowledgeable and well read. However, since the whole of the Confessions is

[14] The only name given to the French tutor is "Mentor" and this too is based on a literary source: the original Mentor was Telemachus's tutor in Homer's *Odyssey*.

[15] The verb "schwärmen" is used to describe the dangerous enthusiasm to which she was subject at this stage. It was a prominent expression in the eighteenth century, applicable to religion, philosophy, and aesthetics and was generally introduced as part of an argument for balance and moderation. The excesses of "Schwärmerei" were to be avoided.

devoted to self-analysis, the irony of accusing this young man of self-absorption is hard to overlook.

The narrator becomes acquainted with Narziss at a dance. This is worthy of mention because dancing represents worldly temptation — at first they dance, and then they both decide to sit out. Significantly, Narziss retreats from the dance floor because of a nosebleed, and it is at that point, rather than when they were actually dancing together, that they become close. The recurring blood imagery, associated with a male character, is a parody of the redeeming blood of Jesus Christ (Strack 58). Through Narziss's loss of blood, the narrator is enabled to turn away from the worldly temptation that dancing represents. Until then, she had been swept along by the frenzied activity, but now, through Narziss's influence, her more intellectual pursuits return. In society, she feels compelled to conceal her inclinations towards self-improvement through reading; this is a further condemnation of that society and an additional reason for her to turn her back on its members.

The transformation of a friendship into something deeper and more romantic comes about as a result of Narziss's spilt blood. His injury was undeserved — a further ironic parallel to Christ's suffering, and it permits the narrator to step into the role of a Mary Magdalene, or good Samaritan (Strack 58), caring for his wounds. Narziss becomes much more closely attached to her as a result and soon asks her father for her hand in marriage (Staiger 141). For her, however, the aftermath of this incident is even more significant. Her own transformation takes place behind the scenes, when her blood-soaked clothing has to be discarded. At that moment, she sees herself naked in the mirror and recognizes her own beauty for the first time. This revelation again invites comparison with that much earlier opposite instance of a mirror image, in which the count sees Wilhelm but thinks it is his own reflection. The count's experience was a deceptive one; he saw what he thought was his own image in the mirror and was led to join the Pietists as a result of the trauma produced by this false reflection (Strack 63). For the beautiful soul, the reflection is the transforming moment of self-knowledge, not through contemplation, or the presence of the Invisible Friend, but through realization of her own erotic potential. In both instances, Goethe throws into question the integrity of the principles of Pietism. In one, conversion is based on a deception and in the other the sacrificial blood does not bring about an increase in piety, but an increased awareness of the physical self. The fact that Narziss's blood spread to her clothing is again a parody of Christ's suffering, which Christians believe benefits all believers. In a final irony, the narrator, in admiring herself in the mirror, is indulging in precisely the pastime for which the original Narcissus received his bad name.

While Narziss regains his health and begins visiting the family regularly again, the narrator tries to restore her relations with the Invisible Friend. In both these relationships there remains a lack of clarity and certainty, but they develop in tandem. By the time Narziss becomes her fiancé, the narrator has also moved closer to God. On moral issues, she holds a steadfast position and is confident of finding favor in the eyes of God, although with hindsight she sees this as self-righteousness. Her world revolves around Narziss and yet her own moral values lead to disagreements between them. In effect she more or less reproduces the earlier situation in which she had two suitors, by pitting Narziss and God against each other as rivals (Beharriell 53).

The engagement hinges on Narziss's ability to procure a better position, and when he is passed over in favor of a weaker candidate, the narrator quickly runs through a succession of feelings. In the end she seems to be relieved because this obstacle to her marriage must have been God's will. Yet her feelings and inclinations remain in a state of contradiction for some time; she is even unclear about whether she enjoys dancing or not. Narziss has contradictory views to match: on the one hand, he wishes her to mask her intellectual interests and on the other, he is proud to talk of her gifts and achievements.

The beautiful soul uses a series of images to explain the final break with Narziss. The tension between pleasure and morality is compared to a preference for fresh air over a plentiful supply of wine. Her bond with her fiancé is like a glass dome, which could easily be broken to allow access to fresher air. She says her feelings resemble a thermometer, which cannot remain standing at a high level on its own. Her determination not to yield to pressure to change her views is compared to a refusal to drink coffee, against all advice to do so, because it is harmful.[16] When the final break comes, it is, significantly, like the feeling of straining to get out of the theater when the final curtain has fallen. This image is an echo of Wilhelm's departure from the theater company.

Now the beautiful soul finds that her case has attracted curiosity. It is said that she prefers God to her betrothed, but she feels she has gained something by giving up a relationship which would have required her to keep pace with society. Narziss was too closely bound up in the world of appearance, and did not want them, as a couple, to be seen as disapproving of entertainment. This difference in perspective is

---

[16] Goethe considered coffee to be harmful; he gave up drinking it and urged his close friend Frau von Stein to do the same.

what led to the break, rather than the apparent rivalry between Narziss and God (Reiss 1963, 118). The kind of society the narrator enters next, where she feels much more comfortable, is composed of members of the nobility and defined by a newfound fashion for piety.

The uncle who now looms large in the story is yet another man with little or no understanding for the beautiful soul's point of view. His generosity and cultivation do little to change her view of him, despite the fact that he procures her a position as a lay canoness. Her sister is introduced at court and so the narrator once again finds herself at the center of much social activity. Thus there are two temptations that stand as obstacles to her proper spiritual growth. One is the companionship of a man and the other is society. The dangers of the latter are now made manifest by her failure in health as she suffers another hemorrhage.

The beautiful soul regards the whole of life from the perspective of her own spiritual health. Her parents' frailty is represented as a test of her endurance; every occasion she has for reassessing her principles reinforces her self-satisfaction. Nevertheless, her inclination for society never quite disappears, and is transformed into membership in a Pietist group. Yet again, she later regrets this step and so the cycle is perpetuated. The hindrance to integration into the Pietist group is her inability to understand the concept of sinfulness. Not only does she reject such a notion in relation to herself, she also rejects offers of assistance in matters of faith, confidently relying on her own direct relationship with God instead. Yet a need for companionship still persists.

The friendship with Philo seems promising because he has a grounding in religious matters. But the headstrong manner in which she ignores advice against this relationship and the assurance with which she assumes she has received divine approval for it do not augur well. Again, a parallel to Wilhelm's early development can be noted: he is convinced, with very little evidence, that he will be successful in a career on the stage. But whereas Wilhelm knows enough to keep his relationship with Mariane secret from his parents, the beautiful soul evidently discusses Philo with her friends and family. As she was warned against Narziss, so now everyone advises her not to become too friendly with Philo. From her own perspective, however, it is through his acquaintance that she is able to reach a new stage in her spiritual journey.

The content of the warnings against Philo is not made explicit, but, since the narrator is a lay canoness, the fears of her family and friends would have had to do with her vow of chastity (FA 1463). The significance of the name Philo now becomes clearer and the erotic theme embodied by Philine in Wilhelm's story is reintroduced. Through Philo's disclosures about his past, she learns the character of sin. So foreign is this thought that she can only relate to it through literary analogy. She thinks of Wieland's hero, Agathon, whose early education was undone by the temptations of the flesh, and seems unaware of the satirical tone of Wieland's work. Agathon is the type for Philo, but when she tries to grasp the idea that she too has the potential for sin, the narrator presumptuously looks to a biblical example and asks whether, like David, who was favored by the Lord, she could succumb to weakness, as he did at the sight of Bathsheba. However, in an attempt to apply the unfamiliar idea of sinfulness to herself, the beautiful soul, in all seriousness, goes to ludicrous extremes. She compares herself to the notorious contemporary criminals Girard, Cartouche, and Damiens, and thus unknowingly makes herself an object of satire.[17]

It should not be forgotten that the Confessions are being read by Wilhelm himself. Just as the narrator draws parallels between certain events in her life and episodes in books, so Wilhelm would find in these pages a story with many similarities to his own. Both have the habit of looking to figures in literature for guidance in life. Individual characters represent similar stages in both lives, both are subject to self-delusion, and both narratives employ circular structures. The Confessions tell of events that predate Wilhelm's own experiences, but since he only reads them afterwards, the reader is justified in identifying parallels without regard for chronology. The ailing prince is one case in point, for the beautiful soul's presence at a young man's scene of suffering is repeatedly associated with the onset of feelings of love.

Through her discovery of the sinful nature of mankind, the beautiful soul acquires renewed faith. Ironically, the experience of being faced with the reality of sin results in a sensation of freedom from the world. She uses the image of a bird: she gains the illusion of having grown wings to lift her above all the things she finds oppressive (Reiss 1951, 130). Her wavering assessment of the use of imagery in one's relation to God follows. She acknowledges how useful imagery can be, but also relates how superficial many of these outward signs seemed to her, so that she is prepared to dispense with them on more than one occasion.

In a parody of the Christian view of temptation, Goethe now has the narrator defy the voice of her conscience, unable to resist reading some of the works of Count Zinzendorf and looking at the hymnals used by Pietists. The next step is conversion to Pietism, but still with a critical stance. The beautiful soul feels that when the customary phrases are used, her understanding of them is much deeper than that of the

---

[17] Girard was accused of seducing a penitent, Cartouche led a band of robbers, and Damiens was put to death for an assassination attempt on Louis XV.

older members. Her association with the group has to be clandestine, for fear of offending the court preacher; she tells an anecdote about a parishioner who had offended the court preacher in just this way, but had since returned to the fold, amid much rejoicing. The details are based on actual events (*FA* 1466), but the parable of the prodigal son is evoked in the telling. Goethe transforms this story into a parody, thus gently poking fun at the church.

The beautiful soul's development is punctuated by the men who acquire significance in her life. The main two are obviously Narziss and Philo, but there are also minor characters against whom she defines her position. Though she respects the court preacher, for example, when he overreacts against the influence of the Pietists, she begins to despise him. Another male character with whom there is no romantic attachment, but whose views need to be grappled with, is the uncle. He arranges for the sister of the narrator to be married at his castle and the narrator, while staying at the castle, finds herself confronted with the aesthetic realm, with which she must now try to come to terms. This is a kind of temptation for her, just as the parties and other social activities were earlier on. She is frankly swept away by the splendor and good taste of everything she finds there. She is forced to admit that the work of human hands must not remain unrecognized, but can stand alongside the beauty of nature, that professional singing is aesthetically more pleasing than the most heartfelt but untrained chanting in church. The conversations she now has with her uncle about her moral cultivation are reminiscent of Wilhelm's discussion with a stranger on the subject of destiny.

At the castle, the narrator is also confronted with fine paintings and the uncle is only too happy to instruct her in the art of visual appreciation. The stumbling block is that she assesses a work of art from the point of view of its moral content and decides its merits according to her own standards. She has no appreciation for artistry. This difference in opinion bears some similarity to that between Wilhelm and his father, for whom works of art are commodities rather than expressions of inspiration. At the castle, paintings, books, and collections of specimens are there to be admired, and the uncle tries to impress upon his niece the advantage of cultivating the senses alongside the nurturing of the moral being. The culmination of this doctrine, in concrete form, is the gift of the cross of her order, which she receives on her departure from the castle. It is a work of art, both delicate and rich, adorned with a large diamond.

The uncle's view of human nature is based on the principle that personal circumstances circumscribe individual development. There is nothing to be gained by straining to achieve more, simply in order to be able to point to one's achievements. Self-cultivation is worthwhile only if one actually learns something; too often, there is little in the way of serious intention behind such activities. To illustrate this point, he mentions the Danaids and Sisyphus, both condemned to futile activity in the afterlife (see note 11). Implicit in this view is a criticism of the beautiful soul's way of life.

Time spent at the uncle's castle is enriching in other ways as well. The volumes in his library provide the proper perspective and the study of her uncle's collection of natural specimens brings its own interest for the narrator. She herself draws the parallel with her childhood convalescence, when her experience of the world was confined to the objects and books that could be brought to her bedside. As then, she emerges from this period of stimulation with a deeper insight into the questions that interest her. Now, she is prepared to acknowledge that certain phenomena in the secular realm can be inspiring in a spiritual sense.

Adverse events in the narrator's family set more tests for the narrator's fortitude. Her elder sister's death affects her deeply, but her father dies peacefully, and with the conviction that he has nothing to fear from death. This is a consolation for the beautiful soul; she was also relieved to have gained more freedom of movement through his death. The circular movement characteristic of the narrative's structure continues: the narrator returns to the Pietists and once again meets a man in opposition to whom she defines her position. Her worldliness is still a factor, since her distaste for this man stems from the fact that, although a bishop, his origins are working class.

More introspection follows, at the end of which she expresses the view that her body is to her soul as a dress is to the body wearing it — a separate entity. The soul, in this vision, thinks on its own, without benefit of attachment to the body. The body will fall away, but the soul, the "I," exists on a different plane. This basically Pietist outlook also has a philosophical grounding. The body stands for the attractions of society, whereas the soul, conscious of itself, represents the Cartesian proof of consciousness, whereby the faculty of thought rather than physical presence is decisive (Schings *Pathologie,* 50). The doctor who had displayed the nature collections in the castle now hastens to correct this one-sidedness by insisting on activity as a central principle of humanity, as well as emphasizing the need to know the external world. Thanks to his influence, equilibrium is restored.

The tension between the physical and the spiritual is repeated ever more frequently as the Confessions draw to a close. The image of the body separated from the thinking soul and somehow superfluous to it is quickly defeated by the doctrine which posits activity as being central to human existence. In relation to the children, the narrator is torn between realizing that her physical weakness would prevent her from taking an active role in their upbringing and a strong desire to influence their education. She takes pleasure in tracing their natural hereditary features, and incidentally bases her deductions on works of art. Hitherto, the interest in a painting was, for her, confined to its moral message. Running somewhat contrary to this trust in family traits is her concern about the principle being applied to their upbringing, namely, that they should follow their natural inclinations and so arrive at their goals with real conviction. She would like to put her own faith into practice, and feels capable of guiding these children through life, but the uncle keeps them from her. On the other hand, she closes with the hope that she would never pride herself on her own abilities, since without God's guidance, the baser side of human nature will flourish. Embedded within this hope is a contradiction: she certainly does consider herself superior to the tutor placed in charge of the children. Her general statement about intolerance in practical matters applies both to the uncle and to herself.

The reader notes that the educational method prescribed for the children traces more or less the path that Wilhelm has taken since he first started out on his journey. He has been following his inclinations and has always been free to make mistakes. This pattern of development for the individual lacks any real plan or control, and to that extent the Confessions stand as an implicit criticism of Wilhelm's progress (*FA* 1448). But the many instances of irony demonstrate that Goethe did not intend the beautiful soul's methods to stand as an ideal.

As part of her concluding remarks, the beautiful soul describes her progress as always tending in a forward direction. Goethe, on the other hand, famously said of this book that it points both forwards and backwards.[18] If this is so, then the book is not so markedly different in its function, at least, from the other books so far. The narrative does prepare for this manuscript to be read; what the reader does not yet know is whether any of the characters introduced here will have significance in the remaining two books, or indeed whether they have already been encountered.

---

[18] The phrase is from a letter he wrote to Schiller, dated March 18, 1795.

Book Seven

Chapter One

WILHELM IS RIDING along, musing at the sight of a rainbow. He wonders why colors need a dark background and if sorrow must precede joy. A moving experience or sight helps define one's destination. He recognizes a fellow traveler as the parson from the boat trip. In fact he is a priest, as his tonsure proves.[1] Wilhelm relates that he stayed too long with the actors and did not benefit from the experience. The priest says every experience leaves impressions, but one should look to the future. Wilhelm is to deliver Aurelie's letter to Lothario;[2] the priest gives him directions and says he will see him at the estate. Wilhelm begins rehearsing his speech.

At the estate, convenience outweighs architectural symmetry. Wilhelm waits in a hall with portraits of aristocratic figures. Lothario's charm is disarming and he accepts the letter, so Wilhelm abandons his speech. Lothario is preoccupied and yet invites Wilhelm to stay the night. In his room, a print of a shipwrecked father and two daughters, one of whom resembles the Amazon, produces strong emotions in him.

Wilhelm dreams of his father, with Mariane, in a garden. Wilhelm approaches Aurelie, who ignores him. Madame Melina is holding a rose, Laertes is counting money, Felix and Mignon are lying in the grass. Philine claps her hands, and Felix runs after her. With the harper pursuing him, the boy becomes frightened and falls into a pond. Wilhelm is paralyzed and the Amazon saves Felix. Felix is burning, and the Amazon puts out the fire, using a white veil from her head.

---

[1] A monk or priest, on entering the order, has his head shaved. He can be instantly recognized by this sign of humility.

[2] The use of allegorical names noted in the last book is still in evidence here. The name Lothario means "a carefree seducer" and is based on the character Lothario in Nicholas Rowe's play *The Fair Penitent* (1703). It is significant that the name of Aurelie's lover is derived from a play, given her tendency to imbue her performances with her personal sufferings (Brown 144).

Wilhelm and the Amazon walk hand in hand through the garden, while Wilhelm's father and Mariane are far off. Suddenly, Friedrich blocks Wilhelm and the Amazon's path, and taunts them, before moving off to the other pair. Wilhelm's father and Mariane flee and the Amazon holds Wilhelm back. With a pleasant feeling, but mixed emotions, he awakes to find the sun shining.

Book Seven opens without even a glance back to the events related in Book Six and yet, in an indefinable way, the intervention of the Confessions seems to have had some influence on the nature of the final two books. The task will be to find how Book Six, despite appearances, does in fact build a bridge between the first five books and the last two (Reiss 1963, 80). Wilhelm's introspective mood at the beginning of the chapter seems to carry over from his reading of the Confessions. He is thinking about the rhythms of fortune, and about how Nature sometimes mirrors features of human life. Inspiration and motivation, he reflects, can come from hearing about good works or contemplating objects of beauty.

As Wilhelm rides off, the reader remembers his earlier departure, in Book Two, Chapter Three, also on horseback and similarly uplifted by the beauty of the countryside and of nature in general. The first parting was from his home, family members, and the world of trade. Now he is leaving the acting world behind, and he again senses that the task he is to perform is less important than the act of leaving. His reflections on contrasts and aims in life are all too apt in their application to his life so far. In contrast to his father's world, the theater seemed bright and attractive and now the sight of a rainbow both evokes past regrets and accentuates the promise for the future.[3] The image of the dark background against which the brighter colors can define themselves evokes both the art of painting and the backdrop of the theater. He seems to have an intuition that his present journey may be bringing him nearer to a goal, as yet ill defined. At the end of the chapter, the sun, significantly, is shining again and Wilhelm, in his dream, has just encountered the beautiful Amazon whom he was once determined to find.

The element of recurrence is in evidence when Wilhelm and the priest meet on the road. At their first meeting (in Book 2, Chapter 9), the company took him for a country parson. This was on an outing, an activity that has no point outside itself; the present journey has a definite purpose and promises, already in this chapter, to bring about some

---

[3] The rainbow image is introduced at the beginning of *Faust II* (l.4721–27) in a similar situation. The events of *Faust I* are forgotten and Faust's mood is one of optimism.

significant events. In both this and his first appearance, the priest offers an insight into life and then departs. In reply to the priest's inquiry, Wilhelm claims he cannot think of any lasting benefit from being with the acting troupe for so long. This is a curious statement, since he certainly learned a considerable amount about acting and stage management and made some close friends as well. The remark seems to arise from the image of the rainbow against a dark background, which set him thinking in the opening paragraph. Wilhelm is looking to the future with optimism and those earlier experiences are merely insignificant memories now. The sorrow he speaks of is no doubt the death of Aurelie, since her loss is the actual cause of his present journey.

The priest corrects Wilhelm, saying that even if we do not notice it at the time, all experience contributes to our development. The word he uses is "Bildung"; if the first five books are still in some sense a novel of the theater, the last two center increasingly on the concept of personal development. Apart from the actual use of the term "Bildung" here, there are also less explicit indications that Wilhelm has developed and is interested in developing further. The priest observes that Wilhelm is not under any misapprehension as to his identity as a Catholic priest, as opposed to the last time they met, and this is a good sign. It means that Wilhelm sees more clearly now. In addition, the reader is surely taken unawares by the decisive way in which Wilhelm speaks of having parted from the actors. The priest tells him he is wrong to believe that the time he spent with them has left no trace. He adds, on the other hand, that it is best not to dwell on what is past, but look to the immediate future. This is, in fact, precisely what Wilhelm is doing, in relegating his acting experiences to the status of a memory.

The speech that Wilhelm has prepared is ironically described as a work of art. He knows it by heart and can deliver it with a high degree of emotional intensity. It symbolizes his life on the stage, and his failure to deliver it is a subtle negative judgment on Wilhelm's abortive attempt to establish an acting career for himself. Again, one is reminded of Wilhelm's previous solo journey, when he recited various poems to himself, including "Pastor Fido."

Wilhelm's arrival at the estate encourages a comparison with the castle belonging to the count and countess in Book Three. The first sight of that edifice was magical, suggesting something out of a fairy tale (Braemer 170). After the initial promise, however, the actors were disappointed by their less than welcoming reception. The building Wilhelm now approaches is irregularly planned and asymmetrical; the extensions have been made not with an eye for architectural elegance, but rather with convenience as the guiding principle. There is an overall lack of ostentation and pretension and this shows as well in the way Wilhelm is received. Although there are some curious, even inexplicable features about his first meeting with Lothario, there is no lack of hospitality. But there is no show or ceremony, and that is why Wilhelm cannot bring himself to deliver his formal speech.

Initially, while Wilhelm was waiting to be admitted to Lothario's presence, he had felt that his speech would fit in well with the formal portraits of the aristocracy hanging in the hall. Later, in his room, the motif associated with paintings recurs. Wilhelm reacts sentimentally to a painting of a father shipwrecked with his two daughters.[4] The reader is reminded of the similarly strong effect produced in Wilhelm by the painting of the ailing king's son (*MA* 812).

Still feeling somewhat uneasy because the meeting with Lothario did not follow the imagined course, Wilhelm unpacks. The discovery of the ghost's veil provides him with a further reason for feeling unsettled, as well as forming a link between Book Five and present events. He cannot, at this point, understand the relevance of the admonition to flee, even though the reader can already relate this to Wilhelm's departure from the stage. Because Wilhelm does not realize the finality of his break with the troupe, he cannot see that this admonition has already, in a sense, been fulfilled. The wording of his response is interesting: he thinks that more fitting advice would have been to turn back into himself. On one level this means that he has become aware that acting was not his true calling. On another, it indicates that he has been influenced by reading the Confessions and is now more inclined towards the analysis and cultivation of the self.

The emotions provoked by the picture of the shipwreck find their way into Wilhelm's vivid and detailed dream, along with other components drawn from his memory. The dream recapitulates a number of features of Wilhelm's life and to this extent it, too, has a unifying influence on the narrative as a whole. Ironically, although this is only a dream, its contents are rather more concrete than either Wilhelm's thoughts at the beginning of the chapter or the fantasies and ambitions that led him to pursue an acting career (Hass 194). The figures who appear to him are distinctly recognizable and even the surroundings of the garden are clearly described. The dream clarifies certain events and

---

[4] The picture commemorates an actual event. In 1786 the "Halsewell" went down off the coast of Dorset, with Captain Pierce and his two daughters. Prints of pictures by Smirke and Northcote were widely known in Goethe's day (*FA* 1475).

suggests future developments, although neither Wilhelm nor the reader can know this yet.

Wilhelm's father allies himself with Mariane in the dream — they both belong irretrievably to the past, and, by the end of the dream, have become almost ethereal. Aurelie's face is not visible, no doubt because there remains something unresolved about his relationship to her: Wilhelm has not produced the desired degree of remorse in Lothario on Aurelie's behalf. Madame Melina plays with a red rose, the symbol of love — she often behaved in a flirtatious manner in Wilhelm's presence. It is not entirely clear why Laertes is handling money, but it accords with his resourceful and enterprising character. Philine's clapping is an echo of the clacking sound made by her slippers, but it is not yet apparent why only Felix reacts and not Mignon. The alarm produced by the appearance of the harper is an obvious reference to his insanity and the threat to Felix that this entailed. The flames in the dream evoke the fire once again. The beautiful Amazon once played the role of savior for Wilhelm; now she saves Felix as well. It is highly significant that she removes a veil from her head, to quench the fire. As a symbol, the veil is allied with the coat she gave to Wilhelm; it expresses her goodness and charity. She appears on the scene like Athene or Minerva, an ancient goddess who intervenes in battle to protect her favorite, enveloping him in a veil or cloud that renders him invisible (Barner 90; Schlaffer *Mythos,* 5). In addition, the Amazon's veil connects with the ghost's veil and binds the dream world to the real world. The identity of the two boys playing is mysterious, but the behavior of Friedrich is in character. He it was who jealously tried to sabotage Philine's dalliance with the stable master by throwing their dinner into their laps and then challenging the stable master to a duel.

At the end of the dream Wilhelm feels great pleasure at the Amazon's touch, but regret at not being able to assist his father and Mariane. In this mixture of emotions, past and future meet. He feels regret at the past, but the two figures who represent it are fading from sight. The beautiful Amazon remains to be sought, but the dream represents her as holding him, which gives him grounds for hope that he will find her again. At least on the level of his subconscious, Wilhelm seems to agree with the priest's words now. The dream enables him to confront the past and shows that his past experiences have indeed imprinted themselves upon him. The image of the rainbow can also be applied to the dream: the sorrow at the loss of Mariane and the death of the father form the dark backdrop against which future joy comes into focus.

In Book One, Chapter Twelve, Mariane describes a dream Wilhelm had told her about. That earlier dream turned out to be prophetic, since it showed Mariane being led away by a stranger. In both these dreams, Wilhelm is paralyzed and unable to help and in both, water constitutes a danger. The content of the earlier dream is much darker: the surroundings are unfamiliar, Wilhelm does not recognize the other man and the final message is of separation rather than reunion. Wilhelm reacts with alarm to the first dream and is falsely reassured by the reality of Mariane's presence beside him. The dream in Book Seven leaves him with conflicting emotions and, despite the lack of any reassuring presence in the room, it has given him grounds for optimism.

Chapter Two

At breakfast the next morning, the abbé, as he is now called, seems withdrawn, but soon some exciting events occur. The abbé wants to hear about Aurelie's death. He speaks again about the steps to becoming cultured and well-rounded. He regrets that her life was so wantonly destroyed. Suddenly a young woman bursts in, rushing up to the abbé. She can hardly speak through her sobs. She demands to know Lothario's whereabouts. The abbé's assurances are to no avail. Lothario has gone to meet his opponent in a duel. A coach approaches. Lothario climbs out, leaning on his companion, none other than Jarno. Jarno compares the events to a play, and Wilhelm asks after Lothario. Jarno thinks his condition is not serious, but a young doctor who examines Lothario says it is critical. He carries a bag with an ornate strap that Wilhelm recognizes from the attack in the woods, but the doctor denies this. When the doctor leaves, Jarno says he lied about Lothario's state of health and the strap. Wilhelm receives an invitation from Baron Lothario to stay a few more days. He hears of the circumstances that led to the duel, and from the moment the story ends, Wilhelm is like one of the family.

The quiet mood at the breakfast table provides the backdrop against which a very melodramatic scene will be played out. It is no accident that Wilhelm has just been talking about Aurelie, whose hysteria led to her demise, when another hysterical young woman bursts in. The outburst is interrupted by the sound of a carriage arriving and the reader recognizes the stage technique employed by Goethe in the very first chapter, when Barbara is waiting impatiently for Mariane's arrival — she listens for the sound of the carriage. Similarities to dramatic events on the stage have occurred to Jarno, too, and he addresses the topic directly, saying that Wilhelm seems unable to escape from theatrical events. Wilhelm has not yet succeeded in making a clean break from the theater, it seems.

Now that Wilhelm has recognized and revived his acquaintance with the abbé, similar incidents begin to accumulate. Reality is beginning to resemble Wilhelm's dream, in which figures from the past join figures from the present and keep company with one another simultaneously. First, Jarno reappears without warning, and then the doctor — whom Wilhelm incidentally does not recognize from any earlier scene — is carrying an object that brings back a memory. This strap forms part of the textile motif; it follows Wilhelm's discovery of the ghost's veil in his suitcase and he hopes it will provide a link to the beautiful Amazon. Jarno's comment on the strangeness of events sums up the whole series of coincidences, but leaves the reader wondering whether some of the incidents were in fact entirely coincidental. The observation that the doctor is a liar is intriguing, but there is no hint as to his motivation — it remains unexplained like the inscription on the ghost's veil and the unidentified and mysterious figures who turn up at regular intervals in Wilhelm's life.

Wilhelm may still have been harboring intentions to deliver his speech to Lothario on this morning, and so complete his moral mission. But the arrival of the hysterical woman and the explanation of the circumstances that necessitated the duel intervene as an ironic comment on Wilhelm's proposed righteous speechifying (Hass 194). The young woman who bursts in — we learn that her name is Lydie — introduces an interesting perspective. She claims she is being controlled by the abbé and others, that the room provided for her is in fact a prison, and that she is being prevented from seeing Lothario. When Lothario extends hospitality to Wilhelm at the end of the chapter, the reader begins to wonder if he will find himself in a similar situation to the one the young woman has been lamenting.

Chapter Three

Wilhelm reads to the invalid Lothario, who is, however, distracted and asks for a break. He is keen to implement changes on his estate. Jarno urges patience, but Lothario insists it will benefit the workers; he wants to transfer some profit to them and fears fate might stymie his plans if he delays. He refers to America; he had felt he could be useful there, but now wants to benefit those close to him. Jarno recalls a line from Lothario's letter: "Here or nowhere is America!"[1]

---

[1] This slogan and its variation, which follows soon afterwards, are an adaptation of a line from Horace's *Epistles* 1.17, l.39: "Hic est aut nusquam quod quaerimus" (Here is what we seek — or nowhere).

Lotario says one should honor the demands of the community. Extraordinary gestures are often foolish. The count is an example: he hoped to buy salvation from the Pietist community at Herrnhut. Lothario plans to give money to benefit others. He adapts his slogan: "Here or nowhere is Herrnhut!" Jarno is no longer a soldier; he says he is shrewd and fears stupidity most. Wilhelm describes his fellow actors as considering themselves unique and always craving new diversions. They were mistrustful, over-sensitive, uncooperative, and self-interested. Jarno says this describes mankind in general; he would be more forgiving of actors, who need to please an audience. Actors should be forgiven human faults; human beings should not be forgiven actors' faults.

The doctor gives a more hopeful report on the invalid. Wilhelm is longing to see the Amazon again and he opens up to Jarno, who reassures him. Jarno thinks Lydie's presence is not helping Lothario and would like to consult the old doctor.

The chapter begins with the device, familiar by now, of a tableau that conjures up other, earlier episodes. Wilhelm has been reading to Lothario, and the reader is reminded of the beautiful soul, whose formation owed so much to the experience of being read to during her convalescence. Her own memoirs, in turn, were to be read out loud by Wilhelm to the suffering Aurelie because of the palliative effect this would have on her condition. Lydie is at Lothario's bedside too, and the picture of the ailing prince again springs to mind, as well as other scenes apparently inspired by that painting — scenes in which a female character presides over a man's suffering. Philine holds Wilhelm's head in her lap after the attack in the woods, Mignon keeps watch beside Wilhelm's bed in the pastor's house after Philine departs, and the beautiful Amazon spreads her coat over the recumbent Wilhelm to protect him.

Lothario is determined to introduce some innovations in the way his lands are managed. He feels there is some urgency about implementing the progressive ideas for social reform. On the one hand, he advocates dismantling the feudal system by undermining the privileges of the nobility and granting some of the profit to the peasants working his lands. He also speaks of increasing production and revenue and of a more efficient way of handling interest. These themes and the enthusiastic way Lothario talks about them call to mind Wilhelm's friend Werner, the representative of bourgeois materialism (Hahn 158). Spoken by Lothario, these proposals argue in favor of social responsibility, whereas Werner's emphasis was on the smooth working of the system (Borchmeyer 166). Once again, the cyclical structure of the novel is in evidence, as a character takes up the theme of business that epitomizes aspects of Wilhelm's upbringing that he thought he had left behind forever.

Lothario's thumbnail sketch of his life provides the reader with a portrait of an individual who has developed a position at the end of a route marked by failures and wrong turnings. Lothario has completed his years of apprenticeship and is now a model for Wilhelm (Baioni 106). Features of Lothario's story have a familiar shape. He had made the mistake of reducing everything to an idea, a mistake that he now accuses cultured people in general, and in particular, Jarno of making. Lothario had put into practice an idea in America, which, he now realizes, should have been implemented at home. He has turned from the ideal to the practical and, in doing so, has virtually reiterated the dictum of the abbé in Chapter One of this book — that one should attend first to what lies immediately in the future. Lothario now chimes in with a very similar idea, and gives the reader and Wilhelm a glimpse of the united front among the inhabitants of the castle. Here, too, in a nutshell, is Wilhelm's own development as he has moved from the elevated idea of founding a theater that would have a reforming and cultivating influence on the nation to the less abstract, more practical considerations of life as an actor.

Here again, in Lothario's story, the wrong turnings taken by the beautiful soul are reproduced in microcosmic form. Lothario has descended from the realms of idealism to a resolve to make a difference in everyday matters; the extraordinary is potentially present every day, he now thinks, and it should not be overlooked while the merely reasonable is allowed to become routine. But neither are extremes encouraged. Just as Lothario does not propose overthrowing the whole social order, so now, prompted by Jarno, he rejects the count's example of acting according to a misguided ideal.

The mention of the count triggers a theme which is occurring with increasing frequency in the novel, that of recognition or anagnorisis.[2] The immediate effect of such revelations is Wilhelm's enlightenment, the understanding of something mystifying or unclear (Barner 92). Sometimes a connection stretches back to Wilhelm's childhood, as it does when the first mysterious stranger speaks to Wilhelm about his father's art collection in Book One, Chapter Seventeen. One function of the recognition, then, is to bring together the past and the present. It also contributes to the characteristics this novel shares with drama,

---

[2] Anagnorisis is a term from Aristotle's *Poetics,* where it relates to the plot of a tragedy. A fault on the part of the hero precedes it, and then the act of recognition gives rise to a reversal of fortune.

since the moment of recognition in ancient drama is the crux that brings about a change in the hero's fortunes. The unexpected turn in the nature of Wilhelm's mission, when his hostile intent is met with hospitality, is first set in motion when Wilhelm and the abbé recognize each other. For the count, however, the recognition and reversal sequence acquires an ironic twist: he is mistaken in thinking he recognizes his own image and allows this error to change and determine the course of his life.

The count is used here to demonstrate the consequences of a radical act, undertaken without regard for the established order. Not only was the count's action misguided, the very mention of his name opens Wilhelm's eyes to his own errors. In addition, there is a dramatic function at work in the reintroduction of the count in the narrative at this point: recognition is at work again in the revelation that the countess is Lothario's sister. There are hints at more revelations, and Jarno uses the opportunity to warn Wilhelm against passing judgment on Lothario's attitude toward affairs of the heart. The juxtaposition and precise wording of this piece of advice are crucial for its ironic impact. Jarno says no one should compose long speeches to criticize others. Such speeches should be delivered in front of a mirror. The reference to a mirror relates again to the count's mistake and suggests that Wilhelm remember his own capacity for making mistakes. The dramatic irony is overwhelming, since the very next time Wilhelm opens his mouth, it is to speak unstoppably about the weaknesses in the actors' characters.

The aristocratic circle he had earlier idolized resurfaces in Wilhelm's consciousness with an interesting effect. It shows that when he encounters members of the nobility again, it is not a mere repetition of those earlier experiences. The first reason is that Lothario does not share the views of his relatives, but has embraced some bourgeois attitudes and is inclined to introduce reforms, sacrificing some of the privileges of his own class. The second reason is that Wilhelm himself has changed. He has given up his idealized views of the aristocracy and his dreams for the theater, as he now explains at some length. Wilhelm is now brought face to face with Lothario's realism and controlled spirit of compromise. In this atmosphere, Wilhelm is only too ready to denounce his fellow actors whose approach to life is the very opposite of Lothario's pragmatism (Hass 195).

This seems to be a very decisive step on Wilhelm's part: he is making explicit his intention of abandoning his dreams of becoming an actor. When Lothario criticizes those who reduce everything to an idea, he targets not only Jarno, but Wilhelm too. Yet Goethe is unwilling to allow any such clear-cut advance in his hero to stand unchallenged.

Jarno undermines the speech with scornful laughter and a deflating remark. Wilhelm's attempt at retaliation, his mildly critical remark about Jarno's intolerance, is feeble by comparison, and the situation is still unresolved when the doctor comes in. This is a technique of the stage: the doctor's quick entrance and exit have the effect of changing the direction of the conversation completely. Wilhelm, frustrated by the mystifying detail involving the doctor's bag, abandons this line of inquiry and turns straight to his principle preoccupation — the whereabouts of the beautiful Amazon.

Chapter Four

The old doctor arrives — the one who provided the manuscript of the Confessions. He is not pleased with the invalid's state but tells Wilhelm that he still hopes to rehabilitate the harper. The harper is almost oblivious to anything external; he has strong feelings of guilt and visions of the abyss and ghosts. He denies the presence of God and that time brings changes. The doctor mentions a moving song the harper sang about his gray hair and Wilhelm asks for a copy of it.

Jarno asks the doctor to explain the harper's case. The doctor's reply is based on assumptions. The harper might have been a priest, which would explain the robe and beard. It is possible that an incident implicated him in the death of a female relative, and that an unfortunate birth caused him to lose his senses. His worst delusion is that he brings bad luck and that an innocent boy will cause his death. Mignon's boyish appearance makes him fear her, but also Felix.

Jarno plans to remove Lydie, since her presence is impeding the healing process. She will travel to meet a friend, Therese, but will be misled. Wilhelm will accompany her in the carriage, but feels uneasy: deceit is not the solution. He does not agree that it is like bringing up a child, but accepts the undertaking out of friendship. Jarno assures him he will like Therese, who really deserves the title Amazon. Wilhelm hopes she might actually be the Amazon he seeks. He sees the hand of fate in his task, and his reluctance is like a shadow from the wing of a bird.

Lydie tells Wilhelm that Lothario and Therese's love suddenly and inexplicably ended. She replaced Therese in Lothario's affections and speaks of him passionately. The travelers pass through several villages seeking Therese but the driver ignores instructions. Eventually he admits he is lost and agrees to go back. They drive until morning when Lydie, surprised to recognize the house and the woman who emerges, faints into Wilhelm's arms.

The physician returns in the first sentence of this chapter and forges another link between this book and Books Five and Six. At the same time, the narrator takes the opportunity of directing a remark to the reader — a reminder that the doctor has already made an appearance. The discussion of the harper dominates the first part, and forms another loop back to earlier episodes. This is particularly fitting, since the harper himself does little besides dwell on the past. The direct speech quoted from the harper shares many characteristics with his songs. Cryptic and melancholy, his words offer no real insight into the cause of his condition. The harper's denial of the passage of time is born of despair: it suggests that there is no escape, either from past guilt or from life itself. It is not typical for the harper to speak about himself at any length and, sensing this, both Wilhelm and Jarno insist on knowing more about the songs, where the true idiom of the harper can be heard. The singing of his songs provides a contrast to that other recent and noted type of performance — the activity of reading out loud to a patient. The songs are cathartic, but they induce introspection and melancholy (Marahrens 148), whereas the reading is therapeutic for the listener in a more positive sense.[1]

The remainder of the chapter looks in a forward direction. In Therese a new character is introduced and the plan to deal with Lydie remains uncompleted, so that the reader is left in suspense at the end. Jarno appeals to Wilhelm for his help, using the transparent pretext of Lothario's health. The first doctor's shiftiness and untrustworthy reports on the patient fit into this plot as well. Wilhelm's initial objection allows him to describe the care of children in rather moving terms. He is compromised by his agreement to the undertaking, however, since he obviously realizes that Lydie is being jilted and yet keeps up the pretense that it is all for the benefit of Lothario's health. Even more striking is the rapid switch in Wilhelm from hostility towards Lothario to a willingness to contravene his own principles out of friendship towards him.

Jarno highly recommends Therese's acquaintance to Wilhelm. He calls her a real Amazon, and distinguishes her from others who only don masculine clothing without possessing the required characteristics. He posits mere appearance over against the real thing and adds that, far from being a sham, Therese is more manly than many men. This description is actually bait, designed to hook Wilhelm and ensure that he goes through with the plan. He thinks he is merely helping to trick Ly-

---

[1] The earlier version of the harper in *Wilhelm Meisters Theatralische Sendung* has undergone an almost total transformation. There he is simply a bard, singing of the joys of life (Krauss 336).

die, whereas he himself is being tricked into believing he will reach his goal. The ambiguous nature of this escapade has parallels with an earlier episode. When Wilhelm advised the actors of the best route, the result was the attack in the woods, for which he was held responsible. For Wilhelm himself, however, the episode brought a benefit, since this was the occasion for his meeting the beautiful Amazon. Choosing the wrong route was unintentional on Wilhelm's part then; now the driver chooses the wrong route deliberately. The route itself, complete with wrong turnings, is of course a metaphor for the individual's progress through life.

Wilhelm is taken in by the false promise and his expectations soar. His thoughts are expressed in exaggerated and poetic language that reminds the reader of some of his earlier unrealistic dreams and flowery speeches. He no longer sees the journey as a morally questionable enterprise, but as a sign that the hand of fortune is guiding him. His former misgivings are poeticized and made harmless in the bird image. As for Lydie, she had complained in Chapter Two of being treated as a prisoner, and yet she now seems unsuspecting of any manipulation as she sets out on her journey. She speaks of her passion and devotion and, ironically, feels guilt at leaving Lothario unattended. The main purpose of her speech for the reader and for Wilhelm, however, is the revelation of the love affair between Lothario and Therese and its mysterious conclusion.

The ending of the chapter is mysterious too. The reader can only assume that the travelers have reached their quarry, but that Lydie had expected to arrive home. However, none of this is made explicit and the reason for Lydie's reaction is not given either. The reader only sees a reversal of the scene with which the attack in the woods concluded: instead of Wilhelm's loss of consciousness and subsequent awakening to find himself being supported by a female companion, it is Lydie who faints and is held by Wilhelm in this dramatic closing scene.

Chapter Five

Wilhelm is led to a room in the small and tidy house. Therese is not the beautiful Amazon; she is very different from her. Wilhelm learns that Lydie is displeased and does not wish to see him. She has forgiven Lothario because he has sent a letter laying the blame on his friends. She suspects Wilhelm prevailed upon Lothario to remove her.

Wilhelm expresses the deepest respect for Lothario, praising him and saying how rewarding his conversations are. Therese, listening to Wilhelm, has a similar experience, and agrees with everything. She tells

Wilhelm that she thinks of Lothario daily, and sheds a tear, but hastily explains this as the result of the removal of a wart. Wilhelm looks into her eye and seems to see right through to her soul. Therese tells Wilhelm her life story and is eager to hear his, since a person's history forms his character. She wishes to stay in touch with Wilhelm. Later, she explains that she handles the estate herself. Wilhelm admires her financial gifts and she recommends combining inclination, opportunity, external motivation, and involvement in something useful. Wilhelm finds both house and garden orderly and practical and attributes much to Lothario's influence. But he now fears that his beautiful Amazon might be Lothario's bride.

The description of the house, with which the chapter begins, has something of the quality of stage directions. The modest and orderly abode is clearly intended to reflect the character of its occupant.[1] Wilhelm's reaction to Therese is also described in terms of neutral interest, rather than emotions. Her concerns are domestic and practical and she seems able to maintain, through her activities, a calm and balance that poor Lydie would do well to emulate. Therese is capable and independent, whereas Lydie is completely at others' mercy. Therese denies her emotions, while Lydie dramatizes hers.

Therese's interest in the administration of lands, both her own and those belonging to her neighbor, resembles Lothario's own interests. Her remarks about the unreliability of the servants tie in with his proposals to preserve the status of the peasant farmers while improving their financial situation. She reinforces the direction in which Lothario had earlier pointed, by reintroducing Wilhelm to the economic matters he had first heard Werner talk about (Ladendorf 123). Because of his admiration for Therese, there is a further subtle sign that Wilhelm may be influenced to turn his back completely on his vague, youthful idealism.

An immediate and fundamental harmony is established between Wilhelm and Therese, based initially on their shared admiration for Lothario. Yet there are also signs that this may not prove to be a completely stable basis for their friendship. Wilhelm is given to hyperbole: in his lively expression of enthusiasm, he claims that he had never had a real conversation before meeting Lothario. He has evidently forgotten how much he enjoyed his exchanges with Serlo and Aurelie when he first joined their company. For Therese's part, the explanation of the tear in her eye is so implausible as to be comic. It is like an announcement that there is a large unresolved element remaining in her relations

---

[1] This technique can also be found in *Faust I,* l.2677. Here Gretchen's room is described in terms that reflect her personality.

with Lothario and it invites comparison with Lydie's claim that her eyes were never dry whenever she was forced to be apart from Lothario. In addition, despite the general adulation for Lothario, the reader cannot overlook his obvious faults, including the latest act of cowardice in blaming Wilhelm and the others for the plot against Lydie.

In this chapter, Therese offers Wilhelm two axioms to live by. The first is that the character is formed by and expressed through the history of one's development. It is remarkable how similar this is to the point of view which led Wilhelm himself to tell Mariane all about his childhood, and urge her to do the same, with such unsatisfactory results. Therese's other formula constitutes an explanation of her managerial abilities, but she expresses it in universal terms. It is a prescription for what is possible in the world and it emphasizes the necessary combination of native talent and the nurturing of this talent by circumstances and practice. From this essentially pragmatic explanation the concept of destiny, to which Wilhelm is so attached, is notably absent. It is also evident to the reader that Wilhelm's pursuits up to this point would be found lacking if measured by this yardstick.

Therese leads a life in conformity with her principles. The dominant image is a garden in which nature and culture are combined. When she thinks about true friendship, she sees it as capable of transforming the world into a garden. In Therese's own garden, Wilhelm admires the features which express her outlook on life: it is modest, yet well stocked, orderly and well-proportioned, but circumscribed.[2]

Wilhelm is fascinated by Therese and her world — he has never met anyone quite like her. His remarks at the end of the chapter make it clear that her attraction for him is partly due to her association with Lothario, and in retrospect he sees this as true of Aurelie too. Whereas the women Wilhelm has encountered so far have been presented in terms of their relation to him, now it is Lothario who stands at the center (Hass 196). Because of Lothario's influence, Wilhelm quickly abandoned the moralizing speech that he had planned to deliver for Lothario's improvement. So complete and instantaneous is Wilhelm's transformation that he no longer thinks of chastising Lothario for the

---

[2] The importance of the garden and Therese's self-sufficiency are reminiscent of Voltaire's *Candide* (1759), which concludes with the advice to cultivate one's own garden.

casual treatment of Aurelie but, against the background of a duel caused by yet another affair of the heart, he immediately becomes Lothario's accomplice in casting off the current amour, Lydie.

Chapter Six

Therese appears dressed as a huntsman to tell the story of her days as a huntress. Under an oak tree, she talks about her upbringing.[1] She was an only child, unloved by her mother. Therese and her father were close, but he was too good-natured about his wife's follies. Her mother attracted a circle of men and founded a theater. Lydie grew up with Therese, and acted in the theater, but Therese felt no attraction for the stage; she trimmed the lights[2] but thought people absurd who expected to play a fictional role convincingly. Therese knew her mother was involved with other men and eventually her father noticed too; there were talks, the mother's lover was unfaithful, and she departed for the south of France.

Therese and her father lived happily until his stroke. He once tried to tell her something important, but died without succeeding. A lady entrusted Therese with control of her large estates; this satisfying situation was interrupted by the arrival of the passionate Lydie. Therese noticed Lothario when he came to hunt, but he seemed attracted by Lydie. One evening he described his ideal wife; Therese identified with the description and wished Lothario could see her qualities. She put on men's clothing the next time Lothario came. She conversed at length with him about the estate and secured his respect. Still, Lydie seemed to attract him more. Then, to Therese's surprise, he suddenly asked her to marry him. He told her about his trip to America and the debts that displeased his uncle who would have to approve the match. Through Lothario's sister, Therese met and won over the uncle. The incredulous Lydie disappeared from sight. When Therese's jewelry case was open, Lothario noticed a medallion with a woman's likeness. On learning that this was a picture of Therese's mother, he rushed away, horrified. Therese has never seen him since.

Later Wilhelm sees Lydie sitting with some children, still holding Lothario's letter. He learns that Therese and Lothario's sister are edu-

---

[1] The odes of Friedrich Gottlieb Klopstock (1724–1803) repeatedly designate the oak tree as the quintessential German tree. Among these odes, one of the most familiar is "Ich bin ein deutsches Mädchen"(1771); the words of that title are echoed here by Therese.

[2] She was responsible for snuffing out the candles at the end of the performance.

cating a group of children. Therese shows him her library and speaks of her mother's reading tastes. But books are not important to Therese.

The narrator explains that Lothario had had a romantic encounter with Therese's mother, which precluded an attachment to her daughter. Eventually Lothario took up with Lydie. Now the conversation turns to marriage and misalliance.[3] Therese says one party can adapt to the social demands of the other's class. A great difference in age between husband and wife can also work. For Therese, a mismatch would mean ceremonies and displays; she would sooner marry the son of a neighboring farmer.

Lydie's violent feelings subside but she still loves Lothario, mistrusts his companions, and resents being denied access to a mysterious tower of theirs. She predicts that Wilhelm will aid them in secret endeavors. He is to take a letter from her to Lothario. On his return, Wilhelm reflects that Mignon and Felix would be happy in Therese's care. He will ask Jarno and the abbé about the tower.

Before Wilhelm had met Therese, he heard her summed up as a true Amazon, and Jarno had gone on to say that her male clothing was functional and therefore more authentic than that worn by other women. The choice of the word Amazon is of course not accidental on Goethe's part; it is his way of tricking Wilhelm into one more mistaken identification (MacLeod 130). At the beginning of this chapter, Therese appears dressed most convincingly in hunting attire. Her appearance also suggests the goddess Diana, representative of chastity and hunting. She is a true Amazon because her sphere of activity includes tasks normally reserved for men: the management of her estate and the handling of finances. She is even called upon for advice by other landowners. But Therese gives the lie to her own appearance by saying that she is merely acting when she wears this costume. This statement is consonant with her explicit opposition to all pretense and show.

Although Therese begins by encouraging Wilhelm to talk about himself, she remarks at the end of the chapter that this is still a desideratum: she herself has dominated the conversation. At this point, however, Wilhelm responds with unusual perspicacity that his life has been a series of mistakes. Earlier, he had admired Therese's success in

---

[3] The connotation of the term misalliance is not simply negative. It mainly refers to matches between two people of different social classes — for example, a nobleman marrying a commoner. People were in the habit of discussing this topic in Germany in the eighteenth century, using the tag "mésalliance." The subject is a favorite in the plays of Molière (1622–1673) and the adoption of the French term in German can possibly be attributed to Molière's influence.

aligning herself with fate without having to reject the whole of her previous life to achieve this. This seems to be a rueful comment on his life.

Despite her opposition to the theater, there is a kind of theatrical frame around Therese's narrative. First, she has thought about the appropriate costume to wear, and then she very consciously leads Wilhelm to the right setting, with the oak tree as a prop. They seat themselves beneath the same tree that had also been her resting place, with Lothario as her companion, during their hunting days. Therese refers to both the tree and herself as German, possibly in order to form a contrast with her mother who has associated herself with France (*FA* 1478).

The theatrical aspects of Therese's preparation for her narrative form an obvious link with a major theme of the novel. Also, her willingness to tell her story places her in line with a number of other characters, including Wilhelm himself, and reinforces the first person narrative as a frequently recurring phenomenon in the novel. Most recent among these, at least from the reader's perspective, is the beautiful soul and her Confessions. In very different ways, both women tell the story of their development and of how they each came to adopt an individual perspective (Hass 196). Isolated features familiar from the Confessions echo in Therese's account of her life. The responsibility of caring for an aged father falls to each respectively. Each of the women receives a gentleman caller, who visits frequently, but does not make his intentions clear for some time. Therese's story, however, is entirely secular and outward-looking; whereas the beautiful soul's formative years were lived through books, Therese associates reading with her mother's frivolous search for entertainment.

Both Therese and Mariane are associated with masculine costume, but Therese stands in contrast to Mariane because of her willingness to talk about her past. Her openness in this regard makes her more similar to Wilhelm, and he is certainly eager to hear her story. On the other hand her practical inclination, her administrative abilities, and her skepticism towards the theater are all polar opposites of Wilhelm's own interests. She occupies an aristocratic version of Werner's world of trade and enterprise (Hass 196). This does not appear to be as evident to Wilhelm as it is to the reader, but Wilhelm is certainly most interested in the personal details of Therese's story, in particular as these refer to Lothario. He expresses no opposition to the economic subject matter and listens without protest to her criticism of the theater.

Within the frame of Therese's narrative is the story of the moral downfall of her mother — a warning to Wilhelm. The passion she developed for the theater is an obvious parallel to his, and the emotional damage she caused by leaving her family is sobering. Therese made herself useful backstage, but could not summon the suspension of disbelief necessary in order to enjoy the performances. Lydie was quite different, indeed, in many ways, she is the exact opposite of Therese (Lösch 293). In Therese's view, passion for the theater leads to lack of restraint in personal matters, a view that Lydie's hysteria and histrionics confirm. As the reader already knows from his conversation with Jarno, Wilhelm has adopted a thoroughly critical attitude towards those who make their living in the acting world.

Wilhelm and Therese disagree fundamentally about the essence of drama, quite apart from the personnel involved in it. They also react in diametrically opposed ways to the offer of an estate to administer and improve. Therese accepted the challenge, rose to the occasion, and gained universal respect for her work. For Wilhelm, the suggestion resulted from his father's death, and as it came through Werner, in rejecting it Wilhelm was rejecting his own mercantile background. In some ways, Wilhelm and Therese are mirror images of each other: both become estranged from a parent — Therese had a difficult relationship with her mother, Wilhelm reacted against his father; Wilhelm's friend Werner was more in tune with Wilhelm's father, and Lydie was closer to Therese's mother than she was herself. The tension between Wilhelm and his father was caused by the father's strict morals and philistine attitude towards the theater. Therese's mother, on the other hand, was a great devotee of the theater and indulged in affairs of the heart. She cruelly remarked that if a mother could be as uncertain as a father, she would deny that Therese was her daughter. Therese has good reason to regret her parentage when, as she explains later in her account, it becomes the reason she loses Lothario.

The literary phenomenon of anagnorisis is present here in subtle forms. Therese hears Lothario describe his ideal wife and recognizes herself in his words, although he is as yet unaware of her qualities. When Lothario learns who Therese's mother is, anagnorisis is shown from its negative side, with Oedipal overtones. Finally, Therese speaks of Lothario's sister and Wilhelm decides to keep to himself the guilty secret that he knows the countess.

The chapter continues to present events in a dramatic way. Therese uses a grand style to refer to Lothario's kiss as his first and his last. Lothario's reaction on learning the identity of the woman whose likeness appeared on Therese's medallion is high melodrama. The tantalizing attempts of Therese's father to reveal some secret to her are left unexplained, while the reader looks forward to a resolution in a later act. Two theories are put forward, both having to do with the fact that Therese did not stand to inherit, but neither is conclusive and the suspense persists. Finally, the resentful Lydie complains about the secretive ways of Lothario and his friends and the closed doors, confusing corridors, and mysterious tower she was never allowed to enter.

The sight of Lydie sitting on a bench in the garden, with two children playing at her feet, is both idyllic and misleading. Far from being at peace with the world, Lydie is nurturing her resentment and keeps Lothario's letter about her person as though it had talismanic power. Benevolence towards the children does not inhere in Lydie but in Therese and in Lothario's sister. In performing this act of charity Therese reenacts the situation from which she herself benefited after her mother's death. Lydie, on the other hand, is like an unhappy version of Philine: both are actresses, and guided by their passions, but whereas Philine has a pleasing manner, is carefree, beguiling, and holds no grudges, Lydie is ruled by jealousy, ill will, and ambition.

Thoughts often come to Wilhelm on a journey. Now, on his way back to the castle, he thinks about Therese's many good qualities and about how happy he would be in her company. He ignores those characteristics that set her at variance with his own principles — her lack of understanding of the dramatic arts, her faith in economics, and her failure to see how books can be an important part of life. But in any case, all such thoughts are swept aside by the sight of the mysterious tower.

Chapter Seven

Dialogue dominates this chapter, after the initial paragraph about Lothario's improved health and state of mind. His conversational skills are restored and a certain delicacy of feeling is perceptible. Jarno finally asks about his mood. Lothario has revisited a former lady friend, Margaret, now married, at her father's house. First he glimpsed a younger cousin through the climbing rose,[1] who perfectly resembled the Margaret he had loved ten years earlier. In sentimental mood, he returned later and was reunited with Margaret. A daughter of hers was also a younger version of Margaret, and Lothario saw past, present, and future all at once.

Lothario's encounter leads to a discussion in which he speaks of the pleasure of finding a new love before finishing with the old. He would forgo this pleasure for Therese. He expects Wilhelm to understand how Therese won him away from Aurelie. Wilhelm criticizes Lothario's treatment of her. Lothario admits that his friendship with Aurelie ought not to have developed into love, since she is incapable of being lovable. Wilhelm asks Lothario why he is not concerned about his son.

---

[1] The rose is a traditional topos for feminine beauty and romantic love.

Lothario has no idea what he is talking about. Jarno explains that an old woman, known to Wilhelm, had brought the child for Aurelie to look after. Mignon will now go to Therese and Wilhelm will look after Felix. Jarno points out that Wilhelm has no talent for the theater anyway. Wilhelm is eager to fetch the two children.

The tone of this chapter is quite distinctive, not only because so much of it is conversation, but also because the speakers are straightforward and open. Even Jarno confines himself to the role of encouraging others to speak, until his critical comment to Wilhelm at the end. The episode related by Lothario, in which he sees his former flame in an idyllic family setting, seems at first to be largely unrelated to the main story. It contributes to Lothario's reputation as a ladies' man and indicates the degree to which he has recovered from his wound. There are, however, other functions. The image of Margaret with her cousin, her children, and her father builds on the scene with Lydie and the children in the previous chapter. It also looks forward to the realization of the plan to fetch Felix and Mignon and place them under the care of Therese. In addition, since Margaret was the daughter of a farmer, this liaison is an immediate example of the topic of mixed marriages discussed by Therese in the previous chapter.

The discussion of the Margaret episode introduces a new element of mysterious irony. First, Margaret's cousin, by her presence in the garden, accompanied by one of Margaret's children, prepares for this. Lothario mistakes her for Margaret and asks where her other children are. When the men later discuss Aurelie, another such mistaken assumption is revealed. Wilhelm accuses Lothario of neglecting his paternal obligations towards Felix. Wilhelm is thereby discharging part of the duty he came prepared to carry out, but he receives a quite unexpected reply. It seems he has jumped to the wrong conclusion: Aurelie is not Felix's mother and Lothario is not his father; his heritage remains tantalizingly unexplained, indeed, the extra details provided only serve to cloak the whole question in romantic, fictional wrappings. An old woman, like some sorceress, presents Aurelie with the child, who might as well be the foundling so popular in eighteenth-century literature, and the suggestion is that his very presence will bestow some magical and beneficial power.

Against the background information about Lothario's frequent love affairs, his praise for Therese stands out in its sincerity. He refers to the same attributes in Therese that she heard him speak about on a theoretical level and says that only fate prevented him from forsaking the pleasures of new loves. Because he speaks of the hand of fate, and because of his statement that a man needs to settle down and not remain a child forever, Lothario is also speaking indirectly to Wilhelm's situation. Jarno reinforces this with his matter of fact advice that Wilhelm should turn away from the theater and take on some responsibility.

The element of time in Lothario's story is worthy of comment as it gives point to the whole episode. At first, he thought he recognized Margaret and that she somehow had cheated time by remaining unchanged, despite the intervention of ten years and despite having given birth to several children. When he later sees the real Margaret he finds her considerably changed. Then, in the presence of Margaret, her daughter, and her cousin, who was like an earlier version of Margaret, Lothario compares the effect to that of being in an orange grove where both blossoms and fruit are present. This particular image of the compression of time is already familiar to the reader from Mignon's song "Kennst du das Land?"(*MA* 817). It offers a vision of the various stages of development side by side, although they cannot be simultaneously present in nature (Seidlin 93). Both the ballad and Lothario's image express a universal affirmation of life as an endless cycle of permanence derived through change (Saine 72–75). Change is necessary, and endurance and survival are achieved through change and development. For Lothario, this means that Margaret has developed through time and he finds it charming to see her surrounded by her children. But he himself has not yet achieved that stage in his development, and he envies her. There is also a message for Wilhelm contained in this image: he too should leave off his dreamy pursuits and seek stability. The ideal image of the family is a familiar one to the reader of *Werther;*[2] it is also prefigured in Wilhelm's allusion to the harper, Mignon, and Friedrich as his family. The sight of Margaret and her family in a domestic setting becomes a kind of realistic symbol of stability and endurance (Dürr 208). With the end of the chapter, Lothario's narrative draws to a close.

Chapter Eight

Wilhelm, preoccupied with thoughts about the women he has known, returns to the company to find Aurelie's old serving woman and the two children in the theater. Mignon is reading to Felix. To his surprise, he recognizes the old woman as Barbara, learns that Felix is his son,

---

[2] The first example of an idealized, romantic depiction of the mother and her children is in Werther's letter dated May 27.

258 ~ WILHELM MEISTER'S APPRENTICESHIP: COMMENTARY

and that Mariane is dead. Wilhelm reads a letter from Mariane and asks Barbara for more details so as to be convinced that Mariane was faithful to him. Barbara will speak to him later. Mignon says the ghost as an inner voice told her that Wilhelm was Felix's father. Wilhelm notices that Mignon is thin and pale. Horatio and Laertes have taken over Wilhelm's roles and introduced opera. Laertes has a connection with a large business through the niece of the owner and Wilhelm is reminded of Laertes counting money in his dream.

Barbara reappears stealthily after midnight; she wants to reenact the evening when they shared a bottle of champagne, and asks for three glasses. She explains the lover's note Wilhelm found in Mariane's scarf. Barbara had encouraged the liaison with Norberg, against Mariane's wishes. Mariane fell in love with Wilhelm and bitterly regretted her predicament. It angers Wilhelm that Barbara used Mariane to ensure a supply of creature comforts for herself.

Wilhelm had no idea that Norberg had been kept away from Mariane on the night he saw him leaving. Mariane, dressed in her officer's costume to please him, had waited in vain for Wilhelm's visit. Wilhelm is finally convinced of Mariane's death and understands why she and his dead father formed a pair in his dream.

Madame Melina displays her fondness for Wilhelm in a conversation about Felix. Wilhelm asks Barbara to take Mignon to Therese, but Mignon will not be separated from Wilhelm and Felix, saying reason is cruel and the heart is better. Wilhelm does not want to lose Felix. In the theater, Wilhelm is no longer convinced by the illusion. This makes it easier to take his leave of the actors. He writes to Werner inquiring about money and sets out in a hopeful mood.

Chapter Seven was rather puzzling in that it lingered over Lothario's meeting with a woman he had loved ten years earlier. For the reader, this comes across as an unimportant interlude, involving a previously unknown and minor character. Chapter Eight is quite different: the information it delivers is crucial for the start of the denouement. In Chapter Eight, however, Wilhelm comes into renewed contact with Mariane's sphere and the parallels between this situation and Lothario's in the previous chapter become clear. Lothario's adventure is an amalgam of romantic, happy memories and Margaret is now the personification of the ideal wife and mother (Staiger 149). Wilhelm's is a bittersweet experience, involving recrimination, sorrow, threats, and painful revelations. Mariane has died in a state of dishonor for which Wilhelm is largely responsible. These two episodes converge most sharply in a moment whose full irony is only now revealed. Wilhelm had accused Lothario of neglecting his son Felix, whereas the true situation is that Wilhelm himself has been neglecting his son Felix.

Chapter Eight begins with Wilhelm's thoughts during his journey and since Mariane is on his mind, it is as though the thoughts give rise to Barbara's revelations. He was thinking about all the women he admired, but the only two mentioned by name are Mariane, who represents a past chapter, and the beautiful Amazon, who stands for his future plans. On arriving, he finds none of his actor friends at home and none at the theater either. This is surely significant; it indicates the emptiness of the theatrical enterprise. And when Wilhelm later sits in on a performance, he is no longer held or persuaded by it. Indeed, instead of finding actors at the theater, Wilhelm finds only non-actors and the dreams and illusions he held involving the theater and Mariane are now shown in a harsh and real light (Hass 197).

There is an idyllic air to the initial vignette: the old woman sits over her sewing while the children are engrossed in a book. Mignon is reading to Felix, an activity which, in this novel, usually imparts great benefit to both the reader and the listener. And yet, as soon as the general parallel between this and the previous chapter is established, the details fit into the same pattern as well. The group Wilhelm now encounters becomes a parody of the ideal family painted, if too rosily, in Chapter Seven. The element of mistaken identity, a version of anagnorisis, is present in both. In Chapter Seven, the young cousin, partly obscured by roses, is at first taken for the former beloved and in Chapter Eight, Aurelie's serving woman, whose face had previously been concealed because of a toothache (Book Four, Chapter Fifteen), turns out to be Barbara. The young cousin, as her representative, gives Lothario some information about Margaret; Barbara, who in a grotesque way represents Mariane, tells Wilhelm about the misfortunes of her former mistress (Hass 197).

The chapter comprises another narrative of a life, only this time it is not related in the first person. It is far from straightforward because of Barbara's deviousness, but is also frequently interrupted by the reading of letters and by a series of events. Mignon again reads aloud to Felix, but this time she reads out Mariane's last letter to Wilhelm, which he flung aside in a state of extreme grief. For Wilhelm, this experience of being read to inexpertly by Mignon, with her words echoed by Felix, is by no means consoling. But it is also a reminder that Wilhelm is back at the theater. This is a technique familiar from the stage: a development in the plot is announced by the device of reading a letter out loud.

The suggestion of fairy tale sorcery continues in this chapter, as Barbara will only come under cover of night and then introduces hocus pocus into her story by setting out a third glass of champagne for the ghost of Mariane, as though she could conjure up her spirit. She suggests as well that Wilhelm should keep secret the information that Felix is his son. Mignon, too, contributes to the eeriness by claiming that the voice of the ghost had already revealed Felix's identity to her. Finally, among other recriminations, Wilhelm accuses Barbara of telling him a fairy tale about Mariane's fidelity.

The chapter opens with Wilhelm thinking about some of the women he has known, and in the ensuing events he again encounters Barbara, Mignon, Madame Melina, and Mariane — though the last only in narrative form. The moment when Wilhelm recognizes Barbara is pivotal. It brings a resolution to the Mariane episode, but along with this closure it simultaneously offers Wilhelm a new direction and responsibility as father to Felix, the chance to turn the fanciful role he once imagined for himself as *paterfamilias* into a reality. In Mignon, Wilhelm notices a change — she looks paler and thinner and the reader has learned to expect an explanation to follow at some point. In Madame Melina's case, by contrast, Wilhelm notices nothing. Although she tries her best to express her amorous feelings towards him, Wilhelm fails to notice — the theater itself and those associated with it do not command his interest as before.

Sections of Wilhelm's significant dream are interpreted in this chapter. The dream recalls the past and points to the future in ways that only gradually become apparent during the course of Book Seven (Storz 1953, 70). Mariane's death was represented in it and so was Wilhelm's concern for Felix. Laertes now unconsciously imitates his own actions in the dream by opening a purse and counting out the coins in it. The transformation of Laertes from actor to capitalist is perhaps suggestive, now that Wilhelm is severing his own ties with the theater. On the other hand, Wilhelm's other dreams — his unrealistic plans and fancies — come face to face with the facts. Instead of a life of happiness with Mariane, he must live with the guilt of having caused her much suffering; instead of a future on the stage, he must accept the fact that he has been effortlessly replaced in the theater company.

In the course of this chapter, Wilhelm is repeatedly confronted with mistakes he has made. He discovers that he has misjudged and wronged Mariane, and that, with a wonderful irony, he has accused Lothario of neglecting Felix, when he himself has been guilty of it all along. He also admits that he has not made up for leading the actors astray. The first realization is the most painful and the route he has to take in order to arrive at it is tortuous. He has to endure Barbara's evasiveness, partial revelations, and reproaches. He retaliates in kind with insults and accusations, at one point even believing that Mariane is still alive and that Barbara simply wants to induce remorse in him before bringing them back together. Wilhelm has to immerse himself in all the letters Barbara has preserved, including those written by Norberg, until the story is complete and in perspective. Wilhelm's reaction to the truth about Felix shows that he has shed some of his youthful naiveté. He restrains himself, is a little afraid of taking on responsibility for Felix, and is torn between affection for the child and the fear of losing him again. In providing for Felix, Wilhelm is settling the score with the memory of Mariane and making up for his misguided criticism of Lothario. His guilt in relation to the actors is to remain as a sobering reminder to himself not to make promises too lightly and he has to resist the attractions of flattery in order to hold to his resolution to leave the theater completely.

Mignon is as cryptic as ever in this chapter. Her claim that she already knew about Felix and Wilhelm's relatedness seems to indicate a gift of clairvoyance on her part. Then, when he suggests that she go on her own to stay with Therese, Wilhelm encounters dogged opposition. Her next statements are all paradoxical. She begs to stay with Wilhelm, because it will be good for her and painful as well. When he suggests that she needs more education she says she is sufficiently educated to be able to love and mourn and she rejects his concern for her health on the grounds that there are so many things to be concerned about. Wilhelm is surprised to hear that her second choice would be to join the harper, and all the more so when she speaks of her attachment to him but also her fear of him. This tendency towards contradictions in combination is a prominent feature of the structure of the novel as a whole (Blackall 1976, 122–23). Mignon also cryptically remarks that reason is cruel and the heart is better. In a sense, this maxim contains the culmination of all her previous puzzling utterances, since in each one there is a contrast between love or happiness and pain or fear. Whereas Felix's existence has been satisfactorily explained in this chapter, Mignon's origins and idiosyncrasies remain a riddle.

Mignon's whole being is deeply divided and at odds with itself. A girl who wants to appear like a boy, she combines a mechanical dexterity with a quirkily passionate nature. She is devoted to Wilhelm and Felix and the harper — a curious set of allegiances. She has very definite natural means of expression, not speech or writing, but song and dance, and yet her origins and her whole being remain inscrutable to others.

The end of the chapter brings its own surprise. Werner's cruelty in keeping Mariane's letters from Wilhelm has been mentioned, but now the reader learns that Wilhelm is writing to him. It is not entirely clear what Wilhelm will communicate to his old friend. All the reader learns is that Wilhelm is about to do what Werner had wanted him to do all along and that he had become interested in his own finances. The letter completes a frame: Wilhelm had first explained his decision to join the theater in a letter to Werner; now his thoughts on leaving the theater are laid out in another letter to Werner (Hass 197). Despite the recent emotional upheaval, Wilhelm is optimistic as he sets out.

Chapter Nine

Lothario has gone to deal with some estates inherited from his uncle; Wilhelm will help Jarno and the abbé purchase some neighboring estates on Lothario's behalf. Another business interested in the same lands will become a partner and Wilhelm is keen to involve Therese in the decisions. The others hear the news about Wilhelm's paternity with indifference.

His companions' secrecy reminds Wilhelm of Lydie's complaints. For him as well, the tower is off-limits. However, one evening Jarno says Wilhelm will be initiated into the secrets. He adds that it is good that a man first think himself capable of acquiring advantages and only later learn to live for others and forget himself in directed activity.

Jarno leads Wilhelm to an impressive door. Wilhelm enters a dark room hung with carpets. When invited to do so, he pulls a carpet aside and steps through. The room looks like a chapel. A table covered in green stands below a curtain concealing a painting. Cupboards with lattice fronts of metal contain scrolls. As Wilhelm sits, the sun streams into his eyes. A man in ordinary clothing asks Wilhelm questions relating to his grandfather's art collection, including the painting of the ailing prince, and hopes they can now agree about fate and the individual character. Suddenly the curtain closes again.

The curtain reopens and Wilhelm, confusingly, sees a figure who resembles both the cleric from the river party and the abbé, and who speaks about education. A teacher should permit error and then offer guidance. Wilhelm thinks his whole life is an erroneous attempt to develop a talent he did not have. An officer, whom Wilhelm recognizes as Jarno's companion, advises him to discover whom he can trust. Wilhelm wonders why none of his observers have pointed him in the right direction. The curtain opens on Hamlet's father, the King of Denmark, in full armor. He identifies himself as the ghost of Wilhelm's father and assures him he has fulfilled his father's wishes. Wilhelm is unable to distinguish the present from memories. The abbé hands him a scroll, his Letter of Apprenticeship.

It begins with a series of maxims — art is long, life is short — and gnomic remarks about development. The abbé interrupts Wilhelm's reading and suggests he look at the other apprenticeships. Wilhelm is assured that Felix is his son and that the boy's mother was worthy. The abbé declares that Wilhelm's apprenticeship is over; nature has released him.

Wilhelm returns to Lothario's estate, and the narrator mentions a great change. Lothario is away on business and Jarno and the abbé involved in administrative and financial matters. But this change heralds an even greater still to come. Wilhelm is drawn into the negotiations over the purchase of neighboring lands, just as he will soon be drawn into the secrets contained in the tower. Wilhelm's news arouses little interest and no surprise in his companions, since they already know everything. He notices their air of secrecy, but seems intrigued rather than embittered by it, as Lydie was. The explanation and initiation are soon forthcoming. Jarno introduces the topic with a statement about the development of an individual, which makes it clear that Wilhelm has reached a turning point. Still speaking in general terms, Jarno approves of the attitude Wilhelm has held so far: having confidence in himself, experimenting, and trying to nurture certain talents. The next stage will be characterized by becoming less prominent, belonging to a larger community, and learning to live and act on others' behalf. The break between the earlier and the later stages is radical and the moment to ask Wilhelm to make these changes is well chosen. He has abandoned his dreams for the theater, taken on responsibility for Felix, and provided for both him and Mignon. He expresses no opposition to being drawn into the land negotiations, whereas all questions involving finance would have been anathema to him before. Wilhelm has reached a stage at which he can be called upon to make a clean break with his past. This new stage, as described by Jarno, is not attained by a gradual process of trial and error or maturation, rather, it is a sudden conversion (Schlechta 17).

The trappings of Wilhelm's initiation are generally considered to be loosely based on Goethe's experiences with the Freemasons.[1] In addition, however, it is evident that Goethe has carefully prepared the

---

[1] The first Freemasons' Lodge was constituted in London in 1717 and from there the movement spread across Europe. Its first appearance in Germany is dated 1737. Several prominent intellectuals, such as Goethe, Herder, Lessing, and Wieland, hoping to put the ideals of the Enlightenment into practice, joined the movement. In June, 1780, Goethe was received into the Masonic Lodge in Weimar, but maintained a certain critical distance to the movement for the next few years. Goethe was not alone in writing a novel with a secret society at its center; English and French examples were the forerunners and Schiller's *Geisterseher* (1786–1789) is also of this type.

ground to integrate the Society of the Tower into his narrative. In *Wilhelm Meisters Theatralische Sendung* there is no hint that Goethe would eventually incorporate material of this type (Barner 86). But the details of Wilhelm's puppet theater are already present and Goethe has built on these, enlarging what first appeared in miniature to a life-size scale. In Wilhelm's account of the first puppet show (Book One, Chapter Two) the opening of the door is momentous: a mystic curtain is drawn aside to reveal a temple and a High Priest steps forward. In the version contained in the *Sendung,* a green rug is hanging down over a table, just as the altar in the tower is covered in green.

Some of Wilhelm's experiences in the theater now seem to have been preparations for his initiation. The curtain is the most obvious shared component of the stage and the scene in the tower. The connection is made much more explicit by the appearance of the ghost last seen on the set of *Hamlet.* More specifically, Wilhelm is dazzled by the sun from where he sits, and not for the first time. In Book Five, Chapter Eight, Wilhelm arrives at the theater for a rehearsal and finds that the props remind him of the stage on which Mariane performed, and the sun streaming in through the window completes the sensation of *déjà vu.* This gives rise to thoughts about Mariane, but also brings home the fact that he has crossed the threshold into the world of the theater for which he entertained such high hopes. Now, in the initiation scene, the light of the sun, which contrasts with the all-pervasive darkness in the antechamber, enables Wilhelm to see the new world he is entering (Neumann 81). It is also symbolic of his enlightenment and of a combination of recognition, comprehension, and recollection. It is as though the theater had rehearsed him for this moment. Jarno's initial statement is couched in universal language and yet, for the reader, the relevance to Wilhelm's life is immediately evident. The initiation process, too, seems, rather surprisingly, to be especially tailored for Wilhelm. The four-part presentation is designed to bring Wilhelm's past memories into the present to prepare for his future. The first speaker asks Wilhelm teasingly where he thinks the ailing prince he remembers from his youth is languishing now. Most remarkable is the ghost that seems once again to speak with his own father's voice, just as Wilhelm imagined when he first heard it on stage. The satisfaction expressed by this character arises, no doubt, from the fulfillment of the advice on the veil: Wilhelm has now actually fled from the theater. He is being guided back to his beginnings, and the scene which so struck Lothario, in which past, present, and future are assembled in Margaret's father's house, can now be seen as a foreshadowing of this moment.

The presentation is made up of specific direct questions, rhetorical questions of a general nature, a statement about how education should be carried out, and commands. At each stage what is missing is the opportunity to reply. Wilhelm is clearly intrigued and would like to ask several questions, both general — about fate — and particular. From these questions, which he does not have a chance to pose, it becomes apparent that Wilhelm recognizes the main error in his life, and that he is ready to submit to firmer guidance.

Although Wilhelm has not had an opportunity to express any of his thoughts out loud, he receives a clear instruction not to argue. This command produces a rather comic effect, and when the next words declare him to be saved, it seems that the reclamation of a chapel was necessary so that these men could play God (Staiger 152).[2] The performance — for that is what this is — had been billed as an initiation into the secrets of the Tower, and by the end of the chapter several mysteries have been cleared up for Wilhelm. He has also been reassured that his father's spirit is content and that he can lay aside all bitterness in relation to Mariane. Nevertheless, Wilhelm is still left with more questions than answers; he is confused and cannot distinguish past from present, memories from actual events, fate from chance. He begins to read the Letter of Apprenticeship.

The document contains a collection of aphorisms, which suggests that it has not been drafted with Wilhelm alone in mind. It fits into a long-standing genre that begins with the ancients, and in fact, the first aphorism is taken directly from Hippocrates.[3] Many of the phrases present pairs of opposites. One that speaks directly to Wilhelm's past situation likens a partial grasp of what it takes to be an artist to bread, which, unlike grain, cannot give lasting satisfaction. This supports the view that Wilhelm was not, in the long run, destined for the stage. Statements with homely comparisons, such as this one, are placed side by side with the more esoteric pronouncements about the roles of spirit and action. The types of people named as those who work from signs alone — pedants, flatterers, and bunglers — seem to have been taken from the stock characters of the stage. But the most interesting lines are those that refer to words and are therefore self-referential. The first of

---

[2] The words are a reminder of the conclusion of *Faust I* when salvation for Gretchen is pronounced from on high by the Lord.

[3] Hippocrates was a Greek physician born around 460 B.C. The Hippocratic oath sworn by doctors, which binds them to upholding the code of medical ethics, was first drawn up, perhaps by Hippocrates himself, in the 4th or 5th century. Goethe also places this aphorism in the mouth of Wagner in *Faust I*, 558.

266   *WILHELM MEISTER'S APPRENTICESHIP: COMMENTARY*

these states that words are good, but are not the best. The second says that when words fail, actions speak. Soon after this, as though to enact the sense of these aphorisms, the reading breaks off (Staiger 155).

Considering the theoretical nature of the document Wilhelm has just been reading, it is remarkable that his question, after he breaks off, does not arise from any of the thoughts that mystified him earlier. Instead, Wilhelm wants to know about Felix — simple information. In confining his question to something factual, he earns praise from the abbé because he is putting into practice the principle that action must take over where words leave off. He is already prepared to live for the sake of others. It is not just the ritual that makes the difference. Now that he can fully acknowledge the bond with Felix, the importance of nature in marking the end of the apprenticeship is emphasized.

Book Eight

Chapter One

BOOK SEVEN CLOSED with Felix and Wilhelm united as father and son, and now Book Eight opens with the same two characters. Felix's curiosity about the plants in the garden pushes Wilhelm beyond his limits; he too is learning about the world around him. In the evening Jarno and the abbé arrive, bringing Wilhelm's old friend Werner with them. To Werner's eyes, Wilhelm seems stronger, straighter, more mature, and to have a better bearing. Werner, on the other hand, appears thinner, balder, and paler, with bowed shoulders. Wilhelm objects to Werner's suggestion that, with his improved looks, he could attract a rich heiress.

Werner's firm is negotiating with Lothario to share the property. The magistrate comes, papers are signed, and Werner reminds the company of Wilhelm's interest in the deal. The abbé and Jarno then join Werner in a game of hombre.[1] Later, the two friends exchange information and Werner mentions some rumors showing Wilhelm in an unfavorable light. Wilhelm listens to news about people at home and Werner expresses pleasure at Wilhelm's changed appearance. He refers to a picture of him with an open-necked shirt, a big ruff, baggy trousers, and loose hair.[2] Werner advises him to tie his hair back or be taken for a Jew and have to pay taxes.[3] Wilhelm decides not to tell Werner who Felix is.

---

[1] Hombre is a card game that originated in sixteenth-century Spain as a four-player game, using a pack without the numbers 8, 9, and 10. By the mid-seventeenth century it had been adapted to a three-player version and spread to France and the rest of Europe. The game is played for stakes.

[2] The picture may have shown Wilhelm in the costume he wore as Prince Harry (Bahr 177). In any case, it suggests the style of dress adopted by writers belonging to the Sturm und Drang movement. The well-known portrait of Schiller by Anton Graff springs to mind.

[3] Orthodox Jews follow the biblical injunction not to cut the hair. In Goethe's day, they had to pay a toll at border crossings to ensure safe conduct on the roads.

During the inspection of the estates, Wilhelm observes Felix's pleasure in the ripening fruit and in nature in general; he remembers his own childhood pleasures. He takes a genuine interest in the buildings and their proposed restoration. Wilhelm feels that as well as taking on fatherhood, he has now become a true citizen. He is aware of nature as the real driving force and sees the demands of morality and bourgeois society as misleading. He used to see the theater and the world in general as being like a pair of dice, whose values needed to be added together to amount to anything. Felix is now like one die, with all aspects of human nature appearing on the surfaces.

Wilhelm begins to see through the eyes of a child. He has to learn in order to satisfy Felix's curiosity. He is unable to discipline Felix, so some bad habits have returned. The boy never closes doors and ignores table manners, eating straight from the bowl and drinking from the bottle. However, he has an endearing habit of pretending to read.

Wilhelm's conscience troubles him: he feels he has neglected both Felix and Mignon and his thoughts turn to finding a mother for the boy in Therese. Fate had set an obstacle between her and Lothario, but Wilhelm is sure she is not against marrying in principle. He decides to tell her about himself although his confessions will show him in a bad light. Finally Wilhelm retrieves the scroll of his apprenticeship from the Tower.

Naturally, Wilhelm faces the perusal of the scroll with trepidation. It is like looking at oneself in the mirror after a long illness. The scroll is a sympathetic and detailed retelling of his life. It is less a reflection than a portrait — not accurate in every feature yet pleasing in its permanence. In planning his story for Therese Wilhelm is ashamed at his lack of virtues. Finally he writes a brief letter asking for her hand. Wilhelm considers this matter too important to discuss with the abbé or Jarno. It is disturbing that so much of his life has been observed, and he now wants his fate to depend on Therese alone.

In overseeing Felix's education and development, Wilhelm is also educating himself again; father and son are progressing in tandem. His activities have a purpose now: the plans for renovation are undertaken with the future, with Felix, in mind. Through Felix, he learns to appreciate nature and comes to see it as the guiding principle of life, rather than an abstract fate.

Anagnorisis is still a strong motif in this chapter, having reached a heady climax in the initiation scene. The meeting with Werner seems coincidental, but, in accordance with the established pattern, it is entirely due to the actions of members of the Tower, as is demonstrated by their lack of surprise. The comparison of the two friends' physiques is a reprise of the theme of the two muses depicted in Wilhelm's youthful poem. The muse of commerce, like Werner now, is by far the less attractive of the two. For the reader, the flattering description of Wilhelm is visible evidence of the result of his development (*HA* 794). At every turn since the scene in the tower, Wilhelm has been reliving his past: through Werner, in his approach to Therese, in the memories of his childhood prompted by Felix, and in reading his scroll.

Despite their delight at finding each other again, Werner and Wilhelm still do not see eye to eye. Werner admires Wilhelm's appearance but disapproves of the portrait he sent home. Wilhelm has become more interested in business matters but is still sensitive to Werner's suggestion that he should find an heiress; he considers this remark to be symptomatic of Werner's excessive interest in money. Whereas Wilhelm expresses his pleasure at having been received by Lothario and the others, Werner feels compelled to dampen his spirits by telling him that an adverse picture was being painted in rumors about him. Finally, while Werner takes it more or less for granted that Wilhelm will return with him and become involved in the business, Wilhelm is planning to marry Therese and establish domestic stability. Werner plays a card game, but Wilhelm does not join in. It is played for stakes, which seems logical, given Werner's financial bent and it is actually Werner's version of how fate works, the counterpart to the dice image that Wilhelm is trying to apply to his own situation.

This chapter repeatedly refers to growing and maturing. While Felix satisfies his curiosity, his father develops new interests and grows observant. Felix is enthusiastic about the berries, which will soon be ripe: they are an image of the maturing process. Wilhelm's interest in the newly acquired buildings is also an interest in developing them for future generations.

Although Wilhelm is very satisfied with the situation in which he finds himself, and with his present occupations, there are still tasks outstanding. Felix flouts table etiquette, and Wilhelm is determined to provide him with a stable home atmosphere. His proposal to Therese will require considerable preparation, and here the circular progression of the novel comes to the surface. Wilhelm has heard Therese's account of her life and wants to reciprocate so that she can know him better. So once again, Wilhelm looks back over his life and plans to recount the events to Therese just as he had done for Mariane. The fact that Therese has already unburdened herself, in distinction to Mariane, who would reveal nothing, seems a good omen. And yet Wilhelm cannot bring himself to produce a straightforward account. He repeatedly evaluates his memories and finds them, and himself, wanting. This reluctance is another indication of the degree to which Wilhelm has changed since the days with Mariane. At last he turns to the written account stored in the tower and is told, somewhat mysteriously, that this is the right moment to read it. The scroll containing an account of Wilhelm's life is always referred to as his "Lehrjahre," and he has seen that there are more of these, marked with others' names. This means that his scroll is marked with the words "Wilhelm Meisters Lehrjahre" — the same as the novel itself — and that Goethe was a modernist writer *avant la lettre* (*HA* 793).

Wilhelm is quite reflective in this chapter and not in his old, dreamy way. He has come to understand much more about the human condition since he began to see the world through a child's eyes. For Felix's sake he has taken on a responsibility and had to learn the answers to factual questions, wrestle with moral dilemmas, and make long-term plans. Wilhelm thinks about reality in terms of dice, thereby reducing the theater to a much more subordinate role than he would ever have allowed before. The traditional association of dice with arbitrariness of fate is surely of significance here too, if only to show that the role of chance is much greater in the sphere of the theater than in the Society of the Tower where Felix belongs.

Wilhelm's life story as related in the scroll turns out to be less painful than he expected. He had thought it would be like a mirror image after an illness — meaning that he now feels fully recovered from the illness of his youth. In choosing the mirror image he confirms the intimate degree of knowledge that the members of the Tower have managed to obtain about him. Most recently, Wilhelm consulted the mirror in a tentative way, to search for similarities between his own features and those of Felix. But the mirror image is transitory, and it sends back a second self, not a different one (Reiss 1951, 127). And so Wilhelm shifts his simile and compares the account to a portrait. The choice of a portrait is not accidental, since Wilhelm has so recently been reminded of the painting of the ailing prince. While he reads it and while he thinks how to address Therese, Wilhelm becomes increasingly estranged from his former self. By the end, he writes something very brief, since he is unable to discern any purpose in his life so far.

Wilhelm recognizes the control exercised over his life by the members of the Tower and welcomes their influence. Indeed, during the initiation scene he wondered why they had not nudged him in the right direction with more force and on more occasions. He tells Werner that he is very fortunate to have become involved with this group. Why, then, does he feel he must conceal from Jarno and the abbé the fact that he wants to propose to Therese? Why not ask their advice? In fact, is it not folly on his part to think that this will escape their attention, when everything else of moment in his life has been observed by them? Not only has Wilhelm recognized and accepted the fact that others have been observing and controlling him, he has also come to see the value of self-control. The narrator refers to him as no longer living his life as a bird of passage: he has come to value permanence (Reiss 1951, 132).

Chapter Two

The letter to Therese is sent and Lothario returns. Wilhelm now has some misgivings about his plan to marry Therese, as Lothario has a prior claim to her affections. But the die is cast; distance casts the only veil between Therese's decision and Wilhelm's receipt of it. Werner is delighted to acquire a good piece of land, but Lothario has qualms about how it was procured. He feels that a nobleman landowner, like a farmer, should be subject to taxation. The interest on the investment would not be reduced if feudal rights still allowed division and disposal of the land. Lothario compares a citizen's relation to the state with a father serving his children first at table.

Lothario tells Wilhelm that his sister wishes him to visit Mignon, whose health is declining. He gives Wilhelm a letter and Wilhelm recognizes the countess's writing. Wilhelm will take Felix along and is to ask Lothario's sister to prepare for the marchese's arrival. Wilhelm is beset by doubts and has no-one to confide in. The sight of Felix asleep is comforting; his affection for his son prompts a display of grandiose sentiments. Before daybreak, they set out, and Felix has his first experience of sunrise. On reaching the inn halfway, Wilhelm rereads the letter. The closing words imply that the writer must be expecting a stranger. He thinks of turning back and then realizes this is not the countess's writing but that of the beautiful Amazon. Lothario must have two sisters, and conversing with himself, Wilhelm proceeds.

Wilhelm deduces that the Amazon is Therese's friend, but still has doubts about the handwriting. On arrival he carries Felix into the house. Statues are displayed there, some from his grandfather's collection, and he is amazed to see the familiar painting of the ailing prince. He enters a chamber and confronts the beautiful Amazon. They sit together, with Felix asleep between them, and Wilhelm hears about Mignon. She is more sensitive and emotional, and experiences pain and irregular heartbeat. The doctor will speak about possible causes. Mignon has begun wearing women's clothing after once dressing as an angel to distribute presents at a party. She spoke strangely then about the wings she wore and the lily she held, and, climbing onto a desk, she played the zither and sang about the dress and her own fate. Now she refuses to give up the white dress. Later Wilhelm lies awake, comparing his image of the beautiful Amazon with the actual woman; the first was created in his mind, while the second seems to be molding him.

The chapter divides into three sections. First, the discussion between Lothario and Werner continues the theme of social reform. Next, Wilhelm embarks on a journey with Felix, which leads to his discovery of Natalie, the beautiful Amazon. Finally, the chapter concludes with the report of Mignon's transformation. Because Lothario is a forceful character, his absence tends to be significant too. It is notable, for instance, that he was not present during Wilhelm's initiation in the Tower. Although Lothario exercises a strong control over events, his realm is less that of the Tower than that of society (Haas 62). Lothario's continued absence has had an impact on Wilhelm. He has taken the step of proposing to Therese, and has done so in a secretive way. The reader suspects that this would never have come about except during Lothario's absence. Now all it takes is Lothario's return in order for Wilhelm to feel regret at this possibly ill-conceived act. Lothario's mind, however, is elsewhere. He is thinking about social reform and is busy exercising his powers of persuasion on Werner, hoping to convert him to a similar way of thinking. Lothario is a free agent, and his influence stretches in all directions, connecting him to a large number of characters (Haas 62). His numerous romantic involvements — with Aurelie, Margaret, Therese, Lydie, and the unnamed woman on whose behalf the duel was fought — constitute only one aspect of this. A measure of his power over other peoples' lives is evident in the fact that it was through him that Wilhelm and Werner were reunited. Since this is the last book of the novel, loose threads need to be tied, and Lothario will be instrumental in bringing this about.

Wilhelm is increasingly preoccupied with thoughts of his fate, and two images are prominent in relation to it. First, the narrator uses the image of threads which are to be separated or joined and presents Wilhelm as a mere spectator, waiting to see how the final design will look. In describing Wilhelm's thoughts about his proposal to Therese, the narrator grants Wilhelm a more active role. The irrevocable quality of Wilhelm's act leads into the image of dice again: the die is cast. Finally, when Wilhelm speculates that Therese may already have reached a decision, he suspects that the physical distance separating them casts a veil obscuring her decision from him. The veil, as image, has the function of obscuring, but it also connects. Threads come together to form the cloth of the veil, linking it aptly to the idea of fate, and indeed the recurring image of the veil or scarf appears at fateful moments throughout the novel. Wilhelm had snatched up Mariane's scarf, which led to the end of their relationship, and the ghost's veil displayed a warning for Wilhelm to leave the stage, which he ultimately saw was the right thing to do.

The financial negotiations fade into insignificance for Wilhelm, as he impatiently anticipates Therese's reply, but these too need to be settled; they are part of the process of determining Wilhelm's fate as well, as Werner tries to remind the assembled company. The broader question, introduced by Lothario, involves taxation and the feudal system. He proposes applying the same levies, regardless of social status, and doing away with what he refers to as feudal hocus-pocus. The use of this phrase is surely ironic, since hocus-pocus, in the form of ritual and visitations, is the principal method employed by members of the Tower to achieve their ends. Lothario's position is that social class should not in the future constitute an impediment to advancement. By suggesting and enacting cooperation between the aristocracy, of which he is representative, and the bourgeoisie, in the person of Werner, Lothario also points to the direction of Therese's thinking about misalliances. The union between two social classes on an individual level, discussed by Therese, is writ large here in Lothario's view of society as a whole.

While some loose threads are tied in this chapter, others are left hanging. It is not known, for instance, whether Werner will be convinced by Lothario's reasoning. Lothario compares the relationship between the landowner and the state to that between a father and his children for whom he provides food at table. This argument may well strike home with Werner, who is a family man, but before he can express a view, events intervene. Wilhelm's two most recent letters are further examples of deferred action. His letter to Werner had not arrived before Werner set out, and Wilhelm will receive no immediate reply to his letter to Therese because his presence has been requested elsewhere.

The threads of Wilhelm's fate become more tangled again during his journey. Wilhelm's other journeys have always had an official purpose, even though he often did not carry out his intended mission. The nature of this journey is different in that Wilhelm is confused about its purpose. The difference in Wilhelm is that he is aware of his confusion and indecision, whereas on earlier journeys he was quite clear about his purpose, but misguided. Now he oscillates between certainty and uncertainty about the identity of the woman he is to visit. More than once he thinks of turning back, but eventually adopts a sort of shaky optimism. Even his entrance on arrival is ambiguous and less than reassuring; Wilhelm's confidence has been severely undermined. Certain pointers help the reader to predict the outcome. Because his previous acquaintance with the countess is on his conscience, Wilhelm has no one in whom to confide his misgivings. He voices his fears to Felix, addressing him as though the boy had an adult's experience and powers of reasoning. In fact, Wilhelm simply uses Felix as a catalyst for the development of his own thoughts. He is speaking to himself, and when Felix experiences with wonder, for the first time, the sun rising, this surely portends a glorious event to come for Wilhelm too.

On his arrival, Wilhelm is confronted by his own thoughts and doubts in concrete form. He seems to recognize some of the features of the statues, busts, and other artifacts in the halls through which he is led. They had once been part of his grandfather's collection. And yet this is not a decisive moment of joyful anagnorisis. The experience is fantastical; it is like living inside a fairy tale. His progress is difficult because, carrying Felix, he stumbles and has to stop to catch his breath and take command of his emotions. Even as he enters the room and sees the seated woman in the lamplight, he cannot tell who it is at first. The statues Wilhelm recognizes both take him back to happy childhood memories and suggest that he is proceeding towards another happy moment of recognition. This suggestion receives supreme confirmation in the antechamber where the picture of the ailing prince is hanging on the wall It is not the first time that the ailing prince and the Amazon have been associated in Wilhelm's mind. This second meeting with the Amazon brings with it a similar visual phenomenon: as before, the Amazon's countenance is encircled by light (*MA* 825). This recognition scene is now described in great detail, especially the position of each of the three people in the room. As if suggested by Wilhelm's rediscovery of the painting, the three are now grouped together as though sitting for an artist to commit them to canvas.

The narrator begins to refer to the Amazon as Natalie without prior announcement. For the reader, then, a minor anagnorisis has been prepared. For not only has Wilhelm realized that Lothario must have two sisters, the reader also realizes that this is the very Natalie described with such affection by the beautiful soul — her aunt — at the end of her Confessions. Natalie tells Wilhelm about Mignon's condition, and the narrator inserts the song. The transformation of Mignon is complicated; it arises as a result of her taking on a role, as an actress. The intention of the performance, as Natalie describes it, is to dispel superstitions. In other words, Mignon dresses up as angel in order to show her playmates that angels are not real — a kind of perversion of the standard attempt to induce a suspension of disbelief through a stage performance — and she explains to the others that the objects she bears are mere symbols of her condition. A symbol she does not mention is the desk from the top of which she sings — it sums up Mignon's attempts to educate herself, to learn to read and write, which went against her nature and required such tremendous effort (Schlaffer *Mythos,* 65). But for Mignon herself, the transition is from boyish clothes, which disguised her true nature, to the white dress which was intended to be recognizable as a mere costume, but with which she now identifies so closely that she will not even consider wearing anything else. She is just as intransigent now as she was when she would wear only masculine clothing, except that now she no longer wishes to appear in human form at all. The dress does not signal an acceptance of herself as a young woman, instead, it elevates her to a level where sexual distinctions fall away (MacLeod 123). This, together with Wilhelm's impression of her increasingly frail appearance, points to Mignon's transposition from the earthly to the ethereal realm. There is an aura not only of otherworldliness but also of death about her (Hass 203).

Mignon's song arises more directly out of the preceding related events than any of the other songs in the novel (Storz 1949, 44). She is explaining why she insists on wearing the angel's dress. Although some words are used in a strange, unidiomatic way, the song is on the whole much more easily comprehensible than the other ones sung by Mignon. In the opening line, the verbs "appear" (scheinen) and "become" (werde) should be read in close conjunction with each other. This means that Mignon is not stressing the opposition between appearance and reality. Her otherworldly appearance is the first stage in her process of becoming what she represents. The verb "to become," which seems at first to lack a predicate, is in fact completed by the first half of the line. Appearing is therefore used as an opposite to becoming, and the caesura that divides this line makes the opposition clearer. This is a more confident song, the tone is not one of hopeless longing, but of determination, and the first two lines are imperatives that, because their natural stress disrupts the iambic structure of the line, gain extra emphasis. In support of the definite tone, the metrical scheme is very regular, and deviations from it are rare.

Up until the last stanza, Mignon uses the present tense, and yet she is describing the progressive stages of her becoming, her transfiguration. The white dress is only a stage in her projected development and it will be abandoned when she reaches a higher realm, the realm of becoming. Like the lily and the wings, the dress is only a symbol, not the actuality it suggests. The break between the first two stanzas seemed to prefigure the theme with which the second stanza opens. There, Mignon speaks of a pause, a period of quiet rest.[1] After this, appearance is

---

[1] These details are based closely on Revelations 6: 11.

altered because sight, or vision, are changed as well. The trappings of Mignon's altered appearance are to be laid aside one by one, until human characteristics are completely superseded. Most importantly, as Mignon mentions in the third stanza, there is no longer any difference between man and woman. Mignon will have been freed from the ambiguity that defined her whole existence to this point.

As the stanzas depict Mignon's imagined progress, there is a discernible alteration in their form as well. The regular beat and rhyme of the first stanza is too pedestrian for the heavenly theme of the third stanza, which is more virtuosic, with anaphora, caesura, and internal rhyme in the third line and three unstressed syllables to open the first line. The lighter beat suits those heavenly beings released from earthly form; the repeated negatives in the third line seem to exult in the newfound freedom from restraint.

The fourth stanza switches to the past tense, and Mignon describes her past life. A heaviness of tone sets in and the cause of her cares and sorrows remains unexplained. This stanza is closer to the darker tones and mysterious allusions of her earlier songs. But the change in tone dominates only the first three lines; it does not persist right until the end. The imperative returns for the final line, asserting itself against the metrical scheme with a stressed opening syllable, to reach a crescendo in the word "ewig" (Storz 1949, 46). Mignon strives not only for a neutral physical being, but for timelessness as well. The gesture of looking back over her life in this stanza was called for by the need to revert to the childhood Mignon says she left behind too soon.

After the song, Natalie describes the practical arrangements she made to accommodate Mignon's wishes by providing a supply of white dresses. Wilhelm leaves, but the association with Natalie's sister, the countess, makes itself felt in Wilhelm's thoughts. He wonders if Natalie has a husband who will suddenly appear from behind a door — the reader remembers Wilhelm's confrontation with the countess's husband. His uncertainty and diffidence persist and he hesitates to pose the questions on his mind. The chapter ends with Wilhelm comparing the image of the Amazon, which he had carried in his mind for so long, with the real woman Natalie. Not only does the image produced and embellished in his imagination fade, but he experiences a sensation as though he were now being created by Natalie (Hass 202). She does represent the goal of his long development, but also, because he meets her in a setting redolent with his own childhood memories, it is as though his story were being refashioned from childhood on.

Chapter Three

Wilhelm admires the architecture of Natalie's house and the familiar artifacts. He is deeply moved and affected by the ailing prince picture but also admires the library and natural specimens.[1] He wonders how he will be able to receive a reply from Therese and is apprehensive at seeing both Mignon and Natalie again.

Wilhelm notices a portrait of Natalie's aunt, the beautiful soul, and recounts how touched he was by her Confessions. Natalie is gratified by Wilhelm's reaction; she sees her aunt as an example, just as Therese's orderly household benefited from a good example: one should not make fun of the cleanliness of Dutch housewives.[2] The remark confirms that Natalie is the friend Therese mentioned. Wilhelm realizes that he has also read about Lothario's childhood and that this very house belonged to the uncle. It seems like a temple, with Natalie as household priestess or spirit.[3] The statues and busts remind him of the statues in Mignon's song. Before seeing Mignon, he must await the arrival of the doctor — the same one mentioned in the Confessions.

The abbé is also mentioned in the Confessions, and Natalie's account of his views on education sounds familiar to Wilhelm: education is an essential means of promoting natural ability; also, it is preferable to stray from the right path rather than to wander aimlessly. Just as Natalie is mentioning another brother, Friedrich, the doctor arrives.

The doctor informs Wilhelm that Mignon's condition stems from a deep longing for her half-remembered home, and for Wilhelm. It appears she was taken from her home near Milan at an early age by a group of tightrope artists. In a moment of despair, Mignon had a vision of the Virgin Mary and swore never to reveal her story. The doctor tells Wilhelm that Mignon was present on the night when a woman joined him in his bed. Her heart stopped beating and she rushed out to join the harper. Wilhelm feels guilty about Mignon's distress but the doctor advises him to

---

[1] "Moved" and "affected" render the German words "reizend" and "rührend." In Immanuel Kant's *Critique of Judgement* the same two terms designate a lack of purity of taste (MA 826).

[2] The high standards of orderliness and cleanliness to be found in a Dutch household seem to be proverbial. A glance at the calm and orderliness of Dutch interiors represented in the paintings of artists such as Vermeer confirms this view (Schama 375-98). Goethe was familiar with Dutch works of art from a young age.

[3] Wilhelm calls Natalie the "Genius" of the house. The term comes from the Latin and it means a protective spirit.

visit her and she receives him warmly. Mignon, in her long white dress, looks like a departed spirit, in contrast to the lively Felix on her lap.

Wilhelm now hears how Natalie is indebted to her uncle for encouraging her natural inclinations. Nevertheless, she applies principles in dealing with the young girls in her care.

Mignon walks with Wilhelm in the garden. She envies the birds their peaceful nests in high places. Wilhelm wonders how she would react if he married Therese. He does not suspect that Natalie knows about the proposal. Wilhelm is uncomfortable on hearing talk of Natalie's sister, the countess, and that she and her husband are expected. The count has dedicated himself to the Pietists completely, has delusions of sainthood, and will be traveling to all the congregations, even perhaps to America, with his wife.

Wilhelm is a keen observer of houses. He is very impressed by the house he has now entered. The architecture pleases him, whereas the outline of Lothario's estate fell short in this regard, because of its lack of plan. The objects that had formerly belonged to Wilhelm's grandfather are pleasing as well; it was this aspect which he missed in his own father's new house. So taken is he with the objects in their present setting that he outlines a theory, linking the forms and limitations of art to those which govern a society. Because of Wilhelm's aesthetic interests, it comes as a surprise to the reader when, at the end of the chapter, Natalie declares her complete lack of interest in art. Wilhelm goes back again to look at his favorite painting, and here his sentiments overcome him as always. When he first referred to the painting, Wilhelm freely admitted that it was not a masterpiece, and yet it still exerts a power over him.

Next, Wilhelm is drawn to a portrait. He thinks it is of Natalie, but, in a device crucial to the unfolding of the plot, he hears that this is a likeness of the beautiful soul. Mistakes and misidentifications are thus still a component of Wilhelm's life, despite the many revelations in this chapter alone. He still remains unsure of the identity of the woman who joined him in his bed, but the chapter makes clear the links between the abbé, the beautiful soul, and Natalie and her siblings. Even the physician who now attends Mignon is the same one familiar from the pages of the Confessions.

The fact that Wilhelm has read the Confessions is all-important in this chapter and the manuscript now seems to be quite securely embedded in the narrative. Because he has read the Confessions, Wilhelm suddenly realizes he is very familiar with Lothario and his family. The sight of his grandfather's artifacts brings back his own childhood, and Wilhelm finds himself on an intimate footing with Natalie because of these revelations. He mentions Mignon in the discussion as well, contrasting the marble statues of her song with the ones he finds here in Natalie's house. Mignon's statues are associated with sorrow and sympathy, whereas the ones Wilhelm now sees link him to happier memories. Mignon's present situation is adumbrated in this contrast; she is depicted as almost lifeless, the very opposite of Felix who is so full of life.

Mignon seems to be preparing to depart from life. Her song at the end of the previous chapter was the first step in an elaborate leave-taking. Even so, there are moments when she clings to her beloved Wilhelm and Felix. Her costume as an angel is as artificial as her boy's clothing; both are signs of her thwarted desire to develop in a direction denied to her. Wilhelm hears that she had planned to achieve woman-hood by crawling into his bed, and now she implies innocence by adopting the guise of an angel (Baioni 95). Both these attempts are un-successful, just as the desire to become a boy could never be realized.

Wilhelm, on the other hand, seems to be on the brink of a new stage in life. After a long quest, he finds Natalie and realizes that he is already acquainted with her childhood through his reading of the beautiful soul's Confessions. There are also parallels between them: Wilhelm re-members being especially favored by his grandfather, and Natalie was the favorite of her aunt; both these older relatives were formative influ-ences in their lives. Both Wilhelm and Natalie have been living under the auspices of the abbé and both now have the responsibility of bring-ing up younger charges. Wilhelm has been giving considerable thought to this, ever since the discovery of Felix as his son, and he is interested to hear that Natalie does not follow the same principles with which she herself was brought up, but rather gives her young charges some direc-tion. The more disciplined method adopted by Natalie is reflected in the ordered architecture of her house, whereas the whimsical sprawling out-line of Lothario's estate, with which the abbé is associated, suits his be-lief in the value of making wrong turnings.

In a sense, Wilhelm has reached the end of his journey, because he has finally met the woman who had become an ideal in his mind. This impression is reinforced by the explanation of a number of mysteries and the tying of loose threads. And yet Natalie remains a somewhat in-distinct character. Mignon's clothing and hairstyle are described in de-tail, but the reader is given no such physical impression of Natalie. There is also as yet no clear replacement in Wilhelm's life for the pro-fession of acting. And Wilhelm himself is unclear about whether his future lies with Therese. Because Wilhelm has learned about Natalie's childhood he immediately feels very close to her, just as happened when he met Therese. (Supplying life histories for the principal charac-ters is one of the notable ways in which Goethe revised the earlier version of the novel [Saine 1991, 136].) But the difference now is that Wilhelm has not heard Natalie's story from her lips; instead, he knows it from reading the Confessions written by her aunt. Indeed, Natalie feels the account is not factual but rather a projection of what she might become. It is an ideal version of Natalie and as such it forms a parallel to those heroes in books — David, Tancred, and Hamlet — by whom Wilhelm was inspired as a boy.

The statues provide a link to Wilhelm's boyhood, but they also relate to Mignon. The other work of art specifically mentioned is the painting of the ailing prince. This picture had come to mind the first time Wilhelm saw Natalie and therefore it seems right that he should see it again on the way to meeting her for the second time. But the reason for Wilhelm's visit is Mignon's condition, and the painting, with its theme of renunciation, also announces the truth about Mignon: that she suffers from an unrequited love for Wilhelm and has decided to renounce him and life.

In the earlier books of the novel, recurring themes and leitmotifs were evident, but now the tempo has increased, and the recapitulations are becoming more and more frequent. Occurrences that seemed isolated at the time, and mysterious, inexplicable encounters come to form a pattern, both for the reader and for Wilhelm (Muenzer 41). Phenomena interpreted by Wilhelm as omens, rightly or wrongly, are now seen in a clearer light. In this chapter Wilhelm finds out the meaning of some of Mignon's songs, he is able to identify his acquaintances with people met in the pages of the beautiful soul's Confessions, he finds connections with his childhood, and he meets the woman whose image has been before him for so long (Saine 1991, 136). In finding elements of his remembered childhood, Wilhelm is also to some extent restored to himself. He retrieves the cultural heritage that his father had dispensed with and repairs the rift — both cultural and emotional — which the sale of those items caused (Baioni 100). The continuity of generations is also guaranteed, with Wilhelm's adoption of Felix, and Wilhelm's growing interest in financial and administrative matters repairs the damage caused by his departure from home.

The chapter ends with another topic that causes uncertainty in Wilhelm. He has learned from Natalie that he will have to confront the countess. Wilhelm's new uncertainty stems from his initiation when it was declared that his apprenticeship was over. The members of the Tower are no longer manipulating his life, nudging him away from or towards a particular course of action. The lack of guidance makes itself felt. He is also unsure where he stands in what will soon become a romantic triangle, formed by Therese, Natalie, and the countess. Here again the ailing prince, consumed with love for his father's bride, is relevant: Wilhelm once desired the count's wife, he proposed to the woman Lothario reveres and would like to marry, and now he wonders, logically, but does not dare ask, whether Natalie has a husband.

For Wilhelm, the way forward is far from clear; he cannot see how to extricate himself from his tangled love interests. The unwelcome news that he will be seeing the countess soon, and the proposal he has made to Therese, make relations with Natalie more guarded. In Natalie's story of the count's conversion, it is easy to see Goethe's irony at work. The count would like to emulate and replace the late founder of the Pietist movement, Count Zinzendorf. He is contemplating a trip to America, simply because Zinzendorf went there and he fancies himself a saint and martyr. Goethe is evidently poking fun at the count and at Pietism; this kind of dedication is a perverse version of *imitatio Christi*.

Chapter Four

Wilhelm is often tempted to tell Natalie that he has proposed to Therese. Eventually his silence is broken when Natalie hands him Therese's letter and teases him for being secretive. Although Therese has accepted his offer, Wilhelm turns pale. Natalie remarks on this reaction, and tells him she has been influencing Therese in Wilhelm's favor. Wilhelm's spirits are restored by Therese's letter but he is increasingly consciousness of an attraction for Natalie. The narrator reproduces excerpts from letters exchanged by the two women.

One section of a letter recounts Wilhelm's views on social classes and the question of misalliance: an imbalance is more often temperamental than social. Then Therese describes Wilhelm and Natalie as sharing a striving for the good.[1] Therese quotes Jarno's assessment of her as lacking faith, hope, and charity; insight, endurance, and trust have replaced them.[2] According to Jarno, Therese trains the pupils, while Natalie educates them. Therese writes that she still thinks of Lothario constantly, regrets the consequences of his youthful peccadillo, and feels unworthy of him. Their blood relationship also prevents Natalie, who would suit him, from becoming his wife.

---

[1] The ideal of striving for the good is also the element in human nature that will immunize Faust against Mephistopheles' influence, and which the Lord confidently expresses in the *Prolog im Himmel*, l. 317.

[2] These three virtues are taken from 1 Corinthians 13: 13. In Book 6 of *Dichtung und Wahrheit* Goethe also describes his sister as lacking them.

Therese, influenced by Lydie to mistrust the members of the Tower, has kept everything secret. Natalie and Wilhelm are about to send a letter to Lothario when Jarno suddenly appears. He has news about Therese and makes them guess. Natalie simply hands Jarno the letter, convinced that he has somehow found out the secret. Jarno is speechless. Eventually he reveals his own news: Therese is not her mother's daughter; he has come to prepare her for marriage with Lothario, as the obstacle is now removed. Seeing their amazed reaction, Jarno suggests parting for an hour to think.

When they reassemble, Wilhelm remarks that his proposal to Therese was an independent act and his happiness seemed assured. But fate has made everything dreamlike: he cannot reach to grasp Therese's outstretched hand. His respect for Lothario, from his very first impression, makes it easier to sacrifice his own happiness, so he urges Jarno to inform Lothario soon. Jarno departs on his own to speak to Lothario.

The next day Natalie receives a letter from Therese, reiterating her intention to marry Wilhelm. She encloses a letter for Wilhelm in which she acknowledges the strangeness of desiring a union that was forged so rationally. Wilhelm becomes more suspicious of Jarno's manipulations but remains divided. Natalie suggests waiting to hear whether the story is a fabrication.

A letter from Lothario states with confidence that Therese is not her mother's daughter. He asks Wilhelm not to come between them. Wilhelm writes to Therese to that effect. Therese replies that she will be arriving soon and resents having to transfer her affections from one man to another. In conversation, Wilhelm and Natalie draw closer and she admits to a skepticism about storybook love: cryptically, she declares she has either never or always been in love.

A rapid succession of exchanged letters makes this chapter resemble a section of an epistolary novel, but there is also a dramatic entrance and a touching duet at the end, which mean that the style has not lost its affinity with the theater. Natalie starts out in the role of go-between, giving her blessing to Wilhelm and Therese. There are two twists which make the situation more complex: one is that Natalie, like the members of the Tower, knew all along what Wilhelm had been doing, and that he had proposed to Therese, a fact he had hesitated to reveal to her. The other is Wilhelm's shock and dismay at having his proposal accepted. Proximity to Natalie appears to have made Therese's presence seem unreal and now, with her letter, the image of Therese floods back into his memory. This fluidity is also characteristic of Wilhelm's consciousness of Natalie; his image of her ebbs and flows in his mind (Graham 201). But Natalie has played a crucial part in Therese's deliberations and she still continues in this pivotal role, since communications are by and large addressed to her, with enclosures for Wilhelm, and, in the case of the first letter, she opens it and tells him what it contains before handing it to him.

The reader thus only becomes further acquainted with the two women at one remove from the narrative voice. Therese's views, in particular about Wilhelm, are transmitted only through a letter addressed to Natalie, not through the narrator's omniscient psychological analysis. Natalie, as befits a go-between, seems to have sublimated her own views for the sake of others' happiness.

Expectations are doubly thwarted when Jarno appears with, he is sure, a very welcome piece of news. Wilhelm and Natalie also think they have happy tidings, but everything ends in consternation. The denouement is delayed and prolonged. It is worth noting that Jarno is the only one to produce no written evidence for his claims. In a chapter dominated by the written word, Jarno is bound to fall under suspicion. Both sides in the conversation offer what ought to be solutions, but the result is more complicated than ever. This is a structural irony, but irony works at the narrative level as well. Therese is open in her letter about her strong feelings for Lothario and her admiration for Natalie. She goes so far as to say that Natalie would have made him a better wife, had they not been related by blood. It is a blood relationship that, in fact, prevents her, not Natalie, from being joined to the man she loves. She wishes that a ban could be lifted for Natalie — the very ban that is about to be lifted for her.

Wilhelm's uncertainty and lack of confidence, apparent at the beginning of this chapter, have escalated into a case of extreme indecision. He must decide whether to grant Therese her wish or delay joining her for Lothario's sake. The consequences of either act will influence the entire course of his future, as he is well aware. He is again faced with the mutually exclusive choices offered by the muses of poetry and commerce from his youthful poem. Wilhelm's strategies for overcoming this difficulty are not refined: he hopes to influence the outcome of the dilemma by keeping information to himself, and his reaction to Therese's acceptance of his proposal is anything but straightforward. He claims, for instance, that his hopes had been fulfilled when Therese accepted his proposal, but his reactions have told a different story.

Both women display self-denial to a degree that matches Mignon's. First, Natalie selflessly encourages the relationship between Therese and Wilhelm. Then Therese, after claiming that his sister would make him a better wife, is not prepared to accept a report that would allow her to be joined with Lothario. Wilhelm's situation is more complex, but even he is ready to go through with a marriage to Therese, although he has strong intimations that this would be a mistake. On the other hand, he would also be ready to renounce his right to Therese's hand out of admiration for Lothario. In fact, this would suit Wilhelm better than he lets on, as the reader knows. He gives the lie to this seemingly selfless offer by pointing out that he agreed to mislead Lydie on Lothario's behalf, as though this were an example of a noble self-sacrifice.

The juxtaposition of Wilhelm's reported views on intermarriage is wonderfully ironic. He says that the only true misalliances are not based on differences in social class, but arise out of contrary characteristics. This is an accurate description of Therese and Wilhelm: she has no appreciation for literature or drama, he has little aptitude for finance or administration. Therese's own description of Wilhelm is odd in that she begins by saying he shares much with Natalie and then points out how his life so far has consisted of misguided but well-meaning searching. Nevertheless, the images of Wilhelm and Natalie merge into one another for Therese. This is not the first incident of images merging: Wilhelm had to contend with his remembered vision of the beautiful Amazon when confronted with Natalie in person. He also had to reconcile the painting of the beautiful soul with the flesh and blood Natalie, who resembled her aunt so closely. The discrepancies between the image and the real woman are also a reflection of the dual or androgynous aspect of the principal female characters, including, though to a lesser extent, Natalie herself (MacLeod 133). Both are instances of an irreconcilable dual nature (Hörisch 65).

The suggestion that Natalie and Lothario would be well suited as man and wife were it not for the fact that they are brother and sister shows that Therese's nature leads her to regard matrimony in rational, mathematical terms. Thus she refers to her bond with Wilhelm as rational. At first sight this strikes an excessively pragmatic note, and yet her remarks are also enlightening. In her comparison of Wilhelm and Natalie she offers the reader an insight and a key to the structure of this final book. It is because Natalie has a similar nature to his own that Wilhelm is able to find her. The act of seeking brings forth the noble object of the search (Schings *Symbolik,* 170).

There is a tension in the chapter between the written word as a means of conveying messages and the use of an intermediary. This too relates to the conventions of the stage, where the contents of a letter need to be conveyed to the audience by some means. So Therese tells Wilhelm what he is about to read in Therese's letter and then she hands him the collection of correspondence between Therese and herself on the subject of Wilhelm. Lothario is certain that a letter from him would be preferable to a verbal message brought by Jarno. This letter, too, is forwarded to Therese. It also should not be forgotten that it was a letter from Natalie that brought Wilhelm into this setting and that he at first thought the letter was from the countess.

The final letter from Therese indicates that Lydie, who believes that Lothario is merely the victim of his manipulative companions, has had some influence on her. It is on Lydie's behalf that Therese hesitates, and her objection that she should not be required to transfer her affections so rapidly is valid, though it too shows the marks of Lydie's influence. For fear of becoming the pawn of the members of the Tower, Therese allows herself to be manipulated by Lydie instead.

Having offered at least partial solutions to some difficult situations, the chapter ends with a riddle for Wilhelm and the reader to solve. This is Natalie's ambiguous statement that she has never or always been in love. She rejects the standard representations of love; they are the products of the imagination and do not translate into reality. For Wilhelm, the rediscovery of the beautiful Amazon has brought her lingering image into the realm of the real; Natalie may be on the brink of a similar experience. One sign of this is that Natalie has laid aside the coat she wore as the beautiful Amazon; there is no longer any suggestion of androgyny. Another is that in Wilhelm's dream on his first night under Lothario's roof Natalie, representing Wilhelm's future, restrained him from pursuing Mariane, the representative of his past.

Chapter Five

While talking, Natalie and Wilhelm have wandered into the garden, where Natalie picks some unusual flowers, favorites of her uncle, whom they are going to visit in the Hall of the Past. She describes her uncle as a remarkable man who emphasized both striving for breadth of understanding and the occasional self-indulgence. He saw Natalie as perfectly balanced.

Natalie now leads Wilhelm up to a doorway flanked by two sphinxes and tapered in at the top, in Egyptian style, with solemn brass doors. Within, art and life predominate. A series of arches contain sarcophagi, and niches in the pillars hold urns. On the walls hang imposing portraits in bright colors with ornate backgrounds. Yellowish-red marble with streaks of blue lends the appearance of lapis lazuli and unites the whole.[1] The effect is to show what man is and what he can become. A

---

[1] Lapis lazuli is an attractive deep blue stone, sometimes veined with gold. The combination of colors present in the hall is prescribed in Goethe's theory of colors, *Zur Farbenlehre* (1810), paragraphs 803–24.

marble likeness of a man reading from a scroll stands on a sarcophagus, with the inscription "Remember to live." Natalie places the flowers on this, her uncle's tomb. Wilhelm seems to recognize his features. He feels that because pictures outlive people and have a universal appeal, this could be called Hall of the Past, Present, and Future. The pictures show the ages of man and his faculties. Wilhelm is inspired by his surroundings, and the narrator adds that if the perfect order of the room could be conveyed in words, the reader would not wish to leave it.

Marble candlesticks stand at the corners of a smaller, ancient sarcophagus Natalie's uncle had particularly liked. He used to remark that fruit can be taken prematurely from the tree, thus predicting Mignon's fate. Wilhelm sees the hidden choir stalls and brasses for hanging tapestries during funerals and learns of the uncle's preference for disembodied music.

Mignon and Felix race up to announce Therese's arrival. Mignon's heart is beating wildly and she remarks that it might as well break. Therese enters, embraces Natalie, Mignon, and then Wilhelm, addressing him as husband. Mignon grasps at her heart and falls. Wilhelm carries her out, but the doctors cannot save her. Therese comforts Wilhelm, but the images of Mignon and Natalie still preoccupy him.

Therese asks Natalie to bless their union there and then, but Natalie reminds them about Lothario. The doctor and his assistant dissuade Wilhelm from viewing Mignon before the embalming. Wilhelm learns that he recognizes the ribbon on the young surgeon's instrument case because it had come from the surgeon's father, the old doctor who had attended to Wilhelm's wounds in the forest. Wilhelm wants the ribbon because of its sentimental associations with Natalie and poor Mignon.

Lothario, Jarno, and the abbé enter and Therese and Lothario greet each other. Lothario says his fate rests in her hands. Despite Wilhelm's resistance, Jarno tells him more about the Tower. It contains only the remnants of a youthful plan and they find it amusing. He assures Wilhelm that the letter of apprenticeship contains useful sayings and he reads some out.

Jarno explains that the most successful members recognize their innate gifts and are released to follow their own course. Wilhelm feels he himself was released too soon, since he has no idea what he could or should do. Jarno offers Wilhelm two maxims: anyone with the potential for development eventually acquires knowledge of himself and the world, and few have the understanding as well as the ability to act. Jarno explains his remark about Wilhelm's acting: Wilhelm is only good in roles that suit his temperament. One should not trust a talent that cannot be perfected. Wilhelm discovers that the abbé was behind the ghost's appearance in *Hamlet* and the message on the veil. Jarno had disagreed with the abbé that this would dissuade Wilhelm from further attempts to become an actor. It is helpful to learn that, although he was there, Jarno does not know whether the abbé or his twin brother played the ghost. Wilhelm is surprised that the members keep secrets from each other, but Jarno explains that they nevertheless understand each other.

He reads that nature holds everything in balance and that development has to come from within. He assures Wilhelm that the members of the Tower are only there for support. Wilhelm feels that people who are in love should be allowed to arrange their own marriages.

Natalie paints a picture of the Hall of the Past not as a mausoleum but as a sun-filled room, so that the reader already expects Wilhelm to undergo an eye-opening experience. Natalie does not make it clear that the uncle she is proposing to visit is lying in a tomb; her description of him as someone intent on broadening his mind, being useful to others but also treating himself well demonstrates how the founding principles of the Tower arose. This description, and the uncle's view of her own balanced nature, present Wilhelm with an ideal to strive for. Much of the rest of the chapter continues this trend: it is composed of further tenets to live by, which Jarno reads out for Wilhelm's edification.

The grandeur of the portal to the Hall of the Past arouses great expectations in the visitor. In this respect it is akin to the stage, and the tapestries that are hung during funerals contribute to this impression as well. The hybrid nature of the sphinx links it to the sexually ambiguous appearance of certain female characters in the novel, and the association of the sphinx with wisdom in the form of terse riddles makes it an appropriate emblem for the Tower and its certificate of Apprenticeship, filled as this is with improving maxims. The Egyptian aspect of this entrance depicts the historical beginnings of art (Schlaffer *Mythos*, 66). Inside, the decorations present a lively and bright appearance to offset the solemn presence of the sarcophagi. Architecture, normally a static art form, is brought to life by the color scheme and the ornamentation. Bright colors and fresh flowers to replace the withered ones insistently declare the continuation of life in the face of death. The culmination is in the explicit inscription on a stone scroll: Remember to live. The very fact that this is written in stone brings together the two principles of life and death, change and permanence, past and an ongoing present. The inscription explicitly contradicts the medieval Christian advice to remember one's mortality: *Memento mori* (Bahr 181). Here any thoughts of death are taken up into the all-pervasive principle of life. A series of pictures shows the stages of human life and Wilhelm points out their universal appeal. He wonders why he should find this perfectly ordered space so inspiring, but the narrator chooses this moment to withdraw, on the pretext that such perfection is indescribable.

Natalie draws attention to one last monument, which had been a favorite of her uncle's. The sarcophagus is only of medium size and, as Natalie herself points out, it suggests that Mignon will not live much longer. The uncle's preference for disembodied music strikes one more blow against the theater in that he disapproved of the subsidiary role to which music is reduced on the stage. Invisible voices imply the unseen presence of angels, a theme already introduced by Mignon in her angel's costume and soon to be continued when Wilhelm expresses his desire to see the body of Mignon, whom he refers to as the departed angel.

Mignon's death is brought on by both physical and emotional causes. Over-exertion places a literal strain on her heart, but unrequited love for Wilhelm has metaphorically broken it. There is irony in her death occurring at the moment when Wilhelm and Therese embrace, because this apparent expression of love is insincere, at least on Wilhelm's part. It is also ironic that Mignon should exert herself by running to announce the arrival of Therese, which will lead to the very scene that causes her death. In this dramatic moment the motifs of life and death represented in the room are brought together again (Hass 204). This is an immediate opportunity for Wilhelm to put into practice the principle to remember to live in the face of death (Neumann 70). In sympathy with Mignon, who will never sing again, Wilhelm is speechless. This constitutes a reversal of the uncle's ideal disembodied voices: the physical is displayed, but the voice is silenced.

Therese tries to salvage something joyous from the scene of grief by suggesting she and Wilhelm be joined together on the spot. Her suggestion is a secular parody of the wedding ceremony. Her fiancé is in mourning, no preparations have been made, and Natalie is not empowered to perform the ceremony. Indeed, her inapposite response paraphrases the biblical injunction that no man should put asunder those whom God has joined together.[2] Nevertheless, there is something of the spirit of the Tower in her idea that life can be reaffirmed in the face of death. But there are absolute impediments as well, since Wilhelm's desire to marry Therese wanes the longer he spends in the company of Natalie. Also, as Natalie points out, Lothario cannot simply be ignored.

Wilhelm is not permitted to view the body until the embalming is complete and it lies in the Hall of the Past. In effect, Mignon will have been turned into a monument. He feels responsible for her death; in rejecting her, he repeats the events that made him partially responsible for Mariane's death as well (Neumann 70). Looked at symbolically, these two women were Wilhelm's connection with the theater, and now Mignon's death reemphasizes the conclusion of Wilhelm's theatrical career.

---

[2] Matthew 19: 6.

The ribbon on the doctor's instrument case has become a symbol for Wilhelm, both because it reminds him of the first time he saw Natalie and because he associates it with Mignon's devotion. In a morbid reprise of the night when he snatched up Mariane's scarf as a keepsake, he now demands to have this ribbon. Objects outlast emotions, says Wilhelm, and, in a way, his words echo the idea of the Hall of the Past. For here, the art on the walls will survive beyond the life span of any individual, as Wilhelm himself observes.

Although the abbé, Jarno, and Lothario, like messengers of Fate, appear at this moment, and although the company divides into pairs, this is not yet a harmonious and operatic finale. For Wilhelm, the outlook seems gloomy: the Tower must have some inscrutable purpose and he resents it. Jarno's history of the Tower begins with a remark that makes light of the whole enterprise. Just as the interior of the Hall is a reversal and a parody of the traditional Christian view of death, so now the solemnity of the ceremony and the trappings in the Tower are undermined by Jarno's remarks. This is reinforced later when Jarno points out that the secrecy is not restricted to the protégés of the Tower, like Wilhelm, but the individual members also keep secrets from each other. His aim is both to lift Wilhelm's spirits and to draw his attention to the importance of the advice contained in the Letter of Apprenticeship. Wilhelm, however, is resilient; he repeatedly asks Jarno to stop reading out the maxims, so great is his disappointment in the workings of the Tower. As the members of the Tower are also members of the aristocracy, Wilhelm's disillusionment appears as a repetition of his earlier experience among the aristocratic circle at the castle, of whom he had entertained such high hopes.

The discussion turns to Wilhelm's role as Hamlet. Jarno's view is that Wilhelm could only play himself. For Aurelie this was true as well, and this was what caused her downfall and ultimately her death. In Wilhelm's case, the remark really applies to his whole endeavor to be an actor, an ambition that stood in contradiction to his true nature. Jarno's theme is in fact a preoccupation of Goethe's: Wilhelm lacks serious purpose, which makes him a dilettante. In reinterpreting Hamlet's personality to suit his own purposes, Wilhelm was compromising the sovereignty of art to accord with his own subjective preferences.[3]

In all Jarno's attempts to enlighten Wilhelm, through reading out maxims and by means of verbal advice, the central idea has to do with

---

[3] Goethe embarked on a scheme with Schiller to produce a detailed analysis of dilettantism, which, however, was never completed. From the standpoint of classicism, the dilettante, who fails to distinguish between the natural and the artistic, is a dangerous influence.

the perfection of the individual. The world is made up of all the individuals who live in it.[4] Each person has talents which have to be acknowledged and developed; there is no attempt to make anyone conform to a standard which does not accord with his true nature. Wilhelm is mistaken in thinking that the Tower's method is to impose change on him, because they only intend to guide him in his free choices. At the close of the chapter, Wilhelm's mood has not improved; he is suspicious of the abbé and resents Jarno's advice.

Chapter Six

A messenger arrives with a letter for Lothario. Wilhelm recognizes him as the one he sent after Philine and, as he supposed, Mariane. In a presumptuous tone, the messenger announces his master's imminent arrival. Immediately, Friedrich — Wilhelm's friend and Natalie's brother — leaps out from behind a bush. In a series of rhetorical flourishes, Friedrich expresses his pleasure at seeing Wilhelm again and they retire to Wilhelm's room. Friedrich remarks on Philine's knife with the inscription and reveals that he was the officer in the red uniform whom Wilhelm took for Mariane. He and Philine are still together and in love, living in a rented castle. They are playfully dipping into the books they found there: a folio Bible,[1] Gottfried's *Chronik*,[2] two volumes of *Theatrum Europaeum*,[3] *Acerra Philologica*,[4] and the works of Gryphius.[5] Wilhelm learns that it was Philine

---

[4] These principles appear to have been inspired by Goethe's reading of Herder's "Ideen zur Philosophie der Geschichte der Menschheit" (1784–91) and his "Über den Charakter der Menschheit" in "Briefe zur Beförderung der Humanität" (1793–97) (*MA* 840–43).

---

[1] The term "folio" refers to the size of the edition. A folio edition is composed of sheets of paper folded once only.

[2] Johann Ludwig Gottfried's history of the world from its beginnings to the present was written between 1630 and 1634.

[3] The *Theatrum Europaeum* (1633–1738) is a history, religious and otherwise, with the main emphasis on Europe.

[4] *Acerra Philologica* (1640), a collection by Peter Lauremberg, is a selection of stories from ancient Greek and Roman authors.

[5] Andreas Gryphius (1725–1799) was a lyric poet and a dramatist who extoled stoicism in his tragedies and displayed linguistic dexterity in his satirical comedies.

who visited him after the *Hamlet* production. She is now pregnant by Friedrich and hates her bloated resemblance to Madame Melina. Friedrich is overcoming his jealousy about that night.

The abbé tells Therese's story. A couple had had a number of still births and the wife's health was now threatened. They continued to live together and she even indulged her husband's attraction for a woman in their employ. When the woman conceived, it was agreed that the couple would adopt her child. This was the information that Therese's father tried to disclose before dying. The abbé provides documentation to support the story and adds that Lydie had to be kept away from Lothario, as long as it remained possible that relations with Therese might be restored. Wilhelm declares his readiness to renounce Therese; he suspects that her show of feeling towards him is not genuine and he wants to free himself from a misalliance.

The chapter contains a number of examples of anagnorisis. First, Wilhelm recognizes the messenger, and soon afterwards, Friedrich himself appears and is revealed as the fourth sibling. The mysterious female visitor to Wilhelm's bed is at long last identified, as well as the officer in the red uniform, and, finally, the mystery about Therese's actual identity is cleared up. Friedrich's reappearance contributes to the growing impression that events are building up to a grand finale; characters from the past are assembling on the stage, as it were. What the reader learns of Friedrich's intervening adventures suggests that Goethe has created in him a superficial semblance of Wilhelm. Like Wilhelm, he is enamored of a woman connected with the theater, and becomes jealous because of her liaison with another man. Like Wilhelm in his boyhood, Friedrich reads a varied selection of books he finds in a library and is influenced by them. Now, having established his paternity, he looks forward to fatherhood, both steps that Wilhelm has also recently taken.

The titles Friedrich mentions are among the important seventeenth-century works that would have been available in an educated household, and were read by Goethe as a young man (*FA* 1495). But the references in Friedrich's animated banter are taken from far and wide: biblical, rhetorical, and mythological sources have all been tapped. To be able to indulge in a show of arbitrary learning is not Wilhelm's goal and indeed it disquiets Natalie to see her brother behave in this way. Friedrich presents a kind of comic version of the sentences Jarno insisted on reading out, and which Wilhelm found so irritating.

Wilhelm finds it hard to believe that Friedrich and Philine are prepared to take on the responsibility of parenthood (Reiss 1963, 124). In fact, Friedrich, like Wilhelm, has had to take it on trust that he is the father of Philine's unborn child. This theme prepares the way for the story of

Therese's provenance. In Therese's case paternity is not in question, but the identity of the natural mother has been kept a closely guarded secret.

Wilhelm's remark in the previous chapter — that inanimate objects outlast human emotions — was a direct comment on the recurring motifs in the novel. Now, in this chapter, Philine's knife, with the inscription "Remember me," announces that he will indeed soon be turning his thoughts to her. The inscription is also a variation on the message that appeared on a stone scroll in the Hall of the Past, "Remember to live." Philine is the very embodiment of a love of life and laughter (Blackall 1965, 66). And at last the reader finds out the reason for Philine's gratuitous remarks about Madame Melina's ungainly appearance in pregnancy at the beginning of Book Four. In a perfectly natural, if ironic, twist of fate, Philine now finds her own reflection an unbearable sight.

In the light of recent revelations, Wilhelm feels justified in suggesting that his engagement to Therese should be dissolved. He would like to act decisively in this matter, partly to prove that he is capable of making up his mind and acting upon it. He complains about not being permitted to exercise this new faculty he has developed. Jarno both argues that such changes should be allowed to develop slowly and ensures that no precipitate action takes place. The end of the engagement is a repetition of its beginning: Wilhelm acted decisively in proposing and then was obliged to wait patiently for Therese's response.

Wilhelm reintroduces the term misalliance to describe his relationship with Therese. He is not thinking of a social misfit, or even a temperamental one, but a misalliance brought about by circumstances. His own part in this should not be underestimated: his first act on being liberated from his apprenticeship is a very definite error (Saine 69). Wilhelm still has a somewhat ambivalent attitude towards the Tower. He renounces Therese and sees this as simply paying his due to Lothario and yet he shifts uneasily under the yoke that prevents him from taking this independent step immediately.

Chapter Seven

Jarno is considering traveling to America, and invites Wilhelm to accompany him. His idea arises from the uncertainty of maintaining property. While it is unwise to keep all one's assets in one place, dispersed assets pose administrative problems. He envisages a society emanating from the Tower and spreading over the world. Such cooperation would prove useful in times of revolution, when property comes under threat. Jarno will build on contacts already made by Lothario, and the abbé will go to Russia.

Wilhelm now regrets his recent interest in his holdings; it causes nothing but concern. Jarno replies that cares properly belong to age. Wilhelm is interested in Jarno's proposed journey; his motto is "the farther away, the better." Friedrich asks to go as well, with Philine and Lydie, to establish a colony, but Jarno refuses. Wilhelm resents being expected to console Lydie, and Natalie admonishes Friedrich for recommending impulsive acts. Wilhelm needs a woman who is not recovering from an attachment, but someone pure in heart, like Therese, who refers to affairs of the heart as a risk. Natalie warns Friedrich against Philine's influence and against attributing faults to a principle. Friedrich sees Philine as a Mary Magdalene figure, and says Natalie would marry only if one bride were missing to complete the picture.[1] Jarno surprises everyone by proposing to Lydie: he knows Lydie is capable of love. The abbé mentions the marchese's imminent arrival and his need for an interpreter. Wilhelm objects to being proposed. He controls his agitation and suggests that Felix accompany him. When this is refused, Wilhelm restrains himself for Natalie's sake.

Wilhelm realizes he is in love with Natalie and does not want to be parted from her. He delivers a soliloquy contrasting the enjoyment of a journey with that of her presence. He tells Felix that he will have to replace Natalie in his life. Seeing Felix lose interest in a toy, Wilhelm thinks of traveling the world together, indulging their whims. Werner, although disapproving, makes the financial arrangements. Natalie does not protest, which saddens Wilhelm.

Two things still detain Wilhelm. Mignon's funeral has not yet taken place and news about the harper is expected. Wilhelm is unsettled. Surrounded by familiar works of art, he sees his life as an incomplete circle where everything reminds him of something else. The paintings symbolize his sense of being deprived of valued possessions. His is unsure of his own existence, as though he were a ghost and is torn between his favorable situation and sorrow at having to leave Natalie.

The marchese arrives. He knew the uncle in the army and from business trips; many works of art now in the house date from their journey through Italy together. The narrator characterizes the Italian attitude towards art as thoughtful and analytic. Wilhelm translates the conversation, while Friedrich makes jokes. The marchese's view is that lasting works of art require talent and tremendous effort. Art apprecia-

---

[1] This is a reference to the story about Mary Magdalen anointing Jesus (Luke 7:36–48).

tion differs from the natural ability to distinguish between flavors. The abbé warns that dissatisfaction results from striving for varied experiences. Works of art should be evaluated on their own terms. A statue is not soft enough for remodeling, neither should a painting be instructive or a play improving. Jarno is not disposed to judge people harshly for drawing benefit in their lives from works of art.

The events of this chapter are almost entirely devoted to the process of retardation: everything seems to be working against a denouement. Jarno plans a journey at the beginning of the chapter and Wilhelm has planned one at the end. The group seems bent on dispersing, rather than coming together in pairs, with the one exception of Jarno's proposal to Lydie. Wilhelm is now considered a useful business partner in Jarno's eyes, which is, despite his own ambivalence, a mark of his development. Wilhelm's mood is unsettled in this chapter. He resents the cavalier way in which the others assume he will agree to anything they decide on his behalf, as well as their habit of announcing plans for him without prior consultation. His proposed journey with Felix is thus a bid for independence, and yet at the same time he is loathe to leave Natalie. The appearance of the marchese on the scene further postpones the final decision.

The chapter encompasses two topics of contemporary debate: it opens with a discussion of finance and social reform, and ends with an analysis of aesthetic judgment.[2] The serious nature of these passages is alleviated by talk of matchmaking and Friedrich's quips (Hass 205). Jarno had previously suggested to Wilhelm that the rituals of the Tower had become a bit of a joke, and he now seems ready to transform the association into a financially secure institution with a realistic outlook. His hopes are pinned to the ideal that America represents. In Book Four, the reader learns that Lothario had fought in the American War of Independence, and in Book Seven, that on his return he had intended to establish the American ideal in Germany. The Pietist movement under Count Zinzendorf also considered America as a country where fewer obstacles to progress would be encountered. The motif is more fully developed in *Wilhelm Meisters Wanderjahre*. Since the Tower is an association founded by members of the aristocracy, an expansion to America would entail breaking down

---

[2] Karl Philipp Moritz's *Über die bildende Nachahmung des Schönen* (1788) established the idea of the autonomy of art, Kant's *Kritik der Urteilskraft* (1790) introduced the dualism required for aesthetic judgment, and Schiller's *Über die ästhetische Erziehung des Menschen in einer Reihe von Briefen* (1795) emphasized the aesthetic regeneration of the individual and criticized the one-sidedness of contemporary culture.

class barriers in a movement parallel to that in Wilhelm and Therese's conversation about misalliances. In both situations the anticipated union is between bourgeoisie and aristocracy.

Wilhelm is irritated by Jarno, who simply assumes he can count on Wilhelm's cooperation in his schemes. He was already exasperated by Jarno's habit of quoting maxims, and Jarno produces one more now. In it he allies concern with age, and youth with a carefree attitude. Wilhelm is also annoyed when Friedrich tries to slot him into a scheme, coupled with Lydie. Wilhelm's discomfort comes to a head with his inability to sleep and his sensation of being somewhere between alive and dead. He can neither attain inner harmony nor bring himself to step into the role in society prescribed for him by the Tower. He tries to put his past life into perspective and hopes that, in doing so, he will find the right way forward. Contemplating his grandfather's paintings, he is led to reassess the value of material possessions that they symbolize for him. In realizing that he loves Natalie as intensely as he had Mariane, he again looks back in an attempt to identify a pattern in his life that he can now complete. By overlaying the image of Mariane with that of Natalie he creates a telescoping effect rather than trying to obliterate earlier experiences by imposing later ones (Graham 191). He takes up his old habit of soliloquy again, one that he has not indulged in for some considerable time.

Wilhelm's idea of setting off with Felix is in fact an attempt at regression. This is clear from the association with Felix's abandonment of a toy he had so recently been interested in. Wilhelm is proposing to treat the world as a child treats his toys, moving on to the next attraction, when the current one does not hold his interest any longer. By keeping Felix with him, Wilhelm will always have a like-minded companion to share his adventures. Wilhelm has taken responsibility for Felix, but two others members of his so-called family are on his conscience. He is unwilling to depart before Mignon's funeral has occurred and the news about the harper makes him anxious. Also, Werner's letter makes it clear that this journey would again constitute an abrogation of other responsibilities, specifically, those which have to do with business and property. In a sense, Wilhelm's departure now is a repetition of when he initially set out, only now, ironically, his purpose is much less clear.

For Wilhelm, the works of art from his grandfather's collection stand for stability, and they conjure up a stable childhood idyll. With the arrival of the marchese, the topic of art is extended and the abbé continues the discussion with Jarno. These conversations replace the section of the Letter of Apprenticeship that Jarno did not read out to Wilhelm. The marchese is something like an ambassador or spokesman who represents what Goethe learned on his journey to Italy. Partly this is an opportunity for Goethe to reiterate his anti-dilettantism stance (*FA* 1497). But for the marchese, as for Wilhelm, the works of art are evocative of a lost era and the presence of the uncle, his friend.

The marchese gives his views on the importance of diligence as well as talent in the making of an artist. The mere ability to produce an illusion is not adequate; without a solid basis in training, mediocrity can be the only result. There is also an oblique comment here on Wilhelm's ill-judged desire to become an actor. Hand in hand with the requirements for true artistry go the prescriptions for art appreciation, provided by the abbé. Art cannot be judged by the same standards as are applied to objects in nature. The cultivation of taste is dependent on the same inner separation that is the essential factor in any development. The obvious parallel is the necessity on the stage for a separation between the actor's own character and the one to be portrayed. Again, despite the theoretical tone of the discussion, the abbé might well have been speaking about Wilhelm and his subjective response to the painting of the ailing prince.

The abbé stresses the importance of the autonomy of art, a favorite theme among Goethe's contemporaries. The aesthetic object is not a piece of clay to be remodeled at will: the statue, painting, song, or play must be appreciated on its own terms. Again the reader perceives an oblique condemnation of Wilhelm's dream of establishing a national theater designed to educate and improve the taste of the general public. The art forms listed by the abbé are sculpture, painting, song, drama, and architecture and they all have relevance for Wilhelm. One of the first pieces of art he recognizes on arrival at Natalie's castle is a statue, and so begins the feeling that this arrival is really a homecoming (Schings 1984, 167). The painting of the ailing prince is a constantly recurring image that seems to be reproduced at various stages by events. The songs performed by Mignon and the harper often capture Wilhelm's own mood even when they are difficult to understand on their own terms. Drama was to be the magic solution to Wilhelm's dissatisfaction with life and in fact it pervades the novel itself. Finally, domestic architecture is used to analyze the personalities of its owners in the cases of Wilhelm's and Werner's fathers, and of Lothario and Natalie, although in her case the building is suffused with her uncle's spirit as well.

Chapter Eight

Mignon's funeral takes place in the Hall of the Past. The walls are covered with sky-blue hangings, and candles are burning at the four corners of the sarcophagus. Four boys stand alongside, dressed in blue and silver, fanning the figure on top of the sarcophagus. Out of sight, two choirs intone a question: who has joined the company of the silent? The boys reply that it is a playmate, who should rest until awakened by the rejoicing of heavenly brethren. The dialogue continues, with the choir also addressing Mignon and describing her angelic appearance — the gown, wings, and golden glow around her head. The boys regret her untimely departure and the choirs offer inspiration. The boys end with a resolve to return to life, encouraged by the choirs.

The abbé now addresses the company, explaining the ritual. He speaks of the incalculable nature of the human life span and the air of mystery that surrounded Mignon. Then he invites them to admire the skill of the embalmer who introduced balsam into her veins.[1] Mignon lies beneath the veil, quite lifelike. Only Wilhelm cannot bring himself to view the body.

The abbé speaks of Mignon's piety and devotion to the Catholic Church; her final act was to kiss the crucifix. Church observances have been followed in the burial preparations. He points to the outline of the crucifix on her arm, beside some other letters and signs. The marchese reacts emotionally on recognizing the crucifix tattoo: Mignon was his long lost niece. The body is lowered and four young men, dressed like the boys, place the cover on the sarcophagus. They sing that Mignon is preserved both in marble and in their hearts and urge the listeners to carry the solemnity of the occasion with them, as this makes life eternal. The invisible choir joins in but everyone is too preoccupied with the latest discovery to pay close attention to the words. When the singing dies away, other feelings rush in and make them long for the sanctity of the Hall.

In the Hall of the Past the hangings conceal the paintings of various scenes from life. The blue color of the hangings suggests the heavens as Mignon's ultimate resting-place. It has already been explained that these hangings are temporary, and the motto "Remember to live" has not been forgotten, even in the funeral ceremony (Storz 1953, 95). As the singers point out, Mignon is clad in her angel dress, complete with wings and halo, a sign that this is not simply the death of a mortal, but a rising above mortality to another sphere (Storz 1953, 94). The choir's lack of physical presence expresses the spiritual life, while the boys' fanning of Mignon's body constitutes a denial of death. They use ostrich feathers to do so, and this detail builds on the exotic Egyptian appearance of the architectural features of the Hall that suggest permanence (Dürr 207).

Mignon's funeral is very theatrical — the hangings, costumes, musical overture, and speeches are all standard fare on the stage. The begin-

---

[1] To embalm is literally to introduce balsam, a resinous oily substance, into the body, for the purposes of preservation.

ning and end of the funeral are marked by song. The opening song is in the form of a dialogue between a rather ethereal chorus and the boys and it resolves into an intention to return to life. In tune with the motto and the paintings of scenes from the ages of man, the singers overcome their sorrow with the thought that life goes on.

The abbé's address dwells on the mystery of Mignon's origins and he unwittingly prepares the ground for the marchese's cry of recognition, contradicting the abbé's words. The abbé characterizes fate as inconsistent and illogical in its workings, because Mignon's life has ended before she could reach maturity. He depicts fate as an arbitrary force, whereas Mignon's songs expressed a different view. She sang of her own fate as something dark and menacing. The view that art should not be judged by the standards appropriate for nature is undermined in the mourners' admiration for the artificially restored natural appearance of Mignon's body: through art, death has taken on a lifelike quality and she seems to be sleeping. The embalming procedure also halts the progress of decay; not only is Mignon transformed into a statue, but this arrest of a natural development is a reminder of her inability to mature in a natural way while alive (Gilby 150).

Mignon's pious and regular attendance at the Catholic Mass was mentioned early on. Now the visible sign of her faith is a tattooed crucifix, which allows the marchese to identify her. Ironically, it is not the highly acclaimed embalmer's art that gives access to the truth. What enables her to be recognized in death is the tattoo that combines conventional with strange symbols. This combination itself sums up the funeral ritual that, the abbé claims, honors Mignon's desire for burial in consecrated ground. In fact there is the merest nod in the direction of church practice, because the only earth present is concealed in Mignon's pillow (*MA* 852). Without the foundation provided by a belief system, the ceremony becomes theatrical and hollow (Minden 204). Christian and pre-Christian elements have been mixed in with the principles of the Tower (*HA* 807). The marchese is unable to express himself further, once he recognizes Mignon. This is a variation on Mignon's predilection for silence, as expressed in the song when she begs not to be obliged to speak, and in the boys' reference to the company of the silent.

Young men replace the boys for the final song, thus emphasizing the inexorable passage of time. Their words speak of the incorruptibility of Mignon's memory, of which her body, lying preserved in marble, is an image. The Hall of the Past is a place where time is suspended, but emotions, as well, are banished from it. The mourners fall prey to their feelings as soon as they step outside and they are filled with a longing to return to the suspended moment.

Chapter Nine

The marchese suggests that Mignon's friends, particularly Wilhelm, should visit him. He has told Mignon's story to the abbé, and he will recount it. The abbé reads from a version he has written out. The countess is unexpectedly present, which disconcerts Wilhelm. Her appearance has altered, and her general remarks do not mask her emotional state. The account begins with the marchese's father — a complex man who held strict principles that he tried to impose on others. His eldest son was to become lord of the estates, the marchese was destined for the church, and his younger brother for the army. His own disposition, however, made him more suited to the army, while his brother was more suited to the church. The father grudgingly allowed his second and third sons to exchange professions.

The father had only one friend, who had lost his wife but had a ten-year old daughter. His will was found to provide for this man and his daughter, Sperata, who grew to be very beautiful and might have made the marchese a good wife. Augustin, the brother in the monastery, had meanwhile fallen prey to ecstasies.[1] When reason returned, he asked to be released from his vows because he was in love with Sperata. The two brothers approached their family confessor, who was surprisingly unwilling to agree. Eventually he revealed that Sperata was their sister, conceived after the normal childbearing years. Their father, ashamed at falling subject to passion at an advanced age, concealed the birth, and the child was cared for first by the father's friend and later by an old woman. Augustin refused to believe he was related to Sperata. Nothing would deter him from his intention to marry her; he argued by analogy with nature, pointing out that the lily bears male and female parts on one stem and that nature would curse and destroy a union that was not meant to be.[2] One evening he escaped from the castle, but a boatman, disobeying his instructions, returned him to the monastery.

Sperata was spared the knowledge that her lover was her brother. Instead, the priest compared her act in giving herself to a priest to in-

---

[1] Augustin exhibits the classic symptoms of Schwärmerei, the cause of which is described by Schiller in his letters "Über die ästhetische Erziehung des Menschen," Letter 13, paragraph 4, in the footnote. Schiller recommends strict principles to be applied to oneself, but says charity should be shown to others. He sees the condition of Schwärmerei as one inevitable result of such strict treatment.

[2] In appealing to the example of the lily, Augustin perverts the biblical text of Matthew 6:28.

cest, and eventually she freely renounced him. The birth of her child was kept secret. The child was unusual — she was agile and musical, but not adept at verbal expression. Sperata's motherly love was gradually transformed into a horror of incest and the child was given to foster parents. Now she exercised her love of climbing and imitated the acts of traveling tightrope walkers. She borrowed clothes from boys and often wandered from home. She always returned to a nearby villa where she admired the statues. One day, she did not return; her hat was discovered floating in the lake but no body was ever found.

Sperata received the news calmly; the child would now be in God's care. But people told her how once the bones of a drowned child had washed up on shore and the child was miraculously restored in a church. Sperata now constantly gathered up animal bones on the lakeshore. People regarded her as religiously inspired and she again returned to her foster mother. Meanwhile Augustin had developed a physical restlessness, relieved only by playing the harp. His mind remained calm except when he thought about death. He was plagued by a vision of a small boy threatening him with a knife.

The actual parts of a child's skeleton were surreptitiously added to Sperata's collection. She pieced these together but one morning, finding the basket with the skeleton empty, Sperata thought it was a miracle and described a vision of her child. She died soon afterwards, in a state of bliss. Sperata had achieved a blessed status; worshippers came to the chapel where her body lay, mentioning other saintly appearances.[3] Hearing of this, Augustin escaped from the monastery, went to the chapel and touched the hand of his beloved, as though she were merely sleeping. He was said to be wandering through Switzerland and Germany, but the intervening war made it impossible to track him down.

The marchese makes his exit at the beginning of the chapter, and hands over to the abbé a role like that of the Greek chorus. He will reveal to the audience the background to present events, speaking on the marchese's behalf. For this performance, the countess joins the others in the auditorium, thus contributing to the impression of a grand finale.

The function of this lengthy account within the novel is partly to dispel the secrecy and mystery that accompany both Mignon and the harper. The details of incest, mistaken identity, and revelations about a character's true origins are standard fare in the eighteenth-century novel. The account also contributes to the thematic structures of the

---

[3] The reference is to Cardinal Carlo Borromeo (1538–1584), whose ascetic and pious life led to his canonization in 1610. An immense statue was erected on the shore of Lago Maggiore to honor his memory.

work. Much of the novel as a whole is rooted in the father's principles, in his desire to control both himself and others. Difficult relations with an authoritarian father had an effect on Wilhelm's childhood as well. In the story as in the novel, the father has strong views about a future profession for his son or sons, and the sons' rebellion against the father does not result in a clearly successful outcome in either case. Both Augustin and Wilhelm recklessly plan to leave home to be united with a beloved woman, despite the lack of prospects for the future. But in the marchese's family, there are further signs of impending disaster. First, the second and third sons feel they have been destined for the wrong professions, that their respective natures would be better suited if they exchanged professions. Then there is a half-serious suggestion that the marchese should propose to Sperata; in retrospect this signals the advent of a misalliance on an extreme scale.

Within Mignon's history, as it is now uncovered, there are recurring themes. The marchese's father succumbs to an onslaught of what he considers to be illicit desire; his son Augustin is unable to control the desire that leads him to commit incest. Sperata's elevation to sainthood and her incorruptible corpse prefigure Mignon's own transfiguration in death (Krauss 348). However, an ironic twist has Sperata believing that in dying she will be following behind her deceased child. Sperata carries relics, supposedly of her child, while Mignon holds onto a scarf and necklace, relics of Mariane (Ammerlahn 1968, 114). The myrtles and citrus groves, epitomizing the idyll Augustin imagines as a setting for his love of Sperata, are familiar from Mignon's ballad. Neither Sperata nor Mignon is literate.

There are also parallels between this account and the "Confessions of a Beautiful Soul." In both cases, the written document is read out aloud and has a considerable effect on the listeners. Both contain a decided critique of organized religion, in the form of Pietism in the Confessions, and in its Catholic and specifically monastic form here. The restrictions of life in the monastery are the partial cause of Augustin's instability. Against the beliefs of the church, he strenuously argues for the dictates of nature, and incest is the most extreme form of this position. The confessor initially upholds the church's doctrine, but later uses deception to produce a state of extreme contrition in Sperata. Superstition is a strong component in the events of her life; the veneration of Sperata's remains also arises from misplaced faith. The legends about children lost in the lake are indistinguishable from church doctrine in the mind of Sperata and her neighbors. The events surrounding the bones and the miracle are told in a way that clearly conveys religious skepticism, and the assessment of Sperata as saintly rather than insane is obviously not in accordance with the narrator's own view.

Not only in their deaths are there similarities between Mignon's story and her mother's. Both were removed from their natural parents at an early age and live rootless lives (Krauss 349). Both lack formal education, but are devoutly pious. In both cases, the crucial relationship to a man is an extreme example of misalliance: Sperata's love for her brother and Mignon's love for Wilhelm are ultimately self-destructive.

A struggle between nature and the church as representative of civilization provides the tone for this story. At first the struggle is confined to an inner conflict from which the father suffers. His suffering takes the form of never being satisfied with any of his achievements. His self-censure reaches a climax in the shame he feels in having loving relations with his wife, even though this is a passion sanctified by the church.

Many of the mysterious features that adhered to the characters of Mignon and the harper are clarified in this chapter. The reader learns about the context in which it was natural for Mignon to develop such strong piety. Her kidnapping by tightrope dancers and her preference for boys' clothing both make sense when one reads how she perfected her natural agility. Mignon's androgyny is explained both in natural terms and as an image of the irregular, incestuous union that resulted in her birth. The statues and citrus groves she sings about are not ideal images, but childhood memories. The harper's robes, his feeling of living under a curse and bringing harm to others, and his fear of Felix are all put into context. Finally, Mignon's claim to find comfort in the harper's company seems less strange now that their relationship is explained.

The figure of Felix constitutes a threat for the harper, both as prefigured in his dream and later during the episode of the fire. Although conceived outside wedlock, Felix is in other respects a normal child — he needs disciplining, appreciates the attentions of a motherly figure, and has a strong desire to learn. He displays the standard signs of development that are not open to Mignon and in this sense is a constant reminder to the harper of the consequences of his misdeed.

The lake is central to the events recounted here. Augustin must cross the lake if he is to join Sperata, Mignon's hat is found floating in the lake, causing everyone to fear the worst, and the legends about children drowning and their remains, returned by the lake, being resurrected, are pivotal in Sperata's path to sainthood. The lake as signifying danger is a recurring component of Wilhelm's dreams; now, in this retrospective account, the lake becomes a real entity.

The harper visits Sperata's shrine and acts as though she were still alive. At first he seems unhinged, and yet other evidence points to her state as something other than literal death. When Sperata departs this life, she is said to be "what we·call dead." This formulation, taken with the fact that her body does not decay, makes the harper's attitude seem more reasonable. At the end of this narrative he disappears on his wanderings, but for Wilhelm and the others he will now become more prominent.

Chapter Ten

The abbé's reading brings tears to the eyes of his listeners. They postpone telling the marchese about the harper pending a report from the doctor. The abbé describes the marchese's gratitude towards Wilhelm for looking after his niece; the money set aside for Sperata could compensate him. Therese remarks that Wilhelm's selflessness is being rewarded, and encourages him to accept the marchese's invitation. Wilhelm resolves to take advice from his friends and not rely on his own judgment. The marchese will go ahead and Wilhelm and Felix follow after receiving the doctor's report about the harper. The doctor, however, arrives in person, with a stranger who is actually the harper, transformed beyond recognition. They hear that the harper has a glass of opium from the pastor's cabinet and regards the possession of this means to end his life as crucial to his recovery. It is decided that the harper should stay with the abbé, while Wilhelm joins the marchese. Strangely, the harper has never overcome his fear of Felix.

The company is increased by several visitors and Felix moves freely among them all. There is no sign of a renewed romance between Therese and Lothario. The count arrives to fetch his wife and mistakes Wilhelm for an English nobleman. The count succeeds in rearranging the rooms to accommodate everyone, despite Jarno's efforts to mislead him. His gentle nature has a good effect on them all and he arranges entertainment for the evenings. Friedrich often irritates Wilhelm by hinting at his feelings for Natalie.

One day the harper rushes in, incoherently stammering that Felix is poisoned. The opium bottle is empty and beside it stands a glass of almond milk and a half-empty carafe.[1] Felix hastily announces that he drank from the glass, not the bottle. The doctor administers vinegar and establishes that the almond milk in the glass contains a large proportion of opium. Felix complains about the vinegar and the doctor is mystified by the lack of adverse symptoms. The harper is found with his throat slit. The wound is treated and there is hope that he might survive. Felix sleeps with his head on Natalie's lap and his feet on Wilhelm's.

---

[1] Almond milk is made by boiling blanched almonds to produce a thin porridge which has the appearance of milk.

In the new household order, the harper, placed in the abbé's room, saw the written account of his youth and wanted to take his life. He added opium to the almond milk and went out for a last look at the world, then returned to find Felix. Later Felix confesses to having drunk from the bottle, which contained no poison. In the night, the harper uncovers his wound and bleeds to death.

The count, convinced that Felix had been saved by his prayers, is ready to depart. The countess squeezes Wilhelm's and Natalie's hands before leaving. The household is upset by the dramatic events and Wilhelm cannot face setting out on his journey. The doctor helps by declaring Wilhelm ill, but Friedrich cannot resist teasing him. With his veneer of learning, he draws parallels in Egyptian or Babylonian history. To everyone's embarrassment, he compares the painting of the ailing prince to Wilhelm's situation and sings a song of wonders soon to be revealed.

Wilhelm finally speaks to Lothario and learns Therese has made his union with Natalie her condition for marrying Lothario. She knows that Wilhelm's heart is Natalie's. Lothario has observed Wilhelm and Natalie's feelings for each other. They should devote their lives to helping people achieve their goals. Natalie would do this well, since she is the true beautiful soul.

Friedrich asks for a reward for telling Wilhelm he can claim Natalie's heart. He has heard her speak of an oath to marry Wilhelm if Felix dies and his survival should not alter anything. As Wilhelm and Lothario approach Natalie and Therese, Friedrich reminds Wilhelm of the day he asked for Wilhelm's bouquet. Now Wilhelm is receiving a wonderful flower from him. Friedrich compares Wilhelm to Saul, son of Kish, who went to look for his father's asses and found a kingdom.[2] Wilhelm agrees that he has found an undeserved happiness.

Far from being a traditional happy ending in which all that remains is for the loose ends to be tied, the final chapter of the novel displays a tremendous tension both in the main character and in some others as well; it contains two dramatic events and ends somewhat inconclusively. For Wilhelm, the tension is caused by the dilemma of the marchese's invitation to join him on his travels. Wilhelm does not want to leave without knowing whether Natalie shares the strong feelings of attraction he experiences in her company. Several times, Wilhelm is described as being ready to leave, or is on the point of departing, and yet at the end of the novel the marchese is presumably still waiting for him to arrive.

Other developments serve to disrupt what might otherwise have been a smooth process of drawing to a close. It is perhaps not surpris-

---

[2] The reference is to 1 Samuel 9–10.

ing that the harper dies in this chapter, but his method of ending his
life is not predictable. The reader is misled into thinking that he will
take opium. Not only does he not do this, but he also fails to kill himself with a razor. Then the countess is reintroduced, bringing tremendous potential for disruption, yet she turns out to be there only in
order to give her tacit blessing to Wilhelm and Natalie.

The abbé's reading has a cathartic effect on his audience; Goethe uses
dramatic impact right to the end of the novel. For the abbé, the most
pressing question is whether to tell the marchese that his brother
Augustin is the harper, but the more important matter, absolutely speaking, is the impact it would have on the harper if he knew that the story of
his past life had been read out to everyone. Only while the story of his
past is unknown to the others is there any hope that the harper can be
cured (Röder 148). In the end, the marchese misses the chance to be reunited with his brother. On the other hand, he seems intent on welcoming Wilhelm as a family member, in a similar gesture to Wilhelm's own
founding of a strange family with Mignon and the harper as members.

Like Mignon before him, the harper has undergone a transformation.
He is now clean-shaven, his hair has been trimmed, and he no longer
wears a robe. Even the words of his songs have become more optimistic.
His outward appearance is a sign that he has gained mental stability, especially since his refusal to shave off his beard had been seen as a major
impediment to his rehabilitation. It is all the more grimly ironic, then,
that the instrument of his death should be a razor. His transformation is a
repeat of Mignon's: for both these curious characters, who are now revealed to be father and daughter, the end is preceded immediately by a
change in outward appearance that seems to indicate a change of nature,
but does not mean that they are better fitted for survival in the world.

From the harper's point of view, the mere possession of the means
to end his life, in the form of the bottle of opium, is a consolation. The
same was true of Aurelie, who carried a dagger. This practice is based
on flawed logic, since the opium is neither a talisman nor an antidote,
and it flies in the face of the Tower's advice, "Remember to live" (*MA*
855). The bottle of opium is an important prop for the story. As the
events of the chapter demonstrate, at least one of the harper's apparent
delusions was in fact prophetic. His vision of Felix brandishing a knife
contains two elements that are instrumental in the harper's downfall. It
is partly because he fears he has harmed Felix that the harper decides to
end his own life, so that Felix is in one sense the cause. The knife corre-
sponds to the razor that, although it does not actually bring about the
harper's death, is nonetheless crucial to the process.

The chapter contains both tragic and comic elements (Röder 147, 154). The comedy is provided by the figures of the count and Friedrich. Wilhelm has had reason to feel apprehension about the count's arrival. He cannot have anticipated that the count would mistake him for an Englishman and a noble one at that. Through this error, Goethe again pokes fun both at the aristocracy and at the kind of piety the count has embraced; he implies that it undermines the normal powers of reasoning. This is later reinforced by the count's inability to grasp that Felix could not have been saved by his prayers because he had not drunk the poison at all. At the same time, Goethe makes the point that class differences are little more than a matter of perception. However, the comic element turns tragic, since the count's billeting arrangements lead to the harper's fateful discovery of the manuscript. Friedrich plays a puckish role, teasing and irritating others, although without real malevolence. His methods are unorthodox, even unethical, and yet in the end it is Friedrich, the nuisance factor, who arranges for Wilhelm and Natalie to open their hearts to each other. One can only assume that, had it not been for Friedrich's eavesdropping, a conspiracy would have arisen between Wilhelm's conscience and the pact between Therese and Lothario, leaving the players in an irresolvable stalemate. Friedrich's role, including his song and dance routine, together with a whole series of misapprehensions, mistaken identities, false starts, and incredible revelations combine to give the novel an ending which seems more suited to a comic play or opera (Reiss 1981, 139).

It is not enough for Felix to cause alarm by leading everyone to believe his life was in danger. The doctor, first perplexed by Felix's lack of symptoms, later becomes an accomplice in Wilhelm's sham illness, only to be rewarded by Friedrich's satirical remarks. Wilhelm's illness plays into Friedrich's hands and allows him to draw attention to the painting of the ailing prince for one final interpretation. Wilhelm's illness is now clearly identified as love for Natalie.

Lothario reports Therese's assessment of Wilhelm's dilemma. Wilhelm's reason had led him to propose to her, but his heart is drawn to Natalie. The reader is inevitably reminded of Mignon's statement that reason is cruel and the heart is better. In Wilhelm's case, the heart appears to be favored in the final solution. However there is still a comment of Friedrich's lingering in the air, which suggests that his sister Natalie might have married more out of a love for symmetry than love for Wilhelm. In addition, there is nothing remotely resembling a romantic love scene between Wilhelm and Natalie at the end: Friedrich is everpresent and Natalie's name is not even mentioned again (Müller 89). The whole scene is understated, and marred for a moment by Friedrich's malicious reminder of Wilhelm's interest in Philine. The lack of real climax contrasts with the many promises of universal rejoicing at the end. This strong seam of realism runs through the more comic and schematic features of the finale. Appropriately, one more comment on social class is permitted before closing, which both asserts that Wilhelm is not a nobleman and at the same time declares this fact to be insignificant.

Finally, a biblical reference offers a parallel to the developments in Wilhelm's life; Friedrich compares Wilhelm to the Old Testament figure of Saul, whose father sends him out on a mission to find his asses. In accordance with the will of God, Saul is anointed king by Samuel and placed in command of the people of Israel. Wilhelm was also sent out on an errand by his father, and the analogy makes it clear that Wilhelm has been chosen and favored. At the same time, however, the biblical reference contains the unstated suggestion that Wilhelm's story could still end badly, since Saul's good fortune ended in suicide (Blair 8). But the comparison has a second function. Here, right at the end of the novel, Wilhelm is again asked to remember the puppet show based on the Old Testament story of David and Goliath, in which the characters of Samuel and Saul also make an appearance. The message is that impressions of childhood remain throughout the later stages in life and leave their indelible imprint (Röder 161).

The narrator has withdrawn for this final scene and with this withdrawal the voice of ironic interpretation disappears as well. The reader is left to rely on the characters' statements. Wilhelm asks Friedrich not to remind him of the days of his infatuation with Philine and his request shows he has not fully grasped that each stage in life is important. He refers to the present as the happiest of moments and this is again a victory for realism against the implausible neatness of the final solution. His words imply that the moment will pass and others will succeed it. Soon afterwards, however, his final sentence shows more of an intuition. He eschews the definite article and speaks of "ein Glück" (a happiness), thus allowing earlier happy moments their own validity and the right to endure (Röder 161). In the whole structure of this last chapter, as here, there are indications that events will not come to an end when the narrative does, but will continue to develop (Müller 89). Both the reader and Wilhelm are encouraged to look back and identify connections with earlier incidents. It is again clear, as it comes to an end, that the narrative operates in both a linear and a circular fashion: the work thus produced is not a completely closed circle but one which leaves the reader with the thought that life will go on precisely because of what has gone before.

Conclusion: Realism and Reading

A COMMENTARY MAKES it abundantly clear that a second reading of *Wilhelm Meisters Lehrjahre* brings definite rewards. T. S. Eliot's suggestion in "Little Gidding" that we "arrive where we started and know the place for the first time" applies even to a Bildungsroman. The reference at the end of *Wilhelm Meisters Lehrjahre* to Saul in the Book of Samuel, for example, gains in perspective when one notices, on re-reading, to what extent Goethe's intertextuality makes use of biblical idiom in this novel. Also, currents of irony undermining Wilhelm's idealistic ambition emerge more clearly when the reader is familiar with the subsequent events of the narrative — there is no doubt that Goethe had fun while writing *Wilhelm Meisters Lehrjahre,* and quite often at Wilhelm's expense. And with subsequent readings, instances of incongruous attention to detail, as well as incidents which initially seemed mystifyingly isolated, now cast light on the later revelations for which they were preparing the ground. From the perspective of hindsight, these are clearly auguries.

The structure of the novel incorporates just such a process of returning, rethinking, and remembering, both when the reader has access to Wilhelm's thoughts and when incidents, themes, characters, and attitudes seem to the reader like echoes of what has gone before. The painting of the ailing prince is among the most striking examples. Wilhelm first recollects it as an enduring memory from his childhood, but the actual painting materializes again at the end of the novel. When first mentioned, it leads into a discussion of aesthetic judgment and taste. On the next occasion, as Wilhelm lies wounded in the woods and his companions watch over him, the assembled group seems to conjure up the configuration of figures in the painting. Finally, when Wilhelm rediscovers the actual painting, his feigned illness is teasingly interpreted by Friedrich in the light of the situation depicted on the canvas.

Sometimes a single object prefigures a later incident: Philine's powder knife, with the inscription "Remember me," recurs in the form of Aurelie's dagger, used to cut Wilhelm's hand, because, as she says, men have to be hurt if they are to become mindful. The textile and costume theme is another case in point: Mariane's scarf reappears in the form of the ghost's veil, and a grubbier version of her negligee clothes Philine when Wilhelm first meets her face to face. The strap on the instrument case carried by Lothario's doctor triggers Wilhelm's memory of the attack in the woods, since he first noticed the same strap in the possession of the surgeon who attended him then. This stimulates Wilhelm to hope for a reunion with the beautiful Amazon, because he first met her on that earlier occasion, and the strap connects these two situations. Eventually, he is in a position to request it from the young surgeon as a keepsake. These are but a few instances of a process that is partly covered by the anagnorisis phenomenon, discussed in relation to the numerous revelations in Book Seven. The insistence on a particular style of clothing and the interest in costume, both inside and outside the theater, shown by several characters, including Wilhelm, Mariane, Mignon, the countess, Therese, and the harper, point at the same time to interconnections and recollections within the narrative, and to the troublesome distinctions between the realms of reality and the imagination that plague Wilhelm from start to finish. The recollection of Mariane's officer's uniform, for example, which he found so becoming on her, leads Wilhelm to jump to a mistaken conclusion when he sees the back view of someone wearing the same uniform. Based entirely on that fleeting and misleading appearance, Wilhelm holds out hope of meeting Mariane again. Eventually, he finds out that the figure he saw from behind was in fact Friedrich.

So at the end of the process of repeated rereading, two observations come to the fore. The first is that, with the problematic tension between appearance and reality as a theme endemic in, though not restricted to, the world of acting, and with the even-handed treatment of contemporary social and cultural issues, the novel comes to constitute its own type of realism, somewhat earlier than the heyday of this movement in the next century. The second observation is that within the actual course of the novel, Goethe, through examples, offers his readers advice on how to read it.

It could be argued that the assessment of the ending of the novel is as potentially divisive an issue as the task of defining the term "Bildungsroman," touched upon in the introduction. Some commentators find the ending satisfactory while others are disappointed. It adopts an operatic convention, with all the main characters paired off, at least in a preliminary way, but it still leaves unfinished business of all sorts: unexplained mysteries, abandoned plans, lost characters. Since Wilhelm's theater prospects have ended in disillusionment, it seems likely that the artificial staginess of the conclusion is an ironic comment on that enterprise, and the unfulfilled character of what remains constitutes some-

thing resembling realism on Goethe's part. Despite superficial indications to the contrary, despite the ironing out of misunderstandings and
the revelation of true identities, this is a far from perfect narrative solution; rather, it is an indecisive one. We might now say without exag-
geration that it lacks "closure."

Working against the contrived artificiality of the closing scene is a
strong seam of social objectivity, seen in the discussions of land reform
and socially mixed marriages. In the affirmation of misalliances, it may
be tempting to detect reflections of Goethe's union with Christiane
Vulpius, who, even though Goethe eventually married her after years of
cohabitation, was never accepted into Weimar society. It is essential to
be aware that the novel's importance stems neither from its autobiographical aspect nor from any tendency towards formulaic prescriptions — for social reform, for instance. This blend of artificiality and
objectivity is precisely what so effectively guards against the didacticism
and doctrinaire stance that other novelists, writing in a similar vein
about the development of a young male hero, have frequently found so
alluring. Wilhelm is no Simplicissimus, starting out with a *tabula rasa*
for a mind and ending with more than an inkling of how humanity relates to the divine will. Neither does Wilhelm resemble the hapless
Agathon who does, in the end, achieve a circumscribed self-fulfillment.

At various points in the narrative, Goethe embeds some advice
about how to read — as well as how not to. He shows Wilhelm as a
boy with an active imagination, who supposes that his sheer enthusiasm
for the story of Tancred and Chlorinda is adequate preparation for a
stage performance. Neither is a feeling of identity with the dramatic
protagonist enough to ensure that Wilhelm will successfully act the part
of Hamlet later on. When Friedrich and Philine reappear in Book
Eight, they have moved into a castle and are working their way through
the library, arbitrarily dipping into volumes and reading passages out
loud to each other as a source of *bon mots* — they have become extremely learned by this method, Friedrich claims. As a consequence of
his act of pillaging, Friedrich is ever ready with a quotation to meet
every circumstance — to the intense irritation of his companions. Here
is an example of satire worthy of Sebastian Brant's *Das Narrenschiff*
(Ship of Fools). The act of reading is yet another of the recurring
themes: letters, both delivered and undelivered, cryptic inscriptions,
misinterpreted notes, and a fabricated journal, to say nothing of the
manuscript of Confessions which constitutes the whole of Book Six, are
all of crucial importance to the direction Wilhelm will take.

The manuscript with the title "Confessions of a Beautiful Soul" is
prescribed as therapy; it is not intended simply as entertainment. Even

though the beautiful soul herself is not an unequivocal shining beacon on the road to piety, Wilhelm, who reads the document aloud to Aurelie, tells Natalie later on that it had a tremendous effect on his life. Then there is also the "Lehrbrief" or Letter of Apprenticeship, that combines a biography of Wilhelm with gnomic pronouncements about life in general, and from which Jarno repeatedly reads out loud to Wilhelm until he can bear it no longer. This document (the reader may deduce) bears, by an inevitable witticism, the title "Wilhelm Meisters Lehrjahre." In other words, by a stroke of pre-emptive post-modernism, Goethe has Wilhelm and the reader of the novel reading the same work. Where Wilhelm finds a distilled version of his own life and useful tenets to live by, the reader of the novel is offered exactly the same fare: an account of a life, and reflections on the nature of life in general. Looking back, the reader realizes that in parodying his various characters' attitudes towards reading — their dilettantism, their failure to distinguish fact from fiction, their excruciating misinterpretations — Goethe demonstrates his intention that the reader's life should be affected by reading this novel, just as Wilhelm benefited from reading the Confessions.

Of course, the situation is not quite so straightforward. Wilhelm maintains a critical distance from his "Lehrbrief"; he recognizes that the account of his life is not exactly a faithful reflection but is written from a particular perspective, and of the aphoristic portion he can only take so much, as he repeatedly tries to make clear to Jarno. Readers of the novel also find that Wilhelm is not being put forward as a paradigm, and that many of the narrator's commonplace observations are ironically intended. The work is anything but moralizing. And here the realism which shows through despite all artifice joins forces with the immanent reflections on reading that form part and parcel of the narrative. During the course of the novel, Wilhelm learned and developed only up to a certain point; already in 1796 Goethe indicated to Schiller that he had a continuation in mind, one that would eventually become *Wilhelm Meisters Wanderjahre oder Die Entsagenden* (final version, 1829).[1] *Wilhelm Meisters Lehrjahre* does not offer solutions, it presents life in the raw, with all its loose threads, all its unfinished business, all its changing facets, and Goethe found it easier to show these through the strivings of an indecisive and sometimes irresponsible dreamer, than by choosing to create a stable, mature, exemplary young man. These

---

[1] Available in English as *Wilhelm Meister's Travels*. Trans. Thomas Carlyle, intro. James Hardin. Columbia, SC: Camden House, 1991.

are the thoughts of Goethe himself, as communicated to Friedrich von Müller on rereading his novel in 1821.[2]

Realism may be a curious term to use when describing a work that predates the actual literary phenomenon officially known by this label, especially since this novel recounts movements and developments in preference to a static state of affairs. On the other hand, a considerable portion of the novel — beginning with Wilhelm's family and ending with his adoption into an aristocratic society — is dominated by tensions between aristocratic and bourgeois interests, much as, say, the works of Fontane are. To that extent, then, *Wilhelm Meisters Lehrjahre* can justifiably be said to uphold the realist aim of being true to life. So Wilhelm's chronic lack of a realistic perspective does not detract from the overall realism of the novel.

Literary theorists and critics have devoted much attention in the last thirty years or more to the question of the implicit reader, the one whose active role in the interpretation of a text is clearly anticipated by the author. Here, we are concerned not with direct communication between the author and a hypothetical reader, but with various acts of reading within the narrative and with the implications these carry over to us as readers.

Realism and reading are only two aspects of the novel that emerged during the compilation of this commentary; other equally worthy and perhaps more prominent features of the work could certainly be put forward. It seemed fit, however, to draw attention to two characteristics of *Wilhelm Meisters Lehrjahre* that display breadth of scope and yet are under-represented in the body of criticism dealing with this important novel.

[2] "Bei jetziger Wiederlesung meines Romans . . . Wilhelm ist freilich ein "armer Hund," aber nur an solchen lassen sich das Wechselspiel des Lebens und die tausend verschiedenen Lebensaufgaben recht deutlich zeigen, nicht an schon abgeschlossenen, festen Charakteren" (*HA* 618).

Works Cited

Primary Literature

Goethe, Johann Wolfgang. *Wilhelm Meisters Lehrjahre. Ein Roman*. Herausgegeben von Goethe. Berlin: Unger, 1795.

———. *Goethes Werke*. Vols. 2, 3. Tübingen: Cotta, 1806.

———. *Wilhelm Meisters Lehrjahre. Ein Roman*. Herausgegeben von Goethe. Stuttgart/ Tübingen: Cotta, 1816.

———. *Wilhelm Meister's Apprenticeship and Travels*. Trans. Thomas Carlyle. 2 vols, London: Chapman and Hall, 1863.

———. *Goethes Werke*. Ed. Carl Schüddekopf. Vol. 21/23. Herausgegeben im Auftrage der Großherzogin Sophie von Sachsen. Weimar: Böhlau, 1898.

———. *Poetische Werke. Romane und Erzählungen*. II, Vol. 10. Ed. Siegfried Seidel. Berlin: Aufbau, 1962.

———. *Wilhelm Meisters Lehrjahre. Ein Roman*. Stuttgart: Reclam, 1982.

———. *Goethes Werke*. Vol. 7. Ed. Erich Trunz. Munich: Beck, 1982.

———. *Sämtliche Werke nach Epochen seines Schaffens*. Vol. 5. Ed. Hans-Jürgen Schings. Munich: Hanser, 1988.

———. *Wilhelm Meister's Apprenticeship*. Ed. and trans. Eric A. Blackall, with Victor Lange. Princeton, NJ: Princeton UP, 1989.

———. *Wilhelm Meister's Travels*. Trans. Thomas Carlyle, intro. James Hardin. Columbia, SC: Camden House, 1991.

———. *Sämtliche Werke I/9*. Ed. Wilhelm Vosskamp, Herbert Jaumann. Frankfurt am Main: Deutscher Klassiker Verlag, 1992.

———. *Wilhelm Meister's Theatrical Calling*. Ed., trans. John R. Russell. Columbia, SC: Camden House, 1995.

General Reference

Brewer, Cobham. *The Dictionary of Phrase and Fable*. London: Galley, 1894.

Dürr, Walther & Andreas Krause. *Schubert-Handbuch*. Bärenreiter: Metzler, 1997.

Garland, Henry and Mary. *The Oxford Companion to German Literature*. 2nd ed. Oxford/New York: Oxford UP, 1993.

Lösch, Michael. *Who's Who bei Goethe*. Munich: Deutsche Taschenbuch Verlag, 1999.

Martini, Fritz. *Deutsche Literaturgeschichte*. 18th ed. Stuttgart: Kröner, 1984.

Parlett, David. *The Oxford Guide to Card Games*. Oxford/New York: Oxford UP, 1990.

Reallexikon der deutschen Literaturgeschichte. Berlin: de Gruyter, 1958–1988.

Ritter, Joachim, ed. *Historisches Wörterbuch der Philosophie*. Darmstadt: Wissenschaftliche Buchgesellschaft, 1971.

Van Rinsum, Annemarie and Wolfgang. *Lexikon literarischer Gestalten*. Stuttgart: Kröner, 1988.

Vivian, Kim, ed. *A Concise History of German Literature to 1900*. Columbia, SC: Camden House, 1992.

Von Wilpert, Gero. *Sachwörterbuch der Literatur*. 7th ed. Stuttgart: Kröner, 1989.

———. *Goethe-Lexikon*. Stuttgart: Kröner, 1998.

Yarwood, Doreen. *The Encyclopedia of World Costume*. New York: Scribner, 1978.

Secondary Literature

Ammerlahn, Hellmut. "'Poesy-Poetry-Poetology,' Wilhelm 'Meister,' Hamlet und die mittleren Metamorphosen Mignons." *Goethes Mignon und ihre Schwestern. Interpretation und Rezeption*. Ed. Gerhart Hoffmeister. New York: Lang, 1993. 1–26.

———. "Goethe und Wilhelm Meister, Shakespeare und Natalie: Die klassische Heilung des kranken Königssohns." *JbFDH* (1978): 47–84.

———. "Puppe-Tänzer-Dämon-Genius-Engel: Naturkind, Poesiekind und Kunstwerdung bei Goethe." *GQ* 54 (1981): 19–32.

———. "Wilhelm Meisters Mignon — ein offenbares Rätsel. Name, Gestalt, Symbol, Wesen und Werden." *DVjs* 42/1 (1968): 89–116.

Anger, Alfred. *Literarisches Rokoko*. Stuttgart: Metzler, 1968.

Bahr, Ehrhard. *Johann Wolfgang Goethe, Wilhelm Meisters Lehrjahre. Erläuterungen und Dokumente*. Stuttgart: Reclam, 1982.

Baioni, Giuliano. "'Märchen' — 'Wilhelm Meisters Lehrjahre' — 'Hermann und Dorothea.' Zur Gesellschaftsidee der deutschen Klassik." *GJ* 92 (1975): 73–127.

Bakhtin, Mikhail. *The Dialogic Imagination: Four Essays.* Austin: U of Texas P, 1981.

Barner, Wilfried. "Geheime Lenkung. Zur Turmgesellschaft in Goethes *Wilhelm Meister.*" *Goethe's Narrative Fiction. The Irvine Goethe Symposium.* Ed. William J. Lillyman. Berlin/New York: de Gruyter, 1983. 85–109.

Becker-Cantarino, Barbara. "Die 'Bekenntnisse einer schönen Seele': Zur Ausgrenzung und Vereinnahmung des Weiblichen in der patriarchalen Utopie von 'Wilhelm Meisters Lehrjahren.'" *Verantwortung und Utopie. Zur Literatur der Goethezeit.* Tübingen: Niemeyer, 1988. 70–86.

Beddow, Michael. *The Fiction of Humanity. Studies in the Bildungsroman from Wieland to Thomas Mann.* Cambridge: Cambridge UP, 1982.

Beharriell, Frederick J. "The Hidden Meaning of Goethe's 'Bekenntnisse einer schönen Seele.'" *Lebendige Form. Interpretationen zur deutschen Literatur.* Munich: Fink, 1970. 37–62.

Blackall, Eric A. "Sense and Nonsense in 'Wilhelm Meisters Lehrjahre.'" *Deutsche Beiträge zur geistigen Überlieferung.* Vol. 5 (1965): 49–72.

———. *Goethe and the Novel.* Ithaca and London: Cornell UP, 1976.

Blair, John. *Tracing Subversive Currents in Goethe's Wilhelm Meister's Apprenticeship.* Columbia, SC: Camden House, 1997.

Blessin, Stefan. "Die radikal-liberale Konzeption von Wilhelm Meisters Lehrjahren." *DVjs* 49 (1975): 191–225.

———. *Die Romane Goethes.* Regensburg: Athenäum, 1979.

Bonds, Mark Evan. "Die Funktion des 'Hamlet'-Motivs in 'Wilhelm Meisters Lehrjahre.'" *GJ* (1979): 101–10.

Borchmeyer, Dieter. *Höfische Gesellschaft und französische Revolution bei Goethe. Adeliges und bürgerliches Wertsystem im Urteil der Weimarer Klassik.* Kronberg: Athenäum, 1977.

Boyle, Nicholas. *Goethe. The Poet and his Age.* Vol. 1, *The Poetry of Desire.* Oxford/New York: Oxford UP, 1992.

———. *Goethe: The Poet and his Age.* Vol. 2, *Revolution and Renunciation, 1790–1803.* Oxford/New York: Oxford UP, 2000.

Braemer, Edith. "Zu einigen Problemen in Goethes Roman 'Wilhelm Meisters Lehrjahre,'" *Studien zur Literaturgeschichte und Literaturtheorie.* Berlin: Rütten & Loening, 1970. 143–200, 346–58.

Brown, Jane K. "The Theatrical Mission of the *Lehrjahre.*" *Reflection and Action: Essays on the Bildungsroman.* Ed. James Hardin. Columbia: U of South Carolina P, 1991.

318 ❦ *WILHELM MEISTER'S APPRENTICESHIP: COMMENTARY*

Bruford, W. H. *The German Tradition of Self-Cultivation. "Bildung" from Humboldt to Thomas Mann.* Cambridge: Cambridge UP, 1975.

Carlyle, Thomas. "Goethe." *Critical and Miscellaneous Essays in Five Volumes.* Vol 1. London: Chapman and Hall, 1899. 198–257.

Debrunner, Hans Werner. *Presence and Prestige, Africans in Europe: A History of Africans in Europe before 1918.* Basel: Baseler Bibliographien, 1979.

Diamond, William. "Wilhelm Meister's Interpretation of Hamlet." *Modern Philology* 23 (1925–26): 89–101.

Dover Wilson, John, ed. *Hamlet.* Cambridge: Cambridge UP, 1969.

Dürr, Volker. "'Wilhelm Meisters Lehrjahre': Hypotaxis, Abstraction and the 'Realistic Symbol.'" *Versuche zu Goethe. Festschrift für Erich Heller.* Ed. Volker Dürr, Géza von Molnár. Heidelberg: Stiehm, 1976. 201–11.

Eichner, Hans. "Zur Deutung von "Wilhelm Meisters Lehrjahren.'" *JbFDH* (1966): 165–96.

Fick, Monika. "Destruktive Imagination. Die Tragödie der Dichterexistenz in *Wilhelm Meisters Lehrjahre.*" *JbDSG* 29 (1985): 207–47.

Flemming, Willi. *Goethe und das Theater seiner Zeit.* Stuttgart: Kohlhammer, 1968.

Gerth, Klaus. "'Das Wechselspiel des Lebens.' Ein Versuch 'Wilhelm Meisters Lehrjahre' (wieder) einmal anders zu lesen." *GJ* 113 (1996): 105–20.

Gilby, William. "The Structural Significance of Mignon in *Wilhelm Meisters Lehrjahre.*" *Seminar,* 16 (1980): 136–50.

Gilli, Marita. "Structure et interprétation du livre I des *Années d'Apprentissage de Wilhelm Meister* de Goethe." *Hommage à Georges Fourier.* Centre de Recherches d'Histoire et Littérature: Paris (1973): 195–205.

Graham, Ilse. *Goethe: Portrait of the Artist.* Berlin: de Gruyter, 1977.

Gray, Ronald D. *Goethe the Alchemist. A Study of Alchemical Symbolism in Goethe's Literary and Scientific Works.* Cambridge: Cambridge UP, 1952.

Gundolf, Friedrich. *Shakespeare und der deutsche Geist.* Berlin: Bondi, 1914.

Guthke, Karl S. "Shakespeare im Urteil der deutschen Theaterkritik." K.G. *Wege zur Literatur.* Bern and Munich: Francke, 1967.

Haas, Rosemarie. *Die Turmgesellschaft in "Wilhelm Meisters Lehrjahre." Zur Geschichte des Geheimbundromans und der Romantheorie im 18. Jahrhundert.* Frankfurt am Main: Lang, 1975.

Hahn, Karl-Heinz. "Zeitgeschichte in Goethes Roman *Wilhelm Meisters Lehrjahre.*" *Deutsche Klassik und Revolution.* Ed. Paolo Chiarini, Walter Dieze. Rome: Edizione dell'Ateneo, 1978.

Hardin, James, ed. *Reflection and Action. Essays on the Bildungsroman.* Columbia: U of South Carolina P, 1991.

Harrison, R. B. *Hölderlin and Greek Literature*. Oxford: Clarendon Press, 1975.

Hass, Hans-Egon. "Goethe. Wilhelm Meisters Lehrjahre." *Der deutsche Roman. Vom Barock bis zur Gegenwart. Struktur und Geschichte*. Ed. Benno von Wiese. Vol. 1, Düsseldorf: Bagel, 1965.

Hörisch, Jochen. *Gott, Geld und Glück. Zur Logik der Liebe in den Bildungsromanen Goethes, Kellers und Thomas Manns*. Frankfurt am Main: Suhrkamp, 1983.

Irmscher, Hans Dietrich. "Beobachtungen zum Problem der Selbstbestimmung im deutschen Bildungsroman am Beispiel von Goethes Roman 'Wilhelm Meisters Lehrjahre.'" *Jahrbuch des Wiener Goethe-Vereins* 86 (1982): 135–72.

Jacobs, Jürgen. *Wilhelm Meister und seine Brüder. Untersuchungen zum deutschen Bildungsroman*. Munich: Fink, 1972.

Janz, Rolf-Peter. "Zum sozialen Gehalt der 'Lehrjahre.'" *Literaturwissenschaft und Geschichtsphilosophie*. Ed. Helmut Arntzen, Bernd Balzer, Karl Pestalozzi, Rainer Wagner. Berlin: de Gruyter, 1975. 320–40.

John, David G. *The German Nachspiel in the Eighteenth Century*. Toronto: U of Toronto P, 1991.

Keppel-Kriems, Karin. *Mignon und Harfner in Goethes 'Wilhelm Meister': Ein geschichtsphilosophische und kunsttheoretische Untersuchung zu Begriff und Gestaltung des Naiven*. Frankfurt am Main: Lang, 1986.

Kieferstein, Georg. "Philine," *Goethe* 3 (1938): 41–58.

Kiess, Martina. *Poesie und Prosa. Die Lieder in "Wilhelm Meisters Lehrjahren."* Frankfurt am Main: Athenäum, 1987.

Kittler, Friedrich A. "Über die Sozialisation Wilhelm Meisters." *Dichtung als Sozialisationsspiel*. Göttingen: Vandenhoeck & Ruprecht. 13–114.

Koch, Manfred. "Serlo, Aurelie, Orest und Cornelia." *Germanisch-Romanische Monatsschrift* N.F. 47 (1997): 399–413.

Kramer, Lawrence. "Decadence and Desire: The *Wilhelm Meister* Songs of Wolf and Schubert." *19th Century Music* 10/3 (Spring 1987): 229–42.

Krauss, Paul. "Mignon, der Harfner, Sperata. Die Psychopathologie einer Sippe in 'Wilhelm Meisters Lehrjahren.'" *DVjs* 22 (1944): 327–54.

Krehbiel, A. R. "Herder als Jarno." *Modern Philology* 17 (1919): 325–29.

Krogmann, Willy. *Wilhelm Meister in Hamburg*. Hamburg: Buske, 1965.

Ladendorf, Ingrid. *Zwischen Tradition und Revolution. Die Frauengestalten in "Wilhelm Meisters Lehrjahren" und ihr Verhältnis zu deutschen Originalromanen des 18. Jahrhunderts*. Frankfurt am Main: Lang, 1989.

Lange, Victor. "Goethe's Craft of Fiction." *PEGS* 22 (1952/53): 31–63.

Larrett, William. "Wilhelm Meister and the Amazons. The Quest for Wholeness." *PEGS,* N.S. 39 (1968–69): 31–56.

Lukács, Georg. *Die Theorie des Romans. Ein geschichtsphilosophischer Versuch über die Form der großen Epik.* Frankfurt am Main: Luchterhand, 1971.

———. *Goethe.* Trans. Robert Anchor. London: Merlin Press, 1968.

MacLeod, Catriona. *Embodying Ambiguity. Androgyny and Aesthetics from Winckelmann to Keller.* Detroit: Wayne State University Press, 1998.

Mahoney, Dennis F. *Der Roman der Goethezeit (1774–1829).* Stuttgart: Metzler, 1988.

Marahrens, Gerwin. "Über die Schicksalskonzeptionen in Goethes 'Wilhelm Meister' Romanen." *GJ* 102 (1985): 144–70.

Martini, Fritz. "Ebenbild, Gegenbild. *Wilhelm Meisters theatralische Sendung* und Goethe in Weimar 1775 bis 1786." *GJ* 93 (1976): 60–83.

Mayer, Mathias. *Selbstbewußte Illusion. Selbstreflexion und Legitimation der Dichtung im 'Wilhelm Meister.'* Heidelberg: Carl Winter Universitätsverlag, 1989.

Minden, Michael. *The German Bildungsroman: Incest and Inheritance.* Cambridge: Cambridge UP, 1997.

Montaigne, Michel de. "On Experience." *Essays.* Trans. M. A. Screech. London: Penguin Classics, 1991.

Mueller, Dennis M. "Wieland's *Hamlet* Translation and Wilhelm Meister." *Jahrbuch der deutschen Shakespeare-Gesellschaft (West)* (1969): 198–212.

Muenzer, Clark S. *Figures of Identity: Goethe's Novels and the Enigmatic Self.* University Park: Pennsylvania State UP, 1984.

Müller, Günther. "Gestaltung — Umgestaltung in Wilhelm Meisters Lehrjahren. Die Metamorphose der Menschen." G.M., *Morphologische Poetik. Gesammelte Aufsätze.* Darmstadt: Wissenschaftliche Buchgesellschaft, 1968. 419–510.

Neumann, Gerhard. "'Ich bin gebildet genug, um zu lieben und zu trauen.' Die Erziehung zur Liebe in Goethes 'Wilhelm Meister.'" *Liebesroman — Liebe im Roman.* Ed. Reinhold Merkelbach, Titus Heydenreich. Erlangen: Schmidt, 1987. 41–82.

Neumann, Michael. *Roman und Ritus. Wilhelm Meisters Lehrjahre.* Frankfurt am Main: Klostermann, 1992.

Nolan, Erika. "Wilhelm Meisters Lieblingsbild: Der kranke Königssohn: Quelle und Funktion." *JbFDH* (1979): 132–52.

Norton, Robert E. *The Beautiful Soul: Aesthetic Morality in the Eighteenth Century.* Ithaca and London: Cornell UP, 1995.

Pascal, Roy. *The German Novel.* Manchester: Manchester UP, 1956.

Ratz, Norbert. *Der Identitätsroman. Eine Strukturanalyse.* Tübingen: Niemeyer, 1988.

Reiss, Hans S. "Lustspielhaftes in *Wilhelm Meisters Lehrjahre.*" *Goethezeit. Studien und Rezeption Goethes und seiner Zeitgenossen.* Bern and Munich: Francke, 1981, 129–44.

———. "On Some Images in *Wilhelm Meisters Lehrjahre,*" *PEGS* N.S. 20 (1951): 111–38.

———. *Goethes Romane.* Bern/Munich: Francke, 1963.

Riemann, Robert. *Goethes Romantechnik.* Leipzig: Seemann, 1902.

Röder, Gerda. *Glück und glückliches Ende im deutschen Bildungsroman. Eine Studie zu Goethes "Wilhelm Meister."* Munich: Max Hueber, 1968.

Saine, Thomas P. "Über Wilhelm Meisters Bildung." *Lebendige Form.* Munich: Fink, 1970. 63–81.

———. "Was *Wilhelm Meisters Lehrjahre* Really Supposed to be a Bildungsroman?" *Reflection and Action: Essays on the Bildungsroman.* Ed. James Hardin. Columbia: U of South Carolina P, 1991. 118–41.

Schama, Simon. *The Embarassment of Riches. An Interpretation of Dutch Culture in the Golden Age.* London: Harper Collins, 1987.

Schings, Hans-Jürgen. "'Agathon,' 'Anton Reiser,' 'Wilhelm Meister.' Zur Pathogenese des modernen Subjekts im Roman." *Goethe im Kontext. Kunst und Humanität, Naturwissenschaft und Politik von der Aufklärung bis zur Restauration.* Ed. Wolfgang Wittkowski. Tübingen: Niemeyer, 1984. 42–68.

———. "Symbolik des Glücks. Zu Wilhelm Meisters Bildergeschichte." *Johann Wolfgang von Goethe: One Hundred and Fifty Years of Continuing Vitality.* Ed. Ulrich Goebel, Wolodymyr T. Zyla. Lubbock: Texas Tech, 1984. 157–77.

———. "Wilhelm Meisters schöne Amazone." *JbDSG* 29 (1985): 141–206.

Schlaffer, Hannelore. *Wilhelm Meister. Das Ende der Kunst und die Wiederkehr des Mythos.* Stuttgart: Metzler, 1980.

Schlaffer, Heinz. *Musa iocosa. Gattungspoetik und Gattungsgeschichte der erotischen Dichtung in Deutschland.* Stuttgart: Metzler, 1971.

Schlechta, Karl. *Goethes Wilhelm Meister.* Frankfurt am Main: Klostermann, 1953.

Scholz, Felix. "Der Brief Wilhelm Meisters an Mariane (Wilhelm Meisters Theatralische Sendung, Buch I, Kap. 22). Eine stilistische Untersuchung." *JbFDH* (1928): 105–124.

Seidlin, Oskar. "Zur Mignon-Ballade." *Euphorion* 45 (1951): 83–99.

Seitz, Erwin. "Die Vernunft des Menschen und die Verführung durch das Leben. Eine Studie zu den 'Lehrjahren,'" *GJ* 113 (1996): 121–37.

Selbmann, Rolf. *Der deutsche Bildungsroman.* Stuttgart: Metzler, 1984.

Sjögren, Christine Oertel. "Pietism, Pathology, or Pragmatism in Goethe's *Bekenntnisse einer schönen Seele.*" *Studies on Voltaire and the 18th Century,* No. 193, Vol. 4. Oxford (1980): 2009–15.

Staiger, Emil. *Goethe.* Vol. 2. Zurich/ Freiburg: Atlantis, 1956.

Steer, A. G. "The Wound and the Physician in Goethe's *Wilhelm Meister.*" *Studies in German Literature of the Nineteenth and Twentieth Centuries.* Ed. Siegfried Mews, Chapel Hill: U of North Carolina P, 1970: 11–23.

Steiner, Jacob. *Goethes Wilhelm Meister. Sprache und Stilwandel,* Stuttgart: Kohlhammer, 1966.

Steiner, Uwe. "Wilhelm Meisters Lehrjahre." *Goethe-Handbuch* 3 (Prosaschriften) Stuttgart/Weimar: Metzler, 1997. 140–43.

Storz, Gerhard. "Die Lieder aus Wilhelm Meister." *Deutschunterricht* 1/7 (1949): 36–56.

———. "Wieder einmal die Lehrjahre." *Versuche zu Goethe.* Ed. Volker Dürr, Géza von Molnár. Heidelberg: Stiehm, 1976: 190–200.

———. "Wilhelm Meisters Lehrjahre." *Goethe-Vigilien oder Versuche in der Kunst, Dichtung zu verstehen.* Stuttgart: Klett, 1953. 61–103.

Strack, Friedrich. "Selbst-Erfahrung oder Selbst-Entsagung? Goethes Deutung und Kritik des Pietismus in 'Wilhelm Meisters Lehrjahre.'" *Verlorene Klassik?* Ed. Wolfgang Wittkowski. Tübingen: Niemeyer, 1986. 52–78.

Swales, Martin. *The German Bildungsroman from Wieland to Hesse.* Princeton, NJ: Princeton UP, 1978.

Thüsen, Joachim von der. "Der Romananfang in 'Wilhelm Meisters Lehrjahren,'" *DVjs* 43 (1969): 622–30.

Viëtor, Karl. "Goethe. 'Wilhelm Meisters Lehrjahre.'" *Deutsche Romane von Grimmelshausen bis Musil.* Ed. Jost Schillemeit. Frankfurt am Main: Fischer, 1966.

Weiss, Gerhard H. "An Interpretation of the Miners' Scene in Goethe's *Wilhelm Meisters Lehrjahre.*" *Lebendige Form.* Festschrift for Heinrich Henel. Ed. Jeffrey L. Sammons, Ernst Schurer. Munich: Fink, 1970. 83–88.

Wertheim, Ursula. "Philosophische und ästhetische Aspekte in Prosastücken Goethes über Shakespeare." *Goethe* 26 (1964): 54–76.

Wilkinson, Elizabeth, and L. A. Willoughby. "Having and Being, or Bourgeois Versus Nobility: Notes for a Chapter on Social and Cultural History or for a Commentary on Wilhelm Meister." *GLL* 22 (1968–69): 101–5.

Willoughby, L. A. "'Name ist Schall und Rauch.' On the Significance of Names for Goethe." *GLL* 16 (1962–63): 294–306.

Winter, Ingrid. *Wiederholte Spiegelungen: Funktion und Bedeutung der Verseinlage in Goethes Iphigenie auf Tauris und Wilhelm Meisters Lehrjahre.* Chapel Hill: U of North Carolina P, 1981.

Wuthenow, Ralph-Rainer. *Im Buch die Bücher oder der Held als Leser.* Frankfurt am Main: Europäische Verlagsanstalt, 1980.

Index